REGIONAL ECONOMIC MODELING:

A SYSTEMATIC APPROACH TO ECONOMIC FORECASTING AND POLICY ANALYSIS

Regional Economic Modeling:

A Systematic Approach to
Economic Forecasting and Policy Analysis

by

George I.Treyz
University of Massachusetts at Amherst

Kluwer Academic Publishers

Boston/Dordrecht/London

Distributors for North America:
Kluwer Academic Publishers
101 Philip Drive
Assinippi Park
Norwell, Massachusetts 02061 USA

Distributors for all other countries:
Kluwer Academic Publishers Group
Distribution Centre
Post Office Box 322
3300 AH Dordrecht, THE NETHERLANDS

Library of Congress Cataloging-in-Publication Data

Treyz, George.
  Regional economic modeling : a systematic approach to economic
forecasting and policy analysis / by George I. Treyz.
     p.   cm.
  Includes bibliographical references and index.
  ISBN 0-7923-9382-1 (alk. paper)
  1. Regional economics--Mathematical models. 2. Regional planning-
-United States--Mathematical models. 3. Economic forecasting-
-United States--Mathematical models. I. Title.
HT388.T74 1993
330.973'00113--dc20   93-22947
                                                         CIP

Printed on acid-free paper.

Printed in the United States of America.

To Sidney

TABLE OF CONTENTS

viii

PART III: APPLICATIONS AND SUMMARY

LIST OF DIAGRAMS

xvi

LIST OF TABLES

PREFACE

Regional economic models are the key to predicting the effects of transportation, economic development, energy, fiscal, and environmental policies. Despite this, the principal regional economic policy analysis model used throughout the United States by government agencies, universities, and the private sector has not been presented in a book until now.

Our approach to building, understanding, and using regional models is progressive. We start with the simplest possible models and conclude with a full presentation of the leading model used by policy makers today. The full details are presented along with facilitating software so that the reader can build a prototype model for any state or county and can perform policy simulations with a full operational model for a sample county. We discuss policy studies that have been carried out with the model, as well as the range of ways in which policies can be tested through policy simulations.

We develop the background necessary for understanding the ways models can be used to improve the basis upon which policies are evaluated, as well as the sensitivity of the predicted effects to the model chosen for the analysis. Our presentation is multifaceted and includes equations, diagrams, and numerical examples. We have integrated the professional literature with introductory materials to produce the first comprehensive book on regional modeling that extends from economic base models to modeling advances that are currently being published in economic journals.

ACKNOWLEDGMENTS

Co-authors of articles that have been drawn upon in some of the chapters in this book include Michael J. Greenwood, Ann F. Friedlander, Gary L. Hunt, Sue Lieu, Dan S. Rickman, Gang Shao, and Benjamin H. Stevens. People who have made contributions to the writing of parts of chapters and preparing the two supplementary programs include Rafael Bradley (chapter 8 and the REMI Demonstration model), Chengfeng Lou (Regional Economic Modeling System), and Frederick Treyz (chapters 1, 2, and 3). Michele Companion prepared the finished copy of this book. Sherri Pierce and Lisa Petraglia read the final manuscript. Many associates and students have made helpful comments.

CHAPTER 1

INTRODUCTION[1]

There are many instances when national government policy changes, international events, national business cycles, or natural disasters have diverse regional effects. In the United States, changes in military spending have direct and indirect effects that are concentrated in the Far West and New England. Output may rise in Texas and Louisiana but decline in other states when the United States faces an oil shortage. Global warming could increase business costs in California and decrease them in Minnesota, leading to shifts in industrial activity. In Japan, a rail link to Tokyo leads to changes in the economy in Hokkaido.

Regional models forecast economic activity and predict the effect of policies and external changes. They encompass single-region models, which represent one subnational area, and multiregional models, which show the interactions between two or more subnational areas. They aid in the choice of national policies that facilitate regional adjustments to national and international changes.

Presently, single-region models are used extensively for policy analysis and forecasting. On the subnational level, decision makers are faced with a number of what-if questions. What would happen if Maine were to increase its state minimum wage? What if Southern California were to impose air pollution control regulations that would increase the cost of electricity? What if Quebec were to provide a tax credit for the electronics industry? What if Minnesota were to shut down a racetrack?

Many types of models are used in regional science. Some focus on the spatial distribution of activity across continuous space, while others deal with subnational areas as regions or sets of regions. The models we consider are of the latter type. They provide forecasts for prices, output, employment, and population. They enable us to project tax revenues, occupational training requirements, and the need for new electrical generation capacity. This type of information is often necessary to make rational decisions and plan for the future.

Regional models should be based on theories that represent the important features of regional economies. Since regional economies are open economies with free movement of goods, services, capital, and people, they require a theoretical treatment that is distinct from international economies, even though the focus on interactions among regions is important to both areas of study. While theories from macroeconomics have some relevance, the open nature of regions and the lack of policy instruments, such as control of the money supply by local governments, means that they must be adapted to a different setting. Other fields that are relevant to the development of regional models include demographics and microeconomics.

Here, we present alternative theoretical frameworks for understanding and modeling the economic and demographic aspects of regions. We show how data is used to calibrate models to any region and how it is used to estimate relationships that are basic to predicting the effects of policies on local economies. Our aim is to integrate theory and evidence in order to improve the quality of regional policy analysis. We focus on

a) the key relationships for understanding open regional economies

b) the proper use of models and

c) informed interpretations of analytical results.

In this book, we do not attempt to survey regional models and approaches. This has been done elsewhere (see Bolton, 1985; Burress, 1988; and Sivitanidou, 1988). Instead, we present general models that can be modified to represent special cases, such as economic base, input-output, and fixed labor supply models. These models, their uses, and special cases are presented for both homogeneous models (e.g., single industry, occupation, age/sex cohort, and type of migrant) and heterogeneous models (e.g., multiple industries, occupations, age/sex cohorts, and types of migrants) in Parts I and II, respectively. The organization of the book is shown in table 1-1.

Parts I and II start with a special case of a more general model in chapters 2 and 6, respectively. In both instances, very rigid assumptions are made, and the policy predictions are static and unrealistic. The next chapter in each part (chapters 3 and 7, respectively) presents a general model with output and employment responses to cost and wage changes. The following chapter in each section (chapters 4 and 8) utilizes the general model for forecasting and policy analysis. The last chapter in each section (chapters 5 and 9) examines the importance of key model assumptions using special cases and alternative closures of the models. Part III reports selective studies that have been carried out with the Regional Economic Models, Inc. (REMI) model (chapter 10), and a summary chapter concludes the book (chapter 11).

TABLE 1-1

Organization of This Book

TOPIC	PART I (Homogeneous)	PART II (Heterogeneous)	PART III
Regional Accounts & Rigid Models	CHAPTER 2 *Economic Base*	CHAPTER 6 *Input-Output*	
Structure of General Models	CHAPTER 3 *Prototype Model*	CHAPTER 7 *Operational Model*	
Forecasting & Simulation	CHAPTER 4 *Prototype Model*	CHAPTER 8 *Operational Model*	CHAPTER 10 *Review of Selected Studies*
Special Cases and Alternative Closures	CHAPTER 5 *Prototype Model*	CHAPTER 9 *Operational Model*	
Summary			CHAPTER 11 *Summary and Strategy for the Future*

A set of menu-driven programs that enables the reader to develop three types of homogeneous models for any subnational area and that includes an operational heterogeneous model for a sample area is available from the author.[2] In an era when regional recessions and even depressions have occurred frequently, an understanding of regional (as well as national) economies is essential. This book provides a framework for explaining the behavior of regional economies and for choosing appropriate policies to mitigate adverse regional developments. We hope to promote research-based public policy. If we can encourage the examination of new policy proposals in a simulation context before they are implemented with real people as the beneficiaries or the victims, we may forestall ill-conceived policies and help to get good proposals implemented. We may also provide a better understanding of the limitations and the possibilities of regional policy initiatives.

NOTES ON CHAPTER 1

1. This chapter was written in part by Frederick Treyz.

2. Send c/o Regional Economic Models, Inc., 306 Lincoln Ave., Amherst, MA 01002 (413-549-1169). Please specify whether or not you can use a 3 1/4 inch, high-density standard floppy disk. The software for the models in part I is the Regional Economic Modeling System (REMS). Its installation is explained in the appendix to chapter 2. The software for the operational model of a sample area in Part II is the REMI Demonstration Model. Its installation is explained in the appendix to chapter 8. Both disks may be included in this book in some instances.

PART I:

HOMOGENEOUS MODELS

CHAPTER 2

ECONOMIC BASE MODELS[1]

Regional models cover a wide range of sizes and employ a variety of techniques in their calibration and estimation. They can be divided into two groups. The first group is composed of *nonstructural models*. Their use includes predictions based on past trends, analysis of regional changes based on national industry changes, and shifts in the local share of these national industries. This group also may employ statistical methods, which search for past regularities in regional data. The second group of models are called *structural models*, because these models include the cause-and-effect relationships in a regional economy. The relationships that explain how participants in the economy respond to changes that affect them, such as the change in consumption that would occur if income changes, are called *behavioral relationships*. Other types of relationships in a structural model would include *definitional* and *technical relationships*.

Since our focus is on how changes in policy, which often involve structural changes, affect a regional economy, we concentrate on structural models. These models range in complexity from those including two or three relationships, to those including thousands of equations. We start with the simplest structural model.

In this chapter, we consider only single-sector models that have fixed prices, wages, and input requirements. These models also assume that all inputs are available in the quantities required. In later chapters, we drop these assumptions in favor of more realistic relationships.

Our first step toward understanding a regional economy is to identify essential economic phenomena that we want to measure and predict. Measured aspects of economic phenomena are called *economic variables*.

We assume that certain variables, called *exogenous* variables, have values that are determined outside of the regional economy. All other variables, called *endogenous* variables, are determined within the economy. We can then develop causal relationships among the variables in the model. To quantify these relationships, we use historical data to estimate *parameters* that are used in the equations of our model to show the magnitude of the causal relationships. The model can then be used to carry out a baseline forecast, as shown in diagram 2-1.

8

In order to generate the *baseline* or *control* forecast, values for all of the exogenous variables need to be specified. The computer program solves the model to find the unique set of values for the endogenous variables that are consistent with the relationships and parameters in the model, as well as the values of the exogenous variables.

Baseline Forecast

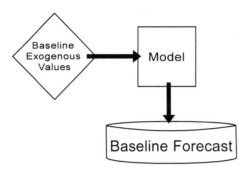

Diagram 2-1

To analyze a particular policy question, the next step is to introduce a change in an exogenous variable or in the structure of the model. This can be accomplished either directly or through *policy variables* that are incorporated in the model program. These policy variables take on a default value of zero in the control forecast if they are additive, or a value of one if they are multiplicative. Thus, at their default values,

Policy Simulation

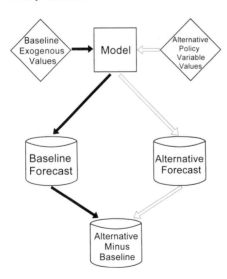

Diagram 2-2

they do not affect the forecast. Alternative values for the policy variables are used as inputs into the alternative forecast. Then, with these new inputs and the baseline exogenous values, the model program generates a complete new set of values for the endogenous variables, as illustrated in diagram 2-2. By subtracting the baseline from the alternative, we find the effect of the policy. This means of producing an alternative forecast is called *policy simulation.*

2-1 ASSUMING INCOME EQUALS OUTPUT

The first task in regional modeling is defining the subnational area to be modeled. Each area is considered to be a point, and spatial location within it is not considered. Thus, each area should be defined to be the smallest geographical area of interest. In the case where a larger geographical entity is also of interest, subareas may be linked in a multi-area model.

A Closed Economy

We begin our model building by defining and showing the accounting relationships among some key economic variables. We start with a simple account for a closed economy that ignores many of the income flows in the real world. As a starting point, we simplify our presentation by assuming that our regional economy is self-sufficient. By way of example, the accounts for a closed economy are shown in table 2-1, although it would be virtually impossible for such an economy to exist.

TABLE 2-1

Income and Product Accounts for a Simplified Closed State Economy

A. State Product Account		B. Personal and Local Government Income and Outlay Account	
Uses	*Sources*	*Uses*	*Sources*
Y (output)	**CG** (consumption and local government spending)	**CG** (consumption and local government spending)	**Y** (output)
	IL (local investment)	**S** (personal savings and local government surplus)	
Y	**Y**	**Y**	**Y**

C. Savings and Investment Account

Uses	*Sources*
IL (local investment)	**S** (personal savings and local government surplus)
IL	**S**

Y   Total state output of goods and services: gross state product (GSP) or gross regional product (GRP)

CG   Total state use of goods and services for consumption, and local (including state) government spending

S   Local savings by individuals, and local (including state) government surplus

IL   Residential and nonresidential construction, new equipment purchases, and inventory changes within the state.

For the time being, we ignore government taxes and transfers, imports and exports, and other economic flows in the accounts. We will include these as we develop our model. The accounts can be represented in equation form. From account A, we have

$$Y = CG + IL, \tag{2-1}$$

where the income earned in the region (Y) comes from sales to the investment sector (IL) and to consumers and local government (CG). From account B, we have

$$Y = CG + S, \tag{2-2}$$

where income (Y) can be spent by consumers and local government (CG) or can be saved by individuals and local governments (S). Setting equation 2-1 equal to equation 2-2 gives us the equation for account C,

$$IL = S, \tag{2-3}$$

in which all local investment (IL) is equal to savings (S), and all savings are used for local investment. Savings could be negative if individuals and local governments are spending more than is earned in the state (CG > Y). In this case, local investment (IL) would also be negative. This would be possible in a closed economy only if inventory reduction exceeds new fixed investment.

An Open Economy

To convert the closed accounts to an open economy, we include imports and exports in the accounts. Savings and investment can now originate or be used in the rest of the country. We are able to develop an account for the rest of the country that shows the interactions between the state and the outside world.

TABLE 2-2

Income and Product Accounts for a Simplified Open State Economy

A. State Product Account		B. Personal and Local Government Income and Outlay Account	
Uses	*Sources*	*Uses*	*Sources*
Y (output)	**CG** (consumption and local government spending)	**CG** (consumption and local government spending)	**Y** (output)
	IL (local investment)	**S** (personal savings and local government surplus)	
	XFG (exports including federal government)		
	– M (imports)		
Y	**Y**	**Y**	**Y**

C. Savings and Investment Account		D. Rest of Country Account	
Uses	*Sources*	*Uses*	*Sources*
IL (local investment)	**S** (personal savings and local government surplus)	**XFG** (exports including federal government)	**M** (imports)
IR (investment, rest of country)			**IR** (investment, rest of country)
I	**S**	**XFG**	**XFG**

XFG   Sales outside of the state of goods produced within the state. This includes federal government spending in the local area.

M   Purchases within the state of goods and services produced outside of the state.

IR   Investment in the rest of the country from the state (a negative value indicates a net flow of rest of country investment into the state).

We can see the difference between a closed and an open economy by comparing the accounts in tables 2-1 and 2-2. Account 2-1A gave us the state product equation for a closed economy ($Y = CG + IL$) in which exports and imports are equal to zero. In an open economy, a state imports part of its consumption and exports part of its production. Thus, account A from table 2-2 gives us

$$Y = CG + IL + XFG - M. \tag{2-4}$$

Output in the state is equal to the value of locally produced goods and services. Consumer and local government spending (CG), local investment (IL), and sales outside of the state (XFG) represent the final sales of the state. To find the value of locally produced goods and services, we must subtract imports (M) from this amount, since part of the final sales of the state are produced outside of the state.

Net exports (XFG - M) can have a negative value within the accounts. From this account, we can see that in an open economy output (Y) can be smaller than CG + IL, as long as imports (M) exceed exports (XFG).

The uses of income in account B are the same in the open economy as in the closed economy.

$$Y = CG + S, \tag{2-5}$$

or

$$S = Y - CG. \tag{2-6}$$

In this account, all output (Y) is assumed to go to households and local government as income (Y).[2] It is then spent for personal or local government use (CG), or it is saved in the form of personal savings and government surpluses (S). Again, federal government taxes, transfers, and spending are implicitly assumed to be zero and are not considered until later in the chapter. Meanwhile, we define all income (Y) that is not used for personal consumption or local government spending (CG) to be equal to savings (S).

In our closed-economy example, all savings are invested locally. In an open economy, savings can be invested locally or in the rest of the country. By including investment in the rest of the country (IR), the closed-economy investment account (IL = S) is converted to the open-economy investment account.

$$I = S = IL + IR, \tag{2-7}$$

or

$$IL = S - IR. \tag{2-8}$$

In an open economy, personal savings and local government surpluses (S) can be invested either locally (IL) or outside of the local area (IR). Local investment (IL) can also exceed local savings (S), if investment in the rest of the country is negative. In other words, if investment in the locality is larger than the amount of local savings, we know that the rest of the country is funding investment in the locality.

We can now develop an account that shows the interactions that the rest of the country has with the region. Account D gives us the equation.

$$XFG = M + IR, \tag{2-9}$$

or

$$IR = XFG - M. \tag{2-10}$$

In this simplified economy, the earnings gained from exports (XFG) are directly or indirectly spent on imports (M) or investment in the rest of the country (IR). The investment in the rest of the country (IR) is therefore equal to the difference between exports (XFG) and imports (M). Regions with positive net exports (XFG - M > 0) will be experiencing a flow of their savings to the rest of the country to finance investment outside of the region. On the other hand, regions with more imports than exports will be financed by savings from the rest of the country.[3]

Before continuing, we look at estimated values for the variables in this model for a representative state. Using methods that are covered later, the following accounts are estimated for Michigan.

TABLE 2-3

Estimated Income and Product Accounts
for Michigan in 1977

A. State Product Account				**B. Personal and Local Government Income and Outlay Account**			
Uses		*Sources*		*Uses*		*Sources*	
Y	80.8	CG	65.0	CG	65.0	Y	80.8
		IL	16.2	S	15.8		
		XFG	83.7				
		– M	84.1				
	80.8		80.8		80.8		80.8

C. Savings and Investment Account				**D. Rest of Country Account**			
Uses		*Sources*		*Uses*		*Sources*	
IL	16.2	S	15.8	XFG	83.7	M	84.1
IR	-0.4					IR	-0.4
	15.8		15.8		83.7		83.7

It may surprise you to find that exports (XFG = 83.7) are greater than total gross state product, or GSP (Y = 80.8). The reason that this is possible is that GSP (Y) is a measure of the total value added to production in Michigan. For example, when a car is produced, the value added in Michigan is equal to the sales price of the car minus the intermediate inputs into production. Many of these intermediate inputs are imported into the state. In contrast, exports are valued at their total final sales price.

Account B assumes that all GSP is available for consumption by individuals and local government. The difference between this spending and GSP is savings (S). The savings and investment account (account C) indicates that a small part of local investment (IL) was financed by a net flow from the rest of the country. In any case, these accounts give a simple view of a state economy, which we enhance when we assemble a more comprehensive set of accounts later in the chapter.

Returning to our accounts, we can show the internal consistency of the accounts by substituting equation 2-6 and equation 2-10 into equation 2-8.

$$IL = Y - CG - XFG + M \tag{2-11}$$

Rearranging this gives us

$$Y = IL + CG + XFG - M, \tag{2-12}$$

which is the same as equation 2-4. Therefore, our four basic equations are

$$Y = CG + IL + XFG - M \tag{2-13}$$

$$Y = CG + S \tag{2-14}$$

$$S = IL + IR \tag{2-15}$$

$$XFG = M + IR \tag{2-16}$$

We can now express local investment as planned local investment (IL_p) and unplanned investment (IL_{up}), which are defined as follows:

$$IL = IL_p + IL_{up} \tag{2-17}$$

IL_p local planned investment: local residential and nonresidential construction, new equipment purchases, and planned changes in inventory. Planned inventory changes are equal to zero in steady state.

IL_{up} local unplanned investment: unplanned changes in inventories, usually caused by failure to set output equal to sales.

This distinction will be useful as a way to allow for a difference between output and demand as we develop our model. Our accounting identities can now be shown as

$$Y = CG + IL_p + IL_{up} + XFG - M \tag{2-18}$$

$$Y = CG + S \tag{2-19}$$

$$S = IL_p + IL_{up} + IR \tag{2-120}$$

$$XFG = M + IR \tag{2-21}$$

An Economic Base Model

The accounts give us definitional interrelationships among the variables that we are examining. This, however, does not tell us how a change in one variable affects the other variables. To build a model for simulations and forecasts, we must develop behavioral relationships between the variables.

First, we choose the exogenous variables (i.e., those that are determined outside the model). As explained previously, the remaining variables are the endogenous variables. Each must be explained by an equation in the model. All equations in the model are solved simultaneously; thus, all endogenous variables are interrelated. After we develop the model, we will then be able to make a forecast or carry out a simulation. A simulation is accomplished by changing the exogenous variables or relationships in the model and evaluating the changes in the endogenous variables.

Our task now is to develop a model that includes all of the variables in the economy that are defined by our accounts. We consider IL_p and XFG to be exogenous.[4] It seems reasonable to assume that planned investment and exports depend on factors determined outside of the local economy, at least in the short run. For example, exports may depend on demand in the rest of the country and world for the commodities produced in the region, while local investment may be due to decisions made in the last few years.

The remaining variables in our accounts, Y, CG, IL_{up}, IR, M, and S, are endogenous variables. All endogenous variables of interest must be explained within the model, either by a behavioral relationship or by an accounting identity.

Total planned purchases (PP) of goods and services produced in the area are

$$PP = CG + IL_p + XFG - M \qquad (2\text{-}22)$$

Note that PP is less than total purchases made in the area because imports are subtracted from total spending. This is due to the fact that some portion of spending by residents and by purchasers of exports is supplied with imported goods. In the case of exports, this occurs because imported intermediate inputs are used in their production.

In the following equation, we assume that the same proportion of all types of purchases are satisfied by imports.

$$M = mCG + mIL_p + mXFG, \qquad (2\text{-}23)$$

where m is the proportion of export and local demand supplied by imported content.

Substituting equation 2-23 into equation 2-22 and simplifying, we obtain

$$PP = (1 - m) CG + (1 - m) IL_p + (1 - m) XFG. \qquad (2\text{-}24)$$

If we now define the parameter r as

$$r = 1 - m, \qquad (2\text{-}25)$$

then r becomes the proportion of local and export planned purchases that is supplied locally. Substituting equation 2-25 into equation 2-24, we obtain

$$PP = rCG + rIL_p + rXFG. \qquad (2\text{-}26)$$

We further simplify the notation by defining the net economic base (BN) and the gross economic base (BG), as follows:

$$BN = rIL_p + rXFG = rBG, \text{ where} \tag{2-27}$$

$$BG = IL_p + XFG. \tag{2-28}$$

Substituting equation 2-27 into equation 2-26, we obtain

$$PP = rCG + BN \tag{2-29}$$

Next, we assume that local personal and government consumption (CG) is some proportion (*b*) of total gross state (regional) product.

$$CG = bY \tag{2-30}$$

We can complete the model by assuming that businesses produce what they can sell. This means that they do not have any change in their inventories, so our assumption is equivalent to assuming that they act to keep $IL_{up} = 0$. The equation that represents both of these assumptions is

$$Y = PP. \tag{2-31}$$

The equations of the model can be summarized in the order in which they appear in the computer program. This program is available to accompany this book.

$$Y = PP \tag{2-32}$$

$$CG = bY \tag{2-33}$$

$$BN = rBG \tag{2-34}$$

$$PP = rCG + BN \tag{2-35}$$

$$IL_{up} = Y - PP \tag{2-36}$$

When stated in this form, it is obvious from equation 2-32 and equation 2-36 that, at equilibrium (i.e., a simultaneous solution for all of the equations), unplanned inventory change IL_{up} will equal zero.

Returning to our specific example for Michigan from equation 2-30, we could estimate *b* as

$$b = \frac{CG}{Y} = \frac{65}{80.8} = .804 \tag{2-37}$$

Likewise, from equations 2-26 and 2-31, we could estimate *r* as

$$r = \frac{Y}{CG + XFG + IL_p} = \frac{80.8}{65 + 83.7 + 16.2} = .490 \tag{2-38}$$

This would enable us to rewrite equations 2-27, 2-29, and 2-30 in the explicit forms

$$BN = 0.49 \, BG \tag{2-39}$$

$$PP = .49 \, CG + BN \tag{2-40}$$

$$CG = .804 \, Y \tag{2-41}$$

$$Y = PP. \tag{2-42}$$

Substituting equation 2-30 into 2-29 and using 2-31, we obtain

$$Y = PP = (rb) Y + BN \tag{2-43}$$

where *rb* is the fraction of Y that is used for locally produced consumption and local government spending. This is obtained when *b*, the proportion of income Y that is spent, is multiplied by the proportion of this spending that is met by locally produced goods (*r*). Output (Y) is expressed as a function of BN (exports (*r*XFG) + local planned investment (*r*IL$_p$)) and the part of Y that is used for local consumption and local government spending [(*rb*)Y]. Note that Y changes if the value of the economic base (BN) changes. When Y increases, (*rb*)Y also increases, further increasing Y, increasing Y again, etc. This is called *induced demand,* or the demand created by the respending of income gained due to changes in output.

We can obtain the explicit form of equation 2-43 by substituting equation 2-41 into equation 2-40.

$$PP = .804 \,(.49) \, Y + BN = .394 \, Y + BN \tag{2-44}$$

Using this equation and equation 2-31, we can also find the value of BN for 1977 in Michigan.

$$BN = 80.8 - 0.394 \,(80.8) = 48.96 \tag{2-45}$$

From equation 2-39 and the value for BN, we can determine that

$$BG = 48.96/0.49 = 99.92 \tag{2-46}$$

A Diagrammatic Representation of the Economic Base Model

The model presented previously is represented graphically in diagram 2-3. The equilibrium output, at which output is equal to planned purchases, is at the intersection of the 45-degree line (Y = PP) and the line showing planned purchases (PP = *rb*Y + BN) at the equilibrium

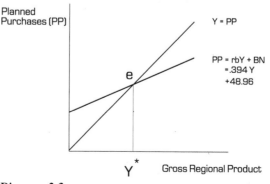

Output Determination for a Region

Diagram 2-3

20

Y*. Since we are only at equilibrium when local output is equal to expenditures on local output, the 45-degree line is used to graphically represent all of the points where the value along the vertical axis is equal to the value along the horizontal axis. The equilibrium is achieved when producers have no reason to increase or decrease their output. Since it is exactly equal to what they can sell (i.e., $IL_{up} = 0$), this must be along the 45-degree line.[5]

The equilibrium must also be on the expenditure on local output line, defined by $PP = rbY + BN$ (from equation 2-43). The points along this line represent the planned purchases of local output that would take place at given levels of output (Y).

The intersection of these two lines gives the actual equilibrium of local output (Y) and of expenditures for local goods and services purchased in the locality (PP). This intersection shows the actual amount of production and expenditure that occurs when all of the behavioral assumptions of the model are fulfilled simultaneously. Diagram 2-4 illustrates how this equilibrium is achieved.

Suppose that the demand were at point a with planned purchases PP** and output Y**. Point b would represent the rate of output on the vertical axes. Then, we would observe an excess of PP over output of a-b at an annual rate. Initially, this causes decreasing inventories ($IL_{up} < 0$). Production is

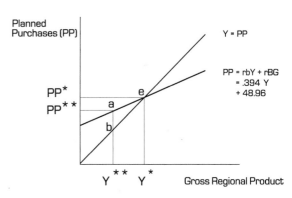

Movement Toward Equilibrium Output

Diagram 2-4

increased by businesses to stem the loss of inventory. This moves output to an equilibrium (e) on the 45-degree line, where inventory no longer changes and producers have no incentive to increase or decrease production.

We can represent the situation at Y** by assuming that output (Y) may momentarily be different than planned purchases (PP). This situation can be modeled by assuming that output at this moment (m) is set, based on sales rate the moment (or day) before ($m - 1$).

$$Y_m = PP_{m-1} \tag{2-47}$$

In this case, inventory change (IL_{upm}) in moment m can be represented as

$$IL_{up, m} = Y_m - PP_m. \tag{2-48}$$

Using the explicit form of the model, which represents the Michigan economy, we can write the following set of equations:

$$Y_m = PP_{m-1} \tag{2-49}$$

$$CG_m = 0.804\, Y_m \tag{2-50}$$

$$BN_m = 0.49\, BG_m \tag{2-51}$$

$$PP_m = 0.49\, CG_m + BN_m \tag{2-52}$$

$$IL_{up, m} = Y_m - PP_m. \tag{2-53}$$

In this model, the subscript m or $m-1$ has been added to each variable. It shows that all of the variables depend on the values of the other variables at the same moment, except output (Y), which depends on planned purchase (PP) a moment before. As is shown in diagram 2-4, the only exogenous variable in this model is BG.

We know from equation 2-49 that $Y_m{}^{**}$ is the output rate that was needed to supply planned purchases (PP_{m-1}) in the previous period. Thus, with PP^*_{m-1} and BG_m, we can solve each of the equations (2-49 through 2-53) above in sequence. Suppose that we select an arbitrary value of PP_{m-1}, say 60. Then, from equation 2-49, we know that Y_m will be equal to 60. We will assign $Y_m{}^{**}$ the value of 60 for the initial period ($m = 0$). Using equations 2-50, 2-51, 2-52, and 2-53 in sequence, we can calculate values for all four endogenous variables in the initial moment ($m = 1$).

$$Y_1\ (60.0) = PP_0\ (60.0) \tag{2-54}$$

$$CG_1\ (48.24) = 0.804\, Y_1\ (60.0) \tag{2-55}$$

$$BN_1\ (48.96) = 0.49\, BG_1\ (99.92) \tag{2-56}$$

$$PP_1\ (72.60) = 0.49\, CG_1\ (48.24) + BN_1\ (48.96) \tag{2-57}$$

$$IL_{up,\ 1}\ (-12.6) = Y_1\ (60.0) - PP_1\ (72.60) \tag{2-58}$$

These calculations locate a, b, and Y^{**} on diagram 2-4. They show that the change of inventory ($a-b$) will be an annual rate of -12.6. Now, we can find PP* and Y* at point e on diagram 2-4, if we can find a way to calculate values of Y** and PP** that get closer and closer to the Y* and PP* values indicated as e on the graph. This can be accomplished by starting the set of calculations again for iteration $m = 2$ at equation 2-59. This time we use the PP_1 value (72.60). The calculations for $m = 2$ are

$$Y_2\ (72.60) = PP_1\ (72.60) \tag{2-59}$$

$$CG_2 \ (58.37) = 0.804 \ Y_2 \ (72.60) \tag{2-60}$$

$$BN_2 \ (48.96) = 0.49 \ BG_2 \ (99.92) \tag{2-61}$$

$$PP_2 \ (77.56) = 0.49 \ CG_2 \ (58.37) + BN_2 \ (48.96) \tag{2-62}$$

$$IL_{up, \ 2} \ (-4.96) = Y_2 \ (72.60) - PP_2 \ (77.56). \tag{2-63}$$

We note that at the end of iteration 2, the value of inventory loss has decreased. This means that we have moved closer to Y*, as shown in diagram 2-5. In this diagram, note how the difference between PP and Y gets smaller after each iteration. By checking this difference, which is also IL_{up} (unplanned inventory change), we can see how close we are to the equilibrium point. When IL_{up} reaches an arbitrary small number, we say we are at the equilibrium point.

An Iterative Approach to Finding Equilibrium

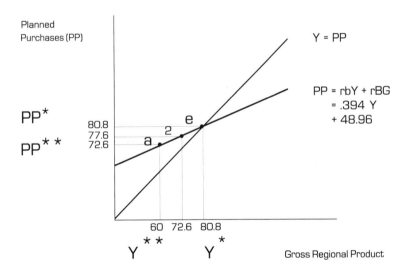

Diagram 2-5

In table 2-4, we show the results of the iteration process at the end of each iteration, as generated with the Regional Economic Modeling System (REMS) computer program that is available with this book. It is clear that IL_{up} gets smaller in absolute value after each iteration, as does the change in Y_m from the previous iteration $(Y_m - Y_{m-1})$. Thus, we can use the size of the change in Y or the size of IL_{up} to decide when we have gotten near enough to the e value. If we had started with PP_0, which was larger than P*, the value of e would still be the final result, because the absolute value of inventory accumulation at every point above e will become smaller after each iteration. The results from a solution using 100 as the starting value are shown on table 2-5. In this case, you will note that IL_{up} is positive, and Y** decreases with each iteration. This table can be reproduced by setting the 1977 initial value of PP at 100 in the "data prep" section in the REMS software.

The iterative process is the algorithm that we use to find the simultaneous solution to all of the equations (i.e., the *e*-value) for each year. It is sometimes called the Gauss-Sidel solution method. The degree of accuracy of the solution can be increased by increasing the number of iterations arbitrarily. It can also be increased by reducing the size of the convergence criteria that is used to test when the difference between PP_{m-1} and Y_m (i.e., the value of IL_{up}) is small enough to assume that equilibrium (*e*) has been reached.

TABLE 2-4

Iterative Solution for an Economic Base Model
for 1977

Iteration	Y	PP	CG	BN	IL_{up}
0	60.00000	60.00000	0.00000	0.00000	0.00000
1	60.00000	72.59840	48.24000	48.96080	-12.59840
2	72.59840	77.56167	58.36911	48.96080	-4.96327
3	77.56167	79.51699	62.35958	48.96080	-1.95533
4	79.51699	80.28731	63.93166	48.96080	-0.77032
5	80.28731	80.59079	64.55100	48.96080	-0.30348
6	80.59079	80.71035	64.79500	48.96080	-0.11956
7	80.71035	80.75745	64.89112	48.96080	-0.04710
8	80.75745	80.77600	64.92899	48.96080	-0.01856
9	80.77600	80.78331	64.94391	48.96080	-0.00731
10	80.78331	80.78619	64.94979	48.96080	-0.00288
11	80.78619	80.78733	64.95210	48.96080	-0.00113
12	80.78733	80.78778	64.95301	48.96080	-0.00045

TABLE 2-5

Iterative Solution for an Economic Base Model
for 1977

Iteration	Y	PP	CG	BN	IL_{up}
0	100.00000	100.00000	0.00000	0.00000	0.00000
1	100.00000	88.35680	80.40000	48.96080	11.64320
2	88.35680	83.76984	71.03887	48.96080	4.58696
3	83.76984	81.96277	67.35096	48.96080	1.80708
4	81.96277	81.25085	65.89807	48.96080	0.71192
5	81.25085	80.97039	65.32569	48.96080	0.28047
6	80.97039	80.85989	65.10019	48.96080	0.11049
7	80.85989	80.81636	65.01135	48.96080	0.04353
8	80.81636	80.79921	64.97636	48.96080	0.01715
9	80.79921	80.79246	64.96257	48.96080	0.00676
10	80.79246	80.78980	64.95714	48.96080	0.00266
11	80.78980	80.78875	64.95500	48.96080	0.00105
12	80.78875	80.78834	64.95415	48.96080	0.00041

Baseline and Alternative Forecasts

To obtain a baseline forecast covering a number of years, the values of BG_t (where t indicates the year) need to be predicted. In the program to solve this model, it is most convenient to use the values of the last year as the starting point for the next year's solution. A computer program to carry this out, as well as other programs shown in this book, are available from the author on a diskette for an IBM-compatible PC. You should try these out on your computer. We extend the exogenous variable (BG_t) forward. In this case, we use changes given in the United States Index of Durable Goods production, since Michigan exports depend heavily on durable goods, to "predict" the changes in the Michigan BG value from 1977 through 1982. This index[6] and the values of BG, if it had moved as the United States durable goods industrial production index did, are shown on table 2-6.

TABLE 2-6

"Prediction" of Michigan's Economic Base Using United States Durable Goods Industrial Production Rates of Change

Durable Goods	1977	1978	1979	1980	1981	1982
U.S. Industrial Production Index	100	106.5	110.7	108.6	111.0	103.1
Michigan Predicted BG	99.92	106.4	110.6	108.5	110.9	103.0

A Simple Michigan Economic Base Model Control Forecast

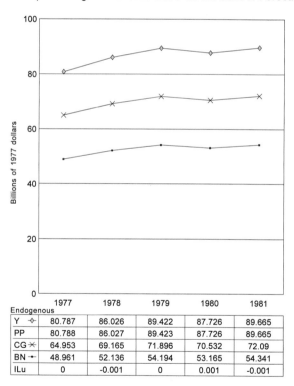

Endogenous	1977	1978	1979	1980	1981
Y ◇	80.787	86.026	89.422	87.726	89.665
PP	80.788	86.027	89.423	87.726	89.665
CG ✶	64.953	69.165	71.896	70.532	72.09
BN ●	48.961	52.136	54.194	53.165	54.341
ILu	0	-0.001	0	0.001	-0.001

Diagram 2-6

Using these projected values, the model can generate the baseline "forecast" shown on diagram 2-6. Note that behind the equilibrium values for each year was an iterative process to find these values. The iterations required and the values of the variables for each iteration are available through your program.

To carry out a policy simulation, we need to consider how a proposed change will alter an exogenous variable or a parameter of the model. Then, we need to make this change and rerun the forecast. The result, obtained by subtracting the control from the alternative forecast, shows the effect of the policy or external change on the local economy. Policy variables can be either multiplicative or additive. The simple economic base model for Michigan can be rewritten to include policy variables as follows:

$$BN = (0.49 \times PVrBGM \times PVrM)(BG + PVBGA) \qquad (2\text{-}64)$$

$$PP = (0.49 \times PVrCGM \times PVrM)CG + BN \qquad (2\text{-}65)$$

$$CG = (0.804 \times PVbM)Y, \qquad (2\text{-}66)$$

where

Variable	Default Values	Definition
PVrBGM	$= 1$	Policy variable for changing the share of gross economic base exports that come from local inputs;
PVrM	$= 1$	Policy variable for changing the share of gross exports and of local CG that are produced locally;
PVrCGM	$= 1$	Policy variables for changing the proportions of local CG supplied locally
PVbM	$= 1$	Policy variable for changing the average and marginal propensity to consume; and
PVBGA	$= 0$	Policy variable for changing gross exports (BG).

The policy variables ending in M are multiplicative, and the policy variables ending in A are additive. This is reflected in their default values. It is easy to see that when all of the policy variables are at their default values, we have the economic base model that was used to generate the control forecast. However, if we increase the default value for a multiplicative policy variable to 1.02, we will increase the parameter (or exogenous variable) by 2 percent. Likewise, if an additive policy variable is increased by 2, it will have the same effect as increasing the parameter or exogenous variable to which it is attached by 2. Much of the work in performing a policy study involves translating the change caused by a policy into appropriate policy variable changes.

The most common change made is to assume that a policy is successful in increasing economic base activity by enough to generate an amount (say 1) of net economic base output. Thus, to increase the gross economic base output (BG) by this amount, we divide the desired change in BN (1) by r (0.49, in this case) to obtain the change in BG required to produce this change in BN (2.04; i.e., 1.00/0.49 = 2.04). In table 2-7, we show the baseline values, and then alternative values with PVBGA equal to 2.04 from 1977 to 1981. We also show the difference between the control and the alternative for each of the years, indicating our predicted policy effect. The results of this simulation are also shown in diagram 2-7.

A Simple Michigan Economic Base Model Simulation

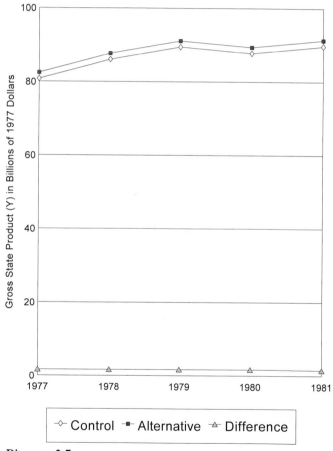

Diagram 2-7

TABLE 2-7

A Forecast and Simulation Using the Michigan Economic Base Model

CONTROL FORECAST

Policies

	1977	1978	1979	1980	1981
PVbM	1.000	1.000	1.000	1.000	1.000
PVrM	1.000	1.000	1.000	1.000	1.000
PVrBGM	1.000	1.000	1.000	1.000	1.000
PVrCGM	1.000	1.000	1.000	1.000	1.000
PVBGA	0.000	0.000	0.000	0.000	0.000

Endogenous

	1977	1978	1979	1980	1981
Y	80.787	86.026	89.422	87.726	89.665
PP	80.788	86.027	89.423	87.726	89.665
CG	64.953	69.165	71.896	70.532	72.090
BN	48.961	52.136	54.194	53.165	54.341
IL_{up}	0.000	-0.001	0.000	0.001	-0.001

POLICY SIMULATION

Policies

	1977	1978	1979	1980	1981
PVbM	1.000	1.000	1.000	1.000	1.000
PVrM	1.000	1.000	1.000	1.000	1.000
PVrBGM	1.000	1.000	1.000	1.000	1.000
PVrCGM	1.000	1.000	1.000	1.000	1.000
PVBGA	2.040	2.040	2.040	2.040	2.040

Endogenous

	1977	1978	1979	1980	1981
Y	82.437	87.676	91.072	89.376	91.314
PP	82.437	87.676	91.072	89.375	91.315
CG	66.279	70.491	73.222	71.858	73.416
BN	49.960	53.136	55.194	54.165	55.341
IL_{up}	0.000	-0.001	0.000	0.001	-0.001

EFFECTS OF POLICY CHANGES
(Alternative Minus the Control)

Policies

PVbM	0.000	0.000	0.000	0.000	0.000
PVrM	0.000	0.000	0.000	0.000	0.000
PVrBGM	0.000	0.000	0.000	0.000	0.000
PVrCGM	0.000	0.000	0.000	0.000	0.000
PVBGA	2.040	2.040	2.040	2.040	2.040

Endogenous

Y	1.650	1.650	1.650	1.650	1.650	1.649
PP	1.649	1.649	1.649	1.649	1.649	1.650
CG	1.326	1.326	1.326	1.326	1.326	1.326
BN	0.999	1.000	1.000	1.000	1.000	1.000
IL_{up}	0.000	0.000	0.000	0.000	0.000	0.000

30

We find that if we divide the change in the endogenous variables Y, PP, and CG by the change in BN (i.e., $0.49 \times BG$), then we obtain the ratio 1.65, 1.65, and 1.32, respectively. These values are the same for each year of the simulation. This ratio of Y to BN is called the *multiplier* and is constant due to the simple linear nature of the model at hand. The value of r (.49) times the consumption multiplier (1.32) is .65, or the amount of extra local production per dollar of increase in BN. This value plus 1 is the Y multiplier.

Returning to our equation 2-43, we represent the baseline or control values as C and the alternative as A. When we subtract the control from the alternative, equation 2-69 expressed in changes is obtained.

$$Y_A = rb\ Y_A + BN_A \quad \text{\textit{Alternative}} \qquad (2\text{-}67)$$

$$-Y_C = -rb\ Y_C - BN_C \quad \text{\textit{Control (Baseline)}} \qquad (2\text{-}68)$$

$$Y_A - Y_C = rb\ (Y_A - Y_C) + BN_A - BN_C \qquad (2\text{-}69)$$

$$\Delta Y = rb\ \Delta Y + \Delta BN \qquad (2\text{-}70)$$

Output Determination After an Exogenous Change

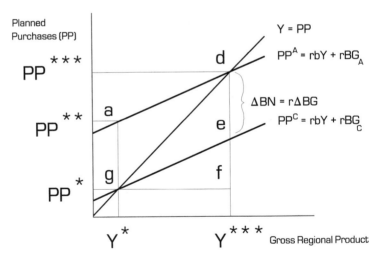

Diagram 2-8

Diagram 2-8 illustrates the effects of such a change. In this diagram, the demand curve shifts up from PP^C to PP^A due to an increase in the exogenous variable BG. The equilibrium expenditure and output, determined by the intersection of the demand curve and the 45-degree line, moves from *g* to *d*. The total equilibrium demand moves from PP* to PP***, corresponding to the equal rise in output from Y* to Y***. Although *r*BG increased by the distance PP** − PP* (*d-e* or *a-g*), the expenditure increased by PP*** − PP* (*d-f*), which is significantly larger than just the exogenous change in *r*BG. The vertical difference PP*** − PP** (*d-a* or *e-f*) is equal to the induced demand caused by increases in Y (*rb*ΔY). If *rb* were equal to zero, the PP line would be horizontal, and the vertical distance PP** to PP*** (*d-a*) would be equal to zero.

The Multiplier (K)

A very important distinction in model building is the difference between structural equations in a model and equations in the model's *reduced form*. The structural equations of a model show causality. They set forth the behavioral assumptions and identities in the model. The reduced-form equations simply have one of the endogenous variables on the left and all of the exogenous variables on the right.

In model building, there is a distinction between *parameters* and exogenous variables in the model. In general, the distinction is that parameters of a model are fixed, whereas exogenous variables take on different values during the sample periods.[7] We illustrate these concepts using the economic base model that we have developed up to this point. The model can be restated as follows:

$$BN = rBG \qquad\qquad (2\text{-}71)$$

$$Y = rCG + BN \qquad\qquad (2\text{-}72)$$

$$CG = bY \qquad\qquad (2\text{-}73)$$

An Economic Base Model

Legend

Y   Output
CG Consumption and Local
    Government Spending
BG Economic Base Output (Gross)
BN Economic Base Output (Net)

☐   Endogenous

◇   Exogenous

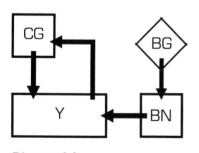

Diagram 2-9

Using equations 2-71, 2-72, and 2-73 as our structural equations, we can identify r and b as the parameters of the model. Y, BN, and CG are the endogenous variables, and BG is an exogenous variable. A causal arrow diagram of the model might be drawn as represented in diagram 2-9.

From diagram 2-9, we can see how a change in the exogenous variable, the economic base (BG and then BN), changes output (Y), which in turn changes individual spending (CG). This circle of causality continues to be repeated until a new equilibrium is reached.

A way to find the value of Y directly for any given BG for the simple economic base model is to find the reduced form of the model, where Y is on the left and only BG is on the right. This approach cannot be generalized to work with the more complicated models, which we will consider later, in the same way that the iterative approach works for almost all economic models. We obtain equation 2-74 by substituting equations 2-71 and 2-73 into equation 2-72.

$$Y = (rb)Y + rBG, \tag{2-74}$$

in which the endogenous variable Y is on both sides of the equation. The similarity between this equation and equation 2-69 should be noted.

We arrange equation 2-74 so that

$$Y = \left[\frac{1}{1-rb} \right] rBG \tag{2-75}$$

This is a reduced-form equation. It shows the endogenous variable (Y) as a function of model parameters (r and b, which would be values estimated from data in an actual model) and the model's exogenous variable (BG). By using the reduced-form equation, we can estimate the effects on output (Y) of a change in the exogenous variable BG.

We use 1977 values from Michigan to develop an economic base estimate.

$$Y = \left[\frac{1}{1 - (.49)(.804)} \right] (.49\,BG)$$
$$= 1.65\,(.49\,BG) \tag{2-76}$$

Equation 2-75 can also be expressed in the form

$$\frac{Y}{rBG} = \frac{Y}{BN} = \frac{1}{1 - rb} \tag{2-77}$$

If we take the derivative of equation 2-75 with respect to BN, or if we apply the same procedure that we used to derive equation 2-70, we obtain

$$\frac{\Delta Y}{\Delta BN} = \frac{dY}{dBN} = \frac{1}{1 - rb} = K \tag{2-78}$$

This gives us the multiplier K. Using the same operations on equation 2-76 for Michigan, we obtain

$$\frac{\Delta Y}{\Delta BN} = \frac{\Delta Y}{\Delta(rBG)} = \frac{dY}{d(rBG)}$$

$$= \frac{dY}{dBN} = \frac{1}{1 - (.49)(0.804)} = 1.65 \tag{2-79}$$

This multiplier shows the change that is required in equilibrium output in response to a change in the BN variable. It confirms the result that we obtained with the iterative approach for each year by subtracting the baseline from the alternative.

The Effect of the Parameter Changes

While r and b are regarded as parameters of our model, it would be interesting to see what would happen to the local economy if r or b were changed. The easiest way to do this is to use the framework that we have set up for an iterative approach to model solution. For example, suppose we undertook policies to increase the local content (r) of goods and services purchased locally (CG) and of gross economic base exports (BG). This can be accomplished by increasing r in the alternative forecast, using the PVrM policy variable. If we wanted to compare increasing BG by 2.04 with a policy to encourage increased local content by enough to raise net demand by 1.00 (e.g., by subsidizing a local person to become a brewer for a local tavern in an area where no beer is currently brewed), we would have to calculate the change in r that is required to accomplish this increase in the base period.

$$\Delta Y = 1.00 = 0.49 \, (PVrM)(BG + CG) \tag{2-80}$$

$$PVrM = \frac{1.00}{0.49 \, (BG + CG)} = \frac{1.00}{0.49 \, (99.92 + 65)} = 0.012375 \tag{2-81}$$

Thus, the value for PVrM in the alternative would be set at 1.012375. The results from this simulation are shown on table 2-8. Comparing this table with table 2-7, we see that raising r (i.e., import substitution) is as effective as expanding BG (the economic base) as a way to stimulate Y (output).

TABLE 2-8

Michigan Economic Base Model

Effects of Increasing r by .012

	1977	1978	1979	1980	1981
PVrM	0.012	0.012	0.012	0.012	0.012
Y	1.612	1.717	1.785	1.751	1.789
CG	1.296	1.380	1.434	1.408	1.439
BN	0.587	0.626	0.650	0.638	0.652

At this point, it might be instructive to do a number of policy simulations using the policy variables in the simple economic base model. In doing these simulations, remember that you need to think of a policy that will lead to an exogenous variable or parameter change. Then, you represent it quantitatively in the model. You must be sure to include all of the effects not shown in the model. For example, increasing spending on local schools or financing a new industrial park with local taxes may change PVbM, PVBGA, and PVrM.

Converting Output (Y) to Employment (E)

Regional economic models are used to make predictions of the changes in economic activity in a local area for the purpose of planning and public policy making. Employment data is the primary source of data for subnational areas, and employment is usually the greatest concern in public policy making. To predict changes in employment, the model is converted from dollar terms to employment terms.

To do this, four new definitions are presented:

E   total employment

EXFG   employment dependent on exports, including the federal government

EIL_p employment dependent on local planned investment

ECG   employment dependent on local consumer and government spending

EBN employment dependent on local investment and exports, including federal government

Algebraically, the terms are defined as

$$E = ECG + EXFG + EIL_p \qquad (2\text{-}82)$$

$$E = ECG + EBN, \qquad (2\text{-}83)$$

where

$$EBN = EIL_p + EXFG \qquad (2\text{-}84)$$

Note that, in employment units, EIL_p and EXFG are already net (not gross) variables, because, by measuring employment input, we capture that portion of investment and exports (BG) that is supplied locally.

To convert the dollar amounts to employment, we must make an assumption about the relationship of value added to employment. We assume that employees per unit of value added in producing Y is equal to the average number of employees per unit of value added. The employees per unit of value added (E/Y) is called *epv*, which produces

$$epv = \frac{E}{Y} \qquad (2\text{-}85)$$

By expressing output in terms of employment and the number of employees per dollar of value added, we obtain

$$Y = \frac{E}{epv} \qquad (2\text{-}86)$$

Thus, the number of employees per unit of value added is assumed to be fixed and the same for all types of production in this simple model.

This means that *epv* is assumed to be the average employment per dollar of local value added in the export sector (EXFG/rXFG), in the investment sector (EIL_p/rIL_p), and in the local consumption and government spending sector (ECG/rCG), producing the equalities

$$rXFG = EXFG/epv \qquad (2\text{-}87)$$

$$rIL_p = EIL_p/epv \qquad (2\text{-}88)$$

$$rCG = ECG/epv \qquad (2\text{-}89)$$

$$rBG = EBN/epv \qquad (2\text{-}90)$$

36

which implies that

$$EBN = epv \times BN \qquad (2\text{-}91)$$

We restate the causal arrow diagram in employment terms in diagram 2-10.

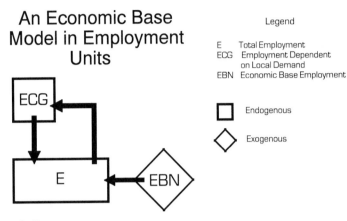

An Economic Base Model in Employment Units

Legend

E   Total Employment
ECG   Employment Dependent
        on Local Demand
EBN   Economic Base Employment

☐ Endogenous

◇ Exogenous

Diagram 2-10

Economic base employment (EBN) is assumed to be the production for export, multiplied by the average number of employees per dollar of value added in all sectors (epv). Using equation 2-43,

$$Y = rbY + BN, \qquad (2\text{-}92)$$

we can substitute for Y and BN to obtain

$$\frac{E}{epv} = rb\frac{E}{epv} + \frac{EXFG}{epv} + \frac{EIL_p}{epv} = rb\frac{E}{epv} + \frac{EBN}{epv} \qquad (2\text{-}93)$$

We can find the reduced form from equation 2-93, as follows:

$$\frac{E}{epv} = \frac{1}{1-rb}\left[\frac{EBN}{epv}\right] \qquad (2\text{-}94)$$

or

$$E = \frac{1}{1-rb} EBN \qquad (2\text{-}95)$$

We divide equation 2-95 by (EXFG + EIL_p = EBN) to obtain

$$\frac{E}{EBN} = \frac{1}{1-rb} \qquad (2\text{-}96)$$

This is the employment counterpart to equation 2-77, which is in output units. To predict the change in total employment, based on the change in exogenous employment (EBN), we take the derivative of E with respect to EBN, or perform the same operation we used to obtain equation 2-70, which yields

$$\frac{\Delta E}{\Delta EBN} = \frac{d(E)}{d(EBN)} = \frac{1}{1 - rb} = K$$

(2-97)

This is the same multiplier (K) in employment units that we previously estimated in output units in equation 2-78.

While the multiplier can be obtained from equation 2-96, the value of r cannot be determined from the reduced form unless the value of b can be found from a different source. This illustrates the problem, in general, with the reduced form relative to the structural approach. When we know K but not r and b, we cannot do simulations that involve changes in r or b. This is especially important in this case, because changing r may be key to stimulating the local economy.

2-2 EMPIRICAL IMPLEMENTATION OF THE ECONOMIC BASE MODEL

We estimated the parameters for the Michigan model, as shown previously, using regional income and product account data developed for a full-scale forecasting and simulation model. An economic base model can also be estimated using primary data sources published by the U.S. government. However, none of the available data explicitly separates employment into basic and nonbasic sectors. Therefore, we must find a way to derive the numbers needed for our economic base model from the published data. To do this, we first develop an adequate database. Then, we determine which employees are economic base employees for each industry. Finally, we add these employees together to find the total number of economic base employees. This becomes a key input into the process of estimating the parameters for all of the single sector models in this book. Our focus here is on United States data. However, similar data issues are likely to exist in other countries.

Using Available Data

Employment data, based on place of employment for states and counties, is tied to either social security records for employees or records from the unemployment insurance program. Data from the Bureau of Labor Statistics (BLS) and the Bureau of Economic Analysis (BEA) are based on unemployment insurance data, often called *ES-202 data*. County Business Patterns (CBP) data, published by the Census Bureau, is drawn from social security records. The BLS also conducts the 790 program, which samples firms and gives current estimates of employment that are benchmarked annually to the ES-202 data. BEA uses some other data sources, including income tax returns, to estimate self-employment and to supplement the ES-202 wage and salary employment data. The other major sources of employment data are the decennial Census Data and the Current Population Survey.

The BLS and the BEA data lack detail. The Census does not provide annual information, and the population sample of the Current Population Survey is too small to yield reliable regional data. For our current purpose, the best data source, due both to its detail and frequency, is County Business Patterns.

County Business Patterns reports March employment figures by industry for every county in the United States. At the detailed level of about 1,400 industries, the annual data gives the number of employees, the first quarter and annual payroll, the total number of establishments, and the number of establishments by employment-size class. Due to their reliance on social security records, CBP tables do not show employment figures for government or self-employed workers.

TABLE 2-9[8]

1987 Employment by Major Sector
Adams County, Colorado

Total	97,009
Agricultural services	365
Mining	550
Contract construction	6,545
Manufacturing	12,807
Transportation and other public utilities	11,643
Wholesale trade	19,940
Finance, insurance, and real estate	3,721
Services	14,041
Unclassified establishments	222
Federal government employment	6,254
State and local government employment	11,059

Total employment in each county is divided into ten major, private nonfarm sectors, as shown by the Adams County, Colorado data in table 2-9.[9] Total wage and salary employment reported by CBP is equal to the sum of the employment in each of the aggregate sectors. The number of government workers is available from the Bureau of Economic Analysis (BEA) Regional Economic Information Systems (REIS). The number of self-employed people in nongovernment sectors is also available in the BEA data, but it is not used in this chapter.

Unlike the BEA county data, CBP reports employment in progressively more detailed levels. This is illustrated by an excerpt from the Adams County data shown in table 2-10. Some detail is left in this table to show the specificity with which CBP defines sectors.

TABLE 2-10[10]

Excerpt from the Construction Sector of County Business Patterns (CBP)
Adams County, Colorado

SIC	Industry	No. of Employees for the Week Including March 12
	CONTRACT CONSTRUCTION	
15	GENERAL CONTRACTORS AND OPERATIVE BUILDERS	6,545
16	HEAVY CONSTRUCTION CONTRACTORS	856
	161 Highway and street construction	207
	162 Heavy construction, except highway	350
17	SPECIAL TRADE CONTRACTORS	5,065
	171 Plumbing, heating, air conditioning	1,049
	172 Painting, paper hanging, decorating	116
	173 Electrical work	864
	174 Masonry, stonework, and plastering	513
	175 Carpentry and flooring	224
	1751 Carpentry	153
	1752 Floor laying and floor work, not elsewhere classified	71
	176 Roofing and sheet metal work	367
	177 Concrete work	935
	179 Misc. special trade contractors	852

Each detailed industry is defined by a number. This is the *standard industrial classification* (SIC) code, in which sectors are categorized at the two-, three-, or four-digit level. The relationship is hierarchical. In other words, two-digit sectors are subcategories of the aggregate sectors, three-digit sectors are components of two-digit sectors, and four-digit sectors are classified as part of three-digit sectors. For example, contract construction in Adams County consists of SIC-15, general contractors and operative builders; SIC-16, heavy construction contractors; and SIC-17, special trade contractors. At the four-digit level, we see that carpentry (SIC-1751) and floor laying and floor work not elsewhere classified (SIC-1752) are components of carpentry and flooring (SIC-175).

If each worker were classified at a detailed level, the sum of subsectors would equal the aggregate sector. However, CBP is sometimes unable to classify employees. For example, the sum of employment in SIC-161 and SIC-162 is 557 (207 + 350). This is less than the total of 604 employees reported at the respective two-digit sector (SIC-16). In this example, 47 workers are reported at the two-digit level but not at the three-digit level. To have a working model, we must somehow classify unidentified employees. Our solution to this problem is, by its nature, somewhat arbitrary. One possible approach would be to allocate unclassified employees among the sub-categories in the same proportion as those who are classified.

A further problem that we encounter is CBP data suppression, which is done to protect the confidentiality of individual companies. Thus, for an industry with a small number of firms or a few firms that employ a large percentage of the total workers, CBP reports the *employment-size class* of the sector rather than the exact number of employees. When data is suppressed in the CBP tables, you will find letters representing employment ranges. In table 2-11, for example, the letters B and C in the employment column represent ranges of 20 to 99 and 100 to 249, respectively.

TABLE 2-11[11]

Grain Mill Products (CBP Data)
Adams County, Colorado

SIC	Industry	No. of Employees (for the week including March 12)	Payroll in Thousands of Dollars		Total No. of Establishments	No. of Establishments by Employment-Size Class							
			1st Qtr.	Annual		1-4	5-9	10-19	20-49	50-99	100-249	250-499	550-999
204	Grain Mill Products	193	1,539	6,668	5	-	2	-	2	-	1	-	-
2041	Flour and other grain mill products	(C)	(D)	(D)	1	-	-	-	-	-	1	-	-
2048	Prepared foods, n.e.c.	(B)	(D)	(D)	3	-	1	-	2	-	-	-	-

Note: Employment-size classes are indicated as follows:

A = 0 to 19	E = 250 to 499	H = 2,500 to 4,999	K = 25,000 to 49,999
B = 20 to 99	F = 500 to 999	I = 5,000 to 10,000	L = 50,000 to 99,999
C = 100 to 249	G = 1,000 to 2,499	J = 10,000 to 24,999	M = 100,000 or more

D = Disclosure Suppression

These employment-size classes can help us approximate employment numbers for suppressed data. We could assume, for example, that employment is equal to the midpoint of the range given for an industry. Accordingly, we would estimate employment in prepared feeds not elsewhere classified (n.e.c.)[12] (SIC-2048) as being equal to 60, which is the midpoint of employment class B. We would also estimate employment in flour and grain mill products (SIC-2041) as being equal to 175, the midpoint of employment class C. These estimates would then need to be adjusted downward, since the sum of estimated employment at the four-digit level (60 + 175 = 235) would exceed the 193 employees reported for SIC-204.

We could also estimate suppressed data as the sum of the employment in individual establishments. The right-hand columns in CBP show the number of establishments in each employment class. In table 2-11, we see that SIC-2048 includes one establishment employing five to nine workers and two others each employing twenty to forty-nine workers. Assuming that the midpoint of the employment-size range is equal to the employment in the establishment, we would estimate SIC-2048 employment as [(1 × 7) + (2 × 35)], or 77 workers, and SIC-2041 employment as 175, for a total of 252 workers. Again, we would need to adjust the four-digit level estimates downward to reflect the total SIC-204 employment given as 193 above.

A final limitation of the CBP data arises because it is first-quarter rather than full-year employment. For an industry that has a large seasonal change in employment, March data could overreport or underreport average annual employment. We could use first-quarter and annual payroll figures to estimate seasonal employment changes. For example, the first-quarter payroll rate in Adams County for grain mill products is less than the total payroll rate for the year. To obtain a seasonally-adjusted annual employment estimate, we might scale up the seasonal employment to reflect the seasonal payroll differences.

Having obtained figures for all types of employment and having compensated for unclassified workers, suppressed data, and seasonal variations in employment, we would like to obtain a numerical solution for the economic base model. The multiplier (K) is given as

$$K = \frac{E}{EBN} , \qquad (2\text{-}98)$$

where E is total employment, and EBN is economic base employment.

Estimating Economic Base Employment

The first step in measuring economic base employment is to find employment by disaggregated industry, as we did previously. Next, we refer back to the behavioral assumption of the model to define the difference between ECG and EBN. Consumption and local government spending (CG) is dependent on local output, as a proxy for income. The values of rXFG and rIL$_p$ are determined exogenously. The activity associated with local output, assuming a uniform employment-to-output ratio in all sectors, is ECG, while that associated with exogenous activity is EXFG and EIL$_p$, or simply economic base employment EBN (where EBN = EXFG + EIL$_p$). Employment directly dependent on consumption by local consumers and government goes in the ECG category, while a commodity produced locally for the national or international market goes into exports, and is, therefore, counted in the EBN category. Employment for a commodity that is produced locally, as an intermediate input for a product that will be sold nationally or internationally, is also in the EBN category because it depends on sales from the area to national and international markets. Having established these definitions, we need a method to divide employment into ECG and EBN. The standard methods used to estimate this economic base are (1) the judgmental approach, (2) the location quotient, and (3) the minimum requirements technique. We present these three approaches in turn.

Judgmental Approach

The first approach is labeled judgmental, because it relies on the judgment of the analyst. He or she simply looks over the industries and categorizes them based on a subjective assessment of whether they are producing for the local market or for direct or indirect export out of the local area. For example, employment in grocery stores or regular dental services is almost certainly for the local market, while employment for the production of guided missiles or airplanes is almost certainly for export. However, other industries present more difficult choices. A printing company, for example, may be printing the local newspaper or it may be printing encyclopedias. In the former case, the industry is local; in the latter, it is almost all export. The classification is also difficult for industries that supply other industries. Here, one must know what industries they serve and what market is served by the industries that use their inputs.

The judgmental approach is a somewhat ad hoc process, and the results may vary from one analyst to another. In many cases, the approach benefits substantially from the analyst's knowledge about the specific area. In this case, we illustrate how we might proceed in a case where we have only the information contained in the CBP publication.

We use an example to illustrate the judgmental method. Table 2-12 shows our division of employment in the mining industry.

TABLE 2-12[13]

Mining Sector
Economic Base and Local Employment
Adams County, Colorado

		ET	EBN	ECG
MINING		550	524	26
13	OIL AND GAS EXTRACTION	278	278	0
	138 Oil and gas field services	278	278	0
	1381 Drilling oil and gas wells	198	198	0
	1398 Oil and gas field services, n.e.c.	80	80	0
14	NONMETALLIC MINERALS, EXCEPT FUELS	132	106	26
	144 Sand and gravel	132	106	26
	1442 Administrative and auxiliary	140	140	0

Most of the employees are economic base employees in the mining sector. We assume that the local consumption of locally produced oil is insignificant, and therefore assign this sector's 278 employees to EBN. Sand and gravel is difficult to transport, so we assume that at least some of the workers in this industry are supplying noninvestment local demand.

The last category, administrative and auxiliary, often refers to employees working in a headquarters office, rather than working directly on the production of the commodity or service in question. We also classify them as EBN employees. On a more aggregated level, table 2-13 shows our complete ECG and EBN assignments.

TABLE 2-13[14]

Major Sector
Economic Base and Local Employment
Adams County, Colorado

	ET	EBN	ECG
Total	97,009	24,573	72,436
Agricultural services, forestry and fisheries	365	65	300
Mining	550	524	26
Contract construction	6,545	4,860	1,685
Manufacturing	12,807	11,847	960
Transportation and other public utilities	11,643	0	11,643
Wholesale trade	9,862	0	9,862
Retail trade	19,940	0	19,940
Finance, insurance and real estate	3,721	0	3,721
Services	14,041	972	13,069
Unclassified establishments	222	51	171
Federal government	6,254	6,254	0
State and local government	11,059	0	11,059

Total economic base employment is 24,573. Total local employment is 72,436. Most economic base employees work in mining, construction, federal government, and manufacturing. Since we are counting investment-dependent employment (IL_p) as EBN, workers involved in building new roads and houses are considered EBN. In the construction sectors, only maintenance and repair workers are classified as ECG.

From examining the detailed sectors, we guess that while some service employees are exporting their production, most are supplying the local market. We divided unclassified establishments to match the proportion of employment found in EBN and ECG among the classified industries. A preponderance of employees work to supply the local market, including some in every large category of industry. ECG workers include all of those working in transportation, wholesale trade, and retail trade.

Location Quotient

The next approach that we present for estimating EBN is called the *location quotient (LQ) method*. This is used to find the EXFG portion of EBN. The location quotient is a measure of the concentration of an industry in a region. This approach assumes that an industry in a region that has a proportion of employment in that industry that is greater than the national average, exports all of the output produced by the employees who are in excess of the national proportion. Local investment, such as contract construction, is still determined judgmentally. We use the following definitions to calculate the location quotient:

LQ(i)   the location quotient for industry i in the local region

E(i)   employment in industry i in the local region

E   total employment in the local region, and

EU   total employment in the United States

LQ(i) is calculated as

$$LQ(i) = \frac{E(i)/E}{EU(i)/EU} \qquad (2\text{-}99)$$

The location quotient is the proportion of employment in industry i relative to the United States proportion of employment in industry i. If two out of one hundred employees in a region are involved in furniture manufacture, for example, and two million out of one hundred million employees in the United States make furniture, then

$$E(i)/E = 2/100 = .02 \qquad (2\text{-}100)$$
$$EU(i)/EU = 2\ million/100\ million = .02 \qquad (2\text{-}101)$$

In other words, both the region and the nation employ 2 percent of their workers in the furniture business. Our location quotient is calculated as follows:

$$LQ(i) = \frac{E(i)/E}{EU(i)/EU} = \frac{.02}{.02} = 1 \qquad (2\text{-}102)$$

A location quotient of 1 indicates that the region employs the same proportion of people in industry i that we find in that industry nationwide. If there is a proportionally high amount of employment in a particular industry within the region, then the location quotient is greater than 1. If there is a proportionally low amount of employment in a particular industry within the region, then the location quotient is less than 1.

Location quotients are calculated at the most detailed level for which data is available. In the mining sector, for example, Adams County data is reported for SIC-1381, SIC-1389, SIC-1442, and administrative and auxiliary employees. We compute a separate location quotient for each of these sectors. Table 2-14 shows Adams County, Colorado and United States employment figures and our computation of the EXFG employment using the location quotient approach for the mining sector.

TABLE 2-14[15]

Mining Sector Location Quotient Determined Local and Economic Base Employment

	Adams County	United States	Location Quotient LQ(i)	Export Employment (EXFG)	Local Employment (ECG)
Total Employment	79696	85483804			
MINING	550	724967		233	327
13 OIL AND GAS EXTRACTION	278	428303		128	150
131 Crude petroleum and natural gas	0	158913	0.00	0	0
132 Natural gas liquids	0	16369	0.00	0	0
138 Oil and gas field services	278	253020		128	150
1381 Drilling oil and gas wells	198	75464	2.81	128	70
1382 Oil and gas exploration services	0	25198	0.00	0	0
1389 Oil and gas field services, n.e.c.	80	152357	0.56	0	80
14 NONMETALLIC MINERALS, EXCEPT FUELS	132	141030		95	37
141 Dimension stone	0	3378	0.00	0	0
142 Crushed and broken stone	0	49264	0.00	0	0
144 Sand and gravel	132	44316		95	37
1442 Construction sand and gravel	132	39210	3.61	95	37
1446 Industrial sand	0	5106	0.00	0	0

	Adams County	United States	Location Quotient LQ(i)	Export Employment (EXFG)	Local Employment (ECG)
14 NONMETALLIC MINERALS, EXCEPT FUELS, cont.					
145 Clay, ceramic and refractory materials	0	11592	0.00	0	0
147 Chemical and fertilizer materials	0	21984	0.00	0	0
148 Nonmetallic minerals services	0	1860	0.00	0	0
149 Miscellaneous nonmetallic minerals	0	8636	0.00	0	0
ADMINISTRATIVE AND AUXILIARY	140	155634	0.96	0	140

We see that Adams County mining employment is proportionally high in drilling oil and gas wells (LQ = 2.81) and in construction sand and gravel (LQ = 3.61). The relative proportion of employment in administrative and auxiliary jobs (0.96) is about the same as found in the rest of the United States, while the relative employment in oil and gas field services n.e.c. (0.56) is lower than in the United States. Location quotients for all four-digit sectors other than those mentioned is zero. We report location quotients of zero at the three-digit level when all of the corresponding four-digit location quotients are zero. The amount [E × (EU(i)/EU)] is the number of employees we assume a region would need in a particular industry to supply itself. If employment is proportionally low compared to the United States, then we assume that there are no exports. If employment in an industry is proportionally high, then the region has employment above the national average for this industry, which is equal to the total employment minus that needed for local supply. We assume that the product of these employees is exported, giving us EXFG(i). Algebraically, we have

$$
EXFG(i) \begin{bmatrix} EXFG(i) = 0 \ \ if \ LQ(i) \leq 1 \\[2ex] EXFG(i) = \left[\dfrac{LQ(i) - 1}{LQ(i)} \right] \times E(i) \ \ if \ LQ(i) > 1 \end{bmatrix}
\tag{2-103}
$$

Thus, in SIC-1442, LQ = 3.61; so

$$
EXFG(i) = \left[\frac{3.61 - 1}{3.61} \right] 132 = 95
\tag{2-104}
$$

The location quotient method of calculating export-dependent employment would only be accurate if several very restrictive assumptions were met: (1) no cross hauling of goods and services; (2) uniform consumption patterns; (3) equal labor productivity across regions; and (4) no international trade. To help focus our discussion of these four assumptions, we use the location quotients for mining in Adams County on table 2-14.

(1) No Cross Hauling

A region may simultaneously import and export a commodity in what is known as cross hauling. The calculation of the location quotient, however, assumes that this never occurs. This assumption is not realistic, particularly at high levels of aggregation. In the Adams County oil-and-gas-wells drilling industry, for example, we find that nearly two-thirds of employees would be classified as EXFG at the four-digit level. At the three-digit level, SIC-1381 employees would not be distinguished from other SIC-138 workers, and their collective location quotient (1.18) would lead us to classify less than one-fifth of the workers as economic base. Classified at the two-digit level (LQ = 0.70) or in the mining sector (LQ = 0.81), we would assume that all of the drilling oil and gas workers are supplying local consumption.

We would be mistaken to assume that no cross hauling occurs in aggregate industries. Even at the four-digit level, this assumption could be unrealistic. While Adams County oil and gas drilling may all be done by Exxon, residents can still buy some of their gasoline at Mobil and Chevron.

(2) Uniform Consumption Patterns

When we assume that relatively high employment in an industry implies the production of export goods, we are implying that all regions consume equal proportions of every good. However, consumption patterns may differ across regions. In the real world, for instance, we might expect Californians to buy proportionally more hot tubs than Iowans.

(3) Equal Labor Productivity

We assume that excess employment creates goods and services that are then exported. In an actual economy, however, the number of employees needed to satisfy local demand depends on their productivity. Regional labor could be more or less productive than the national average, affecting the accuracy of our economic base estimation.

(4) No International Trade

We compare employment in a local industry to the percentage of employment in that industry for the country as a whole to infer export employment. Implicitly, we assume that there are no international imports or exports. However, United States employment in the industry could be higher or lower than the amount needed to supply the total demand of the nation. If the United States exports college educational services to foreign students, for example, a state that has a location quotient of 1 might appear to be satisfying only local demand when, in fact, it is exporting by teaching an average proportion of foreign students. Conversely, a state with a location quotient of 1 for video equipment could in fact be importing this equipment, since no VCRs are made in the United States.

Despite these drawbacks, the location quotient is a frequently used measure of local and export production. In comparison to the ad hoc determination of exports in the judgmental approach, the location quotient is straightforward and well documented. Before extending the economic base model, we will discuss a third method of estimating EBN, called minimum requirements.

Minimum Requirements

The minimum requirements (MR) approach sets the least amount of production needed to meet local demand. Everything else is assumed to be exported. Unlike the LQ, this approach allows for cross hauling. The MR approach assumes that the region having the lowest location quotient for any given industry can be used as an estimate of the proportion of that industry that is used to satisfy local markets. For example, there are some states that do not produce any oil and gas. Thus, the minimum requirement of oil and gas production is zero, and all oil and gas production (in any region in the country) is assumed to be for national markets. If banking services for any state are as low as one-half of the national average of banking to total employment, then we assume that only one-half of the banking industry in a state with the average proportion of banking services is tied to the local market.

The minimum requirements approach bases an industry's exports on the concentration of the sector in the *minimum requirements region*. This is in contrast to the location quotient, which bases exports on an industry's concentration in the Unites States as a whole. We use the following equation to calculate MR exports:

$$EXFG(i) = E(i) - \left[\frac{EM(i)}{EM} \times E \right] \tag{2-105}$$

EM(i)   the employment in industry (i) in the state with the minimum LQ(i) (i.e., the minimum E(i)/E)

EM   the total employment in the minimum-requirement region

The difference between this approach and the LQ approach can be more easily seen if we rearrange the location quotient equation 2-103. We start by repeating and rearranging equation 2-103,

$$EXFG(i) = \left[\frac{LQ(i) - 1}{LQ(i)} \right] \times E(i) = \left[E(i) - \frac{E(i)}{LQ(i)} \right]$$

(2-106)

We then substitute equation 2-99 for $LQ(i)$ to obtain

$$EXFG(i) = E(i) - \left[\frac{EU(i)}{EU} \times E \right] .$$

(2-107)

In the LQ approach, we assume that the proportion of local employment required to supply local demand is the same proportion of total employment that is devoted to this industry nationally. By comparing equation 2-107 with equation 2-105, we can see that the only difference between the LQ approach and the MR approach is that the United States ratio in equation 2-107 is replaced by the ratio of that industry in the minimum requirement region in equation 2-105.

In the MR approach, the proportion of employment in industry i in the state with the lowest proportion of any state in the country $EM(i)/EM$ is multiplied by the employment (E) for the state in question. This gives us the amount of employment used to satisfy local demand in that region. We assume that any employment over this amount is equal to the exports for that state. The most surprising feature of the minimum requirements is that the ratio of E to EXFG is the same for every area. The reason for this can be deduced by starting with equation 2-105 and setting the minimum requirement for each industry in a particular year equal to its proportion $p(i)$.

$$p(i) = \frac{EM(i)}{EM}$$

(2-108)

We restate equation 2-105 as

$$EXFG(i) = E(i) - [p(i) \times E] ,$$

(2-109)

where $p(i)$ is the same in every region. Now, summing over all industries for any region, we obtain

$$\sum_{i=1}^{n} EXFG(i) = \sum_{i=1}^{n} E(i) - \left[\left(\sum_{i=1}^{n} p(i) \right) \times E \right]$$

(2-110)

Next, let $\sum\limits_{i=1}^{n} EXFG(i)$ equal EXFG, $\sum\limits_{i=1}^{n} E(i)$ equal E, and $\sum\limits_{i=1} p(i)$ equal p. Over all, we find

$$EXFG = E - (p \times E) = (1 - p) \times E \qquad (2\text{-}111)$$

Solving this equation for E/EXFG, we find that

$$\frac{E}{EXFG} = \frac{1}{1 - p} \qquad (2\text{-}112)$$

Since the summation of p(i) over all i is the same for each region, the multiplier, if it is based only on EXFG rather than on EBN, is the same for each region.

Another way to see why E/EXFG is the same for all regions is to imagine moving an employee from one industry to the next. Equation 2-111 shows that unless this region is the one used to define EM(i)/EM in that year, this transfer does not change the total export employment for that year. Thus, E/EXFG remains at a fixed value for all areas in a given year.

Calculating the Multiplier

Once the EBN (EXFG + EIL$_p$) and ECG values have been determined, we can calculate the multiplier (K). We do this using the equation for the economic base model,

$$K = \frac{EBN + ECG}{EBN} = \frac{E}{EBN} \qquad (2\text{-}113)$$

For example, we can estimate K using the judgmental numbers from Adams County. We obtain

$$K = \frac{97,009}{24,573} = 3.95 \qquad (2\text{-}114)$$

The multiplier 3.95 is high compared to the Michigan multiplier of 1.65 that we estimated in equation 2-79. This is especially surprising because, in general, we would expect a large state to have a larger multiplier than a small county. In this case, the judgmental approach gives us a high multiplier compared to one derived from the data that was constructed in the process of building a fully operational model (explained in chapter 7). More importantly, this K could be used to find the structural parameters of the employment economic base model, if we can estimate b. Using United States data for consumption (3,052) plus state and local government spending (497) and dividing by gross domestic product (4,540)[16], we calculate $b = 3549/4540 = .78$.

$$\frac{1}{1 - r(.78)} = 3.95 \quad as \tag{2-115}$$

$$1 = 3.95 - r \times .78 \times 3.95 \tag{2-116}$$

$$\frac{1 - 3.95}{.78 \times 3.95} = -r \tag{2-117}$$

$$r = \frac{3.95 - 1}{.78 \times 3.95} = .96 \tag{2-118}$$

This value of r is obviously unrealistically high. The economic base may be incorrectly estimated. As we find in the next section, it is due to a problem with the specification of the model, which happens to be important for this county. We return to estimating this model using an extended and more accurate economic base model in section 2-4. In this section, we extend our economic base model to incorporate the fact that output by place of work is not the same as income by place of residence. Before proceeding to extending the model, we first consider the forecasting accuracy of the simple economic base model, expressed in employment units, in the next section.

2-3 FORECASTING WITH AN ECONOMIC BASE MODEL

If a model is an accurate representation of the system being modeled, it should replicate the observed values of the endogenous variables providing that it uses the observed values of the exogenous variables. If the model is accurate and complete, we should also find evidence that the values of the parameters of the model have remained constant.

Making a Forecast

While we need to know the structural equations in the model for most policy simulations, it is possible to make economic forecasts based on the reduced form model. From equation 2-97, we find that the reduced form for the economic base model stated in employment terms is

$$\Delta E = K \times \Delta EBN, \tag{2-119}$$

where

$$K = \frac{1}{1 - rb} \tag{2-120}$$

Providing that r and b are parameters that remain constant, equation 2-119 can be used as our forecasting equation. If we use this equation on historical data and there is evidence that K changes or that ΔE is not accurately forecast, then this would be evidence that the model is not an accurate representation of the local economy being modeled.

Here, we present two versions of a forecasting model using the employment version of the simple economic base model. We start by restating equation 2-97 as equation 2-121.

$$E_{t+1} - E_t = K_t \times (EBN_{t+1} - EBN_t) \tag{2-121}$$

The subscripts t and $t + 1$ indicate the present year and the following year, respectively. The change in employment from one year to the next ($E_{t+1} - E_t$) is the multiplier for year t (K_t), which is multiplied by the change in economic base employment ($EBN_{t+1} - EBN_t$). Forecasted employment in this model, which we will call model A1, is given by equation 2-122.

$$F1_{t+1} = \left[K_t \times (EBN_{t+1} - EBN_t) \right] + E_t \tag{2-122}$$

Predicted employment in forecasting model A1 ($F1_{t+1}$) is equal to the change in employment given in equation 2-121 plus the initial employment in year t.

The accuracy for past years of the model (equation 2-122) can be tested using historical data. To test the validity of the model in 1968, for example, we use values for K_{1967}, EBN_{1967}, EBN_{1968}, and E_{1967} and compare the model ($F1_{1968}$) results to actual 1968 employment. If we wish to forecast future employment, however, we find that no regional data can help us estimate future economic base employment (EBN_{t+1}). Thus, we need to adjust our model to create a forecasting model, which will be named model A2.

Model A2 uses model A1, but it also assumes that some regional variables are a fixed proportion of national variables. A number of national economic models can provide us with predictions of national employment for sectors in the CBP and BEA data. We can then use these national forecasts to derive our regional forecasting model.

This type of model can also be called the *share t model*, where exogenous regional variables are assumed to be a fixed share of national variables. The economic base employment for each industry (i) in each time period (t) can be calculated using the following formula:

$$EBN_{i,t} = S_{i,t} \times E_{i,t}^{u} ,$$

(2-123)

in which the employment in the economic base industries ($EBN_{i,t}$) is given as a proportion ($S_{i,t}$) of United States employment in the same industries $E_{i,t}^{u}$. The share coefficient is computed for industry i in year t as

$$S_{i,t} = EBN_{i,t}/E_{i,t}^{u} ,$$

(2-124)

which follows directly from equation 2-123. The change in employment in industry i is given by

$$EBN_{i,t+1} - EBN_{i,t} = S_{i,t} \left[E_{i,t+1}^{u} - E_{i,t}^{u} \right] ,$$

(2-125)

in which we use the share coefficient, regional employment, and national employment values for year t. We obtain an estimate of the increase in United States employment in industry i from a national economic forecast. To estimate the change in aggregate economic base employment, we sum across all industries.

$$EBN_{t+1} - EBN_{t} = \sum_{i=1}^{n} S_{i,t} \left[E_{i,t+1}^{u} - E_{i,t}^{u} \right]$$

(2-126)

The complete A2 model, corresponding to the A1 model shown in equation 2-122, is given by

$$FA2_{t+1} = K_{t} \sum_{i=1}^{n} S_{i,t} \left[E_{i,t+1}^{u} - E_{i,t}^{u} \right] + E_{t} ,$$

(2-127)

in which we multiply the change in economic base employment by K_{t} and add baseline employment E_{t} to derive our forecast of employment in year $t + 1$.

Measuring Forecast Error

The purpose of this book is to present a comprehensive approach to regional policy analysis and forecasting models. A key part of evaluating a model is assessing its validity. Therefore, we want to test the validity of forecasting Models A1 and A2.

One way to evaluate the accuracy of a model is to test it using historical data.

We obtain data from past years and run an *ex post forecast* for an historical year. The predictions from our models are compared against the actual change in economic activity. We can measure the error of the models in terms of percentage, mean percentage, or absolute percentage.

The *percent error (PE)* is calculated as

$$PE_{(t+1)} = \frac{F_{(t+1)} - E_{(t+1)}}{E_{(t+1)}} \times 100 \tag{2-128}$$

The forecast error in year $t + 1$ is equal to the forecasted employment F, minus the actual employment found in historical data (E). The result is expressed as a percentage by dividing it by the actual employment, and multiplying the result by 100. If the forecasted employment in year $t + 1$ is 103 and the actual employment in year $t + 1$ is 100, we would have

$$PE_{(t+1)} = \frac{103 - 100}{100} \times 100 = 3 , \tag{2-129}$$

where the error in the employment is 3 percent.

To develop a procedure for estimating the *mean percent error (MPE)* over a number of years, we use the following definition: MPE is the mean percent error of the model in predicting employment. We compute the MPE by taking the summation of the percent error over the *n*-year span. Algebraically, we have

$$MPE = \sum_1^n \frac{F_{(t+1)} - E_{(t+1)}}{E_{(t+1)}} \times \frac{100}{n} = \sum_1^n \frac{PE_{(t+1)}}{n} \tag{2-130}$$

In a three-year period where the percent error of the forecast are PE (year 1) = 2.2%, PE (year 2) = -1.8%, and PE (year 3) = 3.2%, the MPE would be

$$MPE = \frac{2.2\% - 1.8\% + 3.2\%}{3} = 1.2\% \tag{2-131}$$

In this example, the mean percent error (MPE) of the model is 1.2%, which shows a tendency of the model to overpredict employment by 1.2%.

The *absolute percent error* is the absolute value of the percent error. Thus, a 2% error and a -2% error would both have an absolute percent error of 2%. The *mean absolute percent error (MAPE)* is the average of the absolute percent error over a given period of time. Algebraically, we have

$$MAPE = \frac{1}{n} \times \sum_{t+1=1}^{n} \left[\frac{|FI_{(t+1)} - E_{(t+1)}|}{E_{(t+1)}} \times 100 \right] \qquad (2\text{-}132)$$

Using the values PE (year 1) = 2.2, PE (year 2) = -1.8, and PE (year 3) = 3.2, the MAPE would be

$$MAPE = \frac{|\;2.2\%\;| + |\;-1.8\%\;| + |\;3.2\%\;|}{3} = 2.4\% \qquad (2\text{-}133)$$

The MAPE shows the average percentage error per year, but it does not show the direction (positive or negative) of the error. Thus, the MAPE is always at least as large in absolute value as the MPE. The MAPE is larger if errors are made in both the positive and negative direction.

To evaluate our forecasting models using these error measurements, we need a basis of comparison. For this, we use a *naive no-change forecasting model*. We compare the economic base model forecast to the simple prediction that employment in a given year is equal to that of the previous year. The naive model can be represented as

$$FN_{t+1} = E_t . \qquad (2\text{-}134)$$

Table 2-15 allows us to examine the change in multipliers over time and to compare the errors of the forecasting models with those of the no-change model.

While model estimation should be applied at the most disaggregate level available, we illustrate error measurements using data derived from a two-digit judgmental approach. All employment in construction, durable and nondurable manufacturing, mining, farming, the federal government, military, and hotel sectors is EBN. All other employment is assumed to be ECG. Models and errors are calculated from 1967–1983. Table 2-15 shows selected states and United States averages based on fifty states plus Washington, D.C.

TABLE 2-15

Ex Post Forecasting Information 1967–1983

	K1967	K1972	K1983	Mean % Error			Mean Absolute % Error		
				Model A1	Model A2	No-Change Model	Model A1	Model A2	No-Change Model
Connecticut	2.0	2.4	2.9	-2.2	-1.5	-1.4	2.2	2.0	2.3
District of Columbia	2.1	2.3	2.4	-0.7	0.5	0.3	1.3	41.1	11.2
Maryland	2.4	2.8	3.4	-2.2	-1.8	-1.7	2.2	1.8	2.1
New York	2.8	3.4	4.0	-2.2	-0.1	-0.2	2.2	2.1	1.2
Illinois	2.3	2.6	3.4	-2.3	-0.2	-0.3	2.3	1.7	1.8
Michigan	2.1	2.4	3.0	-2.0	-0.7	-0.6	2.7	1.4	3.2
Nebraska	3.0	3.2	3.8	-1.5	-1.8	-1.9	1.6	1.9	2.2
Florida	2.9	3.2	3.8	-1.6	-3.9	-4.3	2.2	4.0	4.7
South Carolina	1.8	1.9	2.2	-1.4	-2.6	-2.2	1.4	2.6	2.8
Colorado	2.7	2.9	3.2	-1.0	-3.8	-4.1	1.4	3.8	4.1
Wyoming	2.6	2.5	2.9	-0.7	-2.6	-3.9	1.9	2.7	4.9
Alaska	1.7	2.1	2.7	-2.8	-4.3	-4.6	2.9	5.9	5.3
U.S. Average	2.4	2.6	3.0	-1.5	-1.9	-2.0	1.9	2.3	2.8

In forecasting model A1, we use past figures for K_t to forecast K_{t+1}. For economic base model A2, we use an estimate of $S_{i,t+1}$, introducing a second potential source of error. Since we use the actual value of past employment, any error in models must originate in either changes in the K values for model A1 or in the K and the S values in model A2.

The first three columns in table 2-15 show the value for each state in 1967, 1972, and 1983, respectively. The K value for Connecticut in 1967 is 2.0. This means that

$$2.0 = \frac{E\ (1967)}{EXFG\ (1967)\ +\ EIL\ (1967)} = K \tag{2-135}$$

In Michigan, in 1972, the value of K was 2.4. Using an estimate from the United States of 0.8 for CG/Y ($b = 0.78$) and equation 2-46, we would infer that

$$2.4 = \frac{1}{1\ -\ r \times b} \tag{2-136}$$

$$2.4\ -\ 2.4 \times r \times 0.78 = 1 \tag{2-137}$$

$$r = (1\ -\ 2.4)\ /\ [-(2.4)\ (0.78)]$$

$$=\ -(1\ -\ 2.4)\ /\ -1.872 = .75 \tag{2-138}$$

The r value (the percentage of local consumption and exports supplied locally) is equal to .75 for Michigan. If this estimate were accurate, it would mean that for every dollar spent in or exported from this state, 75¢ goes to locally produced goods. It should be contrasted with our estimate of .49 for r in 1977, using data from the regional accounts that were derived from an operational model of the Michigan economy.

From equation 2-119, we have

$$\Delta E = 2.4\ \Delta EBN \tag{2-139}$$

This means that for each export or investment employee (EBN) in Michigan, there are also 1.4 employees whose jobs depend on local demand.

The average multiplier across all states increased from 2.4 in 1967 to 3.0 in 1983. This value increased fastest for northeastern and midwestern states, and slowest for southern and western states. Because the change in our multiplier is our source of error in forecasting, it deserves some discussion.

The K value is calculated as [(ECG + EBN)/EBN], in which we have judgmentally decided that most services are ECG, while most manufacturing is EBN. Service employment relative to manufacturing employment increased over the 1967 – 1983 period across the country and especially in northern and midwestern states. This sectoral shift from manufacturing to services might be explained by

- a decline in manufacturing without a corresponding decline in use of services, because the existing population increasingly uses savings, social security payments, etc., to buy local services;

- growth in services, such as banking and education, which are assumed by our judgmental model to be entirely for local use, yet may in fact include export services; or

- an increase in workers earning income outside of the state, which is then spent within the state.

The slowest growing K values in western and southern states could be explained by

- a decline in residents' spending of savings and social security payments for local services;

- a low amount or decline in exports of services such as banking and education; or

- an increase in workers' earning income in basic industries in these states that is then spent for services in other states.

The high value of K (3.8) for Florida in 1983 could be explained by a large number of retirees spending savings and social security payments on local services. Other high K values might be explained differently. Nebraska's high value, for instance, could be due to the high amount of sales per export employee. The high K value in New York could be due to services exported from New York, which we did not include in EBN. Wyoming was the only state over this period that showed only a small increase in its K value. This was possibly caused by an increase in workers' earnings in mining that were then spent outside of the state. The lowest K values were 1.7 (Alaska) and 1.8 (South Carolina) in 1967. Only 0.7 jobs in Alaska and 0.8 jobs in South Carolina were dependent on local demand for every one job dependent on exogenous demand. In the case of South Carolina, this might have been due to low wages for employees in manufacturing, which would lead to a high EBN value, but a low ECG value, since workers in manufacturing would have little to spend. The low K value of Alaska can be explained by looking at one of the unique characteristics of its economy — a high percentage of its consumption is supplied by imports.

The percentage error in the models shows the difference between predicted and actual employment. In the naive model, percentage error shows the rate of economic growth. Thus, the growth rate over the 1967 – 1983 period ranges from -0.3 in Washington, D.C., to 4.6% in Alaska. On average, the state and district economies expanded at a rate of 2% per year over the period.

The percentage error in economic base models A1 and A2 is somewhat lower than that of the naive model. As expected, model A1 produces more accurate forecasts than A2 because shifts in the multiplier account for all error in model A1, while changes in shares are an additional source of error in model A2. Although A1 produces better forecasts, we can only estimate this model if we know EBN_{t+1}. To project employment into the future, we must rely on model A2, for which we can obtain the necessary data from historical records and national forecasts.

In either case, the underprediction of employment is caused by sectoral shifts. We use multipliers estimated in year t to develop forecasts for year $t + 1$. Since the older multipliers are smaller than the actual multipliers, employment is systematically underestimated. In addition to this multiplier shift, the share of total United States employment changed in each state over the period of the forecast.

Model A2 underestimated employment by a great deal for states with high growth levels, such as Florida, Wyoming, and Alaska. We can infer that the use of the year t share coefficient led to a systematic underestimation of economic growth. If we observe that multipliers were growing quickly in these same states, we can see that the underestimation of the share coefficient and the multiplier would interact in our model, leading to a large underestimation of economic growth. On average, model A2 underestimated growth by 1.9%, which is only slightly better than the 2% error in our naive, no-change forecast.

The MAPE is the average of the absolute value of the percentage errors for each year of the forecast period. Colorado shows the same magnitude MAPE and MPE for the naive forecast. This indicates that all the errors were in the same direction. In this case, the no-growth forecast underestimated employment change in each of the years from 1967 to 1983. For almost all of the states and all forecasting models, however, the magnitude of the MAPE is greater than the MPE, indicating that errors of overprediction, as well as those of underprediction, occur.

Measured by the MAPE, forecasting models A1 and A2 both represented an improvement over the naive forecast. The MAPE is 2.8% for the naive model, 2.3% for model A2, and 1.9% for model A1. Again, we see that model A1 produces the least error. Unfortunately, it cannot be used for actual forecasts because we do not know the EBN values. However, it can be used for what-if scenarios if we hypothesize changes in EBN.

2-4 RECOGNIZING THAT REGIONAL OUTPUT AND INCOME DIFFER

The model developed in section 2-3 is designated as economic base model A hereafter. In that model, we consider income to be equal to output in an area. Yet, the income generated by production in a local area may often go to residents outside of the area. Conversely, the income of an area's residents may come from outside of the area. In making an economic prediction or carrying out a simulation for a region, it is vital that we take this distinction into account. For example, many people earn income in a city and live in the suburbs in a different county or state. Thus, when the economy of the city is stimulated, a high proportion of the generated income is respent in the suburbs and does not lead to further induced spending in the city. In the suburbs, induced demand using economic base model A would overestimate induced spending because a high proportion of spending depends on income earned outside of the region. This income is mainly exogenous instead of local, as assumed in economic base model A.

The amount of economic activity that is generated may be overestimated because we have the wrong model. In economic base model B, we separate income by place of work (Y) from income by place of residence (YP), recognizing the following three reasons for the discrepancy: 1) government transfers, 2) income earned from capital invested outside the place of residence, and 3) income earned by working outside of the place of residence. In this model, consumption and local government spending (CG) are a function of exogenous income (RDV), as well as output (Y). This allows for the differentiation between output and income.

Accounts

The accounts for economic base model B are built on economic base model A, with place-of-work income separated from place-of-residence income and with some additional flow variables added. In the accounts for model B, account A is defined on a place-of-work basis, while account B is defined on a place-of-residence basis. We show both the simple account A for economic base model A and the parallel account for economic base model B.

TABLE 2-16

Comparison of Account A for Models A and B

Account for Model A

Account for Model B

A. State Product Account

A. State Product Account
    (Place of work)

Uses	*Sources*	*Uses*	*Sources*
Y (output)	CG (consumption and local government spending)	YLPL (local earnings by local residents)	CG (consumption and local government spending)
	IL (local investment)	YLPU (earnings locally by nonresidents)	IL (local investment)
	XFG (exports, including federal government)	H (profits)	XFG (exports, including federal government)
	− M (imports)		− M (imports)
Y	Y	Y(gross state product)	Y(gross state product)

YLPL   Labor and proprietors' income earned in the state that stays in the state

YLPU   Labor and proprietors' income earned in the state by nonresidents of the state

H   Profits earned in the state

The source of local output (Y), i.e., gross state or gross regional product, is consumer and local government spending (CG), plus local investment (IL), plus exports including federal government spending (XFG), minus imports (M). The use of local income is now divided into laborers' and proprietors' income earned by residents (YLPL) and nonresidents (YLPU) of the state and the residual profits (H = Y − YLPL − YLPU).

TABLE 2-17

Comparison of Account B for Models A and B

Account for Model A

Account for Model B

B. Personal and Local Government
   Income and Outlay Account

B. Personal and Local Government
   Income and Outlay Account
   (Place of residence)

Uses	Sources	Uses	Sources
CG (consumer and local government spending)	Y (output)	CG (consumer and local government spending)	YLPL (local earnings by local residents)
S (personal savings and local government surplus)		SETC (residual, Account B)	UYLP (income earned rest of country by local residents)
			DIR (dividends, interest, rent)
			V (transfer payments)
Y	Y	YP (Personal Income)	YP (Personal Income)

UYLP	Labor and proprietors' income earned outside of the state by residents of the state
DIR	Dividends, interest, and rent received by residents of the state
SETC	Personal income not spent for consumption or state and local government expenditures. SETC includes federal taxes.
V	Net transfer payments including payments to and from the social security system

In table 2-17, account B for model B is a place-of-residence account, and both sides of the account are equal to the income of residents of the state. Output (Y) from our simple account is replaced by all sources of income for residents of the region: labor and proprietors' income earned within the state (YLPL) and outside of the state (UYLP); dividends, interest, and rent received by residents of the state (DIR); and net government transfers to residents of the state (V). The uses for the income are consumer and regional government spending (CG) and the residual (SETC), which includes federal taxes and local savings. The sum of both sides of the equation gives us the personal income of the residents of the state (YP). In account CD shown in table 2-18, we combine accounts C and D for model A into a residual account for model B. This catch-all account shows the uses and sources of funds for savings and investment and the rest the country. We show the residual account (CD) to complete the accounting system, but we do not enter it into our models directly.

TABLE 2-18

Comparison of Accounts C and D for Model A to Account CD for Model B

Accounts for Model A   Account for Model B

C. Savings and Investment Account   CD. Residual Account

Uses	*Sources*	*Uses*	*Sources*
IL (local investment)	S (personal savings and local government surplus)	XFG (exports including federal government)	M (imports)
IR (investment, rest of country)		UYLP (income earned rest of country by local residents)	YLPU (earnings locally by nonresidents)
I	S		H (profits)
		DIR (dividends, interest, rent)	SETC (residual Account B)

D. Rest of Country Account

Uses	*Sources*	V (government transfers)	
XFG (exports including federal government)	M (imports)	IL (local investment)	
XFG	IR (investment, rest of country)		
	XFG		

The complete accounts for economic base model B are shown in table 2-19.

TABLE 2-19

Social Accounts for a State or Other Local Area

A. State Product Account
(Place of work)

B. Personal Income and Outlay Account
(Place of Residence)

Uses	Sources	Uses	Sources
YLPL	CG	CG	YLPL
YLPU	IL	SETC	UYLP
H	XFG		DIR
	– M		V
Y	Y	YP	YP

CD. Residual Account

Uses	Sources
XFG	M
UYLP	YLPU
DIR	H
V	SETC
IL	

The New Equations

The equations behind these accounts can be used as part of the basis for building regional economic base model type B. To assign values to the equations for economic base model B, we must use the available data, which is in the following form:

YLP   *earned income by place of work.* The income earned in a region; and

RA   *residence adjustment.* The net amount of the excess of earnings by local residents outside of the local area (UYLP) and earnings of out-of-area residents in the local area (YLPU).

Algebraically, these are

$$YLP = YLPL + YLPU \tag{2-140}$$

and

$$RA = UYLP - YLPU \qquad (2\text{-}141)$$

Adding equations 2-140 and 2-141, we obtain

$$YLP + RA = YLPL + UYLP, \qquad (2\text{-}142)$$

which we substitute into account B. By also substituting equation 2-141 into account CD, we have a slightly altered set of accounts so that we can use the existing data. These accounts and their measured values for Michigan in 1977 are shown in table 2-20.

TABLE 2-20

**Social Accounts for Any Region with Specific
Estimates for Michigan in 1977**

A. State Product Account   B. Personal Income and Outlay Account
   (Place of Work)   (Place of Residence)

Uses		Sources		Uses		Sources	
YLP	55.0	CG	65.0	CG	65.0	YLP	55.0
		IL	16.2			RA	0.3
H	25.8	XFG	83.7			DIR	8.1
		−M	84.1	SETC	4.2	V	5.8
Y	80.8	Y	80.8	YP	69.2	YP	69.2

CD. Residual Account

Uses		Sources	
XFG	83.7	M	84.1
RA	0.3	H	25.8
DIR	8.1	SETC	4.2
V	5.8		
IL	16.2		
	114.1		114.1

YLP   Labor and proprietor's income earned in the state.

RA   Residential adjustment (UYLP-YLPU): The net of income earned in the rest of the country by state residents and the earnings in the state of nonresidents.

Using these accounts, we develop model B as an alternative to model A. We first recall the equations for model A, where equation 2-27 becomes equation 2-143, equations 2-35 and 2-40 are combined with equation 2-31 to become equation 2-144, and equations 2-33 and 2-41 are modified to become equation 2-145

$$BN = rXFG + rIL_p \qquad (2\text{-}143)$$

$$Y = rCG + BN = 0.49\ CG + BN \qquad (2\text{-}144)$$

$$CG = bY = 0.804\ Y \qquad (2\text{-}145)$$

For our type-B model, the equations for BN and Y remain the same. However, the equation for CG must be changed, since the determinant (Y) of local spending does not differentiate between local output and local income. It is much more appropriate to make local personal consumption and local government spending (CG) depend on local personal income (YP) rather than on local output. Thus, for model B, we use the relationship

$$CG = cYP \qquad (2\text{-}146)$$

The equation for YP can be written from account B as

$$YP = YLPL + UYPL + DIR + V \qquad (2\text{-}147)$$

$$= YLP + RA + DIR + V$$

$$= YLP + RDV,$$

where

$$RDV = RA + DIR + V \qquad (2\text{-}148)$$

To obtain the equation for YLP, we must assume that labor and proprietors' income remains at a constant proportion (p) of output (Y). Then, we can represent YLP $\div$ Y $= p$ as a constant. Thus,

$$YLP = p\ Y \qquad (2\text{-}149)$$

This makes the model complete, or more formerly closed, assuming that RDV is exogenous. We would not assume that the RA components of RDV in equation 2-148 are exogenous if the residential adjustment (RA) is negative. In that case, changes in Y would be expected to lead to changes in local earnings by workers who live outside of the region. In the case of a negative RA, it should be removed from equation 2-148 and included with YLP in equation 2-149. Other components of RDV are made endogenous in later models but offset each other somewhat, since V increases when Y decreases.

The New Multiplier

By substitution, we now write

$$BN = rXFG + rIL_p \qquad (2\text{-}150)$$

$$Y = rCG + BN \qquad (2\text{-}151)$$

$$CG = c(YLP + RDV) \qquad (2\text{-}152)$$

To solve economic base model B, we can derive the multiplier. Alternatively, we can incorporate the new equations in an extended economic base model and solve it using an iterative solution method, as is shown at the end of this chapter. For the interested reader, we present a derivation of the multiplier for model B. We start by substituting equation 2-152 into equation 2-151.

$$Y = r \times c \ (YLP + RDV) + BN \qquad (2\text{-}153)$$

Next, we substitute equation 2-149 into equation 2-153 to obtain

$$Y = r \times c(pY + RDV) + BN \qquad (2\text{-}154)$$

Solving for Y gives us

$$Y - r \times c \times pY = (r \times c \times RDV) + BN \qquad (2\text{-}155)$$

$$Y = \frac{(r \times c \times RDV) + BN}{1 - (r \times c \times p)} \qquad (2\text{-}156)$$

The multiplier shows the change in output that occurs due to a change in exogenous variables. In economic base model B, we have an exogenous income multiplier (K_{RDV}) and an economic base multiplier (K_B). To determine K_{RDV}, we take the partial derivative of Y with respect to RDV or perform the same operations that we carried out for equation 2-70 with $BN = 0$, which yields

$$\frac{\Delta Y}{\Delta RDV} = \frac{\partial Y}{\partial RDV} = \frac{r \times c}{1 - (r \times c \times p)} = K_{RDV} \qquad (2\text{-}157)$$

Similarly, the economic base multiplier is found by taking the partial derivative of Y with respect to BN or by performing the equation 2-70 operations with $RDV = 0$. This is

$$\frac{\Delta Y}{\Delta BN} = \frac{\partial Y}{\partial BN} = \frac{1}{1 - (r \times c \times p)} = K_B \qquad (2\text{-}158)$$

The equation for Y is then

$$Y = (K_{RDV} \times RDV) + (K_B \times BN) \qquad (2\text{-}159)$$

This equation shows that if RDV = 0, then Y = K_B × BN. If we note that, from equations 2-157 and 2-158, K_{RDV} = r × c × K_B, then we can express equation 2-159 as

$$Y = K_B [(r \times c \times RDV) + BN]$$ (2-160)

Substituting the parameters used to estimate K_B from equation 2-158 into equation 2-160, we solve the model for the reduced form in equation 2-161.

$$Y = \frac{1}{1 - (r \times c \times p)} [(r \times c \times RDV) + BN],$$ (2-161)

where

$$r = \frac{Y}{CG + IL + XFG} = 0.49 \text{ as before}$$ (2-162)

$$c = \frac{CG}{YP} = \frac{65}{69.2} = 0.94$$ (2-163)

$$p = \frac{YLP}{Y} = \frac{55}{80.8} = 0.68$$ (2-164)

We now determine the Michigan economic base model B multiplier.

$$K_B = \frac{1}{1 - r \times c \times p} = \frac{1}{1 - 0.313} = \frac{1}{0.686} = 1.46$$ (2-165)

The exogenous income multiplier is calculated as

$$K_{RDV} = K_B \times r \times c$$
$$= 1.46 \times 0.49 \times 0.94$$
$$= 0.67$$ (2-166)

Note that both of the multipliers are lower than the model A multiplier of 1.65. We can infer that using 1.65 as the K multiplier would substantially overestimate the impact of a change in the economic base.

The smaller economic base multiplier estimated in economic base model B recognizes that some local spending is supported by income that is not related to local output. This lower multiplier also reflects that a portion of locally generated value added goes to outside owners of local capital (e.g., the shareholders of General Motors who live outside of Michigan and who, therefore, own part of that state's capital).

Even when we do not have the values in the accounts in table 2-16, we can still estimate the K_B value in terms of the data available for every state and county in the United States. We determine K_B in terms of RDV, YLP, and the K value in economic base model A. We begin by solving equation 2-153 for $r \times c$.

$$r \times c = \frac{Y - BN}{YLP + RDV} \tag{2-167}$$

Next, we substitute this expression into the model B economic base multiplier equation 2-158 and simplify.

$$\begin{aligned} K_B &= \frac{1}{1 - \left[\dfrac{Y - BN}{YLP + RDV}\right] \times p} \\[2ex] &= \frac{1}{\dfrac{YLP + RDV - Y \times p + BN \times p}{YLP + RDV}} \\[2ex] &= \frac{YLP + RDV}{YLP + RDV - Y \times p + BN \times p} \end{aligned} \tag{2-168}$$

Since $p = YLP/Y$ from equation 2-149,

$$\begin{aligned} K_B &= \frac{YLP + RDV}{YLP + RDV - Y\left[\dfrac{YLP}{Y}\right] + BN\left[\dfrac{YLP}{Y}\right]} \\[2ex] &= \frac{YLP + RDV}{RDV + (BN/Y)\,(YLP)} \end{aligned} \tag{2-169}$$

Multiplying through by Y/BN, we obtain

$$K_B = \frac{(YLP + RDV)\,Y/BN}{RDV\,(Y/BN) + YLP} \tag{2-170}$$

Recognizing from equation 2-77 that $Y/BN = K$, we simplify this expression to

$$K_B = \frac{(YLP + RDV)\,K}{RDV \times K + YLP} \tag{2-171}$$

In the case of Michigan where RDV = 14.2 and YLP = 55.0 and K = 1.65, this yields

$$K_B = \frac{(55.0 + 14.2)\, 1.65}{(14.2)\,(1.65) + 55.0} = 1.46 ,$$

(2-172)

which confirms our results from direct calculation in equation 2-165.

Thus, even for simple economic base studies, we can use RDV and YLP data that is publicly available from the Bureau of Economic Analysis (BEA) to improve the accuracy of the multiplier. Note that only in the case where RDV equals zero are K and K_B identical. We can apply this to the Adams County, Colorado multiplier above. Referring to the personal income table for Adams County, we find that for 1986 RDV = 730 (Residence Adjustment) + 306 (Dividends, Interest, and Rent) + 390 (Transfer payments of 519 less Social Insurance Contributions of 129) = 1,426 and YLP = 2,231. Therefore,

$$KB = \frac{(2,231 + 1,426)\, 3.95}{(1,426)\, 3.95 + 2,231} = 1.84$$

(2-173)

This dramatic reduction in the multiplier from 3.95 to 1.84 indicates how important it may be to use model B in some situations. In this case, from the size of the residential adjustment (730), it is clear that many Adams County residents work outside of the county.

2-5 REPRESENTING AN EXTENDED ECONOMIC BASE MODEL

We conclude this chapter by summarizing economic base model B and extending this model to show the determination of personal income, employment, and the economic base. We also undertake to estimate values for the parameters of the model, the exogenous variables, and initial starting values for the endogenous variables. With these estimates in place and projected values for the exogenous variables, we have calibrated a model for forecasting and policy analysis. The model represented in the flow chart in diagram 2-11, in which arrows indicate causality, is a version of the model before we include employment explicitly.

Output (Y) is determined by the economic base (BN), consumption and local government spending (CG), and the local share of local sales (r). Local consumption and local government spending (CG) depend on personal income (YP) and the marginal propensity to consume (c). Output (Y), along with the proportion of output in income (p), and exogenous income (RDV) determine consumption and local government spending (CG).

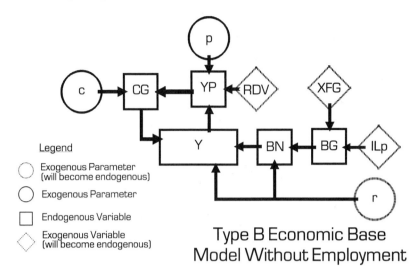

Type B Economic Base Model Without Employment

Diagram 2-11

We begin with the output equation shown earlier in this chapter. Here, output (Y) is equal to the sum of locally produced local consumption and government spending (rCG), plus the economic base (BN) in equation 2-144, which we repeat here.

$$Y = rCG + BN \qquad (2\text{-}174)$$

Consumer and government spending (CG) are shown as a proportion of personal income (cYP) in

$$CG = cYP \qquad (2\text{-}175)$$

The determinants of personal income (YP) can now be shown by substituting equation 2-149 into equation 2-147, giving us

$$YP = pY + RDV \qquad (2\text{-}176)$$

in which personal income is a proportion of output (pY) plus the residence adjustment; dividends, interest, and rent; and transfer payments (RDV). This concludes the model in diagram 2-11.

Next, we extend this model by showing personal income (YP) as a function of employment (E) and earned income per employee (w). We also extend it by determining employment endogenously. This complete economic base model B is shown in diagram 2-12, which shows the complete linkages. As in diagram 2-11, output is shown as a function of the local share of local sales (r), consumption and government spending (CG), and economic base (BN). Local government spending and consumption (CG) depend on personal income (YP) and the marginal propensity to consume (c). This measure of income is determined by the earnings rate (w), by employment (E), and by exogenous income (RDV). Employment is calculated with the labor per unit of output parameter (epv) in combination with endogenously determined output (Y). The economic base (BN) is shown as a function of United States interregional and international trade (XFG"), local planned investment (IL_p), and their respective share coefficients (s and r).

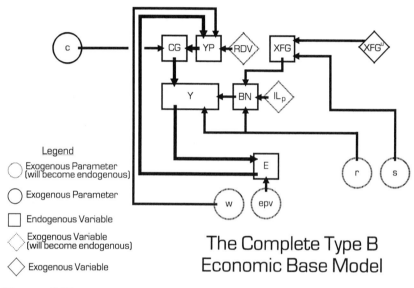

Legend

◌ Exogenous Parameter (will become endogenous)

○ Exogenous Parameter

▢ Endogenous Variable

◇ Exogenous Variable (will become endogenous)

◇ Exogenous Variable

The Complete Type B Economic Base Model

Diagram 2-12

The equation for output is the same as that given previously.

$$Y = rCG + BN \tag{2-177}$$

Consumer and government spending is determined by

$$CG = cYP, \tag{2-178}$$

and YP is found by substituting for YLP in equation 2-147. It is given in the following equation:

$$YP = (E \times w) + RDV, \tag{2-179}$$

where $w = $ YLP/E (annual earnings (w) per employee are equal to labor and proprietors' income divided by employment in the last year for which data is available). Employment is endogenously determined as

$$E = epv \times Y, \tag{2-180}$$

where *epv* was also determined in the last year of data as $epv = E/Y$.

We show the economic base (BN) in terms of United States interregional and international trade and planned local investment.

$$BG = XFG + IL_p \tag{2-181}$$

$$BN = rBG, \tag{2-182}$$

where we show the economic base (BN) as the sum of the locally produced share of exports and federal government spending (rXFG) and local investment spending (rIL$_p$). To derive an expression for exports in terms of total United States international and interregional trade, we show the following relationship:

$$XFG = s \times XFG^u \tag{2-183}$$

    s regional share of interregional and international trade
    XFG^u total United States interregional and international trade and
              federal government spending.

The value of s is also determined with the latest available data as $s = XFG/XFG^u$. We can then substitute equations 2-183 into equation 2-28 to give us

$$BG = (s \times XFG^u + IL_p) \tag{2-184}$$

Thus, the gross economic base (BG) is equal to the region's exports ($s \times$ XFG^u) plus planned local investment (IL$_p$).

The link between one area and the rest of the nation in this economic base model is through demand for interregional and international trade in the rest of the country and federal government spending (XFG^u) and through investment (IL$_p$), as it affects the local area's economic base (BG). It also depends on direct income payments from the rest of the country to households in the local area (RDV). Employment and output, as well as consumption and local government spending, are all determined within the local system. Therefore, a change in the economy is the result of changes in interregional trade, investment, or exogenous income.

This model will produce exactly the same results as economic base model B. When w is substituted into the YP equation (2-179), E $\times$ w becomes E $\times$ (YLP $\div$ E) = YLP, as it was originally in equation 2-147. The purpose for breaking out w, epv, and E is to present the economic base model in a way that integrates the employment and dollar units in the same model. It also allows us to see what parts of the economic base model may be unduly rigid. With explicit parameters and exogenous variables, it is possible to closely examine the assumptions that led to the choice of the endogenous variables for the model.

A variable should not be classified as an exogenous variable or parameter instead of an endogenous variable if it is influenced by the values of endogenous variables. There are many cases where this situation exists in this model. Investment (IL_p) is influenced by local activity and relative factor costs. Both the share of national markets (s) and the region's share of goods and services purchased in the region (r) are influenced by cost and profitability conditions, and (r) may also be influenced by the size of the local market. The employees per unit of value added (epv) are affected by relative factor costs and productivity changes. The residence adjustment, property income, and transfer payments (RDV) change as the size of the population and economic conditions change. Finally, the earnings rate (w) is sensitive to the supply-and-demand conditions for labor in the area. When we further extend modeling in the following chapter, we explain more variables endogenously.

We can see that there are inherent shortcomings in the economic base model that must be overcome before we can do realistic forecasting or policy analysis. On the other hand, the economic base model serves as a good starting point. It is the simplest regional economic model possible. It can be stated in its structural form and in its reduced form. The reduced-form multiplier K can be measured using available data for any county or state in the United States. Finally, we can build on the economic base model by developing equations to explain some of the exogenous variables and parameters in the model, making them into endogenous variables. We undertake this task in the next chapter.

The final tasks in this chapter are to gather the equations for the model, to find the values for the parameters, exogenous variables, and initial values of the endogenous variables, and then to use them in a program to create a baseline forecast and a simulation. The equations are

$$Y = PP \tag{2-185}$$

$$XFG = sXFG^u \tag{2-186}$$

$$BG = XFG + IL_p \tag{2-187}$$

$$BN = rBG \tag{2-188}$$

$$E = epv\ Y \tag{2-189}$$

$$YP = YLP + RDV \tag{2-190}$$

$$YLP = E \times w \tag{2-191}$$

$$CG = cYP \tag{2-192}$$

$$IL_{up} = Y - PP \tag{2-193}$$

$$PP = rCG + BN \tag{2-194}$$

Parameters	Exogenous Variables	Endogenous Variables	
s		Y	E
r	XFG^u	PP	YP
epv	IL_p	XFG	YLP
w	RDV	BG	CG
c		BN	IL_{up}

To have a complete model, we need to find values for the parameters and for the exogenous variables. In general, for an iterative approach to model solution, it facilitates matters to have starting values for the endogenous variables as well. The best way to find the values for the parameters, the exogenous and initial endogenous variables is to look first for values that are key and that we can find easily. We then use these values to determine more values, and so on, until all the necessary values have been obtained.

A key value to find is the employee (E) to output (Y) ratio (epv), because this will make it possible to estimate the values for many of the other variables. Since output is only measured for states and not for counties, we turn to Colorado data. To be consistent with the way in which data was obtained for Adams County in 1987, we find 1,169 thousand Colorado private employees from the 1987 CBP for Colorado and add 323 thousand government employees in 1987 from the BEA Regional Economic Information System for Colorado (REIS) data set (table CA 5, 6/22/92) to obtain total Colorado employment of 1,492 thousand. The gross state product (Y) for 1987 for Colorado is 59.630 billion dollars.[17] Thus,

$$epv = 1,492 \text{ thousand employees}/59.630 \text{ billion dollars}$$
$$= 25.0 \text{ thousand employees per billion dollars of output}$$
(or 25 employees per million dollars of output).

Since the same epv is used for all types of output in this model, we can use this to convert employment numbers from table 2-13 into value added output numbers using equations 2-87 – 2-90.

$$Y = E/epv = 97.009/25.0 = 3.880 \text{ billion dollars} \tag{2-195}$$
$$BN = EBN/epv = 24.573/25.0 = .983 \text{ billion dollars} \tag{2-196}$$
$$rIL_p = EIL_p/epv = 4.860/25.0 = .194 \text{ billion dollars} \tag{2-197}$$

$$rXFG = EXFG/epv = (24.573 - 4.860)/25.0 = .789 \text{ billion dollars} \quad (2\text{-}198)$$

$$rCG = ECG/epv = 72.436/25.0 = 2.897 \text{ billion dollars} \quad (2\text{-}199)$$

$$PP = Y = 3.880 \text{ billion dollars} \quad (2\text{-}200)$$

$$rBG = BN = .983 \text{ billion dollars} \quad (2\text{-}201)$$

Next, if we can estimate the value of r the other values will be easy to find. First, we find c and YP in order to calculate CG with equation 2-192. After finding CG, we can then calculate r from the equation $rCG = 2.897$ above.

The value of c can be observed at the United States level by taking the ratio of consumption ($\$3,052$[18]) plus state and local government spending ($\$497$[19]) divided by personal income ($\$3,802$[20]).

$$c = (3,052 + 497)/3,802 = .93 \quad (2\text{-}202)$$

The values for YP and RDV are found from the REIS, BEA data set and are the values used at the end of section 2-4.

$$RDV = 1.426$$

$$YP = RDV + YLP$$

$$= 1.426 + 2.231 = 3.657 \quad (2\text{-}203)$$

Thus,

$$CG = .93 \times 3,657 = 3,401, \quad (2\text{-}204)$$

and

$$rCG = 2.897$$

$$\therefore r = 2.897/3.401 = .85 \quad (2\text{-}205)$$

From the above, we can also find

$$IL_p = .262/.85 = .308 \quad (2\text{-}206)$$

$$XFG = .721/.85 = .848 \quad (2\text{-}207)$$

$$BG = .983/.85 = 1.156 \quad (2\text{-}208)$$

Note that $r = .85$ is lower than our previous estimate of $r = .96$. However, it still seems high for a county.

We have now completed all of the values for the endogenous variables, except inventory change (IL_{up}), which we assume to be zero. The exogenous values for IL_p and RDV are established for the base year.

For the value of XFG^u, we will use the fraction of nonfederal government U.S. output going to interstate and international trade, estimated as 43.7% using a model of the type presented in chapter 7 for all states plus federal government expenditures. For 1987 through 1991 in 1987 dollars, this is[21]

1987	$2,200 = .437 \times (4540 - 385) + 385$
1988	$2,275 = .437 \times (4719 - 377) + 377$
1989	$2,325 = .437 \times (4837 - 375) + 375$
1990	$2,349 = .437 \times (4885 - 381) + 381$
1991	$2,336 = .437 \times (4850 - 385) + 385$

Using the 1987 value and equation 2-186, the value of the parameter s is established as

$$s = XFG/XFG^u = .848/2,200 = .000385 \qquad (2\text{-}209)$$

The parameter value w is calculated from equation 2-191 as

$$w = YLP/E = 2.231 \text{ billion}/97.009 \text{ thousand} \qquad (2\text{-}210)$$

$$= .0230 \text{ billion per thousand}$$
(or million per employee)
(i.e., \$23,000 per employee).

To make a five year forecast, it is necessary to project all of the exogenous variables forward for five years. If we use United States growth proportions in lines 1 and 3 in table 2-21 to project IL_p and RDV in lines 2 and 4 of the same table over the period, we would project the following:

TABLE 2-21[22]

"Projections" of IL_p and RDV based on United States Data

	1987	1988	1989	1990	1991
I^u_t/I^u_{1987}	1.00	1.032	1.053	.994	.900
IL_p (in 1987 dollars)	.308	.318	.324	.306	.277
RDV^u/RDV^u_{1987}	1.00	1.035	1.055	1.076	1.074
RDV (in 1987 dollars)	1.426	1.476	1.504	1.534	1.532

This completes that calibration of the model.

To facilitate policy simulations with the model, we introduce multiplicative and additive policy variables. The model with these policy variables is as follows:

$$Y = PP \qquad (2\text{-}211)$$

$$XFG = (s \times PVsM)(XFG^u + PVXFGUA) \qquad (2\text{-}212)$$

$$BG = XFG + (IL_p + PVILPA) \qquad (2\text{-}213)$$

$$BN = r(PVrM \times PVrBGM)(BG + PVBGA) \qquad (2\text{-}214)$$

$$PP = r(1 + PVvM) CG + BN \qquad (2\text{-}215)$$

$$E = (epv \times PVeM) \times Y \qquad (2\text{-}216)$$

$$YLP = E \times (w \times PVwM) \qquad (2\text{-}217)$$

$$YP = YLP + (RDV + PVRDVA) \qquad (2\text{-}218)$$

$$CG = c(PVcM)YP + PVCGA \qquad (2\text{-}219)$$

$$IL_{up} = Y - PP \qquad (2\text{-}220)$$

The default values for the policy variables and the baseline forecasts using these values is shown in table 2-22.

TABLE 2-22

Policy Variables
Baseline Values

	YEAR 1	YEAR 2	YEAR 3	YEAR 4	YEAR 5
PVrM	1	1	1	1	1
PVrBGM	1	1	1	1	1
PVsM	1	1	1	1	1
PVeM	1	1	1	1	1
PVwM	1	1	1	1	1
PVcM	1	1	1	1	1
PVBGA	0	0	0	0	1
PVCGA	0	0	0	0	0
PVILPA	0	0	0	0	0
PVRDVA	0	0	0	0	0
PVXFGUA	0	0	0		0
Y	3.868	3.998	4.078	4.108	4.054
PP	3.867	3.999	4.079	4.109	4.054
XFG	0.847	0.876	0.895	0.904	0.899
BG	1.155	1.194	1.219	1.210	1.176
BN	0.982	1.015	1.036	1.029	1.000
E	96.693	99.958	101.946	102.698	101.361
YP	3.650	3.775	3.849	3.896	3.863
CG	3.394	3.511	3.579	3.623	3.593
ILup	0.001	-0.001	-0.001	-0.001	0.001
YLP	2.224	2.299	2.345	2.362	2.331

Table 2-23 shows the alternative less the baseline (or control) forecast with policy variable PVBGA increased by 1.176 (1.00/.85) in the alternative, which increases BN by 1.00. This shows the effect of increasing BN by one, which increases Y by approximately 1.84 and confirms the multiplier calculated in section 2-4. Table 2-24 shows the effects of increasing PVRDVA by 1.00 in each forecast year. This gives us the multiplier for increased exogenous income.

TABLE 2-23

Adams County Extended Economic Base Model

Effects of Increasing BN by Approximately 1.00

	1987	1988	1989	1990	1991
PVBGA	1.176	1.176	1.176	1.176	1.176
Y	1.830	1.833	1.832	1.833	1.833
PP	1.831	1.833	1.832	1.832	1.832
XFG	0.000	0.000	0.000	0.000	0.000
BG	0.000	0.000	0.000	0.000	0.000
BN	0.999	0.999	1.000	0.999	1.000
E	45.745	45.814	45.815	45.815	45.814
YP	1.052	1.054	1.053	1.054	1.054
CG	0.979	0.980	0.980	0.980	0.980
IL_{up}	-0.002	0.000	0.000	0.000	0.000
YLP	1.052	1.054	1.053	1.054	1.054

TABLE 2-24

Adams County Extended Economic Base Model

Effects of Increasing RDV (Exogenous Income) by 1.00

	1987	1988	1989	1990	1991
PVRDVA	1.000	1.000	1.000	1.000	1.000
Y	1.446	1.450	1.449	1.449	1.450
PP	1.448	1.449	1.449	1.449	1.449
XFG	0.000	0.000	0.000	0.000	0.000
BG	0.000	0.000	0.000	0.000	0.000
BN	0.000	0.000	0.000	0.000	0.000
E	36.169	36.231	36.231	36.231	36.230
YP	1.832	1.833	1.833	1.833	1.834
CG	1.704	1.705	1.705	1.705	1.705
IL_{up}	-0.002	0.000	0.000	0.000	0.000
YLP	0.832	0.833	0.833	0.833	0.834

Comparing the two simulations, we find that the output multiplier for changes in net exports (BN) is 1.83, while the multiplier for exogenous income (RDV) is 1.45. The main effect of the RDV increase shows up in increased YP and CG. This demonstrates that extra exogenous income can be as important as an increase in exports in expanding the size of the local economy and the number of jobs in that economy.

Note that both of the simulations show the same effect each year. This is because the model is entirely linear and does not reflect any of the dynamic elements that are almost certainly a part of regional economies.

The extended economic base model in this chapter is our starting point in the next chapter. All of the key elements of model building have been presented in the context of this model. Even though the extended economic base model is not realistic enough to be of much value for policy analysis, it provides a framework on which to build. It also allows us to show how a model can be specified, calibrated, and used for forecasting and policy analysis. The reader is encouraged to try out other policy analysis experiments with this model and to develop interpretations of the resulting predicted effects.

APPENDIX: Chapter 2

The Regional Economic Modeling System (REMS): Information on Installation and Execution

Installation Procedures

The REMS system is available from the author, as noted previously. It includes models for the chapters in part I. The REMS is on 1 high-density floppy disk and, depending on the size of the diskette drive, is either 1.2MB (5' inch) or 1.44MB (3' inch) capacity. The REMS can only be executed on the hard-drive, so it should be installed on the hard-drive first. Approximately 2MB of hard-disk space is required, and 4MB is recommended. To install the REMS, please follow these steps:

1. Make a working copy of the master REMS floppy disk, using either a 1.2MB or a 1.44MB empty diskette.

2. Insert the working copy disk in either drive A: or B:. Switch the system prompt to "A:" or "B:" where the floppy disk is inserted, then type INSTALL < Enter >.

3. Indicate the drive and directory on the hard disk where the REMS is to be installed when the REMS Installation dialogue box is shown on the screen. For example, an answer would look like the following:

    Target Drive and Directory: C:\REMS < Enter >

4. It should take three to five minutes for the installation process to be completed. The program indicates when the REMS is completely installed. Call Regional Economic Models, Inc. (REMI) at 413-549-1169 if the installation takes more than fifteen minutes.

5. Changes to the **CONFIG.SYS** (the system configuration file) may be necessary to properly run the model. The REMS runs best with **FILES=30** and **BUFFERS=20** or greater. Please refer to your DOS manual for more information about how to change the **CONFIG.SYS**.

Using the REMS

Move to the target drive and directory where the program has already been installed, and type **REMS<Enter>** to execute the software. The REMS is menu-driven and easy to use. Once the REMS is executed, use the arrow keys to move the cursor bar to select a choice. Press < **Enter** > to run the selection. The instruction menu should be read for an introduction to REMS, its models, data, tables, and other utilities before executing any other functions.

NOTES ON CHAPTER 2

1. This chapter is adapted in part from George I. Treyz (1986). The chapter was also written in part by Frederick Treyz.

2. The identity output = income assumes that all value added by local production (wages, profits, rents, etc.) is paid out to households or to local governments (through local taxes). This assumption is dropped later in the chapter.

3. Note that net inflows to the state could be used to finance CG rather than IL, if they exceed the value of local investment (IL).

4. In the traditional economic base model, IL_p is combined with CG and considered endogenous. We do not combine them because it is difficult to envision IL_p, which includes investment to build new capital stock, to be a fraction of a flow variable, such as income.

5. Any points off the 45-degree line imply that output exceeds expenditure or expenditure exceeds output. If this were the case, we would observe an unplanned inventory increase (or decrease), which would lead businesses to lower (or raise) output until output reached the equilibrium point.

6. *Business Statistics 1961-88* (December 1989), page 3.

7. For a more complete treatment of this subject see Marschack, J. (1953).

8. The source for this table (2-9) is 1987 County Business Patterns, Bureau of the Census, U.S. Department of Commerce for the first ten sectors and Regional Economic Information Systems (REIS) from the Bureau of Economic Analysis (BEA) for the last two sectors.

9. The complete data for any county or state are available in university libraries and directly from the Bureau of the Census by calling (202) 763-4100 or writing Customer Service Branch, Data Users Service Division (DUSD), Washington Plaza, Bureau of the Census, Washington, D.C. 20233.

10. Source for table 2-10: 1987 County Business Patterns, Bureau of the Census, U.S. Department of Commerce.

11. Source for table 2-11: same as 10 *supra*.

88

12. Hereafter, the abbreviation *n.e.c.* will appear in place of the phrase "not elsewhere classified."

13. Source for table 2-12: 1987 County Business Patterns, Bureau of the Census, U.S. Department of Commerce.

14. Source for table 2-13: 1987 County Business Patterns.

15. Source for table 2-14: 1987 County Business Patterns.

16. All from the *Survey of Current Business* (SCB) Vol. 72, No. 1, table 1.1, January, 1992, p. 25.

17. *Survey of Current Business*, Vol. 71, No. 12, December 1991, table 4, p. 50.

18. *Survey of Current Business*, Vol. 72, No. 1, table 1.1, p. 25.

19. Idem.

20. Ibid, Table 2.1, p. 33.

21. All data from *Survey of Current Business*, Vol. 72, No. 1, January 1992, p. 5 and 25.

22. Ibid, table 1.2, p. 25; 2.1, p. 33; 1.1, p. 5.

CHAPTER 3

A PROTOTYPE MODEL[1]

In a typical regional economy, thousands of people and businesses conduct a multitude of transactions every day. Ultimately, all of these transactions are interrelated. The task of a model builder is to identify the key causal paths through which changes in one part of the regional economy influence the other parts of the economy. The blocks in diagram 3-1 show the main components of the operational model that we present in this book. They are general enough so that the structure of almost any operational regional model can be represented in this framework. In some models, one of the blocks may be omitted or replaced by exogenous variables; in others, one of the blocks may be developed, justifying breaking it into two blocks. In any case, any model that does not include some of the elements from each of the five blocks can be represented as a special case in this more general framework.

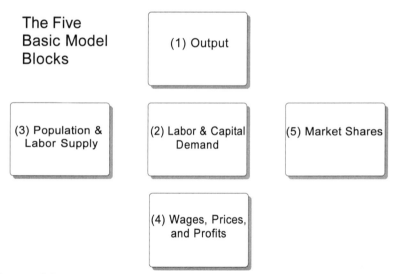

The Five Basic Model Blocks

(1) Output

(3) Population & Labor Supply

(2) Labor & Capital Demand

(5) Market Shares

(4) Wages, Prices, and Profits

Diagram 3-1

Diagram 3-1 shows the basic groupings of endogenous variables found in regional models. The output sector (1) includes output, consumption, and local government spending, which are the key variables in the simple economic base model. More elaborate models would also include output by industry, endogenous investment, export by industry, and different types of consumption spending. The labor and capital demand sector (2) includes derived employment (as in the extended economic base

90

model) and capital demand. In more elaborate models, other factor demands may be included and some of the demands are industry specific. The population and labor supply sector (3) could include migration and population by cohort, as well as the available labor force. The wages, prices, and profits sector (4) includes relative employment opportunity, wage rates, sales prices, and profitability. The market shares sector (5) includes variables for the proportion of local and external markets that are supplied by a given region. Again, in operational models, these variables are usually determined for each industry. In a completely developed regional model, the sectors interact with each other, and the equations in all sectors are solved simultaneously. Our extended economic base model, as developed at the end of the last chapter, is shown within this framework in diagram 3-2.

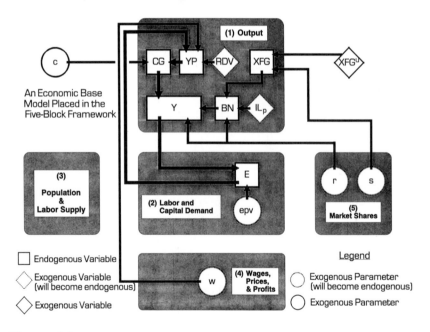

Diagram 3-2

In this diagram, we find that the economic base model is located almost entirely in the output sector (1). The shares of local and national markets (r, s) are parameters in the economic base model, but are determined endogenously in the prototype model in this chapter. Employment (E) is included endogenously instead of making a link directly from output (Y) to personal income (YP), as we did in earlier economic base models. We use a fixed parameter, the employees per unit of output (*epv*) from sector 2, to convert output into employees. We use a fixed parameter of earnings per employee (*w*) from sector 4 to link employment to personal income (YP).

United States interregional and international trade (XFG^u) is exogenous and remains so in future models. Along with the share parameter (*s*) from block 5, it determines exports (XFG). Local planned investment (IL$_p$) is exogenous here, but is incorporated in later models as a variable that is determined endogenously by a behavioral equation. Thus, we can see that the economic base model represents a special case of a more general model. Some of the variables in the economic base model may be split into their components. However, some of the exogenous variables and some of the parameters in the economic base model are made into endogenous variables in later models.

From diagram 3-2, it can be seen that the economic base model ignores important interrelationships in regional economies. In this chapter, we begin to develop a more complete economic model. We develop a single sector, single region, single occupation, single age/sex cohort model with four components of aggregate demand, and two factors of production. This model captures the interaction among economic variables in a regional economy and serves as a prototype for the more detailed operational models. The key linkages in this model are shown in diagram 3-3.

Basic Model Linkages

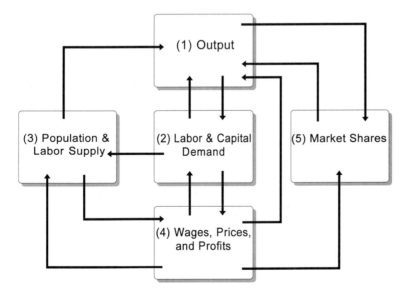

Diagram 3-3

Diagram 3-3 shows the endogenous linkages in our prototype model. The same linkages are also found in the detailed operational model that we present in Part II of this book. In the output sector, population, employment, and the wage rate are all determinants of local consumption and government demand. In addition, local capital demand is an important determinant of local investment. These final demands together determine output (sector 1). The market share variables, showing the proportion of markets supplied by the region, come from sector 5.

The output determined in sector 1 and the employees per dollar of output in sector 2 determine employment. Employees per dollar of output, in turn, depends on the wage rate and capital costs in sector 4. Capital demand also depends on the relative cost of capital and labor, as well as output. In sector 3, population and labor supply depend on labor demand (from sector 2) and the wage rate from sector 4. In sector 4, the demands and supplies interact to determine wages, prices, and profits. Finally, prices and profits from sector 4, as well as the size of the local market from sector 1, are key determinants of the shares of the local and extra-regional markets. All of the specific behavioral assumptions are discussed in the remainder of this chapter.

Before reading the next five sections, which develop each of the blocks of the model in detail, you may want to refer to diagram 3-17 and diagram 3-18 at the end of this chapter. These diagrams show the linkages among the key endogenous variables in the model. They also serve as a useful reference as you read about each block.

3-1 OUTPUT LINKAGES

The output sector is similar to the output demand sector in the economic base model. We can begin to develop the structure for the prototype model by combining equations 2-26 and 2-31 in chapter 2,

$$Y = rCG + rIL_p + rXFG, \qquad (2\text{-}26, 2\text{-}31)$$

where

Y	value added output (gross regional product)
CG	personal and local government consumption
IL_p	planned local investment
XFG	exports from the region
r	the proportion of planned purchases supplied locally

Here, we will split CG into its two components: personal consumption (C) and state and local government spending (G). We also change the parameter (r) into a variable (R) that is explained in another block of the model. These changes produce the following output equation:

$$Y = R \times (C + IL_p + G + XFG) \qquad\qquad (3\text{-}1)$$

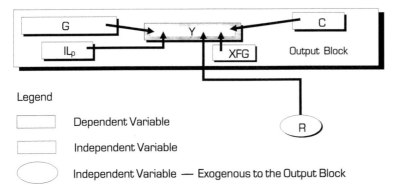

Determination of Gross Regional Product (Y)

Diagram 3-4

Note that we are using a form of the equation that no longer includes the economic base variable (BN), because we explain IL_p and XFG separately in this model. In this expanded version, IL_p will no longer be part of the economic base. Equation 3-1 is represented in diagram 3-4. In this diagram, we note that the determinants of Y are C, G, IL_p, XFG, and R. The R variable is used to account for the fact that a certain portion of the demand represented by the other four variables is filled by imports.

94

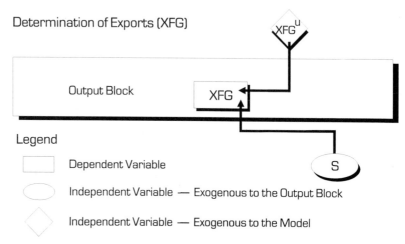

Determination of Exports (XFG)

XFG^u

Output Block

XFG

Legend

☐ Dependent Variable

S

⬭ Independent Variable — Exogenous to the Output Block

◇ Independent Variable — Exogenous to the Model

Diagram 3-5

Exports are explained by multiplying the variable S, which represents the region's share of interregional and international trade and federal government purchases, by XFG^u. This is shown in the following equation:

$$XFG = S \times XFG^u \qquad (3\text{-}2)$$

This simple relationship is also shown in diagram 3-5.

Consumption (C), planned investment (IL_p), and state and local government spending (G) are determined endogenously in conjunction with corresponding United States values, which serve to capture shifts in spending patterns that affect the region and the nation. Each is driven by a local endogenous variable, as follows: C is driven by local real disposable income (i.e., personal income after taxes that is expressed in dollars of constant purchasing power); IL_p is explained by the gap between the local optimal capital stock and the actual capital stock (i.e., structures and equipment); and G depends on the size of the local population. We start with the determination of consumption, which we represent in diagram 3-6.

Consumption is determined by real disposable income (RYD), the ratio of U.S. consumption (C^u) to U.S. real disposable income (RYD^u), and a constant (k_C). The equation for consumption is given as

$$C = k_C \times \left[\frac{C^u}{RYD^u} \right] \times RYD \qquad (3\text{-}3)$$

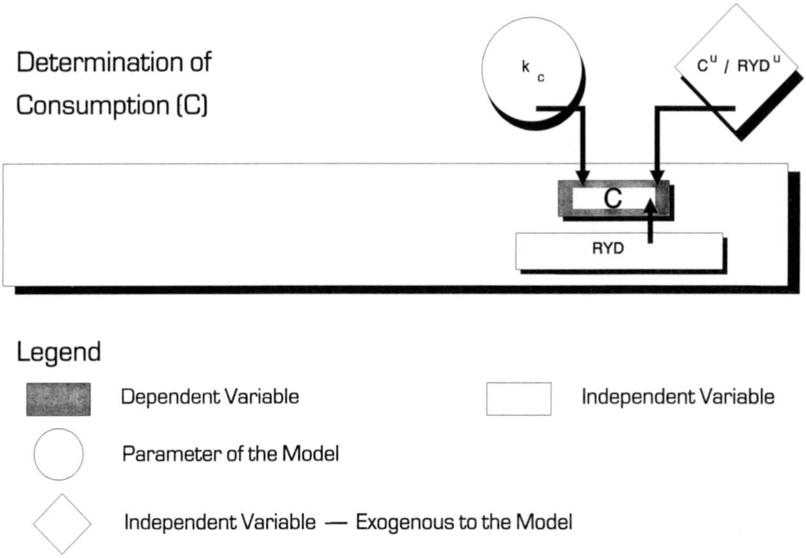
Determination of
Consumption (C)
k c
C u / RYD u
C
RYD
Legend
Dependent Variable
Independent Variable
Parameter of the Model
Independent Variable — Exogenous to the Model

Diagram 3-6

In diagram 3-6, consumption is driven by local real disposable income (RYD). If the constant (k_C) is equal to one, then the proportion of real disposable income used for consumption (C^u/RYD^u) is the same in the region as it is in the nation. A constant that is higher than one indicates a relatively high propensity to consume, while a low regional propensity to consume is indicated by a constant that is less than one. The value of the constant can be estimated by using consumer expenditure surveys for regions of the United States. It is important to note that C^u/RYD^u changes over time but serves the role usually filled by a parameter of the model.

The determination of real disposable income (RYD) involves a number of definitional equations. These equations, in turn, include a number of variables. While a large number of variables are involved, this section of the model is very straightforward. The derivation of real disposable income, starting with labor and proprietor's income by place of work, is shown in table 3-1.

TABLE 3-1

Derivation of Real Disposable Income

Function	Definition	Abbreviation
	Earnings by Place of Work	YLP
LESS(−):	Personal Contributions for Social Insurance (Part of RDV)	VSS
PLUS(+):	Adjustment for Residence (Part of RDV)	RA
PLUS(+):	Dividends, Interest, and Rent (Part of RDV)	DIR
PLUS(+):	Transfer Payments (Part of RDV)	VP
EQUALS(=):	Personal Income by Place of Residence	YP
LESS(−):	Tax and Nontax Payments	TAX
EQUALS(=):	Disposable Income	YD
DIVIDED BY:	Price Index	CP
EQUALS(=):	Real Disposable Income	RYD

The definitional equations used in the prototype model to derive real disposable income are

$$YLP = (E \times W) \div 1000 \quad \text{Labor and Proprietors' Income Eq.} \quad (3\text{-}4)$$

$$YP = YLP + RDV \quad \text{Personal Income Equation} \tag{3-5}$$

$$RDV = - VSS + RA + DIR + VP \quad \text{RDV Equation} \tag{3-6}$$

$$RYD = [YP \times (1 - tx)] \div CP \; \text{Real Disposable Income Equation} \; (3\text{-}7)$$

These equations are also shown in diagram 3-7. $E \times W$ is divided by 1000, because E is in thousands and W is in thousands, but YLP is in billions. All of the right-hand side variables are endogenous. However, the parameter tx has been included in equation 3-7, assuming that tax and nontax payments are a certain fraction of personal income. Thus,

$$TAX = tx \times YP, \tag{3-8}$$

and since

$$YD = YP - TAX; \text{therefore,}$$

$$YD = YP - (tx \times YP) = (1 - tx) \times YP, \tag{3-9}$$

and YD is divided by a consumer consumption deflator[2] (CP) to obtain real disposable income (RYD).

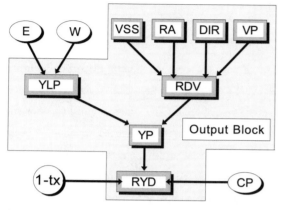

Derivation of Real Disposable Income (RYD)

▬ Dependent Variable ◯ Parameter of Model

◯ Independent Variable – Exogenous to the Block

Diagram 3-7

The equations that determine the four components of RDV are in the output block. The residential adjustment (RA) equation differs, depending on whether or not RA is positive or negative. A positive RA means that, on balance, this area has more residents who work outside the region than nonresidents who commute into the region. In this case, RA is a function of outside of region income (YLP^u). If RA is negative, the preponderance of commuters take income from the region, making RA a function of local area income (YLP). Thus,

$$RA = \begin{cases} k_{RA} \times YLP \ if \ k_{RA} < 0 \ (i.e., \ RA < 0) \\ k_{RA} \times YLP^u \ if \ k_{RA} > 0 \ (i.e., \ RA > 0) \end{cases} \qquad (3\text{-}10)$$

so that in a central city area, where suburban commuters work, some part of any increase in YLP goes to the suburbs. In bedroom communities, local income increases when outside of region earnings (YLP^u) increase.

The other three components of RDV are predicted based on using national rates of payment as parameters in the model. The three equations are

$$VSS = k_{VSS} \times \left(\frac{VSS^u}{YLP^u} \right) \times YLP \qquad (3\text{-}11)$$

$$VP = k_{VP} \times \left(\frac{VP^u}{N^u - E^u} \right) \times (N - ER) \qquad (3\text{-}12)$$

$$DIR = k_{DIR} \times \left(\frac{DIR^u}{N^u} \right) \times N \tag{3-13}$$

In each case, if the rate of payment were the same in the region as in the nation, the k values would be equal to one. In the first case, social security taxes (VSS) are based on the average U.S. social security tax rate multiplied by labor and proprietors' income earned in the area (YLP). In the second equation, transfer payments, which include unemployment, social security, and welfare, are a function of the number of people in the population (N) less the number of people employed by place of residence (ER). Since older people receive a considerably larger share of transfer payments than those under 65, this will be broken down further in the operational model. Finally, property income (dividends, interest, and rent) is predicted on a per capita basis.

Next, we turn to *planned investment* (IL$_p$). It is similar to the other components of aggregate demand, because it represents a flow of economic activity (i.e., billions of 1987 dollars of construction *per year*). However, it is different, because it is the only one out of the four final-demand components that is a function of the difference between an actual and a desired stock, rather than a flow variable. This process, which drives investment, is called the *stock adjustment process*. We represent the driving force behind investment as the optimal capital stock (K*) less the actual stock of capital (K). The actual stock of capital is the stock of capital at the end of last year (K_{t-1}) less depreciation (i.e., the depreciation rate (dr^u) times K_{t-1}). The speed with which this gap is filled is the *adjustment speed* (α) estimated for all states in the United States simultaneously. Any regional differences in capital preference are represented by k_1. This relationship and the determination of IL$_p$ are shown in equation 3-14 and diagram 3-8.

$$IL_{p,t} = \alpha \left[(k_1 K_t^*) - (1 - dr^u) K_{t-1} \right] \tag{3-14}$$

K_{t-1} is the capital stock in the last period, thus $(1 - dr^u) K_{t-1}$ is capital stock at the beginning of period t. To calculate the value of K_{t-1} for the next year of forecast or simulation, we use the following capital stock updating equation:

$$K_t = IL_{p,t} + (1 - dr^u) K_{t-1} \tag{3-15}$$

Investment (ILp): Stock Adjustment Determinants

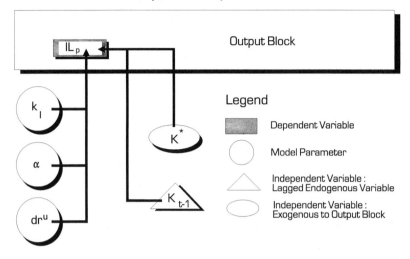

Diagram 3-8

The determinants of *state and local government spending* are shown in diagram 3-9. State and local government spending (G) depends on the population (N), the

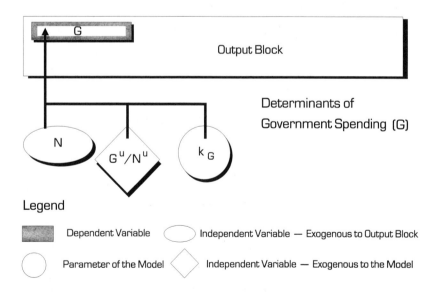

Diagram 3-9

government spending constant (k_G), which represents regional preferences, and total

U.S. state and local government spending per capita (G^u/N^u). The equation for state and local government spending follows:

$$G = k_G \times \left[\frac{G^u}{N^u}\right] \times N$$

(3-16)

State and local government spending (G) is equal to the average national per capita state and local government spending rate, adjusted for regional differences, and multiplied by the regional population. Again, the national ratio functions as a parameter but will automatically change if a new national forecast replaces an old one. The constant (k_G) is the locally observed ratio of per capita government spending to the corresponding average value in the United States.

To conclude this section, see block 1 in diagram 3-17. Note that this block (1) is a simplified version of the equations presented previously. In the diagram, RDV and its components are regarded as exogenous variables and, therefore, are not included.

3-2 LABOR AND CAPITAL DEMAND LINKAGES[3]

The derived demand for basic factors of production are determined next. In this simple model, we consider demand for labor and capital. In our complete model, fuel is also considered as a factor of production. The optimal levels of labor and capital are determined by a cost-minimizing procedure using a *constant returns to scale*[4] Cobb-Douglas production function. This function (see equation 3-17) is commonly used to relate changes in output to changes in factor inputs. We show the factor demand linkages in diagram 3-10 — the only diagram we use to illustrate block 2.

The EPV variable is employees per million 1987 dollars of value-added output. It is determined by the following: total productivity of factor use in the region (A) relative to the United States (A^u); the capital share of output (d); U.S. employees per million 1987 dollars of output (E^u/Y^u); the relative cost of capital (c/c^u); and the relative cost of labor (W/W^u). The relative cost of capital is exogenous to the model, while the relative cost of labor is represented by the local earnings rate relative to the national rate, which is determined in sector 4. We can determine *employment* (E) from workers per unit of output (EPV) and output (Y). *Optimum capital stock* (K*) depends on employment (E), the relative costs of capital (c/c^u) and labor (W/W^u), and the ratio of U.S. employment (E^u) to the U.S. optimal capital stock (E^u/K^{u*}).

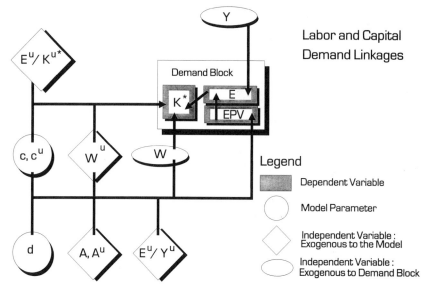

Diagram 3-10

We begin by deriving the optimal levels of employment and capital from a Cobb-Douglas production function. We show the function as

$$Y = A \times E^a \times K^d \tag{3-17}$$

where $a + d = 1$ indicating constant returns to scale (i.e., $2 \times E$ and $2 \times K$ would yield $2 \times Y$), and

        A   average factor productivity

        a   labor share of output

        d   capital share of output

Output is determined by the use of labor (E) and capital (K), their share in production (a, d), and the overall productivity of factor use in the region (A), which may be thought of as the level of technology. We use this function and the assumption that firms maximize profits to derive several of the equations in the prototype model.

We take the partial derivatives of the Cobb-Douglas production function, with respect to labor and capital, which shows the marginal change in output, with respect to employment and capital. We multiply the marginal change in output by the sales price per unit of output (SP). For cost minimization, we set these variables equal to the cost per unit of labor (W) and the cost of capital (*c*) in nominal (i.e., current) dollars.

Marginal Labor Product $=$

$$\frac{\partial Y}{\partial E} = \left[A \times (a \times E^{a-1}) \times K^d \right] \times SP$$

$$= \left[\frac{A \times (a \times E^a) \times K^d}{E} \right] \times SP = W \tag{3-18}$$

Marginal Capital Product $=$

$$\frac{\partial Y}{\partial K} = \left[A \times E^a \times (d \times K^{d-1}) \right] \times SP$$

$$= \left[\frac{A \times E^a \times (d \times K^d)}{K} \right] \times SP = c \tag{3-19}$$

Substituting the production function 3-17 into equations 3-18 and 3-19, we derive

$$SP \times \frac{Y \times a}{E} = W , \tag{3-20}$$

and

$$SP \times \frac{Y \times d}{K} = c \tag{3-21}$$

Dividing equation 3-20 by equation 3-21 and solving for K, we obtain the optimal capital stock (K*).

$$K^* = \left[\frac{W}{c} \right] \times \left[\frac{d}{a} \right] \times E \tag{3-22}$$

The U.S. optimal capital stock is determined by a similar formula.

$$K^{u*} = \left[\frac{W^u}{c^u} \right] \times \left[\frac{d}{a} \right] \times E^u \tag{3-23}$$

From dividing equation 3-22 by 3-23, we produce the optimal capital stock formula. This is given as

$$K^* = \left[\frac{W}{W^u} \right] \times \left[\frac{c^u}{c} \right] \times \left[\frac{E}{E^u} \right] \times K^{u*} \tag{3-24}$$

The optimal capital stock (K*) is determined by the relative cost of labor (W/W^u), the inverse relative cost of capital (c/c^u), the relative use of labor (E/E^u), and the U.S.

optimal capital stock ($K^{u}*$).

Substituting equation 3-22 (the equation for K^*) into the production function 3-17 for K and remembering that $a + d = 1$, we obtain the following equation:

$$Y = A \times E \times \left[\frac{d}{a}\right]^d \times \left[\frac{W}{c}\right]^d \tag{3-25}$$

A similar equation for the United States is

$$Y^u = A^u \times E^u \times \left[\frac{d}{a}\right]^d \times \left[\frac{W^u}{c^u}\right]^d \tag{3-26}$$

Dividing equation 3-25 by equation 3-26 and solving for E/Y, we find the equation for employees per dollar of value added (GRP), which we call EPV. This is now the variable in the model that replaces the parameter *epv*, which was originally used for the same concept in the economic base model.

$$EPV = \left(\left[\frac{c}{c^u}\right]^d \times \left[\frac{W}{W^u}\right]^{-d} \times \left[\frac{E^u}{Y^u}\right]\right) \div \left[\frac{A}{A^u}\right] \tag{3-27}$$

This equation shows, for example, that EPV will increase if relative capital costs (c/c^u) increase. EPV decreases if the relative labor costs (W/W^u) increase, and EPV will also decrease if relative productivity (A/A^u) increases. However, labor intensity only changes over time as new equipment is purchased. This can be captured in the model by making the relative labor intensity part of equation 3-27 change gradually as new equipment replaces old equipment. Therefore, while the optimal labor intensity for current purchases of equipment is $(c \div c^u)^d \times (W \div W^u)^{-d}$, the labor intensity for the average of old and new equipment can be established by the following equation:

$$LIA_t = LIA_{t-1} + salia \, [(c \div c^u)^d (W \div W^u)^{-d} - LIA_{t-1}], \tag{3-28}$$

or

$$LIA_t = (1 - salia) \times LIA_{t-1} + salia \, (c \div c^u)^d (W \div W^u)^{-d} \tag{3-29}$$

In the first version, it is clear that each year the average labor intensity (LIA) is adjusted by the speed of adjustment (*salia*) multiplied by the difference between the old average (LIA_{t-1}) and the optimal labor intensity for new equipment ($(c \div c^u)^d (W \div W^u)^{-d}$). The value of *salia* must be greater than zero and less than or equal to one. The second equation is simply an algebraic transformation of the first. Equation 3-27

104

for EPV can now be reformulated to take into account the lagged adjustment as

$$EPV = \left[LIA \times \left(\frac{E^u}{Y^u} \right) \right] \div \left(\frac{A}{A^u} \right) \tag{3-30}$$

The equation to determine employment is simply the employees per unit of value added (EPV) multiplied by the total value added (Y).

$$E = EPV \times Y \tag{3-31}$$

In summary, we have derived equations for the optimal stock of capital (K*) and employees per unit of value added (EPV) by assuming cost-minimization, using a constant returns to scale Cobb-Douglas production function. The optimal level of capital stock is used to explain regional investment. The optimal number of employees per unit of gross regional product (EPV) and gross regional product (Y) determine employment (E). The fact that EPV is reduced when W increases means that less labor will be used if labor costs increase relative to capital costs. In the following section, we present the population and labor supply linkages. These linkages give us the labor supply curve in our model.

3-3 POPULATION AND LABOR SUPPLY LINKAGES[5]

This set of linkages gives us an increase in the supply of labor when wages or

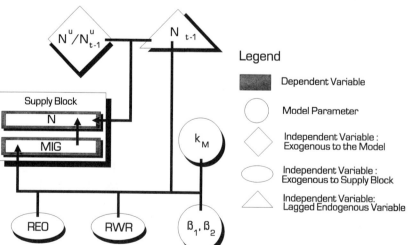

Population and Labor Supply Linkages

Diagram 3-11

the probability of employment increases. The labor supply of an area depends upon the population, the proportion of people who want to work, and the migration into or out of a region. The population and labor supply linkages are shown in diagram 3-11.

The region's *population* (N_t) is determined by the population in the previous history or forecast year (N_{t-1}), the rate of growth in the national population $N_t^u \div N_{t-1}^u$, and the migration into or out of the region (MIG). The ratio of the current population to its value last year approximates the effect of exogenous population changes in the nation. The inclusion of a demographic module would more precisely estimate population by including explicit international migration, returning military personnel, retirement migrants, and rates of natality and survival. *Migration* (MIG) is determined by the last time period population (N_{t-1}), the migration amenity constant (k_M), and the natural logarithm of the relative wage rate (ln(RWR)) and of relative employment opportunity (ln(REO)), and econometrically estimated coefficients (β_1, β_2) that show the effects of RWR and REO. The RWR and REO equations are fully shown and explained in the Wage, Price, and Profit Linkages section.

Migration determines the changes in a region's population in response to economic conditions. The equation is given as

$$MIG = \{ k_m + [\beta_1 \times ln(REO)] + [\beta_2 \times ln(RWR)] \} \times N_{t-1} \quad (3\text{-}32)$$

The determinants of migration are based on the assumption of utility maximization. Migration is estimated as a proportion of the population in the last historical time period (N_{t-1}). The migration constant (k_M) is estimated over a sample period to take into account migration explained by quality of life or amenity factors. The coefficients β_1 and β_2 are estimated in a study conducted outside of the model to explain the effect of the relative employment opportunity and the relative wage rate on migration. High relative employment opportunity, or a relatively large proportion of employment in the population, encourages people to migrate into an area, since this lowers the chance of unemployment for a prospective migrant. A high relative real wage rate also encourages migration into an area, because people move in order to obtain or improve their chances of obtaining a job that pays well. The relative employment opportunity (REO) and the relative wage rate (RWR), along with the relative wage mix introduced in our multi-industry model, are the components that determine expected earned income. In the absence of industry mix, the product of the relative probability of being employed (REO) and the relative real wage rate (RWR) is expected income. Thus, if expected earned income increases, it is captured by these variables.

The population in the region (N) forms the basis of the supply of labor. We can estimate the population using last year's value as a starting point. Changes from the last year are caused by economic migration into or out of the area, demographic processes, and other migration. These latter effects are captured in part by the growth in the United States population, as indicated previously. In a model that includes a cohort-survival model, these can be calculated explicitly. In the prototype model, the population equation is given as

$$N_t = N_{t-1} \times \left[\frac{N_t^u}{N_{t-1}^u} \right] + MIG \tag{3-33}$$

The population gives us the labor supply in this model. In a model with explicit population by age/sex cohort, a potential labor force can be calculated with the aid of estimated participation rates by cohort. Combined with the demand for labor, shown in the second block, we have the supply and demand response of the model. The determination of wages, prices, and profits in response to these conditions is discussed in the next section.

3-4 WAGE, PRICE, AND PROFIT LINKAGES

This set of linkages shows how supply and demand variables determine wages, prices, and profits. These variables are ultimately determined by the relative cost of the factors of production estimated in the Cobb-Douglas production function. We separate wage, price, and profit linkages into three categories: (A) prices and profits, (B) wage rates, and (C) wage rate changes due to changes in labor demand and supply. The following flow chart shows the interrelationships among these linkages.

Simplified Wage, Price, and Profit Linkages

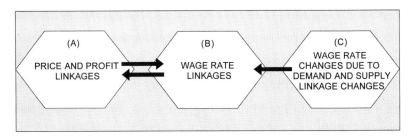

Diagram 3-12

Price and profit linkages (A) are determined by wage rate linkages (B), since relative production costs and other measurements of prices and profits change due to changes in the wage rate. *Wage rate linkages* (B) include wage rate changes, which depend on relative consumer prices, which are, in turn, determined in the price and profit linkages (A). The wage rate itself is endogenously determined by the wage effects from B and wage changes due to changes in demand and supply (C). *Wage changes due to changes in demand and supply* (C) depend on the population and the employment level. First, we show the equations in linkages for prices and profits (A), then wage rates (B), and finally, wage changes due to changes in demand and supply (C).

For the first time, our equations are divided into two parts, as follows: one part is for the part of our industry that has regional industry characteristics; the other is for the part that has national industry characteristics. Therefore, we begin with a general comparison of national and regional industries before presenting the detailed formulas. *Regional industries* are defined as those that, on average across all states, sell more than 50 percent of their output in their own state. *National industries* are defined as those that, on average across all states, supply more than half of their output to national and international markets. An example of a national industry is the automobile industry, since, on average, over 50 percent of the cars produced in any state are exported from that state. Grocery stores, on the other hand, would be considered a regional industry, because more than half of the output of these establishments is used to supply local demand.

Regional industries in a particular area generally have a significant locational advantage over the same type of business in a neighboring region. Each regional industry also tends to be found, to some extent, in almost all regions. Grocery stores, for example, can best serve a local clientele and are found in every county in the United States.

A national industry that is located in a particular region has only a slight locational advantage over similar producers in other locations. A national industry, therefore, competes on a national level, and must sell its output at the national price. Automobiles produced in a particular region, for example, are sold at the price that prevails on a national level. National industries are not necessarily located in every region, and we find that such industries, like the automobile industry, are concentrated in a few counties and nonexistent in others.

108

The price of the output in national industries depends on national production costs. Thus, if the cost of producing an automobile increases across the nation, we would consequently expect the price of automobiles to also increase across the United States. An increase in production costs in one region relative to the rest of the country, however, would not change the price of cars in that region. Within the region, consumers would be able to buy automobiles at the national price. Thus, producers within the region would be forced to sell at the national price, and, when faced with increasing relative production costs, would then be less profitable. In general, national industries sell at the national price, and relative production costs determine their profitability.

Producers in regional industries, however, are competing primarily with other producers within that region. Therefore, the price of output depends on the regional, rather than the national, cost of production. If the regional production costs in eating and drinking establishments increase, we would expect local prices to increase. However, a national increase in production costs without a corresponding regional change would not directly affect the price charged by local restaurants.

We can show the specific determination of price and profit linkages for national and regional industries. We start by showing the flow chart for price and profit linkages.

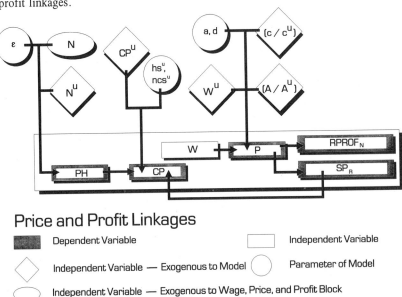

Price and Profit Linkages

■ Dependent Variable		☐ Independent Variable
◇ Independent Variable — Exogenous to Model		◯ Parameter of Model
◯ Independent Variable — Exogenous to Wage, Price, and Profit Block		

Diagram 3-13

We use *relative terms* to explain profitability and production costs. The relative profitability of a national industry (RPROF$_N$) depends on relative production costs (P). The relative sales price of a regional industry (SP$_R$) also depends on relative production costs. If we were to use only the national industry assumption in the model, consumer prices (CP) would depend solely on the U.S. consumer price deflator (CP") and relative housing prices (PH). If we were to use only the regional industry assumption, the local consumer price level (CP) would be determined by the national consumer price deflator (CP"), the relative sales price for the regional industry (SP$_R$), and by relative housing prices (PH). Changes in housing prices (PH) depend on changes in the ratio of the local to the U.S. population (N/N"), which serves as a proxy for measuring changes in relative density. The parameter ε is the estimate of that response. The parameters hs" and ncs" are the weights of housing and the relative weight of national to regional products in CP.

Relative production costs (P) are derived from the Cobb-Douglas production function, and, therefore, depend on the relative cost of labor (W/W"), the relative cost of capital (c/c"), the share of labor and capital in production (a and d), and the relative factor productivity of the region (A/A"). To derive relative production costs, we begin by stating the accounting equation for total costs.

$$TC = (W \times E) + (c \times K) \tag{3-34}$$

Total costs (TC) equal the total labor costs (W × E) plus total capital costs (c × K). Substituting K* in equation 3-22 for K in equation 3-34, and remembering that $a + d = 1$, we obtain

$$TC = (W \times E) \div a \tag{3-35}$$

Solving for E in equation 3-25 and substituting it into equation 3-35, we obtain

$$TC = Y \times A^{-1} \times \left[\frac{c}{W}\right]^d \times \left[\frac{a}{d}\right]^d \times \frac{W}{a} \tag{3-36}$$

The partial derivative of TC from this equation with respect to value added is the marginal cost, and is

$$Marginal\ Cost = \frac{\partial TC}{\partial Y} = A^{-1} \times \left[\frac{c}{W}\right]^d \times \left[\frac{a}{d}\right]^d \times \frac{W}{a} \tag{3-37}$$

Dividing by a similar function for the United States, we obtain the relative cost of production (P) equation.

$$P = \left[\frac{W}{W^u} \right]^a \times \left[\frac{c}{c^u} \right]^d \div \left[\frac{A}{A^u} \right] \tag{3-38}$$

in which the relative cost of production is determined by relative wage and capital costs, allowing for substitutability,[6] and by the relative level of technology.

In the case of a national industry, the relative profitability of the industry determines whether it locates in the area or not. Relative profitability for a national industry is dependent on the cost of production, as follows:

$$RPROF_N = (1 - P) + 1 \tag{3-39}$$

Thus, the higher the cost of production, the lower the relative profitability of the national industry. Since it competes in a national market, the sales price is set equal to the national sales price, which is given as one (1).

$$SP_N = SP_N^u = 1 \tag{3-40}$$

Since regional industries compete primarily in the local market, their selling prices depend on the relative cost of production. In order to have a determinate price for regional production, we assume that, at the margin, the productivity of regional firms is equal in all localities (i.e., $A = A^u$) and that these firms sell at the marginal cost of production. The sales price for regional industries (SP_R) is

$$SP_R = \left[\frac{W}{W^u} \right]^a \times \left[\frac{c}{c^u} \right]^d \tag{3-41}$$

Changes in housing prices are dependent on changes in the density of the population.

$$PH = \varepsilon \times \left(\frac{N_t \div N_t^u}{N_{t-1} \div N_{t-1}^u} - 1 \right) + PH_{t-1} + UPH \tag{3-42}$$

The *housing price* (PH) is shown as a percentage change in the local to U.S. housing price ratio. The elasticity of response (ε) shows how much housing prices will change as relative population density changes. If the local population increases faster than the national population, then the relative housing price will rise. If the relative population density doesn't change, then relative housing prices will not change.

In the case of a regional industry, the price level depends on the regional industries' sales prices in the local area. In the case of a national industry, the price level depends on the price in the nation and would not be affected by local changes in relative production costs. However, since SP for national industries always equals one (1) and the share of the nonhousing portion of the consumption deflator that is not regional is national, we adopt equation 3-43. In our prototype model, we assume that some of the production in the area comes under each of the previous assumptions. Thus, the *consumer price deflator* has weights for the nonhousing proportion of consumption of the regional and national industry types.

$$CP = [(1 - hs^u) \times ((1 - ncs^u) \times SP_R + ncs^u) + (hs^u \times PH)] \times CP^u \quad (3-43)$$

hs^u proportion of consumption in housing

ncs^u national industry proportion of nonhousing consumption

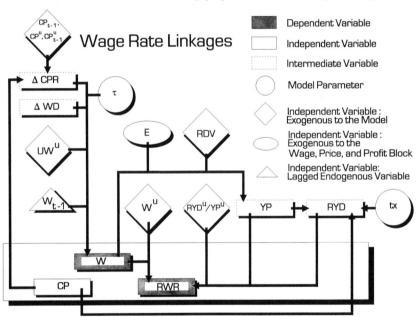

Diagram 3-14

We now turn to Part B, (see diagram 3-14) where wage rates are determined. *The earnings rate* (W) is determined by the change in wages due to demand (ΔWD), the shift in the local consumer price deflators relative to the nation (CP, CP_{t-1}, CP^u, CP^u_{t-1}), the portion of the U.S. wage change that is not due to demand shifts (UW^u), and wages in the last year period (W_{t-1}). Lagged wages and prices are determined by the history or forecast conducted for the previous year. As a result, they are endogenously estimated by the model but are exogenous to the year that is being evaluated.

In showing the wage determination equations, we start with the equation for the wage rate.

$$W = (1 + \Delta WD)(1 + \Delta CPR)^{\tau} (1 + UW^u) \times W_{t-1} \qquad (3\text{-}44)$$

W   the wage or earnings rate

τ elasticity of wage changes to price changes determined from an econometric study (see equation 7-95)

ΔWD the change in the earnings rate due to demand

ΔCPR changes in the relative consumer price deflator

UW^u changes in U.S. wages not explained by changes in employment demand and supply

In this equation, the earnings rate from the previous year (W_{t-1}) is used as the starting point. It is adjusted for the change in earnings due to demand changes (ΔWD), relative changes in consumer prices (ΔCPR), and changes in U.S. wages not explained by demand (UW^u).

Changes in consumer prices affect wages as follows:

$$\Delta CPR = \left[\frac{CP \div CP^u}{CP_{t-1} \div CP_{t-1}^u} \right] - 1 \qquad (3\text{-}45)$$

The ratio $CP \div CP^u$ shows the relative consumer price level of the region during the current time period. If local consumer prices are relatively high, this value is greater than one. The corresponding ratio ($CP_{t-1} \div CP_{t-1}^u$) gives us relative prices from last period. If relative prices are increasing, the ratio $[(CP \div CP^u) \div (CP_{t-1} \div CP_{t-1}^u)]$ is greater than one. If relative prices are decreasing, the value is less than one. By subtracting one from this expression, we obtain a positive value for increasing prices and a negative value for declining prices. Thus, if ΔCPR is greater than one, then increasing relative prices in the region raises the earnings rates with an elasticity of τ. If ΔCPR is less than one, then decreasing prices in the region reduce earnings rates with the same elasticity.

The *relative real earnings rate* (RWR) is determined by the earnings rate (W), the regional and U.S. average income tax rates (tx, tx^u), which include state and local income taxes, and relative consumer prices (CP/CP^u). As we demonstrate later, all of these factors are included if we use the following formula:

$$RWR = \left[\frac{W \times (RYD \div YP)}{W^u \times (RYD^u \div YP^u)} \right] \tag{3-46}$$

This equation adjusts the relative real after-tax wage rate to reflect the relative price levels and tax rates of the region compared to the country as a whole. This can be demonstrated if we recognize that $RYD = (YP - TAX) \div CP$, where TAX represents all income based tax collections, and that $(1 - tx) YP = YP - TAX$. Thus, RYD is equal to $(1 - tx) YP \div CP$. Substituting for RYD and RYD^u in equation 3-46, we obtain

$$RWR = \frac{\dfrac{W(1-tx)YP}{CP \times YP}}{\dfrac{W^u(1-tx^u)YP^u}{CP^u \times YP^u}} = \frac{W(1-tx) \div CP}{W^u(1-tx^u) \div CP^u} \tag{3-47}$$

Thus, equation 3-46 is used for RWR in the migration equations in block 3.

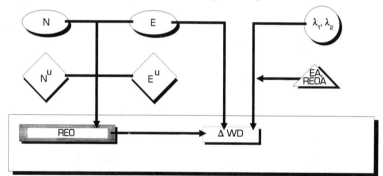

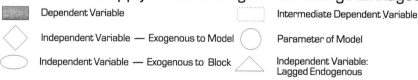

Demand and Supply Related Wage Rate Change Linkages

	Dependent Variable		Intermediate Dependent Variable
Independent Variable — Exogenous to Model		Parameter of Model	
Independent Variable — Exogenous to Block		Independent Variable: Lagged Endogenous	

Diagram 3-15

Finally, we turn to Part C — the demand and supply related wage rate linkages, as shown in diagram 3-15. The changes in the wage rate due to changes in demand[7]

(ΔWD) are caused by employment (E), relative employment opportunity (REO), weighted averages of previous employment and relative employment opportunity (EA, REOA), and model parameters (λ_1, λ_2). The *relative employment opportunity* of a region (REO), which shows the demand for labor relative to its supply, is determined by the relative population (N/N^u) and employment (E/E^u) of the region.

These changes can be shown in a simple form.

$$\Delta WD = (\lambda_1 \times \Delta E) + (\lambda_2 \times \Delta REO) \qquad (3\text{-}48)$$

ΔE	changes in employment (the complete equation is given in equation 3-49)
ΔREO	changes in relative employment opportunity (the complete equation is given in equation 3-54)
λ_1	an econometrically estimated parameter that shows the effect of employment changes on wage rates
λ_2	an econometrically estimated parameter that shows the effect of the relative employment opportunity changes on wage rates.

Estimates for the parameters λ_1 and λ_2 are based on time series data over all states from 1970 to 1989, as described in the appendix (page 137) and in chapter 7 (page 318) . The positive parameter λ_1 indicates that increasing employment will increase wage rates and that decreasing employment will lower wage rates. The parameter λ_2 is an estimate of the effect on wage rates of changes in relative employment opportunity. Thus, it is a representation of the interaction of the demand and supply of labor. Increasing relative employment opportunity, for example, is associated with increasing demand for labor relative to its supply.

Changes in employment (ΔE) and in the relative employment population ratio (ΔREO) are now specified. Changes in employment (ΔE) are specified as

$$\Delta E = \left[\frac{E}{EA} - 1 \right] \qquad (3\text{-}49)$$

$$EA_t = (1 - saea) \times EA_{t-1} + saea \times E_{t-1} \qquad (3\text{-}50)$$

The *moving average of employment* (EA) is a weighted historical average of employment that gives higher weights to the more recent years. It follows the form of equations 3-28 and 3-29. The *saea* value is the speed of adjustment of EA and is greater than zero and less than or equal to one. A ratio of E/EA that is greater than one shows increasing employment. When we subtract one, positive values for (E/EA) − 1 show increasing employment. Negative values for this ratio show declining employment.

The ΔW in equation 3-48 is also calculated for the United States (where ΔREO is zero by definition). Any wage changes observed (in the United States) that are not explained by these demand conditions are used in calculating UW^u for equation 3-44. Thus, UW^u captures changes in U.S. wage rates, due to factors other than ΔE. Next, we show the determination of the *relative employment opportunity* (REO) of a region.

To look at the labor market for residents in the locality, we must convert the employment from a place-of-work to a place-of-residence basis. We do this using the following formula:

$$ER = \left(\frac{YLP + RA}{YLP} \right) \times E \tag{3-51}$$

If the residence adjustment is positive (net outward commuting to work), employment by place of residence (ER) is larger than employment by place of work (E). For negative RA, the opposite holds true.

Next, the concept of the *employment participation rate* (EP) is introduced.

$$EP = ER \div N \tag{3-52}$$

The employment participation rate (EP) is the proportion of the population that is employed. It is a measurement of the employment opportunity of a region, because it indicates the percentage of people who are working. The potential labor force would be preferred instead of population (N), if it were available. If we take the ratio of the employment participation rate to the national employment participation rate (assuming the $E^u = ER^u$), we obtain the relative employment opportunity of the region.

$$REO = \frac{EP}{EP^u} = \left[\frac{ER}{N} \right] \div \left[\frac{E^u}{N^u} \right] \tag{3-53}$$

If the relative employment participation rate of the region is high, the value for the REO will be greater than one. The changes in the relative employment opportunity used to determine wage changes are given as

116

$$\Delta REO = \left[\frac{REO}{REOA} - 1 \right] \tag{3-54}$$

$$REOA_t = (1 - sareo) \times REOA_{t-1} + sareo \times REO_{t-1} \tag{3-55}$$

REOA a weighted moving average of the historic relative employment opportunity

sareo the speed of adjustment, which is greater than zero and less than or equal to one

Thus, if the relative employment opportunity of the region is higher this year than in the past, the value of REO/REOA − 1 is positive. We can now show the complete wage change due to labor supply and demand equation.

$$\Delta WD = \left[\lambda_1 \times \left(\frac{E}{EA} - 1 \right) \right] + \left[\lambda_2 \times \left(\frac{REO}{REOA} - 1 \right) \right] \tag{3-56}$$

This is the basic determination of the effect of the interaction of the supply and demand for labor on the wage rate in the model. The next section shows the determination of the market shares of the region.

3-5 MARKET SHARE LINKAGES[8]

Industries in a region sell to the local and the national market. *Market share linkages* show the proportion of the regional or national market that is captured by an industry. This section considers two types of industries: regional and national. Although regional industries primarily supply local markets and national industries primarily supply

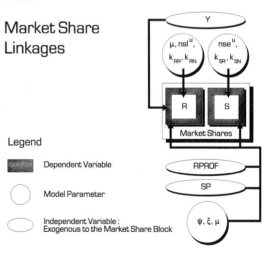

Diagram 3-16

the national market, both types of industries supply both markets. We show the determination of the extraregional (S) and local (R) market shares for both types of industries. However, since our model has only one sector, we will combine these two types of industry responses into a single equation for R and for S. An overview of this sector is shown in diagram 3-16.

First, we discuss the determination of national industry market shares. The *regional supply proportion* (R_N) is determined by the relative profitability of the industry (RPROF), the parameter showing the response of location to relative profitability (ψ), and the regional supply proportion constant (k_{RN}). The *regional share of interregional and international trade coefficient* (S_N) is determined by the relative profitability of the industry (RPROF), the location response parameter (ψ), and the regional share constant (k_{SN}). We start with the regional supply proportion equation for national industries.

$$R_N = k_{RN} \times RPROF_N^{\psi} \tag{3-57}$$

However, since firms cannot move instantly in response to changes in profitability, a speed of adjustment (*sapr*) is added to take this delay into account. It is incorporated in equation 3-57 by first defining a moving average formulation for the profit decision variable.

$$RPROFA_t = (1 - sapr)\, RPROFA_{t-1} + sapr\, RPROF_{N,\,t} \tag{3-58}$$

This is used to transform equation 3-57, as follows:

$$R_N = k_{RN} \times RPROFA^{\psi} \tag{3-59}$$

The regional supply proportion for national industries (R_N) is determined by an industry's decision to locate in a region. If locating in the region becomes profitable, then there is an incentive for more industries to locate there. This increase leads to more local demand being satisfied from within the region. The regional supply proportion depends on relative profitability (RPROF) and the econometrically estimated parameter (ψ) that estimates the response of R_N to a change in profitability. A regional supply proportion constant (k_{RN}) is shown as a third determinant of the regional supply proportion, to account for ongoing regional differences and changes in response to changes in the United States regional supply proportion.

The regional share of interregional trade coefficient for national industries is similarly determined, as shown in the following equation.

$$S_N = k_{SN} \times RPROFA^{\psi} \tag{3-60}$$

The regional share of the interregional trade for national industries (S_N) depends on the interregional share constant (k_{SN}), relative profitability (RPROF), and the econometrically estimated parameter that estimates the effect of relative profitability on the share coefficient (ψ). As in the case of the regional supply proportion, profitability will determine industrial location in a region. Increased profitability of an industry in a region will lead to higher exports, and vice versa (as is shown in the share equation). The k_{SN} parameter is originally calculated by determining exports as a residual in the base year.

In our model, we combine the two types of industries into a single sector. Before doing this, we discuss regional industries, i.e., those that supply mostly local markets and that can pass on increased costs by increasing prices, as opposed to national industries that must sell at the national price.

The *regional supply proportion* (R_R) is determined by output (Y), the regional supply proportion constant (k_{RR}), and the econometrically estimated parameters μ and ξ. The parameter μ is the industry diversity response, and ξ is the elasticity of response to price changes. The regional share of interregional and international trade coefficient (S_R) is determined by the sales price (SP_R), the calibrating coefficient for the regional share of interregional trade constant (k_{SR}), and the price elasticity response (ξ). We start by showing the regional supply proportion equation (R_R).

$$R_R = k_{RR} \times Y^\mu \times SP_R^\xi \qquad (3\text{-}61)$$

An increase in output is expected to increase the regional supply proportion (R_R). Thus, the parameter μ is positive because larger regions are able to satisfy a higher proportion of final demand locally. However, this result is based on on-going research and the equation needs to be specified more carefully. Therefore, $\mu = 0$ for the default version of the current model. The local share of the local market will also respond to changes in the local sales price (SP_R). If this increases, the parameter ξ determines how much of the local share of the market will be lost to imports. The regional industries share of extraregional markets equation follows:

$$S_R = k_{SR} \times SP_R^\xi \qquad (3\text{-}62)$$

Again, since market shares take time to adjust as purchasing patterns change and as business relocates, we use a speed of adjustment (*sasp*) in the response to sales price.

$$SPA_t = (1 - sasp) \times SPA_{t-1} + sasp\ SP_{R,t} \qquad (3\text{-}63)$$

The equations for R_R and S_R become

$$R_R = k_{RR} \times Y^u \times SPA^\xi, \tag{3-64}$$

and

$$S_R = k_{SR} \times SPA^\xi \tag{3-65}$$

The regional share of interregional and international trade for regional industries depends on a constant (k_{SR}) estimated in the base year as a residual, a moving average sales price (SPA_R), and an econometrically estimated parameter (ξ). Although they primarily supply regional markets, regional industries also supply production to surrounding regions. The sales price, which depends on production costs, determines the amount of export trade the industry is able to obtain. If the sales price increases, this reduces the share of extraregional trade as determined by the estimated elasticity of demand response (ξ).

Now that the share equations for both national (price taking) and regional (price setting) industries have been developed, we must integrate them into single equations for R and S in order to incorporate them into our single sector model. We do this by using a weighted average of the two types of industries. So, the local share (R) of ($C + IL_p + G + XFG$) is calculated as a weighted average of R_R and R_N, and the extraregional share value (S) is a weighted average of S_R and S_N. The equations follow.

$$R = nsl^u \left(k_{RN} \times RPROFA^\psi \right) + (1 - nsl^u)\left(k_{RR} \times Y^\mu \, SPA^\xi \right) \tag{3-66}$$

$$S = nse^u \left(k_{SN} \times RPROFA^\psi \right) + (1 - nse^u)\left(k_{SR} \, SPA^\xi \right) \tag{3-67}$$

In the equations, nsl^u and nse^u are the national industry shares of the local and extraregional trade markets, respectively.

Market share linkages are the last set of linkages that we show for the model. Market shares are fundamental determinants of output (our first set of linkages) which brings us full circle. In the next section, we summarize the equations of the model and show complete endogenous linkages in a flow chart.

3-6 SUMMARY

In this chapter, we have developed a single sector, single region, single occupation, single age/sex cohort model with four components of aggregate demand, and two factors of production. This model combines an industry type (national) that

120

supplies primarily to a national market, and an industry type (regional) that supplies more than half of its production to the regional market. In the case of a national industry, the market shares are determined by the relative profitability of the industry. In the case of a regional industry, the market shares are determined by the sales prices and output. National industries' prices depend on the national price, while regional sales prices depend on local production costs. Our market share equations include a weighted average of both characteristics.

We can represent the key endogenous linkages in the model in two summary flow charts. The flow charts show the key endogenous variables for each set of linkages: (1) output, (2) labor and capital demand, (3) population and labor supply, (4) wages, prices and profits, and (5) market shares (building upon the basic linkages shown in diagram 3-3). Diagram 3-17 uses only symbols, while diagram 3-18 includes names in addition to symbols. This makes a transition to the diagram used for the operational model in chapter 7.

Endogenous Linkages in the Prototype Model

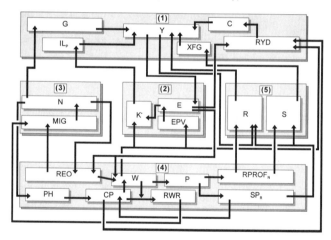

Diagram 3-17

Output linkages (sector 1) include output (Y), consumption (C), real disposable income (RYD), investment (IL$_p$), state and local government spending (G), and exports (XFG). Output is endogenously determined by consumption, investment, state and local government spending, exports, and the regional supply proportion (R). Consumption depends on real disposable income, which is determined by the endogenous level of employment (E), the earnings rate (W), the consumer price deflator (CP), and other income components and taxes that are not shown here but are included in the calculation of RYD. IL_p is endogenously determined by the optimal capital stock (K^*). State and local government spending (G) is determined by the population (N), while XFG depends on the extraregional trade coefficient (S).

Endogenous Linkages

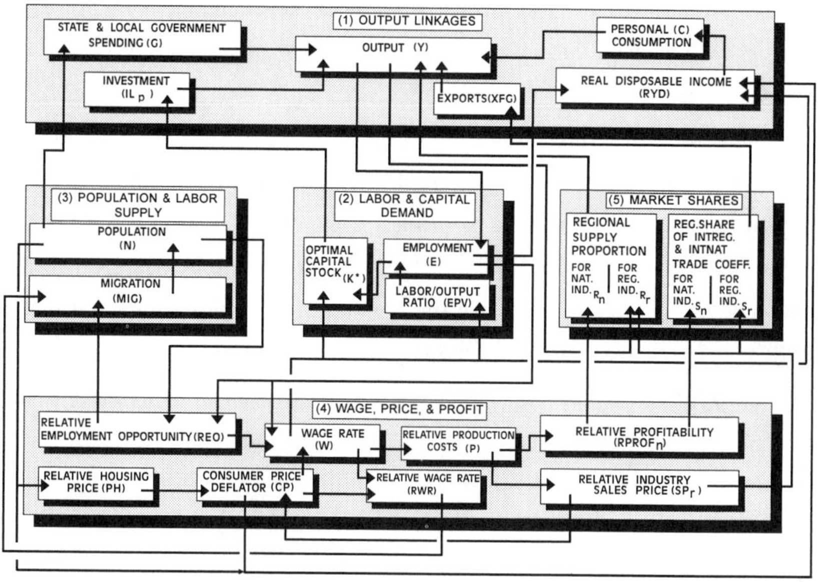

Diagram 3-18

Labor and capital demand linkages (sector 2) include K^*, employment (E), and employees per unit of value added (EPV). The earnings rate (W) relative to capital costs determines the labor per unit of value added (EPV) and K^* per employee. Employment depends on EPV and gross regional product (Y).

The supply determinants in our model are given by the *population and labor supply linkages* (sector 3), where population (N) is determined in part by migration (MIG). Migration is a function of the region's relative employment opportunity (REO) and relative real after tax wage rate (RWR).

Wage, price, and profit linkages are shown in sector 4 of the model. These linkages include relative production costs (P), relative profitability ($RPROF_N$), the regional sales price (SP_R), housing prices (PH), the consumer price deflator (CP), the earnings rate (W), relative employment opportunity (REO), and the relative wage rate (RWR). REO depends on N and E of the area, relative to the United States. REO and E determine the wage rate changes due to labor supply and demand, which, along with

CP, determines W. In turn, W is the endogenous determinant of relative production costs. These costs (P) determine relative profitability for national industries ($RPROF_N$) and the sales price (SP_R) for regional industries. Relative housing prices (PH) are determined by the region's relative population (N) density changes and relative housing prices in the previous period. PH and SP determine the consumer price deflator. The relative real after tax rate wage rate (RWR) depends on CP, W, and the personal tax rate.

Market share linkages (sector 5) include the regional supply proportion (R) and the regional share of interregional and international trade coefficient (S). Market shares determine the proportion of markets captured by an industry. They are determined for both regional and national industry characteristics. The local supply proportion (R_N) for the national industries portion depends on relative profitability ($RPROF_N$). The regional industry portion is determined by the level of output (Y) and relative cost (P). Relative profitability determines the regional share of interregional and international trade (S_N) for the national industry portion. The regional industry share of extraregional markets (S_R) is determined by the sales price (SP_R) for the regional industry.

The endogenous linkages in diagrams 3-17 and 3-18 show the relationships among the variables in the basic model equations. Thus, changes in a variable can be traced throughout the modeling system. The prototype model equations are listed at the end of this chapter. There is also a glossary. In the appendix, we show how this model can be calibrated to any region. The prototype model in the Regional Economic Models System (REMS) program, which is available from the author, can be used for forecasting and policy analysis either with its default calibration to Massachusetts or with a recalibration for another area. The program can also be used to check the recalibration of the model by replicating the last historical year.

SUMMARY EQUATIONS

for the
Single Sector, Single Region,
Single Occupation, Single Age/Sex Cohort Prototype Model with
Four Components of Aggregate Demand and
Two Factors of Production

(1) OUTPUT LINKAGES

Output

$$Y = R \times (C + IL_p + G + XFG) \tag{3-1}$$

Exports

$$XFG = S \times XFG^u \tag{3-2}$$

Consumption

$$C = k_C \times \left[\frac{C^u}{RYD^u} \right] \times RYD \tag{3-3}$$

Labor and Proprietor's Income

$$YLP = E \times W \div 1000 \tag{3-4}$$

Personal Income

$$YP = YLP + RDV \tag{3-5}$$

Adjustment for Residence, Dividends, Interest, and Rent, and Net Transfer Payments (VP − VSS)

$$RDV = - VSS + RA + DIR + VP \tag{3-6}$$

Residential Adjustment

$$RA = \begin{cases} k_{RA} \times YLP & \text{if } k_{RA} < 0 \\ k_{RA} \times YLP^u & \text{if } k_{RA} > 0 \end{cases} \tag{3-10}$$

Social Security Taxes

$$VSS = k_{VSS} \times \left(\frac{VSS^u}{YLP^u} \right) \times YLP \tag{3-11}$$

Transfer Payments

$$VP = k_{VP} \times \left(\frac{VP^u}{N^u - E^u} \right) \times (N - ER)$$

(3-12)

Dividends, Interest, and Rent

$$DIR = k_{DIR} \times \left(\frac{DIR^u}{N^u} \right) \times N$$

(3-13)

Real Disposable Income

$$RYD = [YP \times (1 - tx)] \div CP$$

(3-7)

Investment

$$IL_{p,t} = \alpha \left[(k_I K_t^*) - (1 - dr^u) K_{t-1} \right]$$

(3-14)

Capital Stock Updating

$$K_t = IL_{p,t} + (1 - dr^u) K_{t-1}$$

(3-15)

State and Local Government Spending

$$G = k_G \times \left[\frac{G^u}{N^u} \right] \times N$$

(3-16)

(2) LABOR AND CAPITAL DEMAND LINKAGES

Optimal Capital Stock

$$K^* = \left[\frac{W}{W^u} \right] \times \left[\frac{c^u}{c} \right] \times \left[\frac{E}{E^u} \right] \times K^{u*}$$

(3-24)

Relative Labor Intensity Average

$$LIA_t = (1 - salia) \, LIA_{t-1} + salia \left[\left(\frac{c}{c^u} \right)^d \left(\frac{W}{W^u} \right)^{-d} \right]$$

(3-29)

Labor/Output Ratio

$$EPV = \left(LIA \times \left[\frac{E^u}{Y^u} \right] \right) \div \left[\frac{A}{A^u} \right]$$

(3-30)

Employment

$$E = EPV \times Y \tag{3-31}$$

(3) POPULATION AND LABOR SUPPLY LINKAGES

Migration

$$MIG = \{ k_M + [\beta_1 \times \ln(REO)] + [\beta_2 \times \ln(RWR)] \} \times N_{t-1} \tag{3-32}$$

Population

$$N_t = N_{t-1} \left[\frac{N_t^u}{N_{t-1}^u} \right] + MIG \tag{3-33}$$

(4) WAGE, PRICE, AND PROFIT LINKAGES

Relative Production Costs

$$P = \left[\frac{W}{W^u} \right]^a \times \left[\frac{c}{c^u} \right]^d \div \left[\frac{A}{A^u} \right] \tag{3-38}$$

Relative Profitability for National Industries

$$RPROF_N = (1 - P) + 1 \tag{3-39}$$

Relative Profit Average

$$RPROFA_t = (1 - sapr)\, RPROFA_{t-1} + sapr\, RPROF_{N,t} \tag{3-58}$$

Relative Sales Price for Regional Industries[9]

$$SP_R = \left[\frac{W}{W^u} \right]^a \times \left[\frac{c}{c^u} \right]^d = P \times \left[\frac{A}{A^u} \right] \tag{3-41}$$

Relative Sales Price Average

$$SPA_t = (1 - sasp) \times SPA_{t-1} + sasp\, SP_{R,t} \tag{3-63}$$

Relative Housing Price

$$PH = \varepsilon \times \left[\frac{N_t \div N_t^u}{N_{t-1} \div N_{t-1}^u} - 1 \right] + PH_{t-1} + UPH \tag{3-42}$$

Consumer Price Deflator

$$CP = \left[(1 - hs^u) \times ((1 - ncs^u) \times SP_R + ncs^u) + (hs^u \times PH) \right] \times CP^u$$

$$\tag{3-43}$$

Wage Rate

$$W = (1 + \Delta WD) (1 + \Delta CPR)^\tau (1 + UW^u) \times W_{t-1} \tag{3-44}$$

in which ΔCPR is given by

$$\Delta CPR = \left[\frac{CP \div CP^u}{CP_{t-1} \div CP_{t-1}^u} \right] - 1 \tag{3-45}$$

Relative Real After-Tax Wage Rate

$$RWR = \left[\frac{W \times (RYD \div YP)}{W^u \times (RYD^u \div YP^u)} \right] \tag{3-46}$$

Employment by Place of Residence

$$ER = \left(\frac{YLP + RA}{YLP} \right) \times E \tag{3-51}$$

Relative Employment Opportunity

$$REO = \left[\frac{ER}{N} \right] \div \left[\frac{E^u}{N^u} \right] \tag{3-53}$$

Change in the Wage Rate Due to Change in Demand

$$\Delta WD = \left[\lambda_1 \times \left(\frac{E}{EA} - 1 \right) \right] + \left[\lambda_2 \times \left(\frac{REO}{REOA} - 1 \right) \right] \tag{3-56}$$

REOA Updating

$$REOA_t = (1 - sareo) \times REOA_{t-1} + sareo \times REO_{t-1} \tag{3-55}$$

EA Updating

$$EA_t = (1 - saea) \times EA_{t-1} + saea \times E_{t-1} \tag{3-50}$$

(5) MARKET SHARE LINKAGES

Regional Share of (C + G + IL$_p$ + XFG)

$$R = nsl^u (k_{RN} \times RPROFA^{\psi}) + (1 - nsl^u)(k_{RR} \times Y^{\mu} SPA^{\xi}) \tag{3-66}$$

Regional Share of Extraregional Markets

$$S = nse^u (k_{SN} \times RPROFA^{\psi}) + (1 - nse^u)(k_{SR} \times SPA^{\xi}) \tag{3-67}$$

GLOSSARY: Chapter 3

Variable Modifiers or Forms:

*	optimal level
Δ	change
∂	partial derivative
k	a constant
A	moving geometric average when used as the last letter of a variable name
N, R	(when used as a subscript) indicates national or regional industry
t	(when used as a subscript) current year of history or forecast
t − 1	previous year of history or forecast
u	(when used as a superscript) indicates United States variable

Model Parameters (Values that have been econometrically estimated):

α	adjustment speed of investment response to a gap between K^* and K
β_1 , β_2	migration response to relative employment opportunity (REO) and relative wage rate (RWR) in the migration equation
ε	elasticity of housing price changes to changes in population density
τ	elasticity of wage response to changes in consumer prices
ψ	the coefficient which gives the effects of relative profitability on the regional purchase coefficient (used here for the regional supply proportion) and the regional share of interregional trade coefficient
μ	economic diversity response
λ_1 , λ_2	employment and relative employment opportunity coefficients in the change in the wage rate due to changes in demand equation
ξ	elasticity of response to price changes

Values that are calibrated or estimated from other sources:

a	employment share of output
d	capital share of output
dr^u	depreciation rate
hs^u	housing share of consumption
k_C	consumption preference
k_G	government spending preference
k_I	investment preference
k_M	amenity term in migration equation
k_{RN}	calibration constant for R equation for national industry share
k_{RR}	calibration constant for R equation for regional industry share
k_{SN}	calibration constant for S equation for national industry share
k_{SR}	calibration constant for S equation for regional industry share
k_{VSS}	calibration for social security taxes
k_{VP}	calibration for transfer payments
$k_{RA\ POS}$	calibration for residential adjustment positive
$k_{RA\ NEG}$	calibration for residential adjustment negative
k_{DIR}	calibration for dividends, interest, and rent
ncs^u	national industry share of nonhousing construction
nsl^u	average national industry share of local purchases
nse^u	average national industry share of exports from the local area
sareo	speed of adjustment for REOA
saea	speed of adjustment for EA
salia	speed of adjustment for labor intensity
sapr	speed of adjustment for profit response

| sasp | speed of adjustment for sales price response |
| tx | personal tax rate |

Other variables:

A	average factor productivity
c	the rental cost of capital
C	consumption
CG	personal and government consumption
CP	price of consumer goods (the consumption deflator)
CPR	relative consumer price deflator
DIR	dividends, interest, and rent
E	employment
EA	a geometrically decreasing moving average of employment
EPV	employees per dollar of value added
ER	residence adjusted employment
G	state and local government spending
IL_p	planned local investment (new buildings, houses, and equipment)
K	capital stock
LIA	a geometrically decreasing moving average of labor intensity
M	imports
MIG	migrants
N	population
P	relative cost of production
PH	relative housing prices
R	regional supply proportion of $C + IL_p + G + XFG$
RA	residential adjustment
RDV	all income and deductions other than wage and salary disbursements,

and total tax payments; composed of VSS, DIR, VP, and RA

REO relative employment opportunity

REOA weighted moving average of relative employment opportunity

$RPROF_N$ relative profitability (for national industries only)

RWR relative real after-tax wage rate

RYD real disposable income

S regional share of interregional and international trade coefficient

SPA weighted moving average of sales price

SP_R sales price (regional)

TAX tax and nontax payments

TC total costs

UPH unexplained changes in housing prices

UW unexplained wage changes

VP transfer payments

VSS social security tax

W the earnings rate

ΔWD the change in the wage rate due to demand

XFG exports from the local area including federal government purchases

XFG^u extraregional purchases in the United States (includes all interstate trade, international trade and federal government)

Y value added output (gross regional product)

YD disposable income

YLP earnings by place of work

YP personal income

APPENDIX: Chapter 3

Calibration of the Prototype Model to a Subnational Area

Three sets of values are needed to create a prototype model for forecasting and policy analysis. These are the exogenous variable set, the parameter set, and the endogenous values in the last history year set. Except for three required lagged endogenous variables, the other values in the endogenous set are required due to the particular algorithm that we use to solve the model. In any case, finding the endogenous values in the last year of history will facilitate finding the parameter values that are needed. The set of values that we find for the last year of history must satisfy all of the equations simultaneously. A feature in the Regional Economic Modeling System (REMS) allows you to confirm that a simultaneous solution has been found by solving the model for the last year of historical data (1989, in this case). This algorithm uses your 1989 solution as the starting set and requires values for nine endogenous variables for the next to last year of historical data (in this case, 1988). The prototype model included in the REMS is for the state of Massachusetts, using 1989 as the last year of history.

In order to recalibrate the prototype model to a new subnational area (county, state, etc.), it is not necessary to change any of the United States values. The following tables indicate the values that are required to calibrate the prototype model to any subnational area in the United States. These tables include the values for Massachusetts and the page references in this appendix where you will find an explanation of how to find the corresponding values for any area.

Exogenous

Name in Text	Name in Program	1989 MA Values	1989 New Area Values	1990 and All Forecast Years	Page Reference
A	A	0.924		Use 1989 Values	Page 155
c	c	1.055		Use 1989 Values	Page 149
UPH	UPH	-0.087		0	Page 161
UW^u	UWu	0.050		Use U.S. Values, see table 3-2	Page 162

Parameter Values

Name in Text	Name in Program	MA Values	New Area Values	Page References
k_C	kC	0.939		Page 159
k_G	kG	0.926		Page 153
k_I	kI	0.850		Page 152
k_M	kM	-0.030		Page 164
k_{RN}	kRN	1.016		Page 165
k_{RR}	kRR	0.738		Page 165
k_{SN}	kSN	0.044		Page 165
k_{SR}	kSR	0.032		Page 165
k_{VSS}	kVSS	0.934		Page 160
k_{VP}	kVP	1.465		Page 160
k_{RA}	kRA	-0.019		Page 160
k_{DIR}	kDIR	1.277		Page 160
tx	tx	0.159		Page 158

Endogenous Values for 1989
(In Equation Order)

Name in Text	Name in Program	1989 MA Value	New Area Value	Page Reference
Y	Y	126.00		Page 151
XFG	XFG	70.923		Page 163
C	C	77.986		Page 159
YLP	YLP	97.825		Page 147
YP	YP	131.5		Page 147
RDV	RDV	33.7		Page 148
RA	RA	-1.9		Page 148
VSS	VSS	6.1		Page 148
VP	VP	18.4		Page 148

Name in Text	Name in Program	1989 MA Value	New Area Value	Page Reference
DIR	DIR	23.3		Page 148
RYD	RYD	87.639		Page 158
IL_p	ILp	18.899		Page 152
G	G	11.577		Page 153
K^*	K*	520.296		Page 154
LIA	LIAt	0.985		Page 155
EPV	EPV	29.968		Page 152
E	E	3,776.0		Page 147
MIG	MIG	-36.9		Page 149
N	N	5,912.5		Page 148
P	P	1.183		Page 156
$RPROF_N$	RPROFn	0.817		Page 156
RPROFA	RPROFAt	0.817		Page 156
$RPROFA_{t-1}$	RPROFAt_1	0.817		Page 156
SP_R	SPr	1.093		Page 150
SPA	SPAt	1.093		Page 150
SPA_{t-1}	SPAt_1	1.093		Page 150
PH	PH	1.67		Page 149
CP	CP	1.262		Page 150
W	W	25.907		Page 147
ΔCPR	CPR_δ	-0.008		Page 151
RWR	RWR	0.950		Page 162
ER	ER	3,700.0		Page 157
REO	REO	1.142		Page 156
ΔWD	WD_δ	-0.0045		Page 158
R	R	0.702		Page 163
$S \times 10^2$	S *10^2	3.050		Page 164

Endogenous Variables Carried as
Lagged Endogenous Variables for 1990
(i.e., $t = 1990$)

Name in Text	Name in Program	MA Value	New Area Value	Page Reference
K_{t-1}	Kt_1	224.912		Page 161
$REOA_{t-1}$	REOAt_1	1.165		Page 156
EA_{t-1}	EAt_1	3,594.0		Page 156
LIA_{t-1}	LIAt_1	0.984		Page 155
$RPROFA_{t-1}$	RPROFAt_1	0.817		Page 156
SPA_{t-1}	SPAt_1	1.093		Page 150

Endogenous Variables Carried as
Lagged Endogenous Variables 1989
(i.e., $t = 1989$)

Name in Text	Name in Program	MA Value	New Area Value	Page Reference
K_{t-1}	Kt_1	221.519		Page 161
$REOA_{t-1}$	REOAt_1	1.166		Page 156
EA_{t-1}	EAt_1	3,547.0		Page 156
E_{t-1}	Et_1	3,787.0		Page 148
N_{t-1}	Nt_1	5,889.5		Page 148
PH_{t-1}	PHt_1	1.76		Page 149
CP_{t-1}	CPt_1	1.215		Page 150
W_{t-1}	Wt_1	24.836		Page 147
REO_{t-1}	REOt_1	1.165		Page 156

This appendix is organized as follows:

In order to recalibrate the prototype model for a local area using 1989 as the last history year, we can start on page 147 and fill in the blanks on the previous tables. The data source required to calibrate the Prototype Model, in addition to the data provided here (assuming that you have already calibrated the economic base model in chapter 2), is the Local Area Personal Income and Employment data set from Regional Economic Information Systems at the U.S. Department of Commerce, Economic and Statistics Administration, Bureau of Economic Analysis, Regional Economic Measurement Division, Washington, D.C. 20230. The telephone number is (202) 254-7714. You can obtain a CD-ROM for all states and counties entitled REIS 1969 – 1990 for $35.00, or you can obtain a hard copy for single counties or states.

In order to use the prototype model for policy analysis, it is necessary to calibrate the model as we calibrated the economic base model in chapter 2. The first part of this process is to assemble the econometrically estimated parameters that have been estimated in studies for all states using time series data. These parameters are represented by Greek letters in the model to indicate that they are key structural, econometric parameters. Their estimation is documented in chapter 7, where the operational model is presented along with information about the studies that were done to estimate these parameters. The values of the parameters and a description of their estimation follows.

Econometrically Estimated Structural Parameters

Value	In Text	In Program	Description
0.08	α	alpha	adjustment speed (equation 3-14)

This is a weighted average of the speed of adjustment of 0.127 for residential and 0.061 for nonresidential from equation 7-32 in chapter 7. The weights are 0.29 for residential and 0.71 for nonresidential, including producers durable equipment.[10]

Value	In Text	In Program	Description
0.296	β_1	beta1	lnREO coefficient (equation 3-32)
0.320	β_2	beta2	lnRWR coefficient (equation 3-32)

These coefficients are drawn from equation 7-61 in chapter 7. They are estimated over the period 1971 – 1988 across fifty states and Washington, D.C. The timing of the size of the effects differ from those in 7-61 due to differences between equations 3-32 and 7-61.

Value	In Text	In Program	Description
0.445	ε	epsilon	elasticity of housing prices (equation 3-42)

The elasticity of the housing price response is obtained from a regression over all states and Washington, D.C., from 1970 to 1988. See equation 7-84 in chapter 7.

Value	In Text	In Program	Description
0.25	τ	tau	elasticity of wages to relative consumer prices (equation 3-44)

This is obtained from structural equation error minimization for all states over the period 1970 – 1988. See equation 7-95 in chapter 7.

Value	In Text	In Program	Description
0.024	λ_1	lambda1	coefficient of change in E (equation 3-56)
0.29	λ_2	lambda2	coefficient of change in REO (equation 3-56)

The λ_1 coefficient comes from $\lambda_{WD3} = 0.1335$ for high-skilled employees in equation 7-76, multiplied by the proportion of high-skill employees (0.178). The λ_2 coefficient comes from a weighted average of $\lambda_{WD1} = .1965$ for low-skilled and $\lambda_{WD2} = 0.7305$ for high-skilled. Thus, $\lambda_2 = 0.29 = 0.822 \times .1965 + 0.178 \times 0.7305$. These estimates are based on the best-fitting equation over all states and Washington, D.C., from 1970 to 1988. See equation 7-96.

Value	In Text	In Program	Description
1.83	ψ	psi	measure of RPROF effect on R and S (equations 3-66, 3-67)

The estimated elasticity for national industries is taken from the estimates for the RPROF2 coefficient in equations 7-101 and 7-102. Again, these are based on time series econometric estimates over all states over the period 1970 – 1988.

Value	In Text	In Program	Description
0.000	μ	mu	response measure of Y on R (equation 3-66)
-0.563	ξ	xi	elasticity of response to price changes (equations 3-66, 3-67)

These estimates are drawn from equations 7-106 and 7-107. They were estimated for the same sample period and the same sample states used for the national industries. The μ value is set at zero for the default model instead of .296, because it has not been verified in subsequent research.

U.S. Exogenous Variables and Structural Parameters

Our next task is to assemble the values of the United States variables and structural parameters. The values of the United States variables for the last history year, 1989 in our case, are needed to calibrate the model. Later, we will need to know their values for the forecast years (1990 — last forecast year), in order to make a projection with our model. The values for 1989 – 1994, based on data and projections, are presented on table 3-2 in the appendix. We proceed in the order that the United States variables or parameters appear in the equation list for the prototype model.

Value	In Text	In Program	Description
2325	XFG^u	XFGu	extraregional (including federal government) purchases (equation 3-2)

This value is calculated using an estimate of the share of United States total output that goes into private international and interstate trade to calculate the amount of extraregional trade for all states and Washington, D.C. This is the value of all extraregional trade, excluding federal government sales. It was 1,950 billion 1987 dollars in 1989.[11] It was estimated using a model for all states and Washington, D.C., similar to the model demonstrated in chapter 7. This value divided by United

States GDP in billions of 1987 dollars in 1989 (4,837)[12] less federal government spending of 375[13] or 4,462 is 43.7%. To obtain XFG^u, we add the $1,950 of extraregional nonfederal trade, plus federal government purchases of $375 to obtain $2,325 (for a future year, multiply 0.437 by GDP less federal government spending, and then add federal government spending).

Value	In Text	In Program	Description
3,223	C^u	Cu	U.S. consumption (equation 3-3)

This value represents consumption in the United States in billions of 1987 dollars.[14]

Value	In Text	In Program	Description
4,367	YP^u	YPu	personal income in the United States (equation 3-5)

This value comes from the U.S. Department of Commerce, Bureau of Economic Analysis (BEA), Regional Economic Information Systems (REIS), April 1991, table CA5.

Value	In Text	In Program	Description
3,401	RYD^u	RYDu	U.S. RYD (equation 3-3)

The variable RYD^u is calculated by dividing Disposable income for 1989 (3,710)[15] by the Implicit Personal Consumption Expenditure Deflator[16] (CP), which is 1.091. This yields 3,401.

Value for 1989 in current dollars	In Text	In Program	Description
212	VSS^u	VSSu	social security taxes (equation 3-11)
3,177	YLP^u	YLPu	labor and proprietors' income (equation 3-11)
637	VP^u	VPu	transfer payments (equation 3-12)
766	DIR^u	DIRu	dividends, interest, and rent (equation 3-13)

All of the above values can be found on table CA5 from REIS, BEA for the United States.

Value	In Text	In Program	Description
525	G^u	Gu	total U.S. state and local government spending (equation 3-16)

Total state and local government spending for all states in billions of 1987 dollars is represented by G^u.[17]

Value	In Text	In Program	Description
248,300	N^u	Nu	U.S. population (equations 3-16, 3-33)
245,800	N^u_{t-1}	Nut_1	U.S. population, last period (equation 3-33)

This estimation of United States mid-year population in millions of people for 1989 comes from BEA, REIS, CA5, April 1991.

Value	In Text	In Program	Description
1	c^u	cu_	U.S. cost of capital (equation 3-38)

This variable is set equal to one (1), because we use the ratio of c to c^u in the program and never use c^u by itself.

Value	In Text	In Program	Description
17,827	K^{u*}	Ku*	U.S. optimal capital stock (equation 3-24)
0.07	dr^u	dru	depreciation rate of capital (equation 3-15)

The equation for K^{u*} is found by rearranging the equation for U.S. investment (equation 3-14) and assigning values $k_I^u = 1$, $\alpha = 0.08$. It is

$$K_t^{u*} = \left[IL_{p,t}^u / 0.08 + (1 - dr^u) \, K_{t-1}^u \right] \tag{3-68}$$

This requires that we find the values on the right hand side of this equation first. The fixed net capital stock in 1989 is \$7,515 billion 1982 dollars.[18] To find the depreciation rate (dr^u) we start with the identity

$$K_t^u = (1 - dr^u) \, K_{t-1}^u + IL_{p,t}^u \tag{3-69}$$

and solve for $(1 - dr^u)$, as follows:

$$(1 - dr^u) = \frac{K_t^u - IL_{p,t}^u}{K_{t-1}^u} \tag{3-70}$$

$$dr^u = 1 - \frac{K_t^u - IL_{p,t}^u}{K_{t-1}^u} = 1 - \frac{7,514.8 - 693.1}{7,331.5}$$
$$= .0695 \tag{3-71}$$

$IL^u_{p89} = 693.1$ 1982 dollars[19]
$K^u_{88} = 7,331.5$ 1982 dollars[20]

Using the ratio of 1987 nominal K^u divided by the 1982 dollar K^u, we get 1.151[21], which is the ratio required to convert capital and investment from 1982 to 1987 dollars. Thus,

$$IL^u_{p89} = 693.1 \times 1.151 = 798 \tag{3-72}$$

$$K^u_{88} = 7,331.5 \times 1.151 = 8,439 \qquad (3\text{-}73)$$

Using equation 3-68, we can calculate $798 \div .08 + (1 - .0695) \times 8,439 = 17,827$ for

K^{u*}_{89} . Using equation 3-69, we calculate

$$K^u_{89} = 693 + (1 - .0695) \times 8439 = 8,545 \qquad (3\text{-}74)$$

for 1989. Values for subsequent years are as follows:

	(1) $IL^u_{p,t}$ [22]	(2) $(1 - .0695) \times K^u_{t-1}$	(3) = (1)+(2) K^u_t	(4) $IL^u_{p,t}/.08$	(5) = (2)+(4) K^{u*}_t
1990	744	7,951	8,695	9,300	17,251
1991	687	8,091	8,778	8,588	16,679
1992	698	8,168	8,866	8,725	16,893
1993	767	8,250	9,017	9,588	17,838
1994	787	8,390	9,177	9,838	18,228

Value	In Text	In Program	Description
0.70	a	a	employment share of output (equations 3-38, 3-41)
0.30	d	d	capital share of output (equations 3-38, 3-41)

From equations 3-20 and 3-21, we show that

$$a = \frac{W \times E}{SP \times Y} \,, \quad d = \frac{c \times K}{SP \times Y} \qquad (3\text{-}75)$$

Therefore, a is the labor share of gross domestic product and d is the capital share (or $1 - a$). The labor share can be formed by dividing labor (3,063) plus proprietors' income (531) by gross domestic product for 1989 (5,165) or $3594 \div 5165 = 0.70$[23], with d calculated as $1 - a$.

Value	In Text	In Program	Description
1.000	sareo	sareo	speed of adjustment for REOA (equation 3-55)
0.200	saea	saeaprsp	speed of adjustment for EA (equation 3-50)
0.063	salia	salia	speed of adjustment for labor intensity (equation 3-29)
0.200	sapr	saeaprsp	speed of adjustment for profit response, saea value used (equation 3-58)
0.200	sasp	saeaprsp	speed of adjustment for sales price, saea value used (equation 3-63)

The speed of response variables are necessary to complete the dynamic structure of the model. The sareo value is taken from the skilled workers response in equation 7-96. The salia value is based on an average equipment life of thirteen years. The sapr value comes from equation 7-103, and sasp comes from equation 7-110. Since these are the same value as *saea*, the same coding is used for all three parameters in the REMS program.

Value	In Text	In Program	Description
0.146	hs^u	hsu	housing share consumption (equation 3-43)
0.259	ncs^u	ncsu	national industry share of non-housing consumption (equation 3-43)
0.214	nsl^u	nslu	average national industry share of local sales (equation 3-66)
0.552	nse^u	nseu	average national industry share of exports from local areas (equation 3-67)

These shares are necessary in our single sector model to reflect the typical shares represented by housing and national industries. These weights make it possible to have a single-sector model that also reflects three different aspects of the economy.

144

The housing share of consumption is 14.6%.[24] The nonhousing share of consumption represented by national industries (i.e., prices set nationally) can be estimated using the distribution of consumption among personal consumption categories[25] and a bridge matrix showing the proportion of each category represented by each industry where the industries are classified as national or regional.[26] The average national industry share of local markets can be determined from the total local self-supply satisfied by national industries. This can be estimated by calculating the sum of national industry supply to local markets for all states (using the operational model in chapter 7)[27] as a share of the total self-supply of local demand. In 1989, this value was 0.214. We use the same source to find the national industry share of exports from all regions to extra-regional markets, yielding .552. This means that 55.2% of the interstate and international trade is in "national" type industry products.

Year	Value	In Text	In Program	Description
1989	1.091	CP^u	CPu	U.S. consumption deflator, 1987 base (equation 3-45)
1988	1.042	CP^u_{t-1}	CPut_1	U.S. consumption deflator, 1987 base (equation 3-45)

This table shows that the consumption deflator on a 1987 base for the United States was 1.091 in 1989 and 1.042 in 1988.[28]

Value	In Text	In Program	Description
136,074	E^u	Eu	U.S. employment (equations 3-24, 3-30, 3-53) by place of work

These numbers are in the REIS table for full-time and part-time employees by major industry for counties and metropolitan areas.[29] For the United States, in this case, we overlook any distinction between place-of-work and place-of-residence employment.

Value	In Text	In Program	Description
4,837	Y^u	Yu	U.S. gross domestic product in billions of 1987 dollars (equation 3-30)

United States gross regional product for the nation is almost identical to gross domestic product.[30] Thus, we can use the 1989 GDP in billions of 1987 dollars here.[31]

Value	In Text	In Program	Description
23.348	W^u	Wu	U.S. earnings rate (equations 3-24, 3-46, etc.)

The earnings rate can be calculated by dividing the total earnings ($YLP^u = 3,177$) in billions of 1989 dollars[32] by total U.S. employment in 1989 in millions of people ($3,177 / 136.074 = 23.348$) or $23,348 thousand dollars per year, per employee or proprietor, for 1989.

Value	In Text	In Program	Description
1.0	A^u	Au	U.S. value for A (equations 3-30, 3-38)

As with c^u, A^u always appears as a ratio with A. Therefore, we set it to one (1) here and discuss the ratio under A in the next section.

Value	In Text	In Program	Description
.049	UW^u	UWu	unexplained wage changes in the United States (or local if historical) (equation 3-44)

When all of the values in equation 3-44 are known, we use UW^u as a residual for the last history year (1989). This is necessary to calibrate the model to the last year of history. However, in future years, we calculate the value for the United States and use it in the regional equation to predict the regional wage. For the future, there is a United States constructed variable. We first start with equation 3-44 for the United States. In this case $\Delta CPR = 0$, because it is a relative regional price change. Thus, the equation is

$$W^u = (1 + \Delta WD^u)(1 + UW^u) \times W^u_{t-1} \qquad (3\text{-}76)$$

Because REO and REOA are equal to 1 for the United States, due to the fact that they are relative concepts, equation 3-56 simplifies to the following:

$$\Delta WD^u = \left[\lambda_1 \left(\frac{E^u}{EA^u} - 1 \right) \right]$$ (3-77)

The EA^u equation is

$$EA_t^u = EA_{t-1}^u + saea \times \left(E_{t-1}^u - EA_{t-1}^u \right)$$
$$= (1 - saea) \times EA_{t-1}^u + saea \times E_{t-1}^u$$ (3-78)

for $saea = 0.2$,

$$EA_t^u = (1 - 0.2) \times EA_{t-1}^u + 0.2 \times E_{t-1}^u$$
$$EA_t^u = 0.8 \times EA_{t-1}^u + 0.2 \times E_{t-1}^u$$ (3-79)

The sareo value of 0.2 was found in a study for the wage determination equation for the operational model described in chapter 7.

We will approximate it by assuming (unrealistically) that the 1984 value has persisted during all previous years. We use this same equation for the local area.

	EU	EUA	0.8 EUA$_{t-1}$	0.2 EU$_{t-1}$
1984	119,485	119,485	95,588	23,897
1985	123,176	119,485	95,588	23,897
1986	125,592	120,223	95,588	24,635
1987	129,006	121,296	96,170	25,118
1988	132,906	122,838	97,037	25,801
1989	136,074	124,851	98,270	26,581
1990	137,600	127,096	99,881	27,215

For 1990, we can calculate

$$\Delta WD^u = \left[0.024 \times \left(\frac{137,600}{127,096} - 1 \right) \right] = 0.002$$ (3-80)

Substituting into equation 3-76 and solving for UW^u for 1990, we obtain

$$UW^u = \left[\frac{24.557}{23.348} \times \left(\frac{1}{1.002} \right) - 1 \right] = 0.049$$ (3-81)

For subsequent years, the values are .038, .043, .039, and .058. This concludes the United States exogenous variable and parameter section.

Values for the Local Variables and Calibrating Parameters

Our next task is to calibrate the model to the local area. Our main use of the model will be for policy simulations in chapter 4. As the reader will recall, for a policy simulation, the baseline result is compared with the simulated value. Since *both* the baseline and the simulation include the same approximations, in many cases the prediction of the effect of the policy may be insensitive to the exact baseline values. Therefore, approximations may be used in the process of calibration to the local area.

In the process of calibrating the model, we need to assign values to all of the endogenous variables in 1989, as well as assigning values to the exogenous variables for 1989 and future years. The reason for this is that our computer algorithm is based on the round-by-round approach presented earlier for the simple economic base model. In our case, this requires starting values for all of the endogenous variables. In the following section, we proceed by first finding the values of variables that are easily available, then we go through the equations, filling in the values that we can. We repeat this process, filling in values that may depend on values in the later equations from the first pass. We continue this process until the values of all the variables are determined. As our example, we use Massachusetts.

The values we need to calibrate the model are from the last history year (1989) for all of the variables, for two previous years for some variables, and for future years for the exogenous variable set.

Value	In Text	In Program	Description
131.5	YP	YP	personal income in billions \$ (equation 3-5)
97.825	YLP	YLP	labor and proprietors' income in billions of dollars (equations 3-4, 3-5, 3-10)
25.907	W	W	nominal earnings rate in thousands of \$ (equations 3-4, 3-24, 3-44, etc.)
24.836	W_{t-1}	Wt_1	nominal earnings rate, lagged one year, in thousands of dollars (equation 3-44)
3,776	E	E	employment in thousands of jobs (equations 3-4, 3-24, 3-51, 3-56)

Value	In Text	In Program	Description
3,787	E_{t-1}	Et_1	employment, lagged one year, in thousands of jobs (equation 3-50)
6.1	VSS	VSS	personal contributions for social insurance, billions of $ (equations 3-6, 3-11)
18.4	VP	VP	transfer payments, billions of $ (equations 3-6, 3-12)
-1.9	RA	RA	residential adjustment, billions of $ (equations 3-6, 3-10)
23.3	DIR	DIR	dividends, interest, and rent, billions of $ (equations 3-6, 3-13)
33.7	RDV	RDV	dividends, interest, rent & net transfer payments (VP − VSS), residential adjustment, billions of $ (equation 3-6)

Value	In Text	In Program	Description
5,912.5	N	N	population, in thousands of people (equations 3-16, 3-33)
5,889.5	N_{t-1}	Nt_1	population, lagged one year, thousands people (equation 3-33)

These values can be found for all states, counties and metropolitan areas from the BEA, Regional Information Systems Data (REIS). Total personal income for Massachusetts was 131.472 billion 1989 dollars.[33] The total earnings by place of work (including proprietors' income) was 97.825 billion dollars. The total employment is 3,776 thousand.[34] Thus, earnings per employee are 25.907 thousand dollars. The residential adjustment, net transfers (i.e., transfer payments less personal contributions for social security), dividends, interest, and rent are 33.7 billion dollars,[35] which is the difference between YP (131.5) and labor and proprietors' earnings by place of work (97.8). Also, According to table CA-5 of the BEA, REIS data (April 1991), the population of Massachusetts in 1989 was 5,912.5 thousand people and 5,889.5 in 1988.

Value	In Text	In Program	Description
-36.9	MIG	MIG	migrants, in thousands of people (equations 3-32, 3-33)

Migrants can be calculated from equation 3-33 and the variable values above as

$$MIG = N_t - N_{t-1}\left(\frac{N_t^u}{N_{t-1}^u}\right)$$

$$= 5{,}912.5 - 5{,}889.5\left(\frac{248{,}300}{245{,}800}\right) \tag{3-82}$$

$$= 5{,}912.5 - 5{,}949.4 = -36.9$$

Value	In Text	In Program	Description
1.76	PH_{t-1}	PHt_1	relative housing price (equation 3-42), $t - 1$ (1988)
1.67	PH_t	PH	relative housing price (equations 3-42, 3-43), t (1989)

The relative price of housing is found from the United States census in decennial census years. The median housing price is reported for metropolitan areas on a current basis by the National Association of Realtors. The median sales price in the United States was reported as $89,300, $93,000, and $95,500 in 1988, 1989, and 1990 respectively.[36] The median prices for the Boston metropolitan area were $181,200, $181,900, and $174,200.[37] Taking the ratio of Boston to the United States, we obtain 2.03, 1.96, and 1.82 for 1988, 1989, and 1990, respectively. These changes in relative price along with the census data were used by REMI to calculate relative housing prices normalized to the United States for each state for 1988, 1989, and 1990. They are shown on table 3-3 in the appendix.[38] For calibrating counties or metropolitan area models, the local relative to the state census price could be used to rescale these values.

Value	In Text	In Program	Description
1.055	c	c	cost of capital (equation 3-38)

The cost of capital (c) depends on local business and property taxes relative to the nation. However, the formulation involves other tax rates and depreciation rates, as well as state and local taxes, because they are deductible from federal taxes. The mathematics involved is presented in the appendix to chapter 7. Here, we will use a value of 1.055 for Massachusetts that was calculated by a REMI model. Relative costs of capital for all states is presented in table 3-3.

Value	In Text	In Program	Description
1.093	SP_R	SPr	relative selling price, regional industry share (equations 3-41, 3-43)
1.093	SPA	SPAt	selling price average, using SP_R as a proxy (equation 3-63)
1.093	SPA_{t-1}	SPAt_1	same definition as SPAt

The selling price for the part of the economy that resembles regional industries is calculated using equation 3-41, which is restated here as equation 3-83.

$$SP_R = \left[\frac{W}{W^u}\right]^a \times \left[\frac{c}{c^u}\right]^d = P \times \left[\frac{A}{A^u}\right] \tag{3-83}$$

$$SP_{R,1989} = \left(\frac{25.907}{23.348}\right)^{0.7}(1.055)^{0.3} = 1.093 \tag{3-84}$$

$$W^u_{1988} = \frac{YLP^u \times 1,000}{E^u} = \frac{2,997,700}{132,906} = 22.555 \tag{3-85}$$

$$W_{1988} = \frac{YLP \times 1,000}{E} = \frac{94,077}{3,787} = 24.842 \tag{3-86}$$

$$SP_{R,1988} = \left(\frac{24.842}{22.555}\right)^{0.7}(1.055)^{0.3} = 1.087 \tag{3-87}$$

Value	In Text	In Program	Description
1.262	CP	CP	the consumption deflator (equation 3-43)
1.215	CP_{t-1}	CPt_1	the consumption deflator, lagged one year (equation 3-45)

Using equation 3-43 and the value in equation 3-87, we now have the values required to calculate CP and CP^u_{t-1} as follows:

$$CP = \{(1 - hs^u) [(1 - ncs^u) (SP_R) + ncs^u] + (hs^u \times PH)\} \times CP^u \quad (3\text{-}88)$$

$$CP_{1989} = \{(1 - 0.146) [(1 - 0.259) (1.093) + 0.259] + (0.146 \times 1.67)\} \times 1.091$$
$$= 1.262 \quad (3\text{-}89)$$

$$CP_{1988} = \{(1 - 0.146) [(1 - 0.259) (1.087) + 0.259] + (0.146 \times 1.76)\} \times 1.042$$
$$= 1.215 \quad (3\text{-}90)$$

Value	In Text	In Program	Description
-0.008	ΔCPR	CPR_δ	change in relative regional consumption (equation 3-45)

Using the relative values under CP above and equation 3-45, we obtain

$$\Delta CPR = \left[\frac{CP \div CP^u}{CP_{t-1} \div CP^u_{t-1}} \right] - 1$$

$$\Delta CPR = \{ [1.262 \div 1.091] \div [1.215 \div 1.042] \} - 1 = -0.0080 \quad (3\text{-}91)$$

Value	In Text	In Program	Description
126.0	Y	Y	gross regional product (value added), billions 87 dollars (equations 3-1, 3-31)

The gross state product for Massachusetts was 144.791 billion dollars in 1989.[39] The nominal GSP values are shown for all states in table 3-3. A way to approximate this nominal value for substate areas would be to multiply the ratio of the local labor and proprietors' income (YLP) to the state's YLP (also included on table 3-3) by the state GSP.

The Y value used in our model is real GRP in 1987 dollars. In order to find this value, we must divide by a deflator that includes both the national GDP deflator (base 1987 = 100) of 108.4 and the local GDP deflator. To obtain the local deflator, we need to find the national industry proportion of Y. This can be found by weighting the national industry proportions of local (nsl^u) and export (nse^u) sales by the proportion of sales nationally that are outside of the state of origin ($pexp^u$). The value of $pexp^u$ is 40.5% and was obtained by dividing the exports in the sum of states data from the REMI state models by the total output.

The national proportion of local output (nply) is

$$nply = (1 - pexp^u) nsl^u + (pexp^u \times nse^u)$$
$$.351 = (1 - .405).214 + (.405 \times .552) \tag{3-92}$$

Thus, .351 is the average proportion of national industries in Y. This makes the formula for Y

$$Y = Y\$ \div [1.084 \times ((1 - .351) \times SP_R + .351)], \tag{3-93}$$

where Y\$ is gross state product in current (nominal) dollars. For Massachusetts,

$$Y_{1989} = 144.8 \div [1.084 \times (((1 - .351) \times 1.093) + .351)]$$
$$= 144.8 \div (1.084 \times 1.060)$$
$$= 126.018 \ billion \ 1987 \ dollars \ at \ U.S. \ average \ prices \tag{3-94}$$

Value	In Text	In Program	Description
29.968	EPV	EPV	employees per million 1987 dollars of value added (equations 3-30, 3-31)

The employees per million 1987 dollars of value added can be calculated from equation 3-31. The values are reported above.

$$EPV = E \div Y$$

$$EPV = \frac{3{,}776.0 \ thousand}{126.0 \ billion} = \begin{array}{c} 29.968 \ employees \ per \ million \ (or \\ thousand \ employees \ per \ billion) \\ of \ 1987 \ dollars \ of \ output \end{array} \tag{3-95}$$

This means that 29.968 thousand employees are required for each billion 1987 dollar of value added.

Value	In Text	In Program	Description
18.899	IL_p	ILp	investment spending, billions of 1987 dollars (equations 3-1, 3-14)
0.85	k_I	kI	investment preference (equation 3-14)

To calculate total local investment, we take the ratio of an estimate of local construction to a similar estimate for the United States multiplied by U.S. investment (IL_p^u). The estimate is made by multiplying construction employment by the output per worker (i.e., the inverse of the EPV).

$$IL_p = \frac{E_{CONST} \times (Y \div E)}{E^u_{CONST} \times (Y^u \div E^u)} \times IL_p^u$$

$$IL_p = \frac{195.4 \times (126.0 \div 3,776.0)}{7,225.6 \times (4,837.0 \div 136,074.0)} \times 744.5$$

$$= \frac{195.4 \times .03337}{7,225.6 \times .03555} \times 744.5$$

$$= 18.8987$$

(3-96)

The employment numbers are from the BEA REIS data[40] and the value 744.5 is U.S. investment in 1989 in billions of 1987 dollars.[41]

Two points should be made here. First, we are using employment ratios for an industry as a proxy for estimating a final demand ratio. This is necessary, because no direct observations of local final investment demand are available. It is only possible because a high proportion of investment demand goes to construction, and a high proportion of construction is used to supply final investment demand. There should be a high correlation between the two. Second, we use output per worker on average in the economy rather than using value added by sector. This is due to the fact that we are assuming, unrealistically, that output per worker is the same in all sectors. This assumption will be dropped in Part II of this book.

In a paper by Rickman, Shao, and Treyz (1993) entitled "Multiregional Stock Adjustment Equations of Residential and Nonresidential Investment," values of k_I have been estimated in table 1 entitled "Nonlinear Least Squares Results: Construction Based." For Massachusetts, the value for nonresidential is 0.81, and the residential value is 0.95. Using U.S. weights (see weights used for α previously), the value is 0.85 ($0.71 \times 0.81 + 0.29 \times 0.95$). These weighted values are shown for every state in table 3-3. For substate areas, the value for k_I for the state could be used or, in the absence of other information, the value might be set at one (1).

Value	In Text	In Program	Description
11.577	G	G	state and local government spending, billions of 87 dollars (equations 3-1, 3-16)
.926	k_G	kG	constant in G equation (equation 3-16)

To calculate state and local government spending in the local area (Massachusetts), we use the same technique that we used for investment (IL_p). Again, we do this because a basic assumption of our model is that the output per worker is the same in all sectors and because government output and government demand may be highly correlated.

$$G = \frac{E_{SRL\,gov't} \times (Y \div E)}{E^u_{SRL\,gov't} \times (Y^u \div E^u)} \times G^u$$

$$G = \frac{347 \times (126 \div 3{,}776)}{14{,}771 \times (4{,}837 \div 136{,}074)} \times 525$$

$$= \frac{347 \times .03337}{14{,}771 \times .03555} \times 525$$

$$= 11.5770$$

(3-97)

The value for k_G is obtained by solving equation 3-16 for k_G. This is the relative difference of per capita government spending in the local area relative to the nation.

$$k_G = \frac{G \div N}{G^u \div N^u}$$

$$= \frac{11.577 \div 5{,}912.5}{525 \div 248{,}300}$$

$$= .926$$

(3-98)

Value	In Text	In Program	Description
520.296	K˙	K*	optimal capital stock, billions of 87 dollars (equations 3-14, 3-24)

Now all of the values in equation 3-24 are known. Thus, K˙ is

$$K^* = \left[\frac{W}{W^u} \right] \left[\frac{c^u}{c} \right] \left[\frac{E}{E^u} \right] \times K^{u*}$$

$$= \left(\frac{25.907}{23.348} \right) \left(\frac{1}{1.055} \right) \left(\frac{3{,}776}{136{,}074} \right) \times 17{,}827$$

$$= 520.29551$$

(3-99)

Value	In Text	In Program	Description
0.924	A	A	relative factor productivity, exogenous (equation 3-30)
0.985	LIA	LIAt	moving average of labor intensity (equation 3-29)

Starting with equation 3-29, we find that we need to calculate the moving average of labor intensity (LIA). The first step is to calculate values for $(c/c^u)^d$ $(W/W^u)^{-d}$ for a number of years in order to build up an average as we did for EA in equation 3-78. In this process, it is necessary to assume that the value at some time represents an unbiased estimate of all past values. In this particular case, we illustrate a short-cut method by assuming that the current value has in fact persisted in the past. This short-cut approach may affect the baseline forecast, but it does not affect the simulation properties of the model. It can be used for any of the situations that use an average based on past values, if the main purpose of our model is policy analysis. Thus, we calculate LIA using only one year of data even though, for the best possible estimate, we could have used more years. Assuming an unchanging value of LIA in the past, we can substitute in equation 3-29 and solve for LIA as follows:

$$LIA = (1 - salia) \left(\frac{c}{c^u}\right)^d \left(\frac{W}{W^u}\right)^{-d} + salia \left[\left(\frac{c}{c^u}\right)^d \left(\frac{W}{W^u}\right)^{-d}\right]$$ (3-100)

$$.985 = \left(\frac{c}{c^u}\right)^d \left(\frac{W}{W^u}\right)^{-d} = (1.055)^{.3} \times \left(\frac{25.907}{23.348}\right)^{-.3}$$

Using this value of LIA and assuming that $A^u = 1$, we can first solve equation 3-30 for A, then substitute in all of the right hand side values to find A, as follows:

$$A = LIA \times \left(\frac{E^u}{Y^u}\right) \div EPV$$

$$.924 = .985 \times \left(\frac{136,074}{4,837}\right) \div 29.968$$ (3-101)

With relative wages higher than relative capital costs, the value of LIA (.985) indicates that it would be expected that Massachusetts would have less employees per dollar of output than on average in the United States. However, there are more. Thus, we infer that productivity is relatively low in Massachusetts. In particular, we infer that the value added output relative to the inputs of capital and labor is only 0.924 of the national average.

Value	In Text	In Program	Description
1.183	P	P	relative production cost (equations 3-38, 3-39)
0.817	$RPROF_N$	RPROFn	relative profit (equations 3-39, 3-58)
0.817	RPROFA	RPROFAt	moving average (relative profit), using $RPROF_N$ as a proxy (equation 3-58)
0.817	$RPROFA_{t-1}$	RPROFAt_1	moving average (relative profit), using $RPROF_N$ as a proxy (equation 3-58)

The relative production costs can now be calculated using equation 3-38.

$$P = \left[\frac{W}{W^u} \right]^a \times \left[\frac{c}{c^u} \right]^d \div \left[\frac{A}{A^u} \right]$$

$$P = \left[\left(\frac{25.907}{23.348} \right)^{0.7} (1.055)^{0.3} \right] \div 0.924 = 1.1828 \qquad (3\text{-}102)$$

$RPROF_N$ follows immediately as $1 - P + 1 = 1 - 1.183 + 1 = 0.817$.

Value	In Text	In Program	Description
1.142	REO	REO	relative economic opportunity (equations 3-32, 3-53)
1.165	REOA	REOAt_1 for 1990	moving average of REO (equations 3-55, 3-56)
1.166	REOA	REOAt_1 for 1989	moving average of REO (equation 3-55)
3,594	EA	EAt_1 for 1990	weighted moving average of E, in thousands of jobs (equations 3-50,3-56)
3,547	EA	EAt_1 for 1989	weighted moving average of E, in thousands of jobs (equation 3-50)

Value	In Text	In Program	Description
3,700	ER	ER	employment by place of residence, in thousands of jobs (equations 3-51, 3-53)

The value for REO can be calculated over the period of 1984 to 1989 using values from BEA REIS, April 1991, table CA5. The value for ER is

$$ER = \left(\frac{YLP + RA}{YLP} \right) \times E$$

$$= \left(\frac{97.825 - 1.9}{97.825} \right) \times 3{,}776 \qquad (3\text{-}103)$$

$$= .98 \times 3{,}776$$

$$= 3700$$

Using the 1989 value as an approximation for past years, we can obtain ER for all years.

	1984	1985	1986	1987	1988	1989
E	3,374	3,495	3,586	3,691	3,788	3,776
ER	3,307	3,425	3,514	3,617	3,712	3,700
N	5,792	5,820	5835	5,856	5,890	5,913
E^u	119,485	123,176	125,592	129,006	132,906	136,075
N^u	236,439	238,698	241,104	243,416	245,803	248,258
ER/N	.571	.588	.602	.618	.630	.626
E^u/N^u	.505	.516	.521	.530	.541	.548
REO	1.131	1.140	1.155	1.166	1.165	1.142
REOA		1.131	1.140	1.155	1.166	1.165

To calculate moving average values, the approach is the same as that used for calculating EA^u in equation 3-78 for the United Sates. We repeat it here, as follows:

$$REOA_t = REOA_{t-1} + sareo \times (REO_{t-1} - REOA_{t-1}) \qquad (3\text{-}104)$$

$$REOA_t = (1 - sareo) \times REOA_{t-1} + sareo \times REO_{t-1} \qquad (3\text{-}105)$$

for sareo = 1,

$$REOA_{t-1} = (1 - 1) \times REOA_{t-1} + 1 \times REO_{t-1} \qquad (3\text{-}106)$$

$$REOA_t = REO_{t-1} \qquad (3\text{-}107)$$

The speed of adjustment coefficient (sareo) was found in the study of wage determination for the operational model in chapter 7. The sareo value of 1 indicates that the adjustment takes place in one year.

The EA value equation is

$$EA_t = EA_{t-1} + saea \times (E_{t-1} - EA^*_{t-1})$$
$$= (1 - saea) \times EA_{t-1} + saea \times E_{t-1} \tag{3-108}$$

for saea = 0.2,

$$EA_t = (1 - 0.2) \times EA_{t-1} + 0.2 \times E_{t-1}$$
$$EA_t = 0.8 \times EA_{t-1} + 0.2 \times E_{t-1} \tag{3-109}$$

We approximate it by assuming (unrealistically) that the 1984 value has persisted all years before. This is the same assumption that we made for the United States. We follow the same procedure as that used for finding EUA following equation 3-79 previously.

Value	In Text	In Program	Description
-.0045	ΔWD	WD_δ	changes in wages caused by labor demand and supply, as a proportion (equation 3-56)

Using equation 3-56, we find

$$\Delta WD = \left[\lambda_1 \times \left(\frac{E}{EA} - 1 \right) \right] + \left[\lambda_2 \times \left(\frac{REO}{REOA} - 1 \right) \right]$$

$$\Delta WD = \left[0.024 \left(\frac{3,776}{3,594} - 1 \right) \right] + \left[0.29 \left(\frac{1.142}{1.165} - 1 \right) \right]$$

$$= (0.024 \times 0.0506) + (0.29 \times -0.0197) \tag{3-110}$$

$$= -0.0045$$

Value	In Text	In Program	Description
87.639	RYD	RYD	real disposable income, billions of $ (equation 3-7)
0.159	tx	tx	tax and non-tax payment rate on YP (equation 3-7)

From the *Survey of Current Business*, April 1991, tables 3 and 5, we find that personal tax and nontax payments in Massachusetts were 15.9% of personal income.

Personal tax and nontax payments as a percent of personal income for every state are included in table 3-3. Therefore, disposable income is

$$RD = YP (1 - tx)$$
$$= 131.5 \times (0.841) = 110.6 \tag{3-111}$$

and real disposable income in 1987 dollars is

$$RYD = 110.6 \div CP$$
$$= 110.6 \div 1.262 = 87.6387 \tag{3-112}$$

Value	In Text	In Program	Description
77.986	C	C	consumption, in billions of 1987 dollars (equations 3-1, 3-3)
0.939	k_C	kC	constant in C equation (equation 3-3)

State measures of consumption are not available as such. However, using the U.S. Department of Labor Statistics data from BLS News,[42] the ratio of consumption to personal income is shown for individual components of consumption, as well as for the total consumption. These ratios, relative to the U.S. average for 1989, are 0.93 for the Northeast, 1.0 for the Midwest, 1.02 for the South, and 1.02 for the West.

The value needs to be further modified by the proportion of personal income paid as taxes and nontax payments[43] (tx) in Massachusetts and the United States from table 3-1, which are 15.9% and 15.1% respectively.

$$.93 = [C/YP \div C^u/YP^u] \tag{3-113}$$

To replace YP with YD, we find

$$YD = (1 - .159)YP \tag{3-114}$$

$$YP = YD/(1 - .159) \tag{3-115}$$

$$YD^u = (1 - .151)YP^u \ \therefore \ YP^u = YD^u/(1 - .151) \tag{3-116}$$

$$.93 = \frac{C}{YP} \times \frac{YP^u}{C^u} = \frac{C}{YD} \times \frac{YD^u}{C^u} \times \frac{(1 - .159)}{(1 - .151)} \tag{3-117}$$

$$k_C = \left(\frac{C}{YD} \right) \div \left(\frac{C^u}{YD^u} \right) = \frac{(1 - .151)}{(1 - .159)} \times .93 = .9388 \tag{3-118}$$

$$C = k_C \left[\frac{C^u}{RYD^u} \right] \times RYD \tag{3-119}$$

$$C = 0.939 \left[\frac{3,223}{3,401} \right] 87.639 = 77.986 \tag{3-120}$$

Values	In Text	In Program	Description
.934	k_{VSS}	kVSS	intercept social security tax (equation 3-11)
1.465	k_{VP}	kVP	intercept transfer payments (equation 3-12)
1.277	k_{DIR}	kDIR	intercept dividends, interest, and rent (equation 3-13)
-0.019	k_{RA}	kRA	residence adjustment parameter (equation 3-10)

Since all of the variables' values in the equations for VSS, VP, and DIR are known except the k values, we can find them directly, as follows:

$$k_{VSS} = \frac{VSS}{\left(\dfrac{YLP}{YLP^u} \right) \times VSS^u} = \frac{6.1}{\left(\dfrac{97.825}{3,177} \right) \times 212} = .934 \tag{3-121}$$

$$k_{VP} = \frac{VP}{\left(\dfrac{N - ER}{N^u - E^u} \right) \times VP^u}$$

$$= \frac{18.4}{\left[\dfrac{(5,912.5 - 3,700)}{(248,300 - 136,074)} \right] \times 637} = 1.465 \tag{3-122}$$

$$k_{DIR} = \frac{DIR}{\left(\dfrac{N}{N^u} \right) \times DIR^u} = \frac{23.3}{\left(\dfrac{5,912.5}{248,300} \right) \times 766} = 1.277 \tag{3-123}$$

Since RA is negative, indicating that there is net commuting into Massachusetts to work,

$$k_{RA} = \frac{RA}{YLP} = \frac{-1.900}{97.825} = -.019 \qquad (3\text{-}124)$$

If RA had been a positive number, indicating that there is net commuting from the rest of the United States into Massachusetts to live, then the calculation would have been

$$k_{RA} = \frac{RA}{YLP^u} = \frac{RA}{3177} \qquad (3\text{-}125)$$

Value	In Text	In Program	Description
221.519	K_{88} or K_{t-1} $t = 89$	K88= Kt_1 if t = 1989	capital stock at the end of last year (equation 3-14)
224.912	K_{89} or K_{t-1} $t = 90$	K89= Kt_1 if t = 1990	capital stock at the end of last year (equation 3-14)

Using equation 3-14, we can solve for K_{t-1}. From the amount of current investment IL_p given our estimate of K_t^*, we can infer the value of K_{t-1}. Thus, K_{t-1}, in some sense, becomes the free parameter in equation 3-14 for purposes of calibration.

$$IL_{p,t} = \alpha\,(k_I K_t^*) - \alpha\,(1 - dr^u)\,K_{t-1} \qquad (3\text{-}126)$$

$$K_{t-1} = \frac{\alpha\,(k_I K_t^*) - IL_{p,t}}{\alpha\,(1 - dr^u)}$$

$$= \frac{0.08\,(0.85)\,520.296 - 18.899}{0.08\,(0.9304)} \qquad (3\text{-}127)$$

$$K_{88} = \frac{35.380 - 18.899}{0.0744} = 221.5188 \qquad (3\text{-}128)$$

From equation 3-15, we calculate

$$K_t = IL_{p,t} + (1 - dr^u)\,K_{t-1}$$
$$224.9117 = 18.899 + .93 \times 221.519$$
$$K_{89} = 224.912 \qquad (3\text{-}129)$$

Value	In Text	In Program	Description
-0.087	UPH	UPH	unexplained change in price of housing (equation 3-42)

In equation 3-42, when all of the values except UPH are known, its value can be calculated. For forecasting, it is set at zero or it is used to return housing prices to a long-term equilibrium.

$$UPH = PH - \varepsilon \left[\frac{N_t \div N_t^u}{N_{t-1} \div N_{t-1}^u} - 1 \right] - PH_{t-1} \qquad (3\text{-}130)$$

$$UPH = 1.67 - .445 \left[\frac{5,912.5 \div 248,300}{5,889.5 \div 245,800} - 1 \right] - 1.76 \qquad (3\text{-}131)$$

$$= 1.67 - 0.445 [0.9937981 - 1] - 1.76$$

$$= -0.08724$$

Value	In Text	In Program	Description
0.050	UW^u	UWU	unexplained wage change, UW^u is used when W is not observed (equation 3-44)

In a case where W, ΔWD, ΔCPR, and W_{t-1} are observed, UW should be calculated as a residual instead of using the unexplained wage change in the United States, as we do in forecasting. From equation 3-44, we obtain

$$(1 + UW) = W \div [(1 + \Delta WD) (1 + \Delta CPR)^r \times W_{t-1}]$$

$$UW = 25.907 \div [(0.9955) (0.992)^{0.25} \times 24.836] - 1 = 0.0499 \qquad (3\text{-}132)$$

Value	In Text	In Program	Description
0.950	RWR	RWR	relative wage rate (equations 3-32, 3-46)

From equation 3-46,

$$RWR = \left[\frac{W \times (RYD \div YP)}{W^u \times (RYD^u \div YP^u)} \right]$$

$$RWR = \frac{25.907 \times (87.639 \div 131.5)}{23,360 \times (3,401 \div 4,367)}$$

$$= \frac{25.907 \times .6664563}{23.348 \times .7787955} \qquad (3\text{-}133)$$

$$= .9495$$

Value	In Text	In Program	Description
70.923	XFG	XFG	exports (equations 3-1, 3-2)

The XFG concept is not a value-added concept but, instead, a value of final sales concept. Therefore, we must identify the total sales made by the local area in question (Massachusetts) to out-of-state buyers. The overall final sales (Q^u)[44] to value added (Y^u) ratio for the United States is found by dividing total output (Q^u) in 1989, including double counting, from intermediate sales of 8,611 billion 1987 dollars for the United States (estimated by REMI) by total value added (Y^u) of 4,837 billion 1987 dollars for the United States. This ratio (Q^u / Y^u) is 1.77 (8,561 ÷ 4,837). With this ratio, our next task is to calculate the number of export employees, then multiply them by output per employee in 1987 dollars (Y / E) and the output to value added ratio (Q^u / Y^u).

The export employees must be estimated next. The best way to do this is to use the calculations used for the Export Base Model in chapter 2. All of the employees estimated to be involved in export production $(EXFG')$ for the private sector or the federal government should be divided by total employment E' in the local area. This ratio should then be multiplied by the total employment, as reported previously. The reason for doing this instead of just starting with the number for $EXFG'$ is that there is a difference in the measurement and definition of employment between the County Business Patterns data used in chapter 2 and the BEA data used here.

For Massachusetts, using the model to be described in chapter 7, we have estimated the ratio $(EXFG' / E')$ to be .318. As a result,

$$XFG = \left(\frac{EXFG'}{E'} \right) \times E \times \left(\frac{Y}{E} \right) \times \left(\frac{Q^u}{Y^u} \right)$$

$$= .318 \times 3{,}776 \times \frac{126}{3{,}776} \times 1.77$$

$$= 70.9232$$

(3-134)

Value	In Text	In Program	Description
0.702	R	R	local share of local output (equations 3-1, 3-66)

We arrive at the value using equation 3-1.

$$R = \frac{Y}{C + IL_p + G + XFG}$$

$$= \frac{126}{77.986 + 18.899 + 11.577 + 70.923}$$

$$= \frac{126}{179.385} = .7023 \tag{3-135}$$

Value	In Text	In Program	Description
0.03050	S	S	share of international exports (equations 3-2, etc.)
3.050	$S \times 10^2$	$S * 10^2$	share in percent

For purposes of the computer program, we multiply S by 100 to avoid a rounding error. Using equation 3-2, we find

$$S = XFG \div XFG^u$$

$$S = 70.923 \div 2325 = 0.030504 \tag{3-136}$$

Value	In Text	In Program	Description
-0.030	k_M	kM	constant in migration equation (equation 3-32)

From equation 3-32, we find

$$k_M = \frac{MIG}{N_{t-1}} - \beta_1 \, lnREO - \beta_2 \, lnRWR$$

$$= \frac{-36.9}{5,889.5} - 0.296\,(0.133) - 0.320\,(-0.05) \tag{3-137}$$

$$= -0.02963$$

The value of -0.02985 means that if REO = RWR = 1, then 29.85 thousand people per year would leave Massachusetts. Only if REO and RWR were high enough to offset the perceived negative amenity level, would net out-migration cease.

Value	In Text	In Program	Description
1.016	k_{RN}	kRN	constant in R equation (equation 3-66)
0.738	k_{RR}	kRR	constant in R equation (equation 3-66)

In order to calculate the k_{RN} and k_{RR} values, we assume that

$$xr = .214 k_{RN} RPROF_{89}^{\psi} + .786 k_{RR} Y^{\mu} SP_{89}^{\xi} \tag{3-138}$$

If we normalize both terms in this equation to equal xr, we can then write

$$R = 0.214\, xr + 0.786\, xr = xr \tag{3-139}$$

Therefore, $R = xr = 0.702$, and

$$k_{RN} = \frac{0.702}{RPROF_{89}^{\psi}} = \frac{0.702}{0.817^{1.83}} = \frac{0.702}{0.6908223} = 1.0162 \tag{3-140}$$

$$k_{RR} = \frac{0.702}{(126)^{0.0}(1.093)^{-0.563}} = \frac{0.702}{(1.0)(0.951)} = .738 \tag{3-141}$$

Value	In Text	In Program	Description
0.044	k_{SN}	kSN	constant in share equation (equation 3-67)
0.032	k_{SR}	kSR	constant in share equation (equation 3-65)

For the regional share of extraregional markets, we assume that

$$xs = .522 k_{SN} \times RPROF^{\psi} + .448 k_{SR} SP_R^{\xi} \tag{3-142}$$

Again normalizing both terms to xs, we can write

$$S = 0.522\, xs + 0.448\, xs = xs \tag{3-143}$$

$$S = xs = 0.03050$$

$$k_{SN} = \frac{0.03050}{0.817^{1.83}} = \frac{0.03050}{.69082} = .04415 \tag{3-144}$$

$$k_{SR} = \frac{0.03050}{(1.093)^{-0.563}} = \frac{0.03050}{0.951} = 0.03207 \tag{3-145}$$

This concludes the calculations that are required to calibrate the prototyp model. In the tables that follow, we assemble the numbers. In the case of the U. exogenous variables, we have extended them to 1994, based on a forecast in Mar 1992 which was made by the Research Seminar in Quantitative Economics (RSQ) at the University of Michigan. In each table, the variables that need to be changed calibrate to a new local area are in bold type.

TABLE 3-2

Variables and Parameters for the Prototype Model: (a) Exogenous Variables

Variable	Hist. 1989	Fcast. 1990	Fcast 1991	Fcast 1992	Fcast 1993	Fcast 1994
A	0.924	0.924	0.924	0.924	0.924	0.924
A^u	1.000	1.000	1.000	1.000	1.000	1.000
c	1.055	1.055	1.055	1.055	1.055	1.055
c^u	1.000	1.000	1.000	1.000	1.000	1.000
C^u	3223.0	3262.0	3256.0	3314.0	3412.0	3494.0
CP^u	1.091	1.146	1.194	1.229	1.273	1.332
DIR^u	766.0	811.0	813.0	804.0	861.0	922.0
E^u	136,074	137,600	136,100	135,400	138,000	140,600
ER^u	136,074	137,900	136,100	135,400	138,000	140,600
G^u	525.0	548.0	552.0	559.0	576.0	591.0

Variable	1989, cont.	1990, cont.	1991, cont.	1992, cont.	1993, cont.	1994, cont.
K^{u*}	17,827	17,251	16,679	16,893	17,838	18,228
N^u	248,300	249,500	251,700	253,900	256,100	258,300
RYD^u	3401.0	3456.0	3533.0	3612.0	3702.0	3786.0
UPH	-.087	0.000	0.000	0.000	0.000	0.000
UW^u	0.050	0.049	0.038	0.043	0.039	0.058
VP^u	637.0	699.0	774.0	885.0	909.0	962.0
VSS^u	212.0	225.4	239.2	247.7	262.1	286.1
W^u	23.348	24.557	25.518	26.640	27.710	29.360
XFG^u	2325.0	2349.0	2381.3	2421.7	2489.7	2523.6
Y^u	4837.0	4885.0	4854.0	4995.0	5151.0	5249.0
YLP^u	3177.0	3378.0	3473.0	3607.0	3824.0	4128.0
YP^u	4367.0	4663.0	4820.0	5019.0	5332.0	5724.0

(b) Endogenous Variables in Equation Order

Name in Text	Name in Program	1989 Value
Y	Y	126.00
XFG	XFG	70.923
C	C	77.986
YLP	YLP	97.825
YP	YP	131.50
RDV	RDV	33.700
RA	RA	-1.900
VSS	VSS	6.100
VP	VP	18.400
DIR	DIR	23.300
RYD	RYD	87.639
IL_p	ILp	18.899
G	G	11.577
K^*	K*	520.296
LIA	LIAt	0.985
EPV	EPV	29.968
E	E	3,776
MIG	MIG	-36.9
N	N	5,912.5
P	P	1.183
$RPROF_N$	RPROFn	0.817

Name in Text, cont.	Name in Prog., cont.	1989 Value, cont.
RPROFA	RPROFA	0.817
SP_R	SPr	1.093
SPA	SPA	1.093
PH	PH	1.67
CP	CP	1.262
W	W	25.907
ΔCPR	CPR_δ	-0.008
RWR	RWR	0.950
ER	ER	3,700
REO	REO	1.142
ΔWD	WD_δ	-0.0045
R	R	0.702
$S \times 10^2$	$S * 10^2$	3.050

(c) Endogenous Variables Used in $t + 1$ Calculation

Name in Text	Name in Program	1989 Value
K	K	224.912
REOA	REOA	1.165
EA	EA	3,594

(d) Parameters

Name in Text	Name in Program	Value
α	alpha	0.080
β_1	beta1	0.296
β_2	beta2	0.320
ϵ	epsilon	0.445
λ_1	lambda1	0.024
λ_2	lambda2	0.290
τ	tau	0.250
ψ	psi	1.830
μ	mu	0.000
ξ	xi	-0.563
a	a	0.700
d	d	0.300
dr^u	dru	0.070
hs^u	hsu	0.146
k_C	kC	0.939
k_G	kG	0.926
k_I	kI	0.850
k_M	kM	-0.030
k_{RN}	kRN	1.016
k_{RR}	kRR	0.738
k_{SN}	kSN	0.044

Name in Text, cont.	Name in Prog., cont.	Value, cont.
k_{SR}	kSR	0.032
k_{VSS}	kVSS	0.934
k_{VP}	kVP	1.465
k_{RA}	kRA	-.019
k_{DIR}	kDIR	1.277
ncs^u	ncsu	0.259
nsl^u	nslu	0.214
nse^u	nseu	0.552
tx	tx	0.159
sareo	sareo	1.000
saea	saeaprsp	0.200
salia	salia	0.063
sapr	saeaprsp	0.200
sasp	saeaprsp	0.200

TABLE 3-3

Key Values from All States for Calibrating the Prototype Model

	Nominal GSP (Y)[45]	Housing Prices Relative to the United States (PH)			Cost of Cap. (c)[46]	Capital Pref. (k_I)	YLP[47]	tx Value[48]
	1989	1988	1989	1990	1989	1989	1989	1989
US	5,164.671	1.0000	1.0000	1.0000	1.0000	-	3,177.124	0.151
CT	88.863	1.9165	1.8162	1.7613	1.0958	0.7490	57.420	0.161
ME	23.474	0.9407	0.8900	0.8658	0.9627	1.4537	14.115	0.129
MA	144.791	1.7576	1.6687	1.6127	1.0551	0.8506	97.826	0.159
NH	24.504	1.3948	1.3217	1.2819	1.0002	1.1698	15.018	0.120
RI	18.807	1.4396	1.3649	1.3225	1.0276	0.5219	12.512	0.155
VT	11.502	1.0277	0.9721	0.9460	0.9626	1.4692	6.699	0.149
DE	15.418	0.9846	0.9634	0.9916	1.0635	1.0085	10.286	0.190
DC	39.363	1.2384	1.1994	1.2274	1.1218	3.1945	26.090	0.179

	(Y), cont.	Housing Prices (PH), cont.			(c)	(k_i)	YLP	tx
MD	99.074	1.1553	1.1246	1.1541	1.0313	0.9328	64.413	0.169
NJ	203.375	1.7494	1.6577	1.6078	1.1122	0.7732	121.767	0.151
NY	441.068	1.4192	1.3457	1.3037	1.0910	0.8358	281.747	0.182
PA	227.898	0.7481	0.7054	0.6905	1.0349	0.8226	146.296	0.141
IL	256.478	0.7842	0.7672	0.8014	1.0696	0.8200	162.470	0.146
IN	105.314	0.5279	0.5136	0.5339	0.9805	1.0168	65.151	0.147
MI	181.827	0.5859	0.5740	0.6003	1.1001	0.6816	119.040	0.153
OH	211.545	0.6248	0.6064	0.6290	1.0057	0.7510	130.329	0.145
WI	93.978	0.6269	0.6022	0.6191	1.0191	0.6903	57.475	0.153
IA	52.574	0.4736	0.4482	0.4547	0.9544	1.0335	31.139	0.146
KS	48.829	0.5160	0.4996	0.5171	0.9637	0.9839	28.579	0.145
MN	93.559	0.7302	0.7076	0.7331	1.0166	0.7871	58.321	0.164

	(Y), cont.	Housing Prices (PH), cont.			(c)	(k_i)	YLP	tx
MO	100.081	0.5734	0.5643	0.5924	0.9618	0.8355	62.757	0.139
NE	31.115	0.5023	0.4841	0.4993	0.9343	0.9945	18.785	0.138
ND	11.231	0.5214	0.4948	0.5032	0.9100	1.6616	6.327	0.111
SD	11.135	0.4573	0.4372	0.4478	0.9021	1.3282	6.833	0.101
AL	67.886	0.5426	0.5219	0.5320	0.9425	0.7539	40.855	0.146
AR	37.169	0.4705	0.4509	0.4587	0.8887	1.2758	21.975	0.128
FL	226.964	0.7739	0.7475	0.7638	0.9701	1.2514	139.479	0.147
GA	129.776	0.7088	0.6889	0.7063	0.9782	1.0171	79.861	0.161
KY	65.858	0.5135	0.4920	0.5003	0.9344	1.2539	36.709	0.136
LA	79.138	0.5997	0.5716	0.5795	0.9622	1.4856	40.297	0.122
MS	38.135	0.4644	0.4445	0.4517	0.9182	1.2987	21.380	0.136
NC	130.085	0.6569	0.6367	0.6518	0.9749	0.9155	77.465	0.145

	(Y), cont.	Housing Prices (PH), cont.			(c)	(k_j)	YLP	tx
SC	60.150	0.6124	0.5921	0.6053	0.9612	0.7726	36.300	0.144
TN	92.267	0.5882	0.5669	0.5785	0.9718	1.0754	55.224	0.125
VA	136.497	0.9060	0.8796	0.9015	0.9898	1.1428	82.572	0.158
WV	27.922	0.4957	0.4697	0.4745	0.9497	1.2362	15.167	0.117
AZ	65.306	0.7728	0.7948	0.7935	0.9815	1.5382	39.264	0.138
NM	25.414	0.6681	0.6957	0.6944	0.9169	1.5845	14.136	0.139
OK	52.342	0.4934	0.4701	0.4765	0.8915	1.2630	31.640	0.180
TX	340.057	0.6043	0.5800	0.5904	0.9672	1.1794	197.455	0.130
CO	66.180	0.8212	0.8201	0.8192	0.9677	1.1506	43.396	0.143
ID	16.339	0.5795	0.5771	0.5765	0.9242	0.9106	10.142	0.121
MT	13.104	0.5702	0.5612	0.5607	0.9066	2.4619	7.367	0.123
UT	28.135	0.6963	0.6831	0.6825	0.9524	1.0897	16.918	0.129

(Y), cont.	Housing Prices (PH), cont.			(c)	(k_i)	YLP	tx
WY	11.115	0.6491	0.6102	0.6102	0.9255	2.9273	4.875	0.145
CA	697.381	1.7332	1.9428	1.9367	1.0785	0.8077	429.366	0.159
NV	27.960	0.9333	0.9494	0.9480	1.0191	1.4099	15.856	0.156
OR	52.118	0.6815	0.6651	0.6647	0.9926	0.8548	32.552	0.155
WA	96.233	0.8887	0.9270	0.9252	0.9785	1.2321	60.363	0.125
AK	19.582	0.9471	0.9360	0.9352	1.1101	2.2941	9.452	0.124
HA	25.755	2.2122	2.4369	2.4300	1.1251	1.1544	15.666	0.156

NOTES ON CHAPTER 3

1. This section and the following section are based in part on George I. Treyz, M. J. Greenwood, G. L. Hunt, and B. H. Stevens (1988). An earlier version of this chapter was written in part by Frederick Treyz.

2. In the National Income and Product Accounts, the consumer price index is used for this purpose. Here, we use an index based on the weights in the consumption column of a national input-output table.

3. Also see George I. Treyz, A. F. Friedlaender and B. H. Stevens (February 1980).

4. For a discussion and illustration of assuming increasing returns to scale, see Treyz and Stevens (1980).

5. This section draws from G. Treyz, D. Rickman, G. Hunt, and M. Greenwood (forthcoming) and from M. Greenwood, G. Hunt, D. Rickman, and G. Treyz (December 1991).

6. We can illustrate how factor substitutability is accounted for by using an example. Suppose $a = .7$, $d = .3$, and $A/A^u = W/W^u = c/c^u = 1$. In this case, P would also equal 1 ($1 = 1^{.7} \times 1^{.3} \times 1$). Now, if $c/c^u = 2$, the value of P would be 1.23 ($1.23 = (1)^{.7} \times (2)^{.3} \times 1$). However, performing the same experiment using fixed inputs ($p = [d (W/W^u) + a (c/c^u)] \times 1$) equals 1 in the initial case ($1 = [.7 \times 1 + .3 \times 1] \times 1$), but it equals 1.3 when $c/c^u = 2$ ($1.3 = [.7 \times 1 + .3 \times 2] \times 1$). The smaller increase using equation 3-38 is due to the fact that some of the effects of the capital cost increase can be mitigated by the substitution of labor for capital.

7. Also see George I. Treyz and Benjamin H. Stevens (1985). This section also draws on recent unpublished quantitative work by G. Treyz, D. Rickman, M. Podgursky, and E. Kruse.

8. This section draws from Rickman, D. and G. Treyz, "Regional Competitiveness and Relative Industrial Growth: A Structural Approach," 1991, unpublished.

9. The determination of the sales price for national industries is given by $SP_N = SP_N^u = 1$, which is not included in our list of equations since it is exogenous.

10. *Survey of Current Business (SCB)*, Vol. 71, No. 12, December 1991, table 1.1, p. 3.

11. Sum of states data for the REMI EDFS model, unpublished.

12. *SCB*, December 1991, table 1.2, p. 3.

13. *SCB*, December 1991, table 1.2, p. 3.

14. *SCB*, December 1991, table 2.1, p. 6.

15. *SCB*, April 1991, table 5, p. 34.

16. *SCB*, December 1991, table 7.1, p. 12.

17. *SCB*, December 1991, table 1.2, p. 3.

18. *SCB*, October 1990, Vol. 70, No. 10, table 4, p. 32.

19. *SCB*, October 1990, table 1.2, p. 5.

20. *SCB*, October 1990, table 4, p. 32.

21. *SCB*, October 1990, Tables 2 + 4, pp. 31 – 32.

22. From REMI forecast based on the BLS forecast published in *Monthly Labor Review*, November 1991 and the Research Seminar in Quantitative Economics forecast at the University of Michigan, Ann Arbor, March 13, 1992.

23. *SCB,* December, 1991, table 4, p. 47.

24. *SCB,* December 1991, table 2.3, p. 6.

25. *SCB,* December 1991, table 2.3, p. 6.

26. REMI Documentation Book, 1991, pages 7 – 11.

27. REMI U.S. state estimates summed over all states.

28. *SCB,* November 1991, tables 2.2 – 2.3, p. 13.

29. Bureau of Economic Analysis, Regional Economic Information Systems, April 1991, table CA25 for the United States.

30. *SCB,* December 1991, table 2, p. 44.

31. *SCB,* December 1991, table 1.2, p. 3.

32. BEA, REIS, table CA5, April 1991.

33. BEA, REIS, April 1991, table CA5.

34. BEA, REIS, April 1991, table CA25.

35. BEA, REIS, April 1991, table CA5.

36. National Association of Realtors. (1990). *Home Sales Yearbook*, table 8, p. 31.

37. Ibid., table 28, p. 48.

38. "State-specific median values of owner-occupied housing units are obtained from the Census of Housing for years 1970, 1980, and 1990. The National Association of Realtors' regional growth rates are then used to interpolate between these three census benchmark years. The National Association of Realtors' metropolitan area data for median sales price of existing single-family homes are used to estimate state housing prices after 1990." Taken from REMI, Volume I, Model Documentation, EDFS-53 sector, March 1992 edition, page 4–17.

39. *SCB,* December 1991, Vol. 71, No. 12, p. 47.

40. BEA, REIS, April 1991, table CA25.

41. *SCB,* December 1991, table 1.1, p. 3.

42. USDL, BLS News, no. 91-607, Consumer Expenditures in 1990, November 22, 1991, table 8.

43.

$$tx^u = \frac{YP^u - YD^u}{YP^u}$$

$$tx^u = \frac{4,367.4 - 3,710.0}{4,367.4} = 15.1$$

These values are from *SCB,* April 1991, table 3, page 32 (4,367.4) and table 5 on page 34 (3,710).

$$tx = \frac{YP - YD}{YD}$$

$$tx = \frac{131.5 - 110.6}{131.5} = 15.9$$

The value 110.6 comes from table 5, page 34 of *SCB,* April 1991.

44. Calculation of Q^u:

Private nonfarm output plus government value added plus farm value added (51.6) divided by the ratio of farm value added to farm output (.26).

$$7892.5 \quad \textit{total output of private nonfarm}$$
$$+ \quad 520.3 \quad \textit{Government}$$
$$\underline{+ \quad 198.5 \quad (51.6 \div .26)}$$
$$8611.3 = Q^u$$

The values 7892.5, 520.3, and 51.6 are from REMI historical data for 1989 as of March 25, 1992: table 46, table 5, and table 5, respectively. These are based on reported BLS output data and BEA final demand data, reconciled or modified by REMI. The value .26 is from a BLS Input-Output table modified by REMI entitled "Technical Coefficient Matrix Table." This can be found in REMI Documentation, March 1992 version of Volume I, EDFS - 53, chapter 7, page 8, 1990.

45. *SCB*, December 1991, pp. 51 – 58.

46. REMI Model, EDFS - 53, from July, 1991.

47. *REIS*, April 1991, table CA5.

48. *SCB*, April 1991, pp. 32 and 34.

CHAPTER 4

FORECASTING AND SIMULATION WITH
THE PROTOTYPE MODEL[1]

The prototype model that we developed in chapter 3 can be used to make forecasts and carry out policy simulations for a subnational area to which it has been calibrated. While the model is presented with U.S. data in mind, it could be calibrated to a subnational area for other countries, where the necessary data is available for calibration and reestimation of key parameters.

To use the model for policy analysis, it is convenient to put multiplicative and additive policy variables in the model as we did for the economic base models in chapter 2. An equation list with these policy variables included is presented at the end of this chapter and in the REMS computer program (table 4-2 on page 211 in the appendix). The multiplicative policy variables end with an M and take on a value of 1 as their default. The additive policy variables end in an A and take on a value of 0 as their default. Obviously, if all policy variables are given their default values, then the model is identical to the model presented at the end of chapter 3.

The steps for forecasting and simulating with the prototype model are the same as those in chapter 2 for the economic base models and those presented in chapter 8 for the REMI demonstration model. The first step is to create a baseline forecast (see diagram 2-1). This is accomplished by using the model as specified along with a preset exogenous value for the policy variable set. Using the Massachusetts model parameters and the exogenous variable set presented in the appendix to chapter 3, a control or baseline forecast was generated with the prototype model (table 4-5, page 216).

4-1 THE CONTROL FORECAST

Before we consider the forecast, we need to examine the method used to solve the prototype model. The method used is the simple iterative method, which was described in chapter 2 for the economic base model (pages 20 – 24). We recall that this method of solution requires an initial set of values for some of the endogenous variables, as well as a forecast set for the exogenous variables. The way to find these values for any county or state is set forth in the appendix to chapter 3.

Using the iterative (Gauss-Sidel) method, each equation is solved using either initial values or those determined by an equation that has already been solved. It is

184

important to arrange the model so that either exogenous variables or those already determined in another equation are used to the extent possible. Ideally, the first equation should depend only on exogenous variables. The second should depend only on exogenous variables and the value determined in the first equation, and so on.

If this method could be continued using only exogenous values and those that have been determined in previous equations, it would be called a *recursive system*. In this case, it would not be necessary to have initial values. However, this cannot be accomplished with the prototype model, which is a simultaneous system of equations. Nevertheless, the solution of this system depends on arranging the equations so that they approximate a recursive system as closely as possible. The numbering in the right-hand column on table 4-2 shows the order in which the equations are solved. It takes approximately 15 to 20 iterations to reach a solution that shows changes in Y, E, N, and RYD of less than .001.

The values by iteration for the first ten variables in the model are shown in Table 4-6. The values for all of the variables in the sixteenth iteration are shown on Table 4-5 for 1990, along with the values that resulted from the same iterative process each year with the appropriate set of exogenous and lagged variables in the rest of the forecast through 1994.

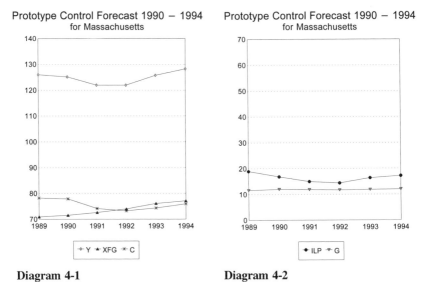

Diagram 4-1   Diagram 4-2

We start by analyzing the forecast for 1990 – 1994, as generated with the prototype model. Later, we consider how a forecaster might have brought information not included in the model into his or her forecast by changing some of the policy variables. The forecast values for all of the variables are shown on table 4-5. The forecast for the components of GRP are shown on diagrams 4-1 and 4-2.

In diagram 4-1, the GRP in Massachusetts is predicted to decline from 1989 through 1992, after which it turns up sharply. The first job of the analyst is to understand the forecast generated by the model. For example, why did GRP in Massachusetts decline in 1990? Looking at diagrams 4-1 and 4-2, it is apparent that the drop in investment was a primary cause of the decline.

Turning to the investment equation, the drop is found to be due to the decline in K^* by 5.2%, which, in turn, is caused by the decline in K^{*u} (see table 3-2 and table 4-4) by 3.2%, the drop of E/E^u (table 3-2 and table 4-5) by 1.7%, and the drop in W/W^u (table 3-2 and table 4-5) by -.4%. Given that investment is a function of the difference between K^* and the depreciated value of K_{t-1}, this decline leads to the much larger percentage decline of 11.2% in investment.

Even more difficult to ferret out is why Massachusetts output (Y) dropped slightly while, at the same time in 1990, Y grew slightly in the United States. The three major reasons are as follows: the bigger drop in investment in Massachusetts (due to the last two factors above reducing K^*); the drop in W/W^u, as it contributed to the holding back in the increase in income; and the outward migration caused in the drop in REOA from 1989 to 1990. The drop in REOA contributed to a one percentage point lower increase in state and local government spending and the lower wage increase. It also appears that the export share (S) has dropped from 1989 to 1990. However, upon examining the calibration of the 1989 values, the calculated value of S is less than the 1990 value shown. The reason for this is that one of the parameters of the S equation had to be rounded to fit into the program. Thus, the calculated value of S actually increased slightly from 1989 to 1990. This would be expected due to the slight increase in average profitability ($RPROFA_t$) and the slight decrease in average sales prices (SPA_t).

In 1991, the Massachusetts GRP (Y) drops again. As before, investment (IL_p) leads this decline for much of the same reasons as in 1990. Another large contributing factor is the drop in consumption (C). This is due to the decrease in consumption as a proportion of disposable income (RYD) and the drop in RYD. The former drop is due to the decrease in the national consumption propensity that is transmitted to Massachusetts through the C^u/RYD^u parameter in the consumption equation. The dynamics of the drop in employment and, thus, wages in Massachusetts are faster than in the United States and continue through 1992, as can be seen on diagram 4-3. This, in turn, leads to higher outward migration, which feeds back on itself to reduce the increase in government spending. In 1993 and 1994, Massachusetts is predicted by the prototype model to have a somewhat faster recovery than in the United States. However, employment in Massachusetts does not return to 1989 levels in 1993 – 1994, even though this happens to U.S. employment in the United States forecast (see table 3-2). Due to the decline in population also predicted by the prototype model, the employment to population ratio in 1989 is restored in 1993 – 1994 in Massachusetts, as shown on diagram 4-4.

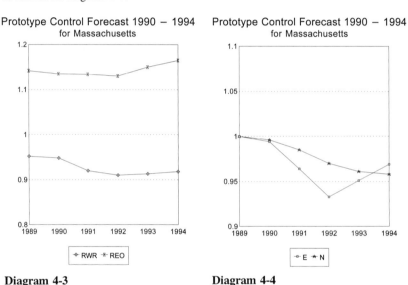

Prototype Control Forecast 1990 – 1994 for Massachusetts

Prototype Control Forecast 1990 – 1994 for Massachusetts

Diagram 4-3   **Diagram 4-4**

As noted above, in making an actual forecast, the forecaster usually adds expert judgement to some of the predictions made by some the equations in the model. For example, by 1990 it was very obvious that minicomputers, which were the mainstay of the high-tech sector of the Massachusetts economy, had fallen into disfavor and that the exports in this sector would drop dramatically. There was also evidence at that time that housing prices were weakening and that this might lead to a decline in the housing sector that would not be captured in the model. As a result, in making an actual *ex ante* (before the fact) forecast, a forecaster might have exogenously reduced exports and investment.[2]

In diagrams 4-5 through 4-8, the prototype forecast is compared with historical data available for 1990 and 1991 and an unadjusted forecast from 1992 to 1994 made with a REMI EDFS-53 model (a 53 sector economic-demographic-forecasting-simulation model, as set forth in chapter 7) for Massachusetts. Since some of the same conditions still existed in 1992 that led to the greater downturns than predicted in 1990 and 1991 with the prototype model, both the prototype and REMI forecasts would be adjusted downwards for a real *ex ante* forecast of 1992 – 1994.

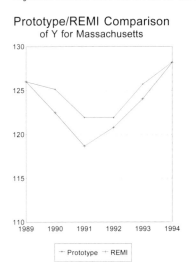

Diagram 4-5

Prototype/REMI Comparison of XFG for Massachusetts

Diagram 4-6

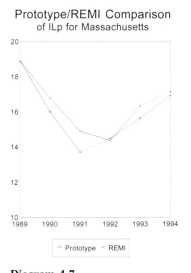

Diagram 4-7

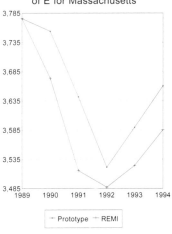

Diagram 4-8

The reason that there is a larger drop in Y on diagram 4-5[3] than was predicted by the prototype model is clear from diagrams 4-6[4] and 4-7[5]. They show the actual drop in XFG when an increase was predicted by the prototype model and the greater than predicted drop in IL_p. Diagram 4-8[6] shows that throughout the period, the prototype prediction of E was higher than REMI. Diagram 4-9[7] shows how personal income (YP), which is a variable in nominal terms that grows in a line with the inflation of over 20% in the period,

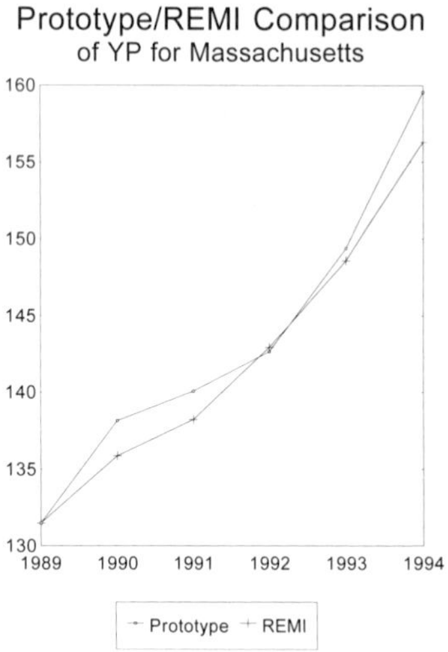

Prototype/REMI Comparison
of YP for Massachusetts

-- Prototype -+- REMI

Diagram 4-9

is so dominated by inflationary growth that the underlying errors in the predictions of the real economy are obscured.

Once the baseline or control forecast is completed, a simulation can be carried out. This can be accomplished with either an adjusted or an unadjusted control forecast.

4-2 THE POLICY VARIABLES

To carry out a simulation, the next step is to change the value of one or more of the policy variables in the model. The policy variables can be placed into five major blocks and sixteen detailed categories, as shown on table 4-1. The first set of policy variables relate to output linkages and their major input through their effects on final demand. The next set are related to factor demand, although in practice, the direct employment policy variable works through export output, which is directly related to employment through the EPV (employment per dollar of value added) variable. The factor productivity variables directly influence both output per employee and production costs.

TABLE 4-1

Categories of Policy Variables
for the Prototype Model

Output Linkages		Name
1)	Industry Output	PVOUTA
2)	Industry Demand	PVDEMA
3)	Disposable Income	PVRAA, PVVSSA, PVVPA, PVDIRA, PVtxA
4)	Consumer Spending	PVCA, PVCM
5)	Government Spending	PVGA, PVGM
6)	Investment Spending	PVIA, PVIM, PVKA, PVKM

Labor and Capital Demand		
7)	Employment	PVEA
8)	Factor Productivity	PVAA, PVEPA

Labor Supply		
9a)	Occupational Supply	PVESA
9b)	Migration	PVMIGA, PVQOLA

Wages, Prices, and Profits		
10)	Production Costs	PVPA
11)	Business Taxes & Credits	PVccA
12)	Fuel Costs	PVPA
13)	Labor Costs (Other than Wages)	PVwcA
14)	Wages	PVwA
15)	Prices (Housing and Consumer)	PVPHA, PVCPA

Market Shares		
16)	Market Shares	PVRA, PVSA, PVRM, PVSM

190

General labor supply is affected primarily by migration, which changes in response to amenity changes. However, labor supply for a particular occupation can also be changed by occupational training. In the wages, prices, and profits block, costs, wages, and taxes can be changed. Market shares can be changed in the final major category.

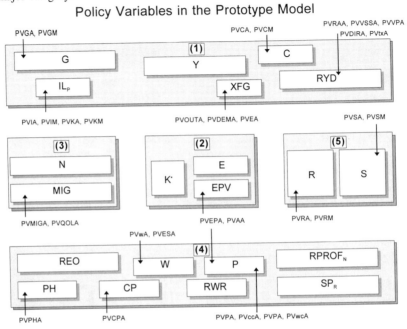

Policy Variables in the Prototype Model

Diagram 4-10

In diagram 4-10, the policy variables are set forth along with an arrow that indicates the point in the flow chart where the direct effect of the policy variable change enters the model. Note that the employment policy variable (PVEA) works through exports. Also, note that the productivity variables directly affect costs and the employees per dollar of output. This diagram, along with table 4-1 and the equation list at the end of this chapter, show you the policy variables available and their direct impact on the economy.

4-3 AN OUTPUT BLOCK SIMULATION

For our first policy simulations, we illustrate the use of the prototype model by making a change in one policy variable for each simulation. This is unrealistic, because almost all policy initiatives involve a change in more than one variable. For example, a change in state or local government spending always has to be matched by cuts in other spending or by tax increases due to the balanced budget constraints under which state and local governments operate. Despite this, it is good practice to see the effect of each of the policy variable changes individually before changing all of the policy variables that are required for the full policy simulation at the same time. The individual simulations are important because the policy analyst gains valuable insights into the final result when he or she understands each of the components.

Suppose that a firm in the state receives a federal government contract to produce one billion 1987 dollars worth of output in that state for each year from 1990 through 1994. In 1989, the task is to forecast what effects this contract will have on the state economy. To do this, we want to increase exogenous output by one billion 1987 dollars from 1990 to 1994.

After examining table 4-1, diagram 4-10, and the equation list, we pick policy variable PVOUTA. As we see in diagram 4-10 and equation 4-44, this variable directly effects the forecast by increasing XFG. Next, the control forecast, as shown in table 4-5, is run using the input and equations in tables 4-2 through 4-4. Following this, an alternative forecast is run. The control forecast is then subtracted from the alternative to show the difference between the two, which represents the effects of the policy change (table 4-7).

The analysis of these effects is the final step in the policy analysis process. It is at this point that the analyst must understand the changes in each variable in the model as they are determined by the interaction of all the variables in the model. The best way to do this is to start with the exogenous change and trace its effects through a few of the causal links. Then, realizing that the effects reported are the result of the entire model interaction, it is important to examine each variable to see how it was changed by its determinates, i.e., the variables on the right hand side of the equation. Diagram 4-11 shows the first year results, and table 4-7 shows the results for all years.

Note that XFG increased by 1.355 billion, not one billion. This difference occurs for two reasons. First, the model assumes that only the R proportion (.702, see control table 4-5) is produced in the area. However, our task was to find the effects of a change of output of one billion, not the change in demand of one billion (see PVDEMA). Thus, PVOUTA was divided by .702 in equation 4-44, yielding 1.425 and providing our increase of one billion to Y ($.702 \times 1.425 = 1.000$). In addition to the exogenous change in output, there was an endogenous response caused by the drop in export market share (S) by -0.003. This, in turn, was caused by a drop in profitability ($RPROF_N$) and an increase in sales prices (SP_R).

First Year Effects of a One Billion 1987 Dollar
Increase in Production for Export

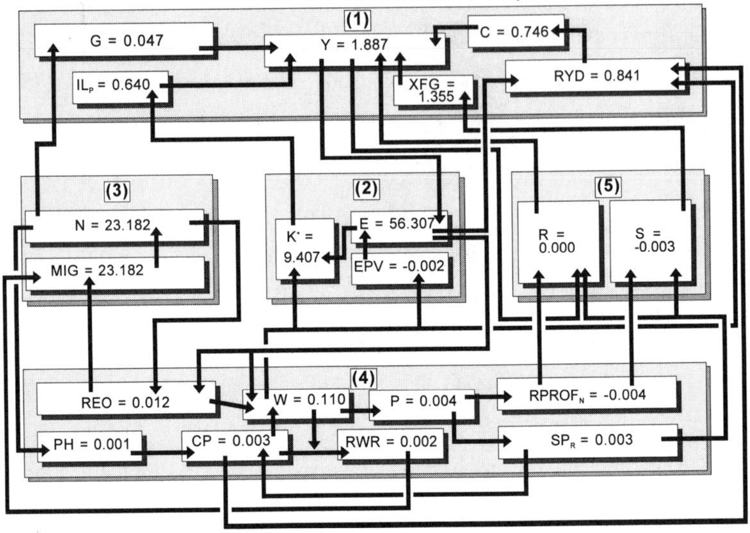

Diagram 4-11

These changes effect the model through RPROFA and SPA. Therefore, XFG was reduced endogenously by .070 (1.425 – 1.355). The Y increase (1.887), caused by the change in XFG, was .951 (.702 × 1.355). The rest of the increase was mainly due to higher consumption induced by increases in income and increases in investment caused by the need to build up the capital stock in order to meet the higher production rates on a continuing basis.

Looking at other details of the simulation, we see that the increase in Y leads to increases in employment (E). This, in turn, leads to wage increases and, with the increase in RWR and REO, to more in migration. Higher migration, in turn, increases population, which adds to the need for government spending.

In addition to the first-year analysis, it is also important to look at the dynamic process that is set into motion. In table 4-7 and diagram 4-12, we notice that the initial increase of 1.887 in Y, which implies a first-year multiplier of 1.887 (1.887/1.000), fades as time passes. This is caused by the drop in XFG as R and S decline over time in response to higher costs and as the increased investment (IL_p) builds up the capital stock, reducing the need for additional investment. However, the effect on Y does not decrease as one would expect looking at the XFG and IL$_p$ declines, due to the fact that these declines are partly offset by increases in government spending that are a result of the population gains and increases in consumer spending that occur as RYD gets larger. RYD grows in response to increases in transfer payments and property income that are also caused by the larger population.

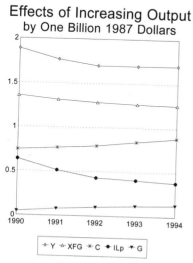

Diagram 4-12

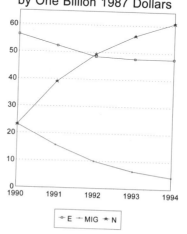

Diagram 4-13

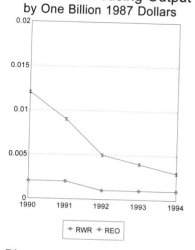

Diagram 4-14

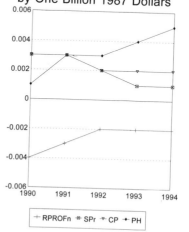

Diagram 4-15

Diagram 4-13 shows how the labor force responds to the increased employment and wage rates. Diagram 4-14 shows how, as migration takes place, the REO and RWR changes diminish. Eventually, any permanent increase in REO has to be offset by a decrease in RWR for inward migration to cease. Diagram 4-15 shows how relative profits (RPROF$_N$) and sales prices (SP$_R$) are restored over time, but housing prices are increased permanently. Thus, CP returns toward normal, but it would only return to its former level if wage decreases offset the effect of the housing price increases. Other policy variables in the output block and employment in the next block work through much the same chain of causality. The reader is encouraged to try changing these using the REMS software.

4-4 A LABOR AND CAPITAL DEMAND BLOCK SIMULATION

The next block on table 4-1 is the Factor Demand Block. Here, we undertake to find out what the implications of increasing labor productivity would be. In this case, we unrealistically assume that this can happen at the stroke of a pen (perhaps by outlawing certain productivity reducing work rules). The policy variable that changes labor productivity is PVEPA. It enters equation 3-30 (4-59) and equation 3-38 (4-63). The way to include this policy variable is demonstrated below.

We first define L as effective units of labor input, F as relative labor productivity, W as wage rate per employee, and E as employment.

$$L = E \times F \qquad \text{effective labor} \tag{4-1}$$

$$W_L = W \div F \qquad \text{cost per unit of effective labor} \tag{4-2}$$

The production function is Cobb-Douglas and is the same as equation 3-17 in chapter 3 with labor included as effective labor units.

$$Y = A \times L^a \times K^d \tag{4-3}$$

$$a + d = 1 \tag{4-4}$$

Following the derivation used in chapter 3 (see equations 3-20 and 3-21) to find minimum cost of production in equilibrium, the real cost of factors are set equal to the marginal factor product.

$$\frac{\partial Y}{\partial K} = \frac{dY}{K} = \frac{c}{SP} \tag{4-5}$$

$$\frac{\partial Y}{\partial L} = \frac{aY}{L} = \frac{W_L}{SP} \tag{4-6}$$

Solving for K, we obtain the optimal capital stock (see equation 3-22)

$$K^* = \left(\frac{W_L}{c}\right)\left(\frac{d}{a}\right) L,$$

(4-7)

which we represent relative to the United States (see equation 3-24) as

$$K^* = \left(\frac{W_L}{W_L^u}\right)\left(\frac{c^u}{c}\right)\left(\frac{L}{L^u}\right) \times K^{*u}$$

(4-8)

With $W_L = W/F$, we have

$$K^* = \left(\frac{\dfrac{W}{F}}{\dfrac{W^u}{F^u}}\right)\left(\frac{c^u}{c}\right)\left(\frac{E \times F}{E^u \times F^u}\right) K^{*u}$$

(4-9)

$$= \left(\frac{W}{W^u}\right)\left(\frac{c^u}{c}\right)\left(\frac{E}{E^u}\right) \times K^{*u}$$

Thus, the relative labor productivity term does not effect optimal capital stock. Substituting equation 4-7 into the production function, we obtain

$$Y = A \times L^a \times \left(\frac{W_L}{c}\right)^d \times \left(\frac{d}{a}\right)^d \times L^d$$

(4-10)

Remembering that $a + d = 1$ and dividing this by the same equation for the United States, we obtain

$$\frac{Y}{Y^u} = \left(\frac{A}{A^u}\right)\left(\frac{W_L}{W_L^u}\right)^d\left(\frac{c^u}{c}\right)^d\left(\frac{L}{L^u}\right)$$

(4-11)

Substituting $W \div F$ for W_L and solving for L, we obtain

$$L = (L^u)\left(\frac{Y}{Y^u}\right)\left(\frac{W^u}{W}\right)^d\left(\frac{F}{F^u}\right)^d\left(\frac{c}{c^u}\right)^d\left(\frac{A^u}{A}\right)$$

(4-12)

Substituting in $L = E \times F$ and solving for E, we obtain

$$E = (E^u)\left(\frac{Y}{Y^u}\right)\left(\frac{W^u}{W}\right)^d\left(\frac{F^u}{F}\right)^a\left(\frac{c}{c^u}\right)^d\left(\frac{A^u}{A}\right)$$

(4-13)

Dividing both sides by Y to express employment per output (EPV), we obtain

$$EPV = \frac{E}{Y} = \left(\frac{E^u}{Y^u}\right)\left(\frac{W^u}{W}\right)^d\left(\frac{c}{c^u}\right)^d\left(\frac{F^u}{F}\right)^a\left(\frac{A^u}{A}\right) \qquad (4\text{-}14)$$

Now, substituting a moving average of labor intensity (see equation 3-29),

$$LIA_t = (1 - salia) \times LIA_{t-1} + salia\left(\frac{c}{c^u}\right)^d\left(\frac{W}{W^u}\right)^{-d} \qquad (4\text{-}15)$$

for $\left(\dfrac{c}{c^u}\right)^d\left(\dfrac{W}{W^u}\right)^{-d}$, and $\dfrac{1}{(1 + PVEPA)}$ for $\dfrac{F^u}{F}$, $\qquad (4\text{-}16)$

into equation 4-14, we obtain

$$EPV = \left(\frac{E^u}{Y^u}\right) \times LIA \times \left(\frac{A^u}{A}\right)\left(\frac{1}{(1 + PVEPA)}\right)^a \qquad (4\text{-}17)$$

Since a change in F does not involve a change in K*, as shown in equation 4-9, it would be inappropriate to include it in the LIA variable. Thus, equation 4-17 provides the basis for inserting PVEPA into equation 3-30 (4-59). In common sense terms, equation 4-17 tells us that an increase in labor productivity means that less people are needed to produce a given output.

Next, we develop the background for inserting PVEPA into the relative production cost equation 3-38 (4-63). We start with an equation similar to equation 3-34 for total cost, which is

$$TC = (W_L \times L) + (c \times K) \qquad (4\text{-}18)$$

Substituting K* from equation 4-7 for K and following equation 3-35, we obtain

$$TC = \frac{W_L \times L}{a} \qquad (4\text{-}19)$$

Substituting for L from equation 4-10 yields

$$TC = \frac{W_L}{a} \times Y \times A^{-1}\left(\frac{c}{W_L}\right)^d\left(\frac{a}{d}\right)^d \qquad (4\text{-}20)$$

Taking the partial derivatives, as in equation 3-37, to obtain marginal cost yields

$$\frac{\partial TC}{\partial Y} = \frac{W_L}{a} \times A^{-1}\left(\frac{c}{W_L}\right)^d\left(\frac{a}{d}\right)^d \qquad (4\text{-}21)$$

Dividing by a similar function for the United States, we obtain

$$P = \frac{marginal\ cost}{marginal\ cost^u}$$

$$= \left(\frac{W_L}{W_L^u}\right) \times \left(\frac{A^u}{A}\right) \times \left(\frac{W_L^u}{W_L}\right)^d \left(\frac{c}{c^u}\right)^d \tag{4-22}$$

$$= \left(\frac{W_L}{W_L^u}\right)^a \times \left(\frac{c}{c^u}\right)^d \times \left(\frac{A^u}{A}\right)$$

Next, substituting for W_L, we obtain

$$P = \left(\frac{\frac{W}{F}}{\frac{W^u}{F^u}}\right)^a \times \left(\frac{c}{c^u}\right)^d \times \left(\frac{A^u}{A}\right) \tag{4-23}$$

$$P = \left(\frac{W}{W^u}\right)^a \left(\frac{F^u}{F}\right)^a \left(\frac{c}{c^u}\right)^d \left(\frac{A^u}{A}\right) \tag{4-24}$$

Since initial $F^u = F = 1$ in the control, we substitute $\dfrac{1}{1 + PVEPA}$ for $\dfrac{F^u}{F}$ and obtain

$$P = \left(\frac{W}{W^u}\right)^a \left(\frac{c}{c^u}\right)^d \left(\frac{A^u}{A}\right) \times (1 + PVEPA)^{-a} \tag{4-25}$$

which is equation 4-63 in the model. In common sense terms, this simply means that, at a given wage, an increase in labor productivity reduces production costs.

We introduce the change by increasing PVEPA by .1, which has the effect of increasing labor productivity by 10% in 1990 and maintaining the new level through 1994. The first year results on table 4-8 show output up slightly but employment down. This result is, of course, due to the labor and cost saving aspects of the productivity increase. Due to the cost savings, profitability is up sharply and sales prices are down. These both increase the market share for exports and the local market. Because of the price drops, real disposable income is up despite decreases in employment and wage rates. Of course, the large drop in employment is due to the fact that we now need ten percent less people to produce any output than we did previously.

The dynamic changes in the effects of this productivity increase are very interesting. In diagram 4-16, we can see employment decrease at first then increase. Inward migration turns positive before employment increases due to the rise in RWR caused by the drop in prices. The changes in RWR and REO are shown in diagram 4-17.

The Effects of a 10% Increase in Labor Productivity for 1990 − 1994

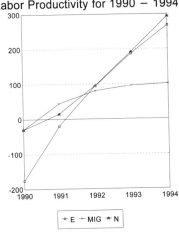

Diagram 4-16

The Effects of a 10% Increase in Labor Productivity for 1990 − 1994

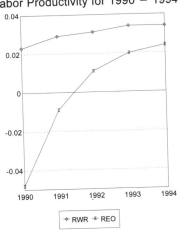

Diagram 4-17

4-5 A POPULATION AND LABOR SUPPLY BLOCK SIMULATION

The next block is the Labor Supply Block. In this case, we consider a policy that would improve the quality of life, such as environmental improvements or public recreational facilities. In this instance, we increased PVQOLA by .02. To find the wage equivalent of this, we refer to equation 4-61. By subtracting this equation with a initial values of $PVQOLA_0$ and RWR_0 from the new values of RWR_1 and $PVQOLA_1$, we obtain

$$\frac{MIG_1}{N_{t-1}} - \frac{MIG_0}{N_{t-1}} = PVQOLA_1 - PVQOLA_0 + \beta_2 \left(lnRWR_1 - lnRWR_0 \right) \quad (4\text{-}26)$$

Setting the net migration change equal to zero and realizing that $PVQOLA_0 = 0$, $PVQOLA_1 = .02$, and that $\beta_2 = .320$, we obtain

$$\frac{0.02}{0.320} = lnRWR_1 - lnRWR_0 = ln\left(\frac{RWR_1}{RWR_0} \right) \quad (4\text{-}27)$$

$$\frac{RWR_1}{RWR_0} = e^{\left(\frac{0.02}{0.320}\right)} \tag{4-28}$$

$$\frac{RWR_1}{RWR_0} = 1.064 \tag{4-29}$$

We obtain $1.064 - 1.000 = .064$ or 6.4% as the change in RWR that is equivalent to PVQOLA $= .02$. To find the probability of employment (REO) equivalent, we find that the coefficient for REO is .296 and then calculate

$$e^{\frac{.02}{.296}} - 1 = .070 \tag{4-30}$$

Thus, the quality of life or amenity effect that we are testing is one that would be valued at 6.4% of the average real after tax wage or at the equivalent of increasing the probability of employment by 7.0%. Of course, this calculation can be done in reverse when it is necessary to model an amenity increase that is worth x percent of the real wage. Then,

$$PVQOLA = .320 \ ln(1 + .01 \times x), \tag{4-31}$$

when $x = 1$ $\quad PVQOLA = .320 \ ln(1.01) = .0032$ $\tag{4-32}$

The results of the increase in PVQOLA by .02 over the period 1990 - 1994 are shown on table 4-9. This simulation represents the "jobs follow people" mechanism in the model, while the output stimulus simulation (PVOUTA) previously discussed represented the "people follow jobs" mechanism.

Looking at the first year, it is clear that increased inward migration leads to more jobs and higher output. Sources include more government services in response to a larger population, more transfer payments, and higher shares (R and S) of markets due to more profits (RPROF$_N$) and lower sales prices (SP$_R$). Lower sales prices are due to lower wages (W), which are caused by an increase in the supply of labor relative to demand (REO). Also, the moving average of labor intensity, LIA, increases by enough to raise EPV but not enough to show at the level reported on table 4-9. This increases employment.

The effects of increasing consumer amenities become even more dramatic over time, as shown in diagram 4-18, where population growth leads employment growth. On diagram 4-19, we see the inevitable effect of declines in REO and RWR caused

200

by the amenities driven policy. Eventually, they drop enough to cut off further inward migration effects.

Effects of Increasing Amenities by a 6.4% Wage Equivalent

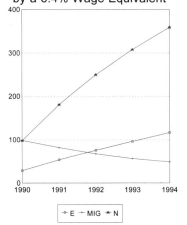

The Effects of Increasing Amenities by a 6.4% Wage Equivalent

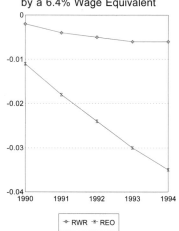

Diagram 4-18   **Diagram 4-19**

4-6 A WAGES, PRICES, AND PROFITS BLOCK SIMULATION

For the next block, which is Wages, Prices, and Profits, we choose a policy where average wage rates are increased by $1,000 due to a government policy, such as raising the minimum wage. Here, the effects shown in table 4-10 demonstrate how, in the first year, the increase in wage rates (W) increases output (Y) and employment (E). This is caused by several factors. First, there is little time for business to relocate or for local people to find new sources of supply, so the decreases in R and S, which reduce employment, are small. At the same time, the wage bill increases and real wage rates increase as wages go up more than prices. This leads to extra consumer spending. Second, people are attracted to move into the state by higher real wages (RWR). This increases government spending. Third, K^* rises dramatically as optimal capital grows due to the increase in wage rates relative to capital costs. This increases investment (IL_p). Thus, the surprising net effect in the first year is to increase output and employment.

As shown in diagram 4-20, however, the situation changes dramatically as time goes on. The drastic reductions in export share are particularly noticeable. On diagram 4-21, the reductions in profits, $RPROF_N$, and increases in sales prices, SP_R, as they are transmitted to the share equations through RPROFA and SPA are shown. Diagram 4-22 shows how these changes decrease market shares over time. This diagram also demonstrates how the employee per dollar of value added (EPV) decreases due to the increase in labor relative to other costs. Finally, the results of all these changes on employment (E), migration (MIG), and population (N) shows how all of the short run effects of the policy are reversed as the forecast span gets longer, as shown in diagram 4-23.

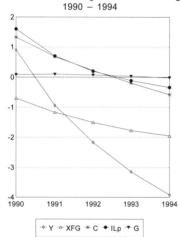

Diagram 4-20

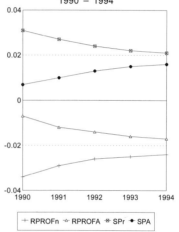

Diagram 4-21

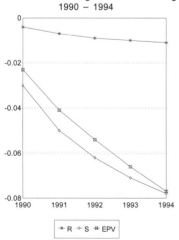

Diagram 4-22

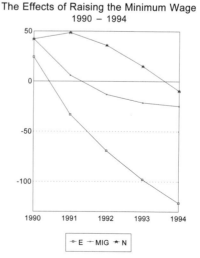

Diagram 4-23

4-7 A MARKET SHARES BLOCK SIMULATION

For the last block, which is market shares, we illustrate how import substitution policy can achieve the same end as a policy increasing the economic base. We start with a policy that increases R by enough to raise output by one billion 1987 dollars. This matches the stimulus in our first simulation case earlier in this chapter (see table 4-7). We do this by solving for ΔR in the equation

$$\Delta Y = \Delta R \ (Y \div R) \tag{4-33}$$

where Y = 125.131 (see table 4-5) and $\Delta Y = 1.000$. Thus, the equation for finding the ΔR that increases Y by one billion 1987 dollars is

$$\Delta R = \left(\frac{1.000}{125.131 \ \div \ .702} \right) = .0056 \tag{4-34}$$

We set PVRA at .006 for the period 1990 – 1994. This rounding is necessary, because the value for PVRA can only be set for three decimal places.

As expected, on table 4-11, we find that the effects on output and employment are very similar to the effects of increasing output for export by one billion 1987 dollars, as in the first simulation in this chapter. Adjusting for the rounding of PVRA by calculating .056 ÷ .060 = .933, the first year change in Y on table 4-11 is 1.897 (.933 × 2.033). This compares with 1.887 for the economic base increased output simulation (table 4-7).

By the last year (1994), the adjusted value of the increase in Y for increasing R is 1.751 (.933 × 1.877) as opposed to 1.702 for the output simulation on table 4-7. Other key variables, such as employment (E), migration (MIG), profits ($RPROF_N$), and sales price (SP_R), are also very similar. The key difference is that R is increased in this simulation, but XFG is not. So, we can conclude that raising self-sufficiency (increasing R), which is sometimes called import substitution, is as effective in raising output and employment as expanding the economic base.

4-8 A BALANCED BUDGET SIMULATION

For our final simulation, we more realistically change more than one policy variable. Since the model does not insure that a proposed policy's simulation include all of the aspects of a policy, it is important for the analyst to make sure that all of the implications of the policy are included. For example, if the analyst is asked to simulate an increase in state spending, it is important to establish how this increase will be funded. Since state governments must balance their budgets, an increase will usually have to be funded by a cut in spending or a rise in taxes. Even expenditures of federal highway funds for one project may mean foregoing another project.

For this simulation, we want to increase government spending by approximately one billion dollars and fund this by raising the income tax rate. To calculate the approximate change that is required in the income tax rate (at the income levels in the control forecast) we extract the following from equation 4-53:

$$\Delta taxes = PVtxA \; (YP \div CP) \tag{4-35}$$

We use the values of YP and CP from the control forecast to find the exogenous change in taxes. If the economy is stimulated by the policy, then population and real income (YP ÷ CP) may grow. The tax revenue increases arising from this endogenous growth are assumed to be required to meet the endogenous increase in government expenditures to provide services to the larger population. Since we want an increase of about one billion 1987 dollars, we set the left-hand side of equation 4-35 equal to one billion and solve for PVtxA.

$$PVtxA = \frac{1.000}{YP \div CP}, \tag{4-36}$$

For 1990 on table 4-5, this calculation is

$$PVtxA = \frac{1.000}{(138.161 \div 1.322)} = .0096 \tag{4-37}$$

Rounding this off, a tax of one percent (.01) on real personal income is decided on. Again, using the control forecast on table 4-5, we calculate .01 times YP/CP for each forecast year, which yields 1.045, 1.019, 1.010, 1.021, and 1.042 for 1990 – 1994, respectively. These are our changes in government spending (PVGA) to accompany the tax rate change (PVtxA) of .01.

The results of this simulation are shown on table 4-12. They show a small decrease in output and employment. This may surprise analysts who are familiar with the simple balanced budget multiplier that can be derived from a simple Keynesian model.

In its simplest form, the balanced budget multiplier starts with a two-equation model:

$$Y = C + G \tag{4-38}$$

$$C = c \; (Y - T), \tag{4-39}$$

where T is taxes, Y is Gross Domestic Product, C is consumption, G is government spending, and c is marginal propensity to consume ($0 < c < 1$). Solving for the reduced form, we obtain

$$Y = \frac{G - cT}{1 - c} \qquad (4\text{-}40)$$

If we propose a balanced budget change,

$$\Delta B = \Delta G = \Delta T \qquad (4\text{-}41)$$

by substituting equation 4-41 into equation 4-40, we can now predict the ΔY as

$$\Delta Y = \frac{1 - c}{1 - c} \Delta B = \Delta B \qquad (4\text{-}42)$$

This shows that an equal increase in both T and G leads to a rise in Y of the amount of that increase. The reason for this result is that consumers will only cut their spending initially by $c\Delta T$ and not by the entire ΔT, while the government increases its spending by the total amount of ΔG. This same process is at work in the prototype model.

Thus, the question is, "Why are there decreases predicted in output and employment by the prototype model that include a consumption function similar to equation 4-39?" A closer examination of table 4-12 shows that the higher tax rate reduces the real after-tax relative wage in Massachusetts by one percent. This leads to substantial outward migration, which has a large negative effect on transfers and on property income and leads to a net decrease in YP and RYD that is large enough to make the drop in consumption larger than the increase in government spending. This is despite the fact that only a portion of disposable income is spent ($\Delta C \div \Delta RYD = 1.028 \div 1.160 = .89$). Also, the decrease in the labor force exceeds the drop in employment, tightening labor markets and causing nominal wages (W) to increase. This, in turn, reduces profits ($RPROF_N$) and increases sales prices (SP_R). These changes lead to a decrease in shares of both the local (R) and national (S) markets. Thus, the open nature of a local economy with respect to the movement of people leads to a different qualitative result then we might have expected from a closed economy.

If we had assumed that the additional government spending would generate a value for people that is equal to the amount of government spending, then we would have increased the amenity term in the migration equation to reflect this. This adjustment would have offset the outward migration in response to the drop in the real after tax wage. The net result would have been a very different than the simulation results reported previously without this adjustment. Thus, we conclude that the outcome in the previous paragraph is based on government spending that does not create any perceived value for the people who are potential migrants into or out of the area.

4-9 CONCLUSION

In this chapter, we have discussed various simulations with the prototype model. The range of potential policy studies is much broader than we have time to present. In the next chapter, we focus on alternative models to investigate how the predicted effects of policy changes would differ depending on the model used. In Part II, we repeat the organizational structure of Part I. At each point in Part II, especially during the interpretation of policy studies, references to the corresponding sections in Part I are important aids. In fact, first running and interpreting policy simulations with the prototype model is good preparation for carrying out a policy study with a multi-industry, multi-occupation, multi-age cohort operational model.

SUMMARY EQUATIONS

for the
Single Sector, Single Region,
Single Occupation, Single Age/Sex Cohort Prototype Model with
Four Components of Aggregate Demand and
Two Factors of Production

(1) OUTPUT LINKAGES

Output

$$Y = [R \times (C + ILp + G + XFG)]$$ (4-43)

Exports

$$XFG = S \times XFG^u + PVDEMA + \frac{PVOUTA}{R} + \frac{(PVEA \div EPV)}{R}$$ (4-44)

Consumption

$$C = k_c \times \left[\frac{C^u}{RYD^u} \right] \times RYD \times PVCM + PVCA$$ (4-45)

Labor and Proprietors' Income

$$YLP = E \times W \div 1000$$ (4-46)

Personal Income

$$YP = YLP + RDV$$ (4-47)

Adjustment for Residence, Dividends, Interest, and Rent, and Net
Transfer Payments (VP − VSS)

$$RDV = - VSS + RA + DIR + VP$$ (4-48)

Residential Adjustment

$$RA = \begin{cases} k_{RA} \times YLP + PVRAA \text{ if } k_{RA} < 0 \\ k_{RA} \times YLP^u + PVRAA \text{ if } k_{RA} > 0 \end{cases}$$ (4-49)

Social Security Taxes

$$VSS = k_{VSS} \times \left(\frac{VSS^u}{YLP^u} \right) \times YLP + PVVSSA \tag{4-50}$$

Transfer Payments

$$VP = k_{VP} \times \left(\frac{VP^u}{N^u - E^u} \right) \times (N - ER) + PVVPA \tag{4-51}$$

Dividends, Interest, and Rent

$$DIR = k_{DIR} \times \left(\frac{DIR^u}{N^u} \right) \times N + PVDIRA \tag{4-52}$$

Real Disposable Income

$$RYD = [\, YP \, (1 - (tx + PVtxA))\,] \div CP \tag{4-53}$$

Investment

$$IL_{p,t} = \alpha \left[(k_I K_t^*) - (1 - dr^u) \times K_{t-1} \right] \times PVIM + PVIA \tag{4-54}$$

Capital Stock Updating

$$K_t = IL_{p,t} + (1 - dr^u) \times (K_{t-1} \times PVKM + PVKA) \tag{4-55}$$

State and Local Government Spending

$$G = k_G \times \left[\frac{G^u}{N^u} \right] \times N \times PVGM + PVGA \tag{4-56}$$

(2) LABOR AND CAPITAL DEMAND LINKAGES

Optimal Capital Stock

$$K^* = \left[\frac{W}{W^u} \right] \times \left[\frac{c^u}{c} \right] \times \left[\frac{E}{E^u} \right] \times K^{u*} \tag{4-57}$$

Relative Labor Intensity Average

$$LIA_t = (1 - salia) \, LIA_{t-1} + salia \left[\left(\frac{c}{c^u} \right)^d \left(\frac{W}{W^u} \right)^{-d} \right] \tag{4-58}$$

Labor/Output Ratio

$$EPV = \frac{\left(LIA \times \left[\frac{E^u}{Y^u} \right] \right) \div \left[\frac{A}{A^u} \right]}{\left[(A + PVAA) \div A^u \right] \times \left[(1 + PVEPA)^{-a} \right]} \tag{4-59}$$

Employment

$$E = EPV \times Y \tag{4-60}$$

(3) POPULATION AND LABOR SUPPLY LINKAGES

Migration

$$MIG = \left[k_M + PVQOLA + (\beta_1 \times \ln(REO)) + (\beta_2 \times \ln(RWR)) \right] \tag{4-61}$$
$$\times N_{t-1} + PVMIGA$$

Population

$$N = N_{t-1} \left[\frac{N_t^u}{N_{t-1}^u} \right] + MIG \tag{4-62}$$

(4) WAGE, PRICE, AND PROFIT LINKAGES

Relative Production Costs

$$P = \left[\frac{W + PVwcA}{W^u} \right]^a \times \left[\frac{c + PVccA}{c^u} \right]^d \div \left[\frac{A + PVAA}{A^u} \right] \tag{4-63}$$
$$\times (1 + PVEPA)^{-a} \div \left(\frac{A + PVAA}{A^u} \right) + PVPA$$

Relative Profitability for National Industries

$$RPROF_N = (1 - P) + 1 \tag{4-64}$$

Relative Profit Average

$$RPROFA_t = (1 - sapr)RPROFA_{t-1} + sapr RPROF_{N,t} \tag{4-65}$$

Relative Sales Price for Regional Industries

$$SP_R = \left[\frac{W}{W^u} \right]^a \times \left[\frac{c}{c^u} \right]^d = P \times \left[\frac{A}{A^u} \right] \tag{4-66}$$

Relative Sales Price Average

$$SPA_t = (1 - sasp) \times SPA_{t-1} + sasp\ SP_{R,t} \tag{4-67}$$

Relative Housing Price

$$PH = \varepsilon \times \left[\frac{N_t \div N_t^u}{N_{t-1} \div N_{t-1}^u} - 1 \right] + PH_{t-1} + UPH + PVPHA \tag{4-68}$$

Consumer Price Deflator

$$CP = \left[(1 - hs^u) \times \left((1 - ncs^u)\ SP_R + ncs^u \right) + (hs^u) \times PH \right]$$
$$\times CP^u + PVCPA \tag{4-69}$$

Wage Rate

$$W = (1 + \Delta WD)(1 + \Delta CPR_t)^\tau (1 + UW^u) \times W_{t-1} + PVwA \tag{4-70}$$

in which ΔCPR_t is given by

$$\Delta CPR = \left[\frac{CP \div CP^u}{CP_{t-1} \div CP_{t-1}^u} \right] - 1 \tag{4-71}$$

Relative Real After Tax Wage Rate

$$RWR = \left[\frac{W \times (RYD/YP)}{W^u \times (RYD^u/YP^u)} \right] \tag{4-72}$$

Employment by Place of Residence

$$ER = \left(\frac{YLP + RA}{YLP} \right) \times E \tag{4-73}$$

Relative Employment Opportunity

$$REO = \left[\frac{ER}{N} \right] \div \left[\frac{E^u}{N^u} \right] \tag{4-74}$$

Change in the Wage Rate Due to Change in Demand

$$\Delta WD = \left[\lambda_1 \times \left(\frac{E - PVESA}{EA} - 1 \right) \right]$$
$$+ \left[\lambda_2 \times \left(\frac{REO}{REOA} - 1 \right) \right] \qquad (4\text{-}75)$$

REOA Updating

$$REOA_t = (1 - sareo) \times REOA_{t-1} + sareo \times REO_{t-1} \qquad (4\text{-}76)$$

EA Updating

$$EA_t = (1 - saea) \times EA_{t-1} + saea \times E_{t-1} \qquad (4\text{-}77)$$

(5) MARKET SHARE LINKAGES

Regional Share of C + G + ILp + XFG

$$R = \left[nsl^u \left(k_{RN} \times RPROFA^\psi \right) + (1 - nsl^u) \left(k_{RR} \times Y^\mu SPA_R^\xi \right) \right] \qquad (4\text{-}78)$$
$$\times PVRM + PVRA$$

Regional Share of Extraregional Markets

$$S = \left[nse^u \left(k_{SN} \times RPROFA_N^\psi \right) + (1 - nse^u) \left(k_{SR} \times SPA_R^\xi \right) \right] \qquad (4\text{-}79)$$
$$\times PVSM + PVSA$$

TABLE 4-2

Prototype Model Equations Summary

Titles	Equations	
	OUTPUT LINKAGES	*
Output	$Y = [R*(C+ILp+G+XFG)]$	02
Exports	$XFG = S*XFGu+PVDEMA+PVOUTA \div R +$	
	$(PVEA \div EPV) \div R$	01
Consumption	$C = kC*[Cu \div RYDu]*RYD*PVCM+PVCA$	15
Labor & Proprietors' Income	$YLP = W*E \div 1000$	07
Personal Income	$YP = YLP+RDV$	13
Exogenous Income	$RDV = -VSS+RA+DIR+VP$	12
Residential Adjustment	$RA = kRA*YLP+PVRAA$; if $kRA<0$	08
	$= kRA*YLPu+PVRAA$; if $kRA>0$	
Social Security Tax	$VSS = kVSS*(VSSu \div YLPu)*YLP+PVVSSA$	09
Transfer Payments	$VP = kVP*[VPu \div (Nu-Eu)]*(N-ER)+PVVPA$	10
Dividends, Interest, and Rent	$DIR = kDIR*(DIRu \div Nu)*N+PVDIRA$	11
Real Disposable Income	$RYD = [YP(1-(TX+PVtxA))] \div CP$	14
Investment	$ILp = \alpha*[(kI*K*)-(1-dru)*Kt\_1]*PVIM+PVIA$	16
Capital Stock Updating	$Kt = ILpt+(1-dru)*(Kt\_1*PVKM+PVKA)$	36
Government Spending	$G = kG*[Gu \div Nu]*N*PVGM+PVGA$	20
	LABOR AND CAPITAL DEMAND LINKAGES	
Optimal Capital Stock	$K* = [W \div Wu]*cu \div c]*[E \div Eu]*Ku*$	15
Labor Intensity Adjustment	$LIAt = (1-salia)*LIAt\_1+salia*\{[c \div cu]^d*$	
	$[W \div Wu]^{(-d)}\}$	04
Labor Intensity	$EPV = LIA*[Eu \div Yu] \div [(A+PVAA) \div Au] \div (1+$	
	$PVEPA)^a$	05
Employment	$E = EPV*Y$	06
	POPULATION AND LABOR SUPPLY LINKAGES	
Migration	$MIG = [kM+PVQOLA+(\beta 1*ln(REO))+(\beta 2*$	
	$ln(RWR))]*Nt\_1+PVMIGA$	18
Population	$N = Nt\_1*[Nu \div Nut\_1]+MIG$	19

	WAGE, PRICE AND PROFIT LINKAGES	
Relative Production Costs	$P = [(W+PVwcA) \div Wu]^a * [(c+PVccA) \div cu^d$ $*(1+PVEPA)^{(a)} \div [(A+PVAA) \div Au] + PVPA$	21
Relative Profitability	$RPROFn = (1-P)+1$	22
Relative Profit Average	$RPROFAt = (1-sapr)*RPROFAt\_1 + sapr* \\ RPROFn$	23
Sales Price	$SPr = P*[A \div Au] = [W \div Wu]^a * [c \div cu]^d$	24
Sales Price Average	$SPAt = (1-sasp)*SPAt\_1 + sasp*SPr$	25
Housing Price	$PH = \varepsilon*[(N \div Nu) \div (Nt\_1 \div Nut\_1)-1] + PHt\_1 + \\ UPH + PVPHA$	26
Consumer Price Deflator	$CP = [(1-hsu)((1-ncsu)*SPr+ncsu)+hsu*PH] \\ *CPu + PVCPA$	27
Wage Rate	$W = (1+CPR\_\delta)^{tau}*(1+WD\_\delta)*(1+UWu)* \\ Wt\_1 + PVwA$	03
Consumer Price Change	$CPR\_\delta = [(CP \div CPu) \div (CPt\_1 \div CPut\_1)-1]$	28
Relative Wage Rate	$RWR = \{[W*(RYD \div YP)] \div Wu*(RYDu \div YPu]\}$	17
Employment by Residence	$ER = E*[(YLP+RA) \div YLP]$	29
Relative Employment Opportunity	$REO = [ER \div N] \div [Eu \div Nu]$	30
Wage Rate Changes	$WD\_\delta = [lambda1*((E-PVESA) \div EA-1)] + \\ [lambda2*(REO \div REOA-1)]$	31
REOA Updating	$REOAt = (1-sareo)*REOAt\_1 + sareo*REOt\_1$	32
EA Updating	$EAt = (1-saea)*EAt\_1 + saea*Et\_1$	33
	MARKET SHARE LINKAGES	
Regional Share Output	$R = [nslu*(kRN*RPROFA^{psi})+(1-nslu)*(kRR* \\ Y^{mu}*SPA^{xi})]*PVRM + PNRA$	34
Share of Extra-Market	$S*10^2 = 100*[(nseu*(kSN*RPROFA^{psi})+(1- \\ nseu)*(kSR*SPA^{XI}))*PVSM] + PVSA$	35

* This column indicates the order in which the equations are solved in each iteration.

TABLE 4-3

Values in the REMS Prototype Massachusetts Model

Endogenous	1989	Endogenous	1989	Endogenous	1989
Y	126.000	ILp	18.899	CP	1.262
XFG	70.923	G	11.577	W	25.907
C	77.986	K*	520.296	CPR_δ	-0.008
YLP	97.825	EPV	29.968	RWR	0.950
YP	131.500	E	3776.000	ER	3700.000
RDV	33.700	MIG	-36.900	REO	1.142
RA	-1.900	N	5912.500	WD_δ	-0.005
VSS	6.100	P	1.183	R	0.702
VP	18.400	RPROFn	0.817	S * 10²	3.050
DIR	23.300	SPr	1.093		
RYD	87.639	PH	1.670		

Parameters		Parameters		Parameters	
alpha	0.080	d	0.300	kVSS	0.934
beta1	0.296	dru	0.070	kVP	1.465
beta2	0.320	hsu	0.146	kRA	-0.019
epsilon	0.445	kC	0.939	kDIR	1.277
lambda1	0.024	kG	0.926	ncsu	0.259
lambda2	0.290	kI	0.850	nslu	0.214
tau	0.250	kM	-0.030	nseu	0.552
psi	1.830	kRN	1.016	tx	0.159
mu	0.000	kRR	0.738	sareo	1.000
xi	-0.563	kSN	0.044	saeaprsp	0.200
a	0.700	kSR	0.032	salia	0.063

Lag-Endogn	1989	Lag-Endogn	1988	Lag-Exogen	1988
Kt_1	224.912	Kt_1	221.519		
REOAt_1	1.165	REOAt_1	1.166		
EAt_1	3594.000	EAt_1	3547.000		
LIAt_1	0.984	Et_1	3787.000		
RPROFAt_1	0.817	Nt_1	5889.500	Nut_1	245800.000
SPAt_1	1.093	PHt_1	1.760		
		CPt_1	1.215	CPut_1	1.042
		Wt_1	24.836		
		REOt_1	1.165		
(used in 1990 calc)		(used in 1989 calc)		(used in 1989 calc)	

TABLE 4-4

United States and Policy Variable Values for the Prototype Model: (a) United States Values

Exogenous	1989	1990	1991	1992	1993	1994
A	0.924	0.924	0.924	0.924	0.924	0.924
Au	1.000	1.000	1.000	1.000	1.000	1.000
c	1.055	1.055	1.055	1.055	1.055	1.055
cu	1.000	1.000	1.000	1.000	1.000	1.000
Cu	3223.000	3262.000	3256.000	3314.000	3412.000	3494.000
CPu	1.091	1.146	1.194	1.229	1.273	1.332
DIRu	766.000	811.000	813.000	804.000	861.000	922.000
Eu	136074.000	137600.000	136100.000	135400.000	138000.000	140600.000
ERu	136074.000	137900.000	136100.000	135400.000	138000.000	140600.000
Gu	525.000	548.000	552.000	559.000	576.000	591.000
Ku*	17827.000	17251.000	16679.000	16893.000	17838.000	18228.000
Nu	248200.000	249500.000	251700.000	253900.000	256100.000	258300.000
RYDu	3401.000	3456.000	3533.000	3612.000	3702.000	3786.000
UPH	-0.087	0.000	0.000	0.000	0.000	0.000
UWu	0.050	0.049	0.038	0.043	0.039	0.058
VPu	637.000	699.000	774.000	885.000	909.000	962.000
VSSu	212.000	225.400	239.200	247.700	262.100	286.100
Wu	23.348	24.557	25.518	26.640	27.710	29.360
XFGu	2325.000	2349.000	2381.300	2421.700	2489.700	2523.600
Yu	4837.000	4885.000	4854.000	4995.000	5151.000	5249.000
YLPu	3177.000	3378.000	3473.000	3607.000	3824.000	4128.000
YPu	4367.000	4663.000	4820.000	5019.000	5332.000	5724.000

TABLE 4-4, cont.

(b) Policy Variable Default Values

Policies	1989	1990	1991	1992	1993	1994
PVOUTA	0.000	0.000	0.000	0.000	0.000	0.000
PVDEMA	0.000	0.000	0.000	0.000	0.000	0.000
PVRAA	0.000	0.000	0.000	0.000	0.000	0.000
PVVSSA	0.000	0.000	0.000	0.000	0.000	0.000
PVVPA	0.000	0.000	0.000	0.000	0.000	0.000
PVDIRA	0.000	0.000	0.000	0.000	0.000	0.000
PVCA	0.000	0.000	0.000	0.000	0.000	0.000
PVGA	0.000	0.000	0.000	0.000	0.000	0.000
PVIA	0.000	0.000	0.000	0.000	0.000	0.000
PVKA	0.000	0.000	0.000	0.000	0.000	0.000
PVEA	0.000	0.000	0.000	0.000	0.000	0.000
PVAA	0.000	0.000	0.000	0.000	0.000	0.000
PVEPA	0.000	0.000	0.000	0.000	0.000	0.000
PVESA	0.000	0.000	0.000	0.000	0.000	0.000
PVMIGA	0.000	0.000	0.000	0.000	0.000	0.000
PVQOLA	0.000	0.000	0.000	0.000	0.000	0.000
PVPA	0.000	0.000	0.000	0.000	0.000	0.000
PVccA	0.000	0.000	0.000	0.000	0.000	0.000
PVwcA	0.000	0.000	0.000	0.000	0.000	0.000
PVwA	0.000	0.000	0.000	0.000	0.000	0.000
PVPHA	0.000	0.000	0.000	0.000	0.000	0.000
PVCPA	0.000	0.000	0.000	0.000	0.000	0.000
PVtxA	0.000	0.000	0.000	0.000	0.000	0.000
PVRA	0.000	0.000	0.000	0.000	0.000	0.000
PVSA	0.000	0.000	0.000	0.000	0.000	0.000
PVCM	1.000	1.000	1.000	1.000	1.000	1.000
PVGM	1.000	1.000	1.000	1.000	1.000	1.000
PVIM	1.000	1.000	1.000	1.000	1.000	1.000
PVKM	1.000	1.000	1.000	1.000	1.000	1.000
PVRM	1.000	1.000	1.000	1.000	1.000	1.000
PVSM	1.000	1.000	1.000	1.000	1.000	1.000

Table 4-5

Baseline Forecast with the Prototype Model of Massachusetts

Endogenous	1989	1990	1991	1992	1993	1994
Y	126.000	125.131	121.931	121.918	125.717	128.229
XFG	70.923	71.522	72.597	73.969	76.090	77.111
C	77.986	77.876	74.123	73.221	74.319	75.928
YLP	97.825	101.850	102.505	103.081	109.724	118.893
YP	131.500	138.161	140.073	142.644	149.389	159.563
RDV	33.700	36.311	37.568	39.563	39.664	40.670
RA	-1.900	-1.935	-1.948	-1.959	-2.085	-2.259
VSS	6.100	6.347	6.594	6.612	7.024	7.696
VP	18.400	20.162	22.086	24.945	24.376	24.811
DIR	23.300	24.432	24.024	23.188	24.397	25.814
RYD	87.639	87.868	85.653	84.990	85.874	87.618
ILp	18.899	16.781	14.919	14.373	16.349	17.146
Kt	224.912	225.950	225.052	223.671	224.364	225.804
G	11.577	11.971	11.828	11.691	11.835	11.999
K*	520.296	492.865	466.615	457.596	485.156	497.623
LIAt	0.984	0.984	0.984	0.985	0.985	0.985
EPV	29.968	30.001	29.869	28.883	28.550	28.547
E	3776.000	3754.095	3641.925	3521.337	3589.218	3660.550
MIG	-36.900	-57.512	-113.548	-140.879	-101.245	-68.483
N	5912.500	5885.956	5824.309	5734.338	5682.779	5663.113
P	1.183	1.179	1.178	1.175	1.178	1.180
RPROFn	0.817	0.821	0.822	0.825	0.822	0.820
RPROFAt	0.817	0.818	0.819	0.820	0.820	0.820
SPr	1.093	1.090	1.088	1.086	1.089	1.091
SPAt	1.093	1.092	1.092	1.090	1.090	1.090
PH	1.670	1.666	1.657	1.647	1.639	1.633
CP	1.262	1.322	1.375	1.412	1.463	1.532
W	25.907	27.130	28.146	29.273	30.571	32.479
CPR_δ	-0.008	-0.002	-0.002	-0.003	0.001	0.000
RWR	0.950	0.948	0.920	0.910	0.913	0.918
ER	3700.000	3682.767	3572.729	3454.431	3521.023	3591.000
REO	1.142	1.135	1.134	1.130	1.150	1.165
WD_δ	-0.005	-0.001	0.000	-0.002	0.005	0.004
REOA	1.165	1.142	1.135	1.134	1.130	1.150
EA	3594.000	3630.400	3655.139	3652.496	3626.264	3618.855
R	0.702	0.702	0.703	0.704	0.704	0.704
S $*10^2$	3.050	3.045	3.049	3.054	3.056	3.056

Table 4-6

**Iterative Solution for the First Ten Variables in the
Massachusetts Prototype Model for 1990**

Iterations	Y	XFG	C	YLP	YP
0	126.00000	70.92300	77.98600	97.82500	131.50000
1	126.43476	71.64450	82.00197	102.37497	138.83911
2	128.43860	71.61259	79.77775	104.39534	141.34043
3	127.08587	71.54614	78.63712	104.30710	139.41646
4	126.07315	71.37596	78.28232	102.88475	139.46291
5	125.58290	71.47614	77.99387	102.45875	138.52981
6	125.30308	71.48056	77.93455	102.06111	138.42188
7	125.20147	71.50949	77.88836	101.95126	138.22533
8	125.15310	71.51412	77.88192	101.87913	138.19955
9	125.13857	71.51972	77.87649	101.86190	138.16820
10	125.13261	71.52065	77.87648	101.85213	138.16527
11	125.13137	71.52149	77.87611	101.85056	138.16137
12	125.13098	71.52159	77.87631	101.84967	138.16144
13	125.13102	71.52168	77.87633	101.84973	138.16111
14	125.13106	71.52168	77.87639	101.84972	138.16124
15	125.13111	71.52169	77.87640	101.84978	138.16124
16	125.13113	71.52168	77.87641	101.84980	138.16127

Iterations	RDV	RA	VSS	VP	DIR
0	33.70000	-1.90000	6.10000	18.40000	23.30000
1	36.46414	-1.94512	6.38021	20.24734	24.54214
2	36.94509	-1.98351	6.50612	20.62982	24.80491
3	35.10936	-1.98183	6.50062	19.19435	24.39747
4	36.57816	-1.95481	6.41198	20.24094	24.70401
5	36.07106	-1.94672	6.38543	19.95218	24.45103
6	36.36077	-1.93916	6.36065	20.17039	24.49019
7	36.27407	-1.93707	6.35380	20.12778	24.43717
8	36.32043	-1.93570	6.34931	20.16412	24.44132
9	36.30630	-1.93538	6.34823	20.15743	24.43247
10	36.31314	-1.93519	6.34762	20.16281	24.43315
11	36.31081	-1.93516	6.34753	20.16160	24.43189
12	36.31177	-1.93514	6.34747	20.16232	24.43207
13	36.31138	-1.93514	6.34748	20.16209	24.43192
14	36.31152	-1.93514	6.34747	20.16218	24.43196
15	36.31145	-1.93515	6.34748	20.16213	24.43195
16	36.31147	-1.93515	6.34748	20.16214	24.43196

Table 4-7

The Effects of Increasing Output by One Billion 1987 Dollars

Endogenous	1990	1991	1992	1993	1994
Y	1.887	1.766	1.698	1.697	1.702
XFG	1.355	1.311	1.283	1.265	1.256
C	0.746	0.770	0.794	0.841	0.885
YLP	1.944	1.811	1.702	1.717	1.803
YP	1.589	1.702	1.780	1.921	2.099
RDV	-0.355	-0.110	0.078	0.205	0.296
RA	-0.037	-0.034	-0.032	-0.032	-0.034
VSS	0.122	0.117	0.109	0.110	0.117
VP	-0.293	-0.120	0.020	0.106	0.170
DIR	0.096	0.161	0.200	0.242	0.278
RYD	0.841	0.890	0.921	0.971	1.021
ILp	0.640	0.513	0.431	0.408	0.382
Kt	0.639	1.108	1.462	1.766	2.025
G	0.047	0.079	0.100	0.117	0.129
K*	9.407	8.245	7.552	7.592	7.548
LIAt	0.000	0.000	-0.001	-0.001	0.000
EPV	-0.002	-0.004	-0.005	-0.006	-0.007
E	56.307	52.268	48.423	47.674	47.692
MIG	23.182	15.672	9.949	6.377	4.287
N	23.182	39.058	49.349	56.154	60.924
P	0.004	0.003	0.002	0.002	0.002
RPROFn	-0.004	-0.003	-0.002	-0.002	-0.002
RPROFAt	-0.001	-0.001	-0.001	-0.001	-0.001
SPr	0.003	0.003	0.002	0.001	0.001
SPAt	0.001	0.001	0.002	0.001	0.001
PH	0.001	0.003	0.003	0.004	0.005
CP	0.003	0.003	0.002	0.002	0.002
W	0.110	0.092	0.080	0.071	0.069
CPR_δ	0.001	0.000	0.000	0.000	0.000
RWR	0.002	0.002	0.001	0.001	0.001
ER	55.238	51.274	47.504	46.768	46.786
REO	0.012	0.009	0.005	0.004	0.003
WD_δ	0.003	-0.001	-0.001	0.000	0.000
REOA	0.000	0.012	0.009	0.005	0.004
EA	0.000	11.261	19.463	25.255	29.739
R	0.000	-0.001	-0.001	-0.001	-0.001
S $*10^2$	-0.003	-0.005	-0.005	-0.006	-0.007

Table 4-8

The Effects of a 10 Percent Increase in Labor Productivity

Endogenous	1990	1991	1992	1993	1994
Y	2.297	7.591	11.781	15.554	18.764
XFG	2.008	3.503	4.651	5.614	6.321
C	0.755	2.608	4.288	5.949	7.599
YLP	-7.262	-2.018	1.981	5.354	8.656
YP	-5.483	-1.453	2.231	5.818	9.641
RDV	1.780	0.564	0.250	0.466	0.985
RA	0.138	0.039	-0.037	-0.101	-0.164
VSS	-0.452	-0.130	0.127	0.343	0.561
VP	1.311	0.336	0.030	0.089	0.371
DIR	-0.122	0.059	0.384	0.821	1.339
RYD	0.851	3.015	4.977	6.874	8.769
ILp	-2.389	-0.447	0.796	1.736	2.451
Kt	-2.390	-2.669	-1.686	0.167	2.607
G	-0.060	0.029	0.193	0.399	0.622
K*	-35.142	-9.186	8.791	23.671	36.232
LIAt	0.001	0.001	0.000	0.000	0.001
EPV	-1.922	-1.908	-1.842	-1.820	-1.822
E	-176.079	-20.299	94.030	186.877	267.909
MIG	-29.486	44.176	80.455	95.368	100.923
N	-29.486	14.429	95.010	191.202	293.767
P	-0.096	-0.087	-0.082	-0.078	-0.076
RPROFn	0.096	0.087	0.082	0.078	0.076
RPROFAt	0.019	0.032	0.042	0.050	0.055
SPr	-0.089	-0.080	-0.076	-0.073	-0.071
SPAt	-0.017	-0.031	-0.039	-0.046	-0.051
PH	-0.003	0.001	0.007	0.014	0.023
CP	-0.064	-0.060	-0.058	-0.056	-0.056
W	-0.694	-0.400	-0.213	-0.096	-0.011
CPR_δ	-0.049	0.005	0.004	0.002	0.003
RWR	0.023	0.029	0.031	0.034	0.034
ER	-172.734	-19.914	92.244	183.327	262.818
REO	-0.048	-0.009	0.011	0.020	0.024
WD_δ	-0.013	0.010	0.006	0.004	0.002
REOA	0.000	-0.048	-0.009	0.011	0.020
EA	0.000	-35.216	-32.232	-6.980	31.792
R	0.012	0.020	0.026	0.031	0.034
S $*10^2$	0.085	0.147	0.192	0.226	0.250

Table 4-9

The Effects of Improving the Quality of Life by a Change that is Valued at 6.4 Percent of the Average Wage

Endogenous	1990	1991	1992	1993	1994
Y	0.945	1.775	2.580	3.324	4.028
XFG	0.041	0.104	0.177	0.257	0.333
C	0.871	1.583	2.268	2.849	3.416
YLP	0.527	1.079	1.655	2.243	2.964
YP	1.534	2.992	4.447	5.785	7.281
RDV	1.007	1.913	2.792	3.543	4.317
RA	-0.010	-0.020	-0.031	-0.042	-0.056
VSS	0.033	0.069	0.106	0.144	0.192
VP	0.642	1.257	1.921	2.407	2.929
DIR	0.407	0.745	1.009	1.322	1.636
RYD	0.982	1.830	2.632	3.292	3.942
ILp	0.174	0.321	0.463	0.607	0.735
Kt	0.173	0.483	0.912	1.454	2.088
G	0.200	0.367	0.508	0.641	0.760
K*	2.552	4.910	7.346	9.916	12.408
LIAt	0.000	0.000	0.000	0.000	0.000
EPV	0.002	0.003	0.006	0.009	0.012
E	28.529	53.454	75.286	96.037	116.582
MIG	98.147	81.641	67.213	56.115	48.629
N	98.147	180.653	249.445	307.723	358.996
P	-0.002	-0.003	-0.005	-0.005	-0.005
RPROFn	0.002	0.003	0.005	0.005	0.005
RPROFAt	0.000	0.001	0.002	0.003	0.003
SPr	-0.002	-0.003	-0.004	-0.005	-0.006
SPAt	0.000	-0.001	-0.001	-0.002	-0.003
PH	0.007	0.014	0.018	0.023	0.027
CP	0.000	0.000	0.000	0.001	0.001
W	-0.065	-0.115	-0.152	-0.189	-0.217
CPR_δ	-0.001	0.000	0.000	0.000	0.001
RWR	-0.002	-0.004	-0.005	-0.006	-0.006
ER	27.987	52.438	73.856	94.212	114.366
REO	-0.011	-0.018	-0.024	-0.030	-0.035
WD_δ	-0.002	-0.002	-0.001	-0.001	-0.001
REOA	0.000	-0.011	-0.018	-0.024	-0.030
EA	0.000	5.706	15.256	27.262	41.017
R	0.001	0.001	0.001	0.001	0.002
S $*10^2$	0.002	0.004	0.008	0.011	0.013

Table 4-10

The Effects of Increasing the Average Wage by One Thousand Dollars Starting in 1990

Endogenous	1990	1991	1992	1993	1994
Y	0.907	-0.941	-2.170	-3.147	-3.920
XFG	-0.698	-1.170	-1.506	-1.772	-1.953
C	1.334	0.680	0.220	-0.195	-0.580
YLP	4.881	2.656	1.197	0.185	-0.677
YP	4.828	3.429	2.379	1.485	0.650
RDV	-0.053	0.773	1.181	1.301	1.327
RA	-0.093	-0.050	-0.022	-0.003	0.013
VSS	0.305	0.171	0.076	0.012	-0.044
VP	0.168	0.794	1.135	1.252	1.314
DIR	0.175	0.200	0.146	0.065	-0.043
RYD	1.505	0.786	0.255	-0.225	-0.670
ILp	1.607	0.703	0.198	-0.111	-0.340
Kt	1.606	2.197	2.241	1.972	1.495
G	0.086	0.099	0.073	0.032	-0.020
K*	23.620	12.089	5.313	0.816	-2.831
LIAt	-0.001	-0.001	-0.002	-0.003	-0.003
EPV	-0.023	-0.041	-0.054	-0.066	-0.077
E	24.344	-33.057	-69.154	-97.926	-121.460
MIG	42.269	5.892	-13.000	-21.297	-24.556
N	42.269	48.532	35.956	14.972	-9.455
P	0.034	0.029	0.026	0.025	0.024
RPROFn	-0.034	-0.029	-0.026	-0.025	-0.024
RPROFAt	-0.007	-0.012	-0.014	-0.016	-0.017
SPr	0.031	0.027	0.024	0.022	0.021
SPAt	0.007	0.010	0.013	0.015	0.016
PH	0.003	0.004	0.002	0.001	0.000
CP	0.024	0.021	0.019	0.018	0.018
W	1.117	0.994	0.934	0.910	0.924
CPR_δ	0.017	-0.002	-0.001	-0.001	0.000
RWR	0.022	0.018	0.016	0.016	0.015
ER	23.882	-32.430	-67.839	-96.065	-119.153
REO	-0.001	-0.019	-0.029	-0.034	-0.037
WD_δ	0.000	-0.005	-0.003	-0.002	-0.001
REOA	0.000	-0.001	-0.019	-0.029	-0.034
EA	0.000	4.869	-2.716	-16.004	-32.388
R	-0.004	-0.007	-0.009	-0.010	-0.011
S $*10^2$	-0.030	-0.050	-0.062	-0.071	-0.078

Table 4-11

The Effect of Increasing the Local Supply
Proportion (R) by 0.006

Endogenous	1990	1991	1992	1993	1994
Y	2.033	1.851	1.777	1.834	1.877
XFG	-0.074	-0.120	-0.147	-0.168	-0.180
C	0.804	0.809	0.834	0.903	0.966
YLP	2.096	1.896	1.779	1.861	1.997
YP	1.713	1.788	1.867	2.066	2.296
RDV	-0.383	-0.108	0.088	0.206	0.299
RA	-0.040	-0.036	-0.033	-0.035	-0.038
VSS	0.131	0.122	0.114	0.119	0.130
VP	-0.316	-0.121	0.025	0.103	0.167
DIR	0.104	0.171	0.211	0.257	0.299
RYD	0.907	0.936	0.967	1.043	1.115
ILp	0.690	0.536	0.449	0.445	0.428
Kt	0.689	1.177	1.544	1.880	2.177
G	0.051	0.084	0.106	0.125	0.139
K*	10.142	8.630	7.896	8.226	8.361
LIAt	0.000	0.000	-0.001	-0.001	-0.001
EPV	-0.002	-0.004	-0.006	-0.006	-0.007
E	60.690	54.754	50.661	51.539	52.638
MIG	24.974	16.226	10.253	7.256	5.337
N	24.974	41.419	52.034	59.742	65.593
P	0.004	0.003	0.002	0.002	0.002
RPROFn	-0.004	-0.003	-0.002	-0.002	-0.002
RPROFAt	-0.001	-0.002	-0.001	-0.001	-0.001
SPr	0.003	0.003	0.002	0.001	0.001
SPAt	0.001	0.001	0.002	0.001	0.002
PH	0.002	0.003	0.003	0.004	0.005
CP	0.003	0.003	0.002	0.002	0.002
W	0.118	0.096	0.083	0.078	0.078
CPR_δ	0.002	0.000	0.000	0.000	0.000
RWR	0.002	0.002	0.001	0.001	0.001
ER	59.537	53.713	49.699	50.560	51.638
REO	0.013	0.009	0.006	0.004	0.003
WD_δ	0.004	-0.001	-0.001	0.000	0.000
REOA	0.000	0.013	0.009	0.006	0.004
EA	0.000	12.138	20.661	26.662	31.637
R	0.006	0.005	0.005	0.005	0.005
S $*10^2$	-0.003	-0.005	-0.006	-0.007	-0.008

Table 4-12

The Effects of a Balanced Budget Increase in State
Government Spending and Income Tax Rates

Endogenous	1990	1991	1992	1993	1994
Y	-0.021	-0.161	-0.313	-0.450	-0.574
XFG	-0.014	-0.031	-0.048	-0.067	-0.082
C	-1.028	-1.104	-1.212	-1.325	-1.439
YLP	0.063	-0.023	-0.136	-0.243	-0.362
YP	-0.158	-0.398	-0.654	-0.883	-1.130
RDV	-0.222	-0.376	-0.518	-0.639	-0.768
RA	-0.001	0.001	0.003	0.005	0.007
VSS	0.004	-0.001	-0.009	-0.015	-0.023
VP	-0.147	-0.252	-0.360	-0.438	-0.524
DIR	-0.070	-0.126	-0.169	-0.221	-0.275
RYD	-1.160	-1.274	-1.408	-1.531	-1.660
ILp	0.021	-0.008	-0.042	-0.070	-0.096
Kt	0.020	0.011	-0.032	-0.101	-0.189
G	1.011	0.957	0.924	0.914	0.914
K*	0.308	-0.104	-0.604	-1.075	-1.514
LIAt	0.000	0.000	-0.001	0.000	0.000
EPV	0.000	-0.001	-0.002	-0.002	-0.003
E	-0.700	-4.942	-9.247	-13.151	-16.774
MIG	-16.772	-13.589	-11.186	-9.376	-8.081
N	-16.772	-30.510	-41.963	-51.701	-60.226
P	0.001	0.001	0.001	0.001	0.002
RPROFn	-0.001	-0.001	-0.001	-0.001	-0.002
RPROFAt	0.000	-0.0001	-0.001	0.000	-0.001
SPr	0.000	0.001	0.001	0.001	0.001
SPAt	0.000	0.000	0.001	0.001	0.001
PH	-0.002	-0.002	-0.004	-0.004	-0.004
CP	0.001	0.001	0.000	0.000	0.000
W	0.022	0.032	0.039	0.044	0.051
CPR_δ	0.000	0.000	0.000	0.000	0.000
RWR	-0.011	-0.010	-0.010	-0.009	-0.009
ER	-0.687	-4.849	-9.071	-12.901	-16.456
REO	0.003	0.005	0.005	0.006	0.007
WD_δ	0.001	0.000	0.000	0.000	0.000
REOA	0.000	0.003	0.005	0.005	0.006
EA	0.000	-0.140	-1.100	-2.729	-4.814
R	0.000	0.000	-0.001	0.000	-0.001
S $*10^2$	-0.001	-0.002	-0.002	-0.002	-0.004

NOTES ON CHAPTER 4

1. The material in this chapter uses the output from the REMS System which was programmed by Chengfeng Lou. Earlier versions were programmed by Rafael Bradley and Frederick Treyz.

2. This can be done using policy variables PVOUTA and PVIA in table 4-1.

3. Prototype model history is 1989 – 1991. REMI EDFS-53 model forecsat is for 1992 – 1994.

4. Historical data is 1990 – 1991. REMI EDFS-53 model forecast is for 1992 – 1994.

5. Historical data is 1990 – 1991. REMI EDFS-53 model forecast is for 1992 – 1994.

6. Historical data is 1990 – 1991. REMI EDFS-53 model forecast is for 1992 – 1994.

7. Historical data is 1990 – 1991. REMI EDFS-53 model forecast is for 1992 – 1994.

CHAPTER 5

ALTERNATIVE MODEL SPECIFICATIONS

Our prototype model assumes that an increase in wages will increase the number of people seeking work and reduce the number of available jobs. Some other regional models assume that the labor market responds differently. In this chapter, we use alternative versions of our prototype model to examine the implications of these alternative assumptions and specifications. We conclude the chapter with a discussion of how a model can help to clarify issues relating to evidence about real wage and nominal wage convergence.

We focus our discussion on labor markets, because wages and employment are key factors in explaining regional economic change. Interest costs are less important, because they are affected by national rather than regional changes in supply and demand. Housing and land prices are determined by the local market. They affect the economy through the cost of living for individuals and the cost of commercial and industrial space for business. These elements will be incorporated at the end of the chapter.

Basic Model Linkages

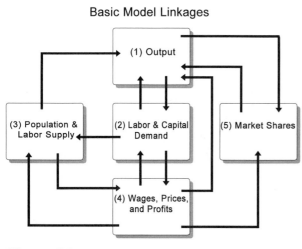

Diagram 5-1

The labor market is given by sectors (2), (3), and (4) in diagram 5-1. Labor and capital demand (2) interact with population and labor supply (3) to determine wages, prices, and profits (4). These, in turn, determine shares of the local and national markets (5).

5-1 THE LABOR MARKET IN THE PROTOTYPE MODEL

In diagram 5-2, the labor market is shown as the intersection of the supply and demand curve for labor. The diagram simplifies the determination of the wage rate and employment change in a regional economy. These variables are shown as the direct market-clearing equilibrium, when in fact, wages and employment changes occur through adjustments that take place gradually over time. These time lags were brought into the wage equation in chapter 3 (equation 3-56) by using current values (E, REO) divided by moving average values (EA, REOA) as explanatory variables. They were brought into the demand curve by introducing LIA, SPA, and RPROFA. They were brought into the supply curve through the time required for migration to change the size of the labor force.

Supply and Demand for Labor

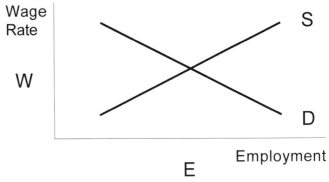

Diagram 5-2

Demand and Supply Curves

Diagram 5-3 shows the key endogenous linkages that give the prototype model a downward sloping demand curve for labor. A downward-sloping demand curve indicates that more people are hired when wages are low. Low wages increase the intensity of labor use and lower production costs. Decreased production costs increase the profitability of national industries and lower the sales prices for regional industries. Both effects lead to an increase in export (S) share and local (R) supply share. These share increases raise employment by increasing output.

The number of people seeking work increases with higher wages, as indicated by the upward-sloping supply curve shown in diagram 5-2. Diagram 5-4 illustrates the linkages that give this slope to the supply curve. An increase in the wage rate causes migration into the region, which increases the number of job seekers. The feedback of this increase through the effects of the population change on relative employment opportunity mitigates but does not reverse the effects of the change in wage on migration and, thus, the number of people seeking employment.

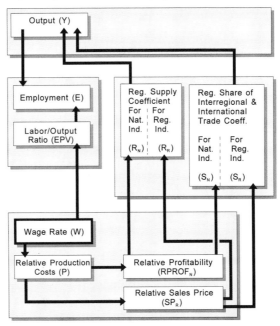

Key Linkages for Downward Sloping Labor Demand Curve

Diagram 5-3

The equilibrium wage rate and employment are determined by the interaction of supply and demand. Therefore, we must simultaneously solve all of the demand and supply relationships. The equilibrium solutions, given the lagged responses along a dynamic time path, are obtained by running our prototype model. This is done in chapters 3 and 4. The effects of exogenous changes can be found as the difference between the alternative and control forecasts. We begin here, however, by analyzing the effects of economic changes using a combination of a static Keynesian diagram and a static regional labor market diagram.

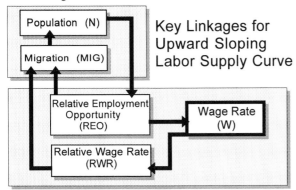

Key Linkages for Upward Sloping Labor Supply Curve

Diagram 5-4

A Representation of Wage and Employment Determination Using Keynesian and Neoclassical Diagrams[1]

Equilibrium wages and employment are determined by the interaction of supply and demand. The responses to economic change are based on macroeconomic theory. Here, we integrate the Keynesian and neoclassical diagrams. We start by showing the effects of an exogenous change in exports in the Keynesian diagram at the top of diagram 5-5.

Determination of Employment and Wage Rate Using Two Static Diagrams

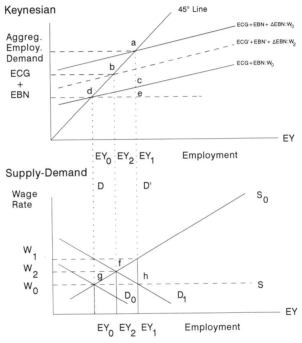

Diagram 5-5

The Keynesian diagram shows the change in aggregate demand caused by an increase in net export employment (EBN). The vertical axis represents the demand for labor (ECG + EBN); the horizontal axis represents the use of labor (EY). Thus, the 45-degree line gives us all of the points at which the demand for employees is equal to employment. The Keynesian demand lines are upward-sloping, because higher employment stimulates consumption and government spending and is therefore associated with increased demand for employment. Before the exogenous change, the equilibrium employment and wage rate is determined by the intersection of the 45-

degree line and the initial aggregate demand line (ECG + EBN) at point d. Assuming that employment for the production of output equals the demand for employment, the initial equilibrium is at EY_0.

To show the effect of an exogenous change, we assume that exports (the economic base) increase by ΔEBN. This shifts the aggregate demand line up to ECG + EBN + ΔEBN (W_0), intersecting the 45-degree line at equilibrium point a. If we assume that wages do not change from the initial level of W_0 in the short run, equilibrium demand for workers and the level of employment is at EY_1.

Part of this increase in employment is caused by the exogenous shift in demand for exports, the distance between the two solid Keynesian demand lines, or the distance between points a and c. The rest of the employment increase is caused by the Keynesian multiplier. This is represented by the upward sloping Keynesian demand curves, so that an endogenous increase in employment is associated with an exogenous shift. The magnitude of this change is given by distance $c - e$, showing the change caused by the movement along the demand curve. Total endogenous and exogenous changes are equal to the distance from $a - e$, which corresponds to the equilibrium change in employment ($EY_1 - EY_0$) given along the horizontal axis.

In our Keynesian diagram, we assume that, in the short run, an exogenous increase in exports will not change wages from their initial level. Next, wages increase to W_2, and the aggregate demand curve shifts downward to ECG' + EBN' + ΔEBN at wage rate W_2. Equilibrium employment is at point b at employment EY_2. Thus, the total equilibrium change caused by the exogenous increase in exports is equal to $EY_2 - EY_0$. In diagram 5-5, we also show how the supply-demand diagram is associated with the Keynesian diagram. The supply-demand diagram shows the wage rate on the vertical axis and employment on the horizontal axis. Initial equilibrium employment is EY_0 at wage rate W_0, corresponding to the initial equilibrium wage and employment in the Keynesian diagram. This is shown as the intersection of the downward-sloping demand curve D_0 and upward-sloping supply curve S_0 at point g.

The increase in exports shifts the demand curve from D_0 to D_1. Assuming that wage rates do not change in the very short term, equilibrium output increases to EY_1, corresponding to the Keynesian determination of output. In the supply-demand diagram, this is given by the demand for workers at wage W_0, shown at point h on demand curve D_1. Since the employment exceeds the supply of employees at W_0 by ($EY_1 - EY_0$), we might assume that workers were fooled in such a way that they thought the real wage was W_1, when in fact it was W_0.

In the next period, wages increase. This is shown in the Keynesian diagram by the downward shift in the aggregate demand curve. In the supply-demand diagram, a labor shortage would occur if wage rates remain at W_0, because only EY_0 workers would be willing to work at this wage, while producers would want to hire EY_1 employees. Thus, as wages increase, the number of employees is reduced. This change is given by the movement along the demand curve from h to f. Equilibrium is given by the intersection of the original supply curve (S_0) and the shifted demand curve (D_1) at point f. This equilibrium is given by wage rate W_2 and employment level EY_2 in both diagrams. This is only a partial answer if the supply curve is a short or intermediate period curve and shifts out in the long run in response to inward migration. We present a more complete theory at the end of this chapter, which includes both wage rates and land prices.

Alternative Versions of the Prototype Model

We can alter the prototype model by suppressing one or more of the equations in the model. Using this process, we can see how sensitive simulation results are to certain assumptions in the model. In this section, we consider an exogenous increase in output by one billion 1987 dollars, as we did in the first simulation in chapter 4. By suppressing a number of key equations, we start with **case 1**, a version of the model where the only equations that are part of the model system are as follows:[2]

$$Y = R \times (C + IL_p + G + XFG) \qquad (3\text{-}1)$$

$$XFG = S \times XFG^u + PVOUTA \div R \qquad (3\text{-}2)$$

$$C = k_C \times (C^u \div RYD^u) \times RYD \qquad (3\text{-}3)$$

$$RYD = (1 - tx)(YP \div CP) \qquad (3\text{-}7)$$

$$YP = YLP + RDV \qquad (3\text{-}5)$$

$$E = EPV \times Y \qquad (3\text{-}31)$$

$$YLP = W \times E, \qquad (3\text{-}4)$$

where IL_p, G, S, R, CP, RDV, EPV, W, and ($C^u \div RYD^u$) are now exogenous variables.

A close comparison of this model with the extended economic base model (see diagrams 2-12 and 3-2 and equations 2-211 through 2-220) indicates that the models are very similar. In this case, G is exogenous instead of being combined with consumption, as it is in the extended economic base model (CG). Taxes are removed from personal income here but not in the base model. Both differences are slight, but they might be expected to reduce the size of the multiplier compared to the extended economic base multiplier. The results of the predicted effects of the one billion 1987 dollar increase in output (PVOUTA = 1.0), using this model, are shown on table 5-1 in the appendix to this chapter.

As expected, an examination of the predicted effects of this policy indicate a fairly consistent effect over the forecast horizon. The one billion 1987 dollars of direct stimulus to the net economic base (BN), as defined in chapter 2, leads to an increase in total output of 1.474 billion 1987 dollars in the first year and amounts between that value and 1.455 billion 1987 dollars in subsequent years. Upon inspection, it becomes apparent that the reason for the slight fluctuation is the change in ($C^u \div RYD^u$) from year to year. From table 2 in chapter 3, the values are .944, .922, .917, .922, and .923 for 1990 through 1994 respectively.

These values, multiplied by the k_C parameter of .939, become the marginal and average propensity to consume in the prototype model. This can be confirmed by dividing the change in consumption (C) by the change in real disposable income (RYD) in table 5-1. It is no surprise that the multiplier changes over the years are in proportion to the change in the marginal propensity to consume. Given the fixed EPV, the employment multiplier is the same as the output multiplier. Since the wage rate is fixed in this model, it would be analogous to the model in diagram 5-5 if the supply curve were horizontal.

For the next case, **case 2**, we add the following equations to the case 1 model:

$$RDV = - VSS + RA + DIR + VP \tag{3-6}$$

$$RA = \begin{cases} k_{RA} \times YLP & \text{if } k_{RA} < 0 \\ k_{RA} \times YLP^u & \text{if } k_{RA} > 0 \end{cases} \tag{3-10}$$

$$VSS = k_{VSS} \times \left(\frac{VSS^u}{YLP^u} \right) \times YLP \tag{3-11}$$

$$VP = k_{VP} \times \left(\frac{VP^u}{N^u - E^u} \right) \times (N - ER) \tag{3-12}$$

$$DIR = k_{DIR} \times \left(\frac{DIR^u}{N^u} \right) \times N \qquad (3\text{-}13)$$

$$MIG = \{ k_M + [\beta_1 \times \ln(REO)] + [\beta_2 \times \ln(RWR)] \} \times N_{t-1} \qquad (3\text{-}32)$$

$$N_t = N_{t-1} \left[\frac{N_t^u}{N_{t-1}^u} \right] + MIG \qquad (3\text{-}33)$$

$$REO = \left[\frac{ER}{N} \right] \div \left[\frac{E^u}{N^u} \right] \qquad (3\text{-}53)$$

$$CP = \left[(1 - hs^u) \times \left((1 - ncs^u) \times SP_R + ncs^u \right) + (hs^u \times PH) \right] \times CP^u \qquad (3\text{-}43)$$

$$W = (1 + \Delta WD)(1 + \Delta CPR)^{\tau}(1 + UW^u) \times W_{t-1} \qquad (3\text{-}44)$$

The last two equations include endogenous feedback terms. However, since ΔWD (equation 3-56) is not activated, there is no feedback to these equations. It was necessary to activate the price equation (CP), because the nonwage portion of personal income is in nominal dollars, not real dollars. It was then necessary to activate the nonendogenous portion of the wage equation in order to have nominal wages grow in line with the price index.[3] In comparing a simulation where W and CP are included to a simulation where both were set at their 1989 values, the results do not differ noticeably. Therefore, the main effect of the change made from case 1 to case 2 is to make the nonlabor income components of personal income endogenous. The results of repeating the same simulation as that run for case 1, except with endogenous nonlabor income components (RDV), is shown on table 5-2 in the appendix.

The difference between case 1 and case 2 is due both to the amount and to the changes over time of the RDV values. In the first year, transfer payments (VP) are reduced substantially by the larger increase in employment than in population. This decrease is only partially offset by the increase in property income (DIR) and is accentuated by the higher social security taxes (VSS) and increased negative residence adjustment (RA). As the population increases, however, VP becomes positive. DIR increases enough so that RDV becomes positive. This makes the predicted output effect in the last year 1.542, as opposed to a value of 1.459 in the case 1 model. In the first year, however, the situation was reversed when the value was 1.474 for case 1 and only 1.325 for case 2. Thus, the addition of RDV, which depends on the stock of population and can only adjust over time in response to the flow of migrants, adds an important dynamic element that shows that a static multiplier, such as the one produced by the economic base model, may not be adequate for planning purposes.

For **case 3**, we repeat all of the assumptions of case 2, with the addition of the government spending equation.

$$G = k_G \times \left[\frac{G^u}{N^u} \right] \times N \tag{3-16}$$

The results are shown on table 5-3 in the appendix. Comparing the results with case 2, we note that the predicted output (Y) change increases by 2% in the first year [$((1.350 \div 1.325) - 1) \times 100]$ and by 7% [$((1.651 \div 1.542) - 1) \times 100]$ in the last year. These results, which are larger and grow as the size of the population increases in response to the reduction in the amount of outward migration, cause increases in government spending.

In **case 4**, we add endogenous investment (IL_p) to the case 3 model. This is accomplished by adding the following equations:

$$IL_{p,t} = \alpha \left[(k_I K_t^*) - (1 - dr^u) K_{t-1} \right] \tag{3-14}$$

$$K_t = IL_{p,t} + (1 - dr^u) K_{t-1} \tag{3-15}$$

$$K^* = \left[\frac{W}{W^u} \right] \times \left[\frac{c^u}{c} \right] \times \left[\frac{E}{E^u} \right] \times K^{u*} \tag{3-24}$$

The effects of adding endogenous investment, on table 5-4 in the appendix, show a dramatic increase in Y and E compared with case 3. The effect on Y in the first year is now 1.815, as opposed to 1.351 for case 3, which is a 34% increase. In the last year, the percentage increase is also 34% [$((2.212 \div 1.651) - 1) \times 100]$. Since investment is a stock adjustment process, it will fall as K grows. In this case, however, the growing Y is enough to offset this trend, so investment stays constant through 1994.

Up to this point, we have maintained a constant wage rate (W). This means that we have been working within the framework of an exogenous wage rate, as in diagram 5-5 before the change in wages, to the extent that this comparative static diagram can represent the dynamic process taking place in the model.

In **case 5**, we introduce an endogenous feedback to wages from changes in the labor market by adding the following equations:[4]

$$\Delta WD = \left[\lambda_1 \times \left(\frac{E}{EA} - 1 \right) \right] + \left[\lambda_2 \times \left(\frac{REO}{REOA} - 1 \right) \right] \qquad (3\text{-}56)$$

$$REOA_t = (1 - sareo) \times REOA_{t-1} + sareo \times REO_{t-1} \qquad (3\text{-}55)$$

$$EA_t = (1 - saea) \times EA_{t-1} + saea \times E_{t-1} \qquad (3\text{-}50)$$

$$RWR = \left[\frac{W \times (RYD \div YP)}{W^u \times (RYD^u \div YP^u)} \right] \qquad (3\text{-}46)$$

The effect of adding these equations is to lead to an endogenous response to changing economic conditions. However, the feedbacks that would reduce employment as wages increase are not yet activated. Thus, in terms of the bottom half of diagram 5-5, the demand curve on the lower half of the diagram will not slope downward, due to competitive effects and factor substitution effects. Furthermore, increasing wages without these feedbacks means that the Keynesian demand curve shifts up even further as wages rise, indicating a demand curve that *increases* employment demand as wages increase. This would be an upward sloping demand curve on the bottom half of diagram 5-5.

The results of case 5 are shown in table 5-5 in the appendix. The effects of the one billion 1987 dollar exogenous output stimulus on Y is 31% more in case 5 than it was in case 4 for the first year [((2.373 ÷ 1.815) − 1) × 100]. It maintains this 31% increase through 1994 [((2.906 ÷ 2.212) − 1) × 100]. A major reason for the increase is the rise in investment caused by the shift toward capital as wage costs are increased in equation 3-24. This shift occurs even though we have not yet activated the shift away from labor in equations 3-29 and 3-30. The other reason for the increase is the wage growth of .4% (.102 ÷ 25.907), or an $118 increase in the average wage in the first year and somewhat less in later years. This increase, applied to all wages in the state, had a very large effect on labor and proprietors' income (YLP), which was 61% (2.380 ÷ 1.477) higher in case 5 than in case 4 in the first year. Of course, this also leads to higher consumption.

For **case 6**, as shown on table 5-6 in the appendix, we introduce a downward sloping demand curve, as in diagram 5-5, for the first time. In this case, as wages increase, we allow the competitive effects to reduce market shares (R and S) and the inflation effect to reduce consumption. We do this by adding the following equations to the case 5 model:

$$P = \left[\frac{W}{W^u}\right]^a \times \left[\frac{c}{c^u}\right]^d \div \left[\frac{A}{A^u}\right] \tag{3-38}$$

$$RPROF_N = (1 - P) + 1 \tag{3-39}$$

$$RPROFA_t = (1 - sapr)RPROFA_{t-1} + sapr\,RPROF_{N,t} \tag{3-58}$$

$$SP_R = \left[\frac{W}{W^u}\right]^a \times \left[\frac{c}{c^u}\right]^d = P \times \left[\frac{A}{A^u}\right] \tag{3-41}$$

$$SPA_t = (1 - sasp) \times SPA_{t-1} + sasp\,SP_{R,t} \tag{3-63}$$

$$R = nsl^u(k_{RN} \times RPROFA^{\psi}) + (1 - nsl^u)(k_{RR} \times Y^{\mu}SPA^{\xi}) \tag{3-66}$$

$$S = nse^u(k_{SN} \times RPROFA^{\psi}) + (1 - nse^u)(k_{SR} \times SPA^{\xi}) \tag{3-67}$$

Now, as the economy expands in response to the policy stimulus, production costs (P) go up, reducing profits ($RPROF_N$) for the part of local industries that must sell at national prices and raising sales prices (SP_R) for the part that sells at locally determined prices. Both movements reduce market shares in local (R) and extraregional (S) markets. The net effect, as shown in diagram 5-5, is to reduce the effect of the stimulus. Here, the effect on Y is 19% lower [((1.917 ÷ 2.373) − 1) × 100] in the first year and 34% lower [((1.914 ÷ 2.906) − 1) × 100] in the fifth year of simulation.

In **case 7**, we also let the increase in wage rates feed back to labor intensity

(LIA) and, therefore, to employees per dollar of value added (EPV) by adding the following equations:

$$LIA_t = (1 - salia)\ LIA_{t-1} + salia\ \left[\left(\frac{c}{c^u}\right)^d \left(\frac{W}{W^u}\right)^{-d}\right] \qquad (3\text{-}29)$$

$$EPV = \left(LIA \times \left[\frac{E^u}{Y^u}\right]\right) \div \left[\frac{A}{A^u}\right] \qquad (3\text{-}30)$$

By comparing tables 5-6 and 5-7 in the appendix, we find that incorporating these equations reduces the predicted effect on Y by a negligible amount in the first year ($1.911 \div 1.917$) when new machinery, embodying the new lower optimum labor capital ratios, is starting to be purchased, and by 6.1% $[((1.797 \div 1.914) - 1) \times 100]$ in the last year.

For **case 8**, we add the price of housing equation (PH) to the case 7 model.

$$PH = \varepsilon \times \left[\frac{N_t \div N_t^u}{N_{t-1} \div N_{t-1}^u} - 1\right] + PH_{t-1} + UPH \qquad (3\text{-}42)$$

This model is now the default model used in chapter 4 (compare tables 4-7 and 5-8). The effect of the negative feedback to the price index (CP) of increases in housing prices (shown on table 5-8 in the appendix) on real disposable income reduced the effect of the stimulus by 1.3% $[((1.887 \div 1.911) - 1) \times 100]$ in the first year and by 5.3% $[((1.702 \div 1.797) - 1) \times 100]$ in the last year. Case 8 represents the situation shown in diagram 5-5, but in a dynamic setting. Note that in a dynamic setting, the supply curve shifts to the right each year as inward migration increases labor supply.

For the final case (**case 9**), we reactivate the effect of changing Y (the diversity effect) on local self-sufficiency (R). This is done by changing the default setting for $\mu_1 = k_{RR} = 0$ in the equation for R (equation 3-66) to $\mu = .296$ and $k_{RR} = .176$. Table 5-9 in the appendix shows that the effect of this change is to magnify the response in the local economy by increasing the share of the local market (R) in response to a growth in the market (Y). While this might be expected, due to increased diversity of goods and services offered and agglomeration economies as the area expands, not enough research has been done to satisfactorily support this theory. The effect of this addition, comparing case 9 to case 8, increases the effect on Y by

76.6% [((3.332 ÷ 1.887) − 1) × 100] in the first year and by 67.6% [((2.852 ÷ 1.702) − 1) × 100] in the last year.

In general, these cases, as summarized on table 5-10 in the appendix, illustrate how sensitive policy analysis is to the model chosen for the analysis. In chapter 9, we examine various model configurations for fifty states over an eight-year post-sample period to test which model has a superior ability to track these economies during this period. This is an approach that may help to select among the models. Another approach is to use several configurations to test the policy and then report the range of results, so that the sensitivity of the results to the assumptions is made known to the people who are exploring the potential economic effects of the policy.

5-2 THE RANGE OF POSSIBLE DEMAND AND SUPPLY CURVE SPECIFICATIONS

In the previous section, we compared various cases for the prototype model. Here, we consider the entire range of demand and supply curve specifications. This will include the extreme cases of zero and infinite elasticities. Diagrammatically, this is equivalent to horizontal or vertical demand or supply curves. If we consider that there are three types of curves, sloping (down for demand, up for supply), horizontal, and vertical, and that two curves are given in each supply-demand diagram, we have 3 × 3 or nine possible model representations. These are shown in diagram 5-6.

Possible Regional Labor Demand and Supply Curves

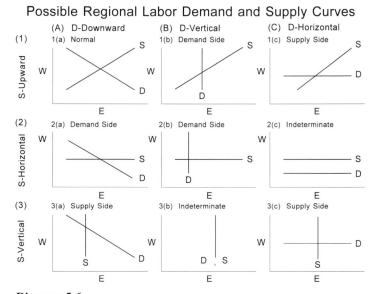

Diagram 5-6

238

Only a change in the national wage rate would cause a strictly upward or downward shift in either the supply or demand curves. Generally, however, we are interested in the relative wage rate compared to that of the United States. We, therefore, assume that supply and demand curves shift either left or right.

In diagram 5-6, model 1(a) is our prototype with normal supply-and-demand curves. This type of model simulates the effect of changes in both supply and demand. Horizontal demand curve shifts change employment in the models represented by figures 1(b), 2(a), and 2(b). These are called demand-side models. The models shown by figures 1(c), 3(a), and 3(c) are supply-side models, since horizontal shifts in the supply curve drive employment changes. Figures 2(c) and 3(b) represent models that do not exist and would not have unique solutions, since, when the supply-and-demand curves are both vertical or both horizontal, they either do not intersect or they coincide exactly. If the demand-and-supply curves do not intersect, as illustrated in the diagram for model 2(c), there is no solution to the model. If the two curves coincide, as shown for model 3(b), then there are an infinite number of solutions to the model.

Demand-Side Models

Demand-side models are quite common in regional analysis. Economic changes always occur due to changes in demand in the economic base model. Input-Output (I-O) models (i.e., Leontief models) assume that all input prices and output prices

The Effects of Demand Curve Shifts in the Demand Driven Input-Output or Economic Base Model

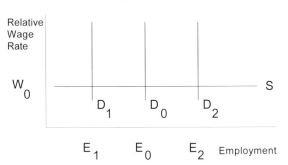

Diagram 5-7

are fixed and that every unit of output requires a fixed amount of inputs. In a demand-side I-O model, fixed input prices correspond to a horizontal supply curve. Demand-driven I-O models assume that output and employment changes occur due to changes in demand. Among the demand-side models (figures 1(b), 2(a), and 2(b) in diagram 5-6), the structure of demand-driven I-O and economic base models is best represented by figure 2(b). This figure is redrawn in diagram 5-7.

In this diagram, we see that shifts in the demand curve do not change the wage rate from W_0. Employment decreases to E_1 when the demand curve shifts inward to D_1, and increases to E_2 when the demand curve shifts to D_2. This is represented previously by case 1 – case 4.

Next, we note, in figure 1(b), in diagram 5-6, that the wage is endogenous. However, demand does not respond when wage rates change because all of the variables needed to represent a downward demand curve are exogenous. In this case, we obtain the same employment and output effects as before, but wages increase. Case 4 represents this approximately, with the exception that the demand curve is upward sloping in case 4, but it is vertical in 1(b).

Supply-Side Models

As noted above, the supply-driven models are represented by figures 1(c), 3(a), and 3(c) in diagram 5-6. Figure 3(c) illustrates the structure of an I-O model in which supply shifts are assumed to cause output and employment changes. The endogenous variable responses are the same in the model pictured in figure 1(c), although this does not represent the I-O structure. The supply-side model in figure 3(a) has a downward-sloping demand curve and represents a model that has some of the properties of a model of Texas built by Thomas Plaut (see Plaut 1981).

This supply-side model, 3(a), with a vertical supply curve and a standard demand curve, means that labor supply will determine output and employment. In this model, the wage adjusts until equilibrium between the demand and supply of labor is found. We illustrate this in diagram 5-8.

Comparison of a Normal [1(a)] and Supply Side [3(a)] Case

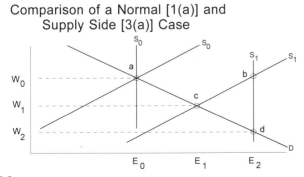

Diagram 5-8

Diagram 5-8 represents an outward shift in the supply curve from S_0 to S_1. In the prototype model with normal supply and demand curves, W_0 drops to W_1, and employment increases from E_0 to E_1. In the model with a vertical supply curve, wages decline to W_2, and employment increases to E_2. The reverse relationship occurs with an inward shift in the supply curve.

To represent the vertical supply curve model, we need to show the effects of a change that increases employment to E_2. This could be accomplished by a programming procedure that would continue to lower the wage rate until employment level E_2 is reached. A model of this type is included in chapter 9 as a GD/VS (General Demand/Vertical Supply) version of a more general model.

Indeterminate Models

The indeterminate models are shown in figures 2(c) and 3(b) in diagram 5-6. If the demand-and-supply curves coincide, there are two possible cases as shown in diagram 5-9. In figure 2(c)′ in diagram 5-9, we can see that there is an adequate

Two Cases of Infinite Number of Solutions

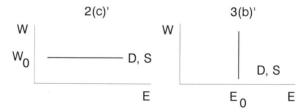

Diagram 5-9

demand and supply of labor for any level of employment. In this case, a nonmarket approach would have to be used to determine E exogenously. In 3(b)′ in diagram 5-9, we have a case where demand for labor will equal the supply of labor at any wage rate. In this case, the wage rate can be set at any arbitrary level without changing the level of employment.

In diagram 5-10, we show four possible cases of no solution. In case 1, the demand for labor is at a higher price than the offer price by potential employees. In such a case, the regional economy should experience explosive growth. In case 2, the reverse is true, and a collapse of employment should be expected, as no one is willing to work at the offered wage. In case 3, supply exceeds demand at every wage. A continual drop in wages should be expected. If a wage rate were fixed, we would expect permanent unemployment. In case 4, the opposite is the case, and the wage rate can be expected to go through the roof. If wages were capped, we would expect to see a continuous shortage of workers and unfilled jobs.

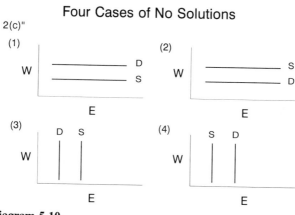

Diagram 5-10

Even though we have only dealt with special cases of prototype models in this chapter, we can gain significant insights into regional economies and operational models. While in reality we would expect all economies (and realistic models) to be best represented by downward sloping demand and upward sloping supply curves for labor, the elasticities of supply and demand may range from zero to infinity $(0 < \text{elasticity} < \infty)$. As the upper or lower limit of these elasticities is approached by either or both of the curves, we approach one of the nonstandard eight figures shown in diagram 5-6. Thus, these special cases may give us insights into real world phenomenon.

While the models illustrated in this section give insights into the behavior of regional economies and the workings of more realistic operational models, they have a serious limitation in their static, short-term orientation. While an increase in demand in the standard model (figure 1(a), diagram 5-6) increases wages and employment along the fixed upward sloping supply curve in the short run, higher wages and a higher employment to labor force ratio attract migrants. This leads to a shift in the supply curve to the right in the long run. If land prices remained constant, the eventual outcome might be closer to 2(a) than 1(a) in diagram 5-6. Thus, in considering realistic models, we need to ask what the effect of a policy change will be along a dynamic time path, not just what it will be in the short run.

In Part II, we turn to operational models that are used for serious forecasting and policy analysis on a year-by-year basis, in both the short- and long-run. It may often be useful to keep in mind the insights provided by the prototype models presented in Part I, because, at the heart of interpreting the result of any policy simulation, there is usually a simple story of causality. Unless this story of causality is understood and presented in a commonsense way, the results of the computer simulations of the model may not be convincing. The simple prototype chains of causality are an important aid in the analysis of policy simulation results generated by complex dynamic operational models. We return to the issue of alternative versions of models in chapter 9, using our operational model.

5-3 THE CONVERGENCE ISSUE[5]

In a multiregional economy in which all people and all businesses are mobile and indifferent to amenity variations, and where land is freely available in all locations, we expect horizontal demand curves and supply curves for labor at the same wage level throughout the country. So, if any area were slightly more attractive to people, the whole country would move to that area because labor would be cheaper. On the other hand, if any area represented above-average productivity, the wage would be higher in that area, and the whole country would move there. In other words, horizontal demand curves and supply curves would yield a system that would lead to a single wage anywhere in the country, and any slight difference in either consumer or producer amenities would suggest a concentration of people and firms in a single location.

In the real world, however, land is immobile, and its price is determined by the demand for that land. Also, some areas are more attractive to live in than others (i.e., they have consumer amenities, such as sunshine), and others are superior locations for business (i.e., producer amenities, such as location advantage). Bringing these elements into a model of location, we can explain how equilibrium nominal and real wages may be determined.

The material presented below draws on the work by Roback (1982) and Beeson and Eberts (1989), as well as joint work by the author with Gary Hunt (University of Maine), Michael Greenwood (University of Colorado), and Dan Rickman (University of Nevada, Las Vegas). It was originally presented at the University of Massachusetts Economic Theory seminar on November 15, 1991.

We start with a utility function for individuals.

$$U = U(X, L, A_c) \qquad (5\text{-}1)$$

It contains three arguments

X = a composite commodity used in consumption

L = land

A_c = consumer amenities.

In other words, consumer utility derived from living in this location comes from the amenity level and the amounts of L and X that they can purchase. Since the amount of L and X will depend on a person's income (W) and the prices of X and L, the consumer faces the following constraint:

$$W = X \times POC + L \times PL, \qquad (5\text{-}2)$$

where POC is the price of the consumption composite, and PL is the price of land. For convenience, we can postulate that the consumer utility function is Cobb-Douglas and can be expressed as

$$U = A_c \times X^{(1-lsc)} \times L^{lsc}, \qquad (5\text{-}3)$$

where *lsc* is the land share of consumption.

To find the indirect utility function for the area relative to the United States, we start by finding the marginal utilities for X and L and then setting their ratio equal to the ratio of their respective prices, as follows:

$$\frac{\partial U}{\partial X} = \frac{(1 - lsc) U}{X} \qquad (5\text{-}4)$$

$$\frac{\partial U}{\partial L} = \frac{lsc \times U}{L} \qquad (5\text{-}5)$$

Equating $\partial U/\partial X \div \partial U/\partial L$ to POC/PL and solving for L, we obtain

$$L = \frac{POC}{PL} \times \left(\frac{lsc}{1 - lsc} \right) \times X \qquad (5\text{-}6)$$

Substituting equation 5-6 into equation 5-3 and solving for X, we obtain

$$X = U \times A_c^{-1} \left(\frac{PL}{POC} \right)^{lsc} \left(\frac{1 - lsc}{lsc} \right)^{lsc} \qquad (5\text{-}7)$$

Substituting equation 5-6 into equation 5-2, we obtain

$$W = \frac{POC \times X}{1 - lsc} \qquad (5\text{-}8)$$

Substituting equation 5-7 into equation 5-8 and solving for U, we obtain

$$U = \left(\frac{W}{POC^{1-lsc} \times PL^{lsc}} \right) \times A_c \times (1 - lsc) \times \left(\frac{lsc}{1 - lsc} \right)^{lsc} \qquad (5\text{-}9)$$

which is the indirect utility function of the local area. Taking the ratio of this function to the same function for the United States, we obtain the following relative indirect utility function.

$$RC = RA_c \times (RW / (RPOC^{(1-lsc)} \times RPL^{lsc})), \qquad (5\text{-}10)$$

where RC is relative consumer utility, RA_c is relative consumer amenities, RW is the relative nominal earnings rate, RPOC is the relative price of the composite consumer commodity, and RPL is the relative price of land. This can be summarized as

$$RC = RA_c \times RRW, \qquad (5\text{-}11)$$

where RRW is the relative real earnings rate.

The interpretation of equations 5-10 and 5-11 is that the relative consumer utility at any location is the product of the amenity level at that location and the real wage at that location. Therefore, if an area was 5 percent more attractive than other areas ($A_c = 1.05$) and the real wage was 2 percent higher than elsewhere (RRW = 1.02), then the relative consumer utility in that area would be 1.071 (1.05 × 1.02). Obviously, everyone would move to that location. In fact, only in the case where RC = 1.00 in every location would the equilibrium location of people be achieved. Thus, in equilibrium, RC = 1. This implies, from equation 5-10, that

$$1/RA_c = RW/(RPOC^{(1-lsc)} \times RPL^{lsc}) \qquad (5\text{-}12)$$

If RA_c = .97 (i.e., a place that is 3 percent less desirable than the rest of the country), then $1/RA_c = 1.031$. This is called the compensating consumer differential. It means that consumers will only move to or remain in this location if they receive 3.1 percent more in real earnings (RRW) than they would in an alternative location. Assuming for simplicity that RPOC = 1, we can write equation 5-12 as

$$CCD = 1/RA_c = RW/RPL^{lsc}, \qquad (5\text{-}13)$$

where the compensating consumer differential (CCD) is inversely related to the relative amenity level in the region. Equation 5-13 is an indirect utility function and is represented graphically in diagram 5-11.

This diagram shows that, for a given level of consumer amenities (i.e., for a fixed CCD), any increase in the relative price of land (RPL) must be offset by an increase in the relative nominal wage rate (RW) to leave the consumer at the same level of utility. It also shows that any decrease in consumer amenities leads to an

A Consumer Indirect Utility Function (V) (RPOC = 1)

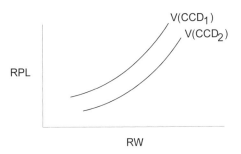

CCD$_2$ > CCD$_1$; CCD = 1/RA$_c$
CCD$_2$ represents a lower amenity level than CCD$_1$

Diagram 5-11

increase in the CCD (CCD$_2$ > CCD$_1$), which requires a higher nominal wage at any given land price to restore an equilibrium level of utility. In other words, the indirect utility curves show the equilibrium combinations of RPL and RW for any amenity level (CCD) in a given location.

To find the equilibrium nominal earnings rates, land prices, and real incomes, we develop a corresponding indirect utility, or relative profit curve, for business. We start with a production function similar to equation 3-17 in chapter 3. However, we replace the local productivity variable with A$_p$ to indicate that it is related to producer amenities. We also replace capital (K) with land (L), to focus on the part of capital that is region specific. Thus, we have the following production function:

$$Y = A_p \times E^a \times L^d \qquad (5\text{-}14)$$

The total cost function equation is similar to equation 3-34 and is

$$TC = W \times E + (PL \times L) \qquad (5\text{-}15)$$

Following the same procedure used from equation 3-34 to 3-38, we obtain the following relative production cost equation:

$$P = [(RW)^a \times (RPL)^d] / RA_p, \qquad (5\text{-}16)$$

or

$$P = RFC/RA_p, \qquad (5\text{-}17)$$

where RFC is relative factor costs. If relative producer amenity (RA$_p$), i.e., relative productivity, is higher than in the rest of the country by 5 percent (RA$_p$ = 1.05) and relative factor costs are equal to those elsewhere (RFC = 1.00), then the relative production costs (P) would be .952 (1/1.05). If this were the case, assuming that all industries are national industries that can charge the same price as in the rest of the nation (1), then all firms would move to this location. Obviously, for equilibrium, P

246

= 1 everywhere. The equilibrium condition for equal profits in all locations will be

$$RA_p = RW^n \times RPL^d \qquad (5\text{-}18)$$

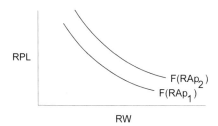

Equal Profit Curves (F)

RPL

F(RAp$_2$)
F(RAp$_1$)

RW

$RA_{p2} > RA_{p1}$, i.e., relative productivity 2 is greater than relative productivity 1

Diagram 5-12

This is represented with the same axes that we used for consumers above in diagram 5-12. This diagram shows that for equal profit, higher relative land prices must be compensated for with lower wage rates for equal profitability. It also shows that with more producer amenities ($RAp_2 > RAp_1$), i.e., with higher productivity, producers can earn equilibrium profits in an area and pay both higher land prices and higher wage rates.

Diagram 5-13 combines diagrams 5-11 and 5-12 and follows the work of Roback. This diagram shows that an equilibrium price of land (RPL) and relative nominal wage (RW) can be determined for a consumer compensating differential (CCD) — inverse of relative consumer amenities – and producer amenity (A_p) level. Only when CCD and

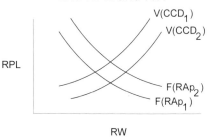

Determination of Equilibrium and RPL and RW

RPL

V(CCD$_1$)
V(CCD$_2$)

F(RAp$_2$)
F(RAp$_1$)

RW

Diagram 5-13

A_p = 1 everywhere would all locations be expected to yield the same relative price of land (RPL) and relative wage rate (RW). Only in that case would we expect both nominal and real wage rates to converge. In the case where all locations had equal producer amenities, any differentials would have to be offset by differences in the relative price of land, based on their proportion of land used in production. We illustrate this by specifying the model in an explicit form.

Returning to equation 5-12 and assuming that RPOC = 1 yields

$$(1/RA_c) = RW/RPL^{lsc} \tag{5-19}$$

Repeating equation 5-18 yields

$$RA_p = RW^a \times RPL^d \tag{5-18}$$

These are the two equations that are necessary to find equilibrium values for RW and RPL. Suppose we assume that 20 percent of consumer costs are land use ($lsc = .2$) and that producers' land and labor inputs are .05 and .95 respectively ($d = .05$ and $a = .95$). Therefore, the explicit equilibrium equations are

$$1/RA_c = RW/(RPL)^{0.2} \tag{5-20}$$

$$RA_p = RW^{0.95} \times RPL^{.05} \tag{5-21}$$

Solving these equations for RW, we obtain respectively

$$RW = \frac{1}{RA_c} \times (RPL)^{0.2} \tag{5-22}$$

$$RW = \left(\frac{RA_p}{RPL^{.05}} \right)^{1/.95}$$

$$= \left(\frac{RA_p}{RPL^{.05}} \right)^{1.0526} \tag{5-23}$$

Setting equation 5-22 and 5-23 equal to each other and solving for RPL, we obtain

$$RPL = \left(RA_p^{1.05} \times RA_c \right)^{3.95} \tag{5-24}$$

Thus, if

$$RA_p = 1 \text{ and } RA_c = 1, \tag{5-25}$$

then from equation 5-24 we obtain

$$RPL = 1 \tag{5-26}$$

and from equation 5-22 or 5-23,

$$RW = 1 \tag{5-27}$$

However, if relative producer amenities equal 1 ($RA_p = 1$) and relative consumer amenities are five percent greater than in other locations ($RA_c = 1.05$), then

$$RPL = (1.05)^{3.95} = 1.21 \tag{5-28}$$

From equation 5-23,

$$RW = [1 \div (1.21)^{.05}]^{1.0526} = .990 \tag{5-29}$$

This makes the real relative wage (RRW)

$$RRW = \frac{W}{(RPL)^{0.2}} = \frac{.990}{(1.21)^{0.2}} = .953 \tag{5-30}$$

In other words, individuals will stop net moves into or out of the area that has an amenity value 5 percent more attractive than other areas when their real relative earnings are 95.3% of the mean in places with average amenities. In this area, relative production costs will be

$$RW^{.95} \times RPL^{.05} = (.99)^{.95} \times (1.21)^{.05} = 1.00, \tag{5-31}$$

so firms facing a relative production amenity level of 1.00 and a relative factor cost of 1.00 are also in equilibrium. This is a result of our simultaneous solution of the two equations in the model.

Now let us suppose that $A_c = 1.00$, but $A_p = 1.05$. Then,

$$RPL = [(1.05)^{1.05}]^{3.95} = (1.05)^{4.15} = 1.224, \tag{5-32}$$

but now the relative wage becomes

$$RW = (RPL)^{0.2} = 1.041. \tag{5-33}$$

In this case, relative factor costs are

$$(RW)^{.95} \times (RLP)^{.05} = (1.041)^{.95} \times (1.224)^{.05} = 1.05, \tag{5-34}$$

so that the producer amenities of 1.05 are offset by higher costs. However, the relative real earnings for consumers are

$$RRW = 1.041/(1.224)^{0.2} = 1.00, \tag{5-35}$$

so they have no incentive to move either.

The above results are equilibrium results. As shown in the prototype model and as demonstrated by the operational model in Part II, the dynamic movement of the system requires long periods before equilibrium, as represented by zero net migration of firms and people, occurs. This time required for a full response is the only way that long term migration flows can be explained, unless it is asserted that endogenous conditions change amenities in a steady way, leading to continuous flows even though the system is in continuous equilibrium (see Graves and Linneman, 1979).

In proceeding to Part II, we move from homogenous models to models that have multiple industries, occupations, age cohorts, and so on. The basic concepts covered in Part I are incorporated into these more complex models.

APPENDIX: Chapter 5

TABLE 5-1

**The Effects of Increasing Output by One Billion 1987 Dollars,
Using the Case 1 Model: Basic Model**

Endogenous	1990	1991	1992	1993	1994
Y	1.474	1.458	1.455	1.458	1.459
XFG	1.424	1.424	1.424	1.424	1.424
C	0.676	0.653	0.648	0.653	0.654
YLP	1.145	1.132	1.129	1.132	1.133
YP	1.145	1.132	1.129	1.132	1.133
RYD	0.763	0.755	0.753	0.755	0.755
E	44.192	43.703	43.614	43.705	43.731

TABLE 5-2

**The Effects of Increasing Output by One Billion 1987 Dollars,
Using the Case 2 Model***

Endogenous	1990	1991	1992	1993	1994
Y	1.325	1.380	1.438	1.493	1.542
XFG	1.424	1.424	1.424	1.424	1.424
C	0.462	0.542	0.623	0.702	0.772
YLP	1.079	1.167	1.267	1.368	1.494
YP	0.821	1.028	1.222	1.420	1.630
RDV	-0.257	-0.139	-0.045	0.052	0.136
RA	-0.020	-0.022	-0.024	-0.026	-0.029
VSS	0.067	0.075	0.081	0.088	0.097
VP	-0.227	-0.147	-0.081	-0.016	0.040
DIR	0.058	0.106	0.141	0.183	0.221
RYD	0.521	0.626	0.723	0.810	0.890
E	39.684	41.362	43.075	44.730	46.187
MIG	14.048	11.398	9.096	7.244	5.820
N	14.048	25.570	34.890	42.436	48.621
ER	38.929	40.576	42.256	43.881	45.310
REO	0.009	0.008	0.006	0.005	0.004

* Case 1 model plus endogenous nonlabor income

TABLE 5-3

**The Effects of Increasing Output by One Billion 1987 Dollars,
Using the Case 3 Model**[*]

Endogenous	1990	1991	1992	1993	1994
Y	1.351	1.430	1.508	1.584	1.651
XFG	1.424	1.424	1.424	1.424	1.424
C	0.471	0.560	0.650	0.739	0.819
YLP	1.100	1.209	1.330	1.451	1.600
YP	0.837	1.062	1.276	1.495	1.731
RDV	-0.263	-0.147	-0.054	0.044	0.131
RA	-0.021	-0.023	-0.025	-0.027	-0.030
VSS	0.068	0.077	0.085	0.092	0.104
VP	-0.233	-0.155	-0.089	-0.026	0.032
DIR	0.060	0.109	0.146	0.191	0.233
RYD	0.531	0.647	0.755	0.854	0.944
G	0.029	0.053	0.074	0.092	0.109
E	40.484	42.861	45.197	47.460	49.473
MIG	14.288	11.851	9.658	7.860	6.468
N	14.288	26.264	36.151	44.324	51.173
ER	39.715	42.047	44.338	46.558	48.533
REO	0.009	0.008	0.007	0.006	0.005

[*] Case 2 model plus endogenous government spending

TABLE 5-4

**The Effects of Increasing Output by One Billion 1987 Dollars
Using the Case 4 Model***

Endogenous	1990	1991	1992	1993	1994
Y	1.815	1.900	2.009	2.127	2.212
XFG	1.424	1.424	1.424	1.424	1.424
C	0.634	0.749	0.871	0.994	1.097
YLP	1.477	1.606	1.772	1.949	2.143
YP	1.128	1.421	1.709	2.010	2.321
RDV	-0.349	-0.186	-0.062	0.062	0.177
RA	-0.028	-0.030	-0.033	-0.037	-0.041
VSS	0.092	0.104	0.114	0.124	0.138
VP	-0.310	-0.198	-0.113	-0.033	0.043
DIR	0.081	0.147	0.197	0.256	0.313
RYD	0.715	0.865	1.011	1.148	1.266
ILp	0.486	0.461	0.467	0.488	0.483
Kt	0.486	0.913	1.316	1.712	2.075
G	0.040	0.072	0.100	0.125	0.146
K*	7.151	7.311	7.862	8.616	8.970
E	54.371	56.940	60.200	63.745	66.266
MIG	19.449	16.013	12.843	10.410	8.508
N	19.449	35.633	48.788	59.621	68.641
ER	53.338	55.858	59.056	62.534	65.007
REO	0.012	0.011	0.009	0.007	0.006

* Case 3 model plus endogenous investment

TABLE 5-5

The Effects of Increasing Output by One Billion 1987 Dollars, Using the Case 5 Model*

Endogenous	1990	1991	1992	1993	1994
Y	2.373	2.439	2.608	2.790	2.906
XFG	1.424	1.424	1.424	1.424	1.424
C	1.109	1.232	1.422	1.610	1.758
YLP	2.380	2.459	2.715	2.997	3.270
YP	1.972	2.338	2.789	3.258	3.717
RDV	-0.410	-0.122	0.074	0.261	0.447
RA	-0.045	-0.047	-0.052	-0.057	-0.062
VSS	0.149	0.158	0.174	0.191	0.212
VP	-0.347	-0.149	-0.007	0.114	0.241
DIR	0.131	0.233	0.308	0.395	0.481
RYD	1.251	1.424	1.651	1.861	2.029
ILp	0.784	0.703	0.713	0.749	0.733
Kt	0.783	1.432	2.044	2.650	3.198
G	0.065	0.115	0.155	0.192	0.224
K*	11.520	11.196	12.053	13.249	13.687
E	71.126	73.084	78.139	83.628	87.093
MIG	31.800	24.372	19.071	15.480	12.562
N	31.800	56.452	76.016	92.156	105.509
W	0.118	0.107	0.100	0.094	0.091
RWR	0.005	0.003	0.003	0.003	0.003
ER	60.775	71.696	76.654	82.040	85.438
REO	0.016	0.011	0.009	0.006	0.004
WD_δ	0.004	-0.001	0.000	-0.001	0.000
EA	0.000	14.226	25.997	36.425	45.866

* Case 4 model plus endogenous wage feedback

TABLE 5-6

**The Effect of Increasing Output by One Billion 1987 Dollars
Using the Case 6 Model[*]**

Endogenous	1990	1991	1992	1993	1994
Y	1.917	1.831	1.845	1.888	1.914
XFG	1.356	1.312	1.286	1.272	1.266
C	0.778	0.836	0.931	1.023	1.097
YLP	1.975	1.891	1.958	2.058	2.182
YP	1.617	1.778	2.005	2.243	2.490
RDV	-0.357	-0.113	0.047	0.185	0.308
RA	-0.038	-0.036	-0.037	-0.039	-0.041
VSS	0.123	0.121	0.125	0.132	0.142
VP	-0.297	-0.125	-0.008	0.085	0.169
DIR	0.100	0.169	0.217	0.271	0.322
RYD	0.879	0.966	1.080	1.182	1.266
ILp	0.649	0.537	0.506	0.502	0.476
Kt	0.650	1.141	1.568	1.961	2.298
G	0.048	0.083	0.110	0.131	0.150
K*	9.556	8.608	8.695	9.099	9.133
E	57.470	54.881	55.295	56.564	57.367
MIG	23.974	16.902	12.149	9.018	6.814
N	23.974	41.087	53.594	63.077	70.431
P	0.003	0.003	0.002	0.002	0.002
RPROFn	-0.003	-0.003	-0.002	-0.002	-0.002
RPROFAt	-0.001	-0.001	-0.002	-0.001	-0.001
SPr	0.003	0.002	0.003	0.002	0.002
SPAt	0.001	0.001	0.002	0.001	0.002
CP	0.002	0.002	0.001	0.002	0.001
W	0.109	0.093	0.082	0.073	0.071
CPR_δ	0.002	0.000	0.000	0.000	0.000
RWR	0.002	0.001	0.001	0.001	0.001
ER	56.377	53.838	54.245	55.489	56.277
REO	0.013	0.009	0.006	0.005	0.003
WD_δ	0.004	-0.001	0.000	-0.001	0.000
REOA	0.000	0.013	0.009	0.006	0.005
EA	0.000	11.494	20.172	27.197	33.070
R	0.000	-0.001	-0.001	-0.001	-0.001
S *10^2	-0.003	-0.005	-0.006	-0.006	-0.006

[*] Case 5 model plus competitive and price feedbacks

TABLE 5-7

The Effects of Increasing the Output by One Billion 1987 Dollars
Using the Case 7 Model*

Endogenous	1990	1991	1992	1993	1994
Y	1.911	1.811	1.760	1.776	1.797
XFG	1.356	1.313	1.286	1.269	1.261
C	0.773	0.818	0.859	0.922	0.982
YLP	1.962	1.844	1.746	1.776	1.880
YP	1.606	1.738	1.837	2.002	2.207
RDV	-0.356	-0.105	0.091	0.226	0.327
RA	-0.038	-0.035	-0.033	-0.034	-0.036
VSS	0.122	0.119	0.112	0.114	0.122
VP	-0.295	-0.118	0.027	0.118	0.187
DIR	0.099	0.167	0.209	0.256	0.297
RYD	0.873	0.945	0.997	1.065	1.132
ILp	0.646	0.522	0.444	0.423	0.401
Kt	0.645	1.123	1.488	1.808	2.082
G	0.049	0.082	0.105	0.124	0.138
K*	9.494	8.393	7.752	7.855	7.872
LIAt	0.000	0.000	-0.001	-0.001	-0.001
EPV	-0.002	-0.004	-0.006	-0.006	-0.007
E	57.059	53.599	50.217	49.957	50.461
MIG	23.760	16.527	10.880	7.293	5.171
N	23.760	40.497	51.731	59.472	65.154
P	0.004	0.003	0.002	0.001	0.002
RPROFn	-0.004	-0.003	-0.002	-0.001	-0.002
RPROFAt	-0.001	-0.001	-0.001	-0.001	-0.002
SPr	0.003	0.002	0.002	0.002	0.002
SPAt	0.001	0.001	0.002	0.001	0.002
CP	0.002	0.002	0.002	0.002	0.001
W	0.108	0.090	0.077	0.068	0.065
CPR_δ	0.002	0.000	-0.001	0.000	0.000
RWR	0.002	0.001	0.002	0.001	0.001
ER	55.975	52.581	49.263	49.008	49.502
REO	0.013	0.008	0.005	0.004	0.003
WD_δ	0.003	-0.001	-0.001	0.000	0.000
REOA	0.000	0.013	0.008	0.005	0.004
EA	0.000	11.412	19.850	25.922	30.730
R	0.000	-0.001	-0.001	-0.001	-0.001
S *10²	-0.003	-0.004	-0.006	-0.006	-0.006

* Case 6 model plus feedback to labor intensity

TABLE 5-8

**The Effects of Increasing Output by One Billion 1987 Dollars
Using the Case 8 Model***

Endogenous	1990	1991	1992	1993	1994
Y	1.887	1.766	1.698	1.697	1.702
XFG	1.355	1.311	1.283	1.265	1.256
C	0.746	0.770	0.794	0.841	0.885
YLP	1.944	1.811	1.702	1.717	1.803
YP	1.589	1.702	1.780	1.921	2.099
RDV	-0.355	-0.110	0.078	0.205	0.296
RA	-0.037	-0.034	-0.032	-0.032	-0.034
VSS	0.122	0.117	0.109	0.110	0.117
VP	-0.293	-0.120	0.020	0.106	0.170
DIR	0.096	0.161	0.200	0.242	0.278
RYD	0.841	0.890	0.921	0.971	1.021
ILp	0.640	0.513	0.431	0.408	0.382
Kt	0.639	1.108	1.462	1.766	2.025
G	0.047	0.079	0.100	0.117	0.129
K*	9.407	8.245	7.552	7.592	7.548
LIAt	0.000	0.000	-0.001	-0.001	0.000
EPV	-0.002	-0.004	-0.005	-0.006	-0.007
E	56.307	52.268	48.423	47.674	47.692
MIG	23.182	15.672	9.949	6.377	4.287
N	23.182	39.058	49.349	56.154	60.924
P	0.004	0.003	0.002	0.002	0.002
RPROFn	-0.004	-0.003	-0.002	-0.002	-0.002
RPROFAt	-0.001	-0.001	-0.001	-0.001	-0.001
SPr	0.003	0.003	0.002	0.001	0.001
SPAt	0.001	0.001	0.002	0.001	0.001
PH	0.001	0.003	0.003	0.004	0.005
CP	0.003	0.003	0.002	0.002	0.002
W	0.110	0.092	0.080	0.071	0.069
CPR_δ	0.001	0.000	0.000	0.000	0.000
RWR	0.002	0.002	0.001	0.001	0.001
ER	55.238	51.274	47.504	46.768	46.786
REO	0.012	0.009	0.005	0.004	0.003
WD_δ	0.003	-0.001	-0.001	0.000	0.000
REOA	0.000	0.012	0.009	0.005	0.004
EA	0.000	11.261	19.463	25.255	29.739
R	0.000	-0.001	-0.001	-0.001	-0.001
S $*10^2$	-0.003	-0.005	-0.005	-0.006	-0.007

* Case 7 model plus the PH equation equals the default model

TABLE 5-9

The Effects of Increasing Output by One Billion 1987 Dollars
Using the Case 9 Model*

Endogenous	1990	1991	1992	1993	1994
Y	3.332	2.910	2.737	2.796	2.852
XFG	1.302	1.245	1.202	1.157	1.135
C	1.317	1.281	1.297	1.393	1.481
YLP	3.427	2.960	2.718	2.826	3.032
YP	2.802	2.818	2.894	3.176	3.515
RDV	-0.625	-0.142	0.176	0.350	0.484
RA	-0.065	-0.056	-0.052	-0.054	-0.058
VSS	0.213	0.191	0.175	0.181	0.196
VP	-0.516	-0.172	0.067	0.184	0.275
DIR	0.171	0.276	0.334	0.401	0.463
RYD	1.486	1.479	1.506	1.609	1.709
ILp	1.128	0.832	0.680	0.669	0.644
Kt	1.127	1.881	2.430	2.929	3.369
G	0.083	0.136	0.168	0.195	0.214
K*	16.585	13.474	12.068	12.496	12.689
LIAt	0.000	0.000	0.000	0.000	-0.001
EPV	-0.004	-0.007	-0.009	-0.010	-0.011
E	99.450	86.112	78.012	78.557	79.932
MIG	41.105	25.531	15.084	10.005	7.216
N	41.105	66.999	82.668	93.390	101.408
P	0.006	0.005	0.004	0.003	0.003
RPROFn	-0.006	-0.005	-0.004	-0.003	-0.003
RPROFAt	-0.001	-0.002	-0.002	-0.003	-0.003
SPr	0.005	0.004	0.004	0.003	0.003
SPAt	0.001	0.002	0.002	0.002	0.002
PH	0.004	0.005	0.006	0.007	0.008
CP	0.004	0.004	0.004	0.003	0.004
W	0.193	0.152	0.127	0.116	0.113
CPR_δ	0.004	0.000	0.000	-0.001	0.000
RWR	0.003	0.002	0.001	0.001	0.001
ER	97.560	84.475	76.530	77.065	78.413
REO	0.022	0.014	0.009	0.006	0.004
WD_δ	0.007	-0.001	-0.001	-0.001	0.000
REOA	0.000	0.022	0.014	0.009	0.006
EA	0.000	19.890	33.134	42.110	49.400
R	0.003	0.003	0.003	0.002	0.003
S *10^2	-0.005	-0.008	-0.010	-0.011	-0.011

* Case 8 model plus the diversity effect on R

TABLE 5-10

Summary of Models Used for Cases 1 – 8[*]

Titles	Equations
	OUTPUT LINKAGES
Output	(1) Y $= [R*(C+ILp+G+XFG)]$
Exports	(1) XFG $= S*XFGu+PVDEMA+PVOUTA \div R +$ $(PVEA \div EPV) \div R$
Consumption	(1) C $= kC*[Cu \div RYDu]*RYD*PVCM+PVCA$
Labor & Proprietors' Income	(1) YLP $= W*E \div 1000$
Personal Income	(1) YP $= YLP+RDV$
Exogenous Income	(2) RDV $= -VSS+RA+DIR+VP$
Residence Adjustment	(2) RA $= kRA*YLP+PVRAA;$ if $kRA<0$ $= kRA*YLPu+PVRAA;$ if $kRA>0$
Social Security Tax	(2) VSS $= kVSS*(VSSu \div YLPu)*YLP+PVVSSA$
Transfer Payments	(2) VP $= kVP*[VPu \div (Nu-Eu)]*(N-ER)+PVVPA$
Dividends, Interest, and Rent	(2) DIR $= kDIR*(DIRu \div Nu)*N+PVDIRA$
Real Disposable Income	(1) RYD $= [YP(1-(TX+PVtxA))] \div CP$
Investment	(4) ILp $= \alpha*[(kI*K*)-(1-dru)*Kt\_1]*PVIM+PVIA$
Capital Stock Updating	(4) Kt $= ILpt+(1-dru)*(Kt\_1*PVKM+PVKA)$
Government Spending	(3) G $= kG*[Gu \div Nu]*N*PVGM+PVGA$
	LABOR AND CAPITAL DEMAND LINKAGES
Optimal Capital Stock	(4) K* $= [W \div Wu]*cu \div c]*[E \div Eu]*Ku*$
Labor Intensity Adjustment	(7) LIAt $= (1-salia)*LIAt\_1+salia*\{[c \div cu]^d*$ $[W \div Wu]^{(-d)}\}$
Labor Intensity	(7) EPV $= LIA*[Eu \div Yu] \div [(A+PVAA) \div Au] \div (1+$ $PVEPA)^a$
Employment	(1) E $= EPV*Y$
	POPULATION AND LABOR SUPPLY LINKAGES
Migration	(2) MIG $= [kM+PVQOLA+(\beta1*\ln(REO))+(\beta2*$ $\ln(RWR))]*Nt\_1+PVMIGA$
Population	(2) N $= Nt\_1*[Nu \div Nut\_1]+MIG$

	WAGE, PRICE AND PROFIT LINKAGES
Relative Production Costs	(6) P $= [(W+PVwcA) \div Wu]\hat{}a*[(c+PVccA) \div cu\hat{}d$ $*(1+PVEPA)\hat{}(a) \div [(A+PVAA) \div Au] + PVPA$
Relative Profitability	(6) RPROFn $= (1-P)+1$
Relative Profit Average	(6) RPROFAt $= (1-sapr)*RPROFAt\_1 + sapr*$ RPROFn
Sales Price	(6) SPr $= P*[A \div Au] = [W \div Wu]\hat{}a*[c \div cu]\hat{}d$
Sales Price Average	(6) SPAt $= (1-sasp)*SPAt\_1 + sasp*SPr$
Housing Price	(8) PH $= \varepsilon*[(N \div Nu) \div (Nt\_1 \div Nut\_1)-1] + PHt\_1 +$ UPH+PVPHA
Consumer Price Deflator	(2) CP $= [(1-hsu)((1-ncsu)*SPr+ncsu)+hsu*PH]$ $*CPu + PVCPA$
Wage Rate	(2) W $= (1+CPR\_\delta)\hat{}tau*(1+WD\_\delta)*(1+UWu)*$ Wt_1+PVwA
Consumer Price Change	CPR_$\delta = [(CP \div CPu) \div (CPt\_1 \div CPut\_1)-1]$
Relative Wage Rate	(5) RWR $= \{[W*(RYD \div YP)] \div Wu*(RYDu \div YPu]\}$
Employment by Residence	(2) ER $= E*[(YLP+RA) \div YLP]$
Relative Employment Opportunity	(2) REO $= [ER \div N] \div [Eu \div Nu]$
Wage Rate Changes	(5) WD_$\delta = [lambda1*((E-PVESA) \div EA-1)] +$ $[lambda2*(REO \div REOA-1)]$
REOA Updating	(5) REOAt $= (1-sareo)*REOAt\_1 + sareo*REOt\_1$
EA Updating	(5) EAt $= (1-saea)*EAt\_1 + saea*Et\_1$
	MARKET SHARE LINKAGES
Regional Share of Output	(6) R $= [nslu*(kRN*RPROFA\hat{}psi)+(1-nslu)*$ $(kRR* Y\hat{}mu*SPA\hat{}xi)]*PVRM+PNRA$
Share of Extra-Market	(6) $S*10^2 = 100*[(nseu*(kSN*RPROFA\hat{}psi)+(1-$ $nseu)*(kSR*SPA\hat{}XI))*PVSM]+PVSA$

* Cases 1 - 8: $\mu = k_{RR} = 0$
Case 9: $\mu = .296$, $k_{RR} = .176$

Case numbers are in parentheses

NOTES ON CHAPTER 5

1. This section draws on a chapter by G. I. Treyz entitled "Policy Simulation Modeling" in Dan Otto (ed.) *Microcomputer Based Input-Output Modeling: Applications to Economic Development*: Westview Press, forthcoming.

2. This is accomplished in the REMS program by shutting off the equations for RDV, IL_p, G, EPV, MIG, P, SP_R, PH, W, and S. Some equations, other than those shown on table 5-1, remain active. However, they do not affect the model, because they only appear on the right-hand side of equations that are suppressed.

3. This was accomplished in the REMS system by activating the RDV, MIG, W, and CP equations, which were suppressed in case 1, and by setting λ_1 and λ_2 equal to zero in the wage change equation (3-56).

4. We activate the ΔWD equations by setting λ_1 and λ_2 back to their original values of 0.024 and 0.290 respectively.

5. For a discussion and the history of wage convergence in the United States, see George I. Treyz (1991).

PART II:

HETEROGENEOUS MODELS

CHAPTER 6

REGIONAL INPUT-OUTPUT MODELS[1]

In chapter 2, we set forth the economic base model and the accounts that accompany it. In the next three chapters, we developed the single-industry model further. To develop a usable regional model, we now expand our purview and consider multiple-industry models. In this chapter, we return to chapter 2 and build on the accounts and models in that chapter in order to develop a rudimentary regional input-output model. In chapter 7, we draw upon this chapter, as well as chapter 3, to specify a full forecasting and simulation model.

6-1 A CLOSED ECONOMY, SINGLE INDUSTRY SPECIAL CASE

In the special case of a closed economy, the accounts for our special input-output case would be just like those in table 2-1, with the addition of intermediate production and use to Account A. In table 6-1, we show two ways in which the table 1 accounts could be rewritten taking intermediate inputs into consideration.

TABLE 6-1

The State Product Account for a Simplified Closed Economy Including Intermediate Inputs

Form 1

Y	CG
	IL
Y	Y
QI	QI
Q	Q

Form 2

	Inputs (down)	Final Demands
Outputs (Across)	QI	+ CG + IL = Q
	+ Y	
	Q	

CG   Total state use of goods and services for consumption and state and local government spending.

IL   Residential and nonresidential construction, new equipment purchases, and inventory changes within the state.

Q   Total sales including sales of intermediate goods from one industry to another

QI   Intermediate goods (i.e., outputs from one industry used as inputs to other industries).

Y   Total state value added output of goods and services: gross state product or gross regional product.

We now have two measures of output. One is value-added output, or GRP (Y), which is in the units used to measure gross domestic product (GDP). The other output variable (Q) measures total sales in the economy. This latter variable, when measured on the input side, includes the purchase of material inputs from other industries (QI), such as the purchase of steel by the auto industry (QI), as well as the usual factor inputs. Likewise on the output side, Q includes the sales of the steel industry to the automobile industry, as well as the sales to final demand sectors, such as CG and IL. Since the intermediate component is added to both sides, we can either simply add it to both sides, as shown in form 1 on table 6-1, or we can set the accounts up, as shown in form 2, so that total sales (Q) is simultaneously the sum of inputs (adding down the column) and the sum of outputs (adding across the row). If we had built a value-added model of the closed economy shown in table 6-1 instead of waiting until exports had been added, it would have had two equations.

$$Y = CG + IL_p \tag{6-1}$$

$$CG = b\,Y \tag{6-2}$$

In this case, planned investment (IL_p) is the only exogenous variable. In equation 6-1, it is assumed that output will be set equal to $CG + IL_p$, as businesses produce what they can sell, and that no unplanned inventory change will occur ($IL_u = 0$). In equation 6-2, consumption plus local government spending (CG) is determined by Y. The reduced form of this model is

$$Y = \frac{1}{1-b}\,IL_p \tag{6-3}$$

Using the interindustry model, we would write

$$Q = QI + CG + IL_p \tag{6-4}$$

$$CG = b\,Y \tag{6-5}$$

$$QI = a\,Q \tag{6-6}$$

$$Y = (1 - a)\,Q \tag{6-7}$$

In this model, a is a fixed parameter showing the proportion of Q that is made up of intermediate inputs (a = QI/Q). This is taken to be a fixed proportion. The counterpart of this assumption is shown in equation 6-7, where $1 - a$ is the proportion of Q that is contributed by value added Y. The reduced form is found by substituting equation 6-7 into equation 6-5, then substituting equations 6-5 and 6-6 into equation 6-4, and solving for Q, as follows:

$$Q = a\,Q + b\,(1 - a)\,Q + IL_p \tag{6-8}$$

$$Q[(1 - a) - b\,(1 - a)] = Q\,(1 - a)\,(1 - b) = IL_p \tag{6-9}$$

$$Q = \frac{1}{(1-a)}\,\frac{1}{(1-b)}\,IL_p \tag{6-10}$$

We then use equation 6-7 to convert equation 6-10 into a multiplier for Y, as follows:

$$Y = \frac{1}{1-b}\,IL_p \tag{6-11}$$

The key point of the derivation of equation 6-11 is to show that the introduction of intermediate inputs yields a total output multiplier, as shown in equation 6-10, but it also yields a value-added multiplier 6-11 that is identical to the multiplier 6-3, which is derived from equations 6-1 and 6-2. In this special case of a closed economy, then, the economic base and input-output models yield an identical multiplier.

6-2 AN OPEN ECONOMY, SINGLE INDUSTRY EXAMPLE

In this section, we will show that, for an open economy, the economic-base model and the regional input-output model are not identical but are still comparable. In table 6-2, the accounts are shown for an open economy. The estimated values for the variables for Michigan in 1977 are also shown.

TABLE 6-2

A One-Industry Social Accounting Matrix: (Michigan 1977)

	Inputs (down)	*Final Demand (F)*						
Outputs (across)	QI + 86.7	CG 65	– M 84.1	+ IL 16.2	+ XFG 83.7	= Q 167.5
Value Added (VA)	YLP 55.0
	H 25.8
	Q 167.5

H   Profits earned in the state.

M   Purchases within the state of goods and services produced outside of the state.

XFG   Sales outside of the state of goods produced within the state. This includes federal government spending in the local area.

YLP   Labor and proprietors' income earned in the state.

In table 6-2, the accounts are written in the second form where the uses side of the accounts is still represented as a column (inputs), while the sources side is represented as a row (outputs). We have now added exports plus federal government spending (XFG) and subtracted imports (M) from the final demand column. Table 6-2 should be compared with Account A in table 2-3.

A Type A model, including the intermediate inputs, has the following equations:

$$Q = QI + CG + IL_p + XFG - M \qquad (6\text{-}12)$$

$$CG = b\,Y \qquad (6\text{-}13)$$

$$QI = a\,Q \qquad (6\text{-}14)$$

$$Y = (1 - a)\,Q \qquad (6\text{-}15)$$

$$M = mn\ QI + mn\ CG + mn\ IL_p \qquad (6\text{-}16)$$

Equation 6-12 is similar to equation 2-22 in economic base model A with the addition of QI to both sides. Equations 6-13 through 6-15 follow equations 6-5 through 6-7 above. Equation 6-16 differs from equation 2-23 in Part I in that it includes intermediate demand QI but excludes exports (XFG). We use *mn* as a new parameter to show that it is different from *m*. The reason for including QI is that intermediate inputs are likely to come from outside of the area in the same proportion as do CG and IL_p. Now that intermediate inputs are included in the model, it is no longer necessary to assume that some portion of exports is imported. The key point here is that XFG includes intermediate inputs (QI) which are imported in part, but that the final items to be exported are not imported directly into the area and then exported.[2]

We now define the regional purchase coefficient (*rpc*) to be

$$rpc = 1 - mn \qquad (6\text{-}17)$$

Substituting equation 6-16 into equation 6-12 and using equation 6-17, we obtain

$$Q = rpc\ QI + rpc\ CG + rpc\ IL_p + XFG \qquad (6\text{-}18)$$

If we now define Local Demand (LD) to equal QI + CG + IL_p, we find that the regional purchase coefficient (*rpc*) is the proportion of local demand (LD) that is supplied locally. The *rpc* will play a key role in the development of our regional input-output models.

Now we follow the type of substitution that we carried out to get equation 6-8 and then solve for the new multiplier (KQ), as follows:

$$Q = rpc\ a\ Q + rpc\ (1-a)\ b\ Q + rpc\ IL_p + XFG \qquad (6\text{-}19)$$

$$Q = \frac{1}{1 - rpc\ a - rpc\ (1-a)\ b}\ (rpc\ IL_p + XFG) \qquad (6\text{-}20)$$

$$\begin{aligned} KQ &= \frac{1}{1 - rpc\ a - rpc\ (1-a)\ b} \\ &= \frac{Q}{rpc\ IL_p + XFG} \end{aligned} \qquad (6\text{-}21)$$

Using the Michigan 1977 numbers from table 6-2, we obtain

$$rpc = \frac{Q - XFG}{QI + CG + IL_p} = \frac{167.5 - 83.7}{86.7 + 65 + 16.2} = 0.499 \qquad (6\text{-}22)$$

$$a = \frac{QI}{Q} = \frac{86.7}{167.5} = 0.518 \quad and \quad (1 - a) = .482 \tag{6-23}$$

$$b = \frac{65}{55.0 + 25.8} = 0.804 \tag{6-24}$$

$$KQ = \frac{167.5}{(0.499 \times 16.2) + 83.7} = 1.82 \tag{6-25}$$

The value added multiplier (KY) using equation 6-15 is

$$KY = (1 - a)\, KQ = 0.482 \times 1.82 = 0.88 \tag{6-26}$$

In other words, each dollar of new exports will only lead to eighty-eight cents of additional value added even after both intermediated inputs and induced spending (from respending of new income) are considered. To see why, we can trace the process over a period-by-period sequence.

Our first step is to assign time subscripts to the variables in the model and then trace the effect through period by period. Using a time subscript (t-1) to indicate a time lag in response for some variables, we have the following model:

$$Q_t = rpc\ QI_{t-1} + rpc\ CG_{t-1} + rpc\ IL_{pt-1} + XFG_t \tag{6-27}$$

$$QI_t = a\ Q_t \tag{6-28}$$

$$CG_t = b\ Y_t \tag{6-29}$$

$$Y_t = (1 - a)\ a_t \tag{6-30}$$

$$Q_t = 0.499\ QI_{t-1} + 0.499\ CG_{t-1} + 0.499\ IL_{pt-1} + XFG_t \tag{6-31}$$

$$QI_t = 0.518\ Q_t \tag{6-32}$$

$$CG_t = 0.804\ Y_t \tag{6-33}$$

$$Y_t = 0.482\ Q_t \tag{6-34}$$

Thus, output responds immediately to export changes but responds with a one period time lag to any other changes. This would be the case if nonexport sources of demand are temporarily filled through inventory changes. Using this model, we now trace through period by period the changes following a permanent increase in XFG of 1000 in period 1. This period-by-period approach yields the following results:

Period	Q	QI	Y	CG	IL	XFG
0	0	0	0	0	0	0
1	1000	518	482	388	0	1000
2	1452	752	700	563	0	1000
3	1656	858	798	642	0	1000
4	1749	906	843	678	0	1000
5	1790	927	863	694	0	1000
6	1809	937	872	701	0	1000
7	1817	941	876	704	0	1000
8	1823	943	877	706	0	1000
9	1824	944	879	707	0	1000
10	1824	945	879	707	0	1000
11	1824	945	879	707	0	1000
12	1824	945	879	707	0	1000

From the period-by-period results, we can see that within the accuracy of our convergence criteria, the multiplier of 1.82 for Q (1.824) and the multiplier of 0.88 for Y (.879) were closely replicated. We can also see that the small multiplier for Y is due to the fact that only 0.482 of Q is value added and that only 0.499 of QI and CG generated by the model is supplied locally.

In the Type A economic base model in chapter 2, the multiplier for the net economic base (BN or r XFG) was 1.65 (equation 2-79). In that model, r was equal to 0.490 (equation 2-38). This means that the XFG increase was 2.04 (1 ÷ 0.49) for a value-added economic base (BN) increase of 1.0. Thus, the multiplier for XFG was 1.65/2.04 = 0.808, which is a little smaller than the 0.88 multiplier here. Of course, for a more accurate multiplier, we would want to turn to the Type B modifications which allow for a divergence between local output and local income.

As a shortcut to a full Type B economic base model, we might try to get a somewhat more reasonable result by using YLP instead of Y in the model. By reference to table 6-2, we find that Y ($=80.8$) can be subdivided into labor and proprietors' income YLP ($=55.0$) and "profits" H ($=25.8$). We can now substitute new equations with new parameters that reflect spending out of labor and proprietors' income for equations 6-13 and 6-15.

$$CG = bn \; YLP \tag{6-35}$$

$$YLP = ay \; Q \; , \tag{6-36}$$

where

$$bn = \frac{65}{55.0} = 1.18 \tag{6-37}$$

and

$$ay = \frac{55}{167.5} = 0.33 \tag{6-38}$$

The bn value is greater than 1, which is unreasonable for a marginal propensity to consume. If we proceed, despite this qualification, and substitute these into equation 2-18 and perform the same operation that we used to get equation 6-21, we obtain

$$KQ = \frac{1}{1 - rpc\,a - rpc\,ay\,bn} = \frac{Q}{rpc\,IL_p + XFG}, \tag{6-39}$$

which is the same as before, with ay replacing $1 - a$ and bn replacing b. Since $(1 - a)\,b = 0.48 \times 0.804 = 0.39$ and since $aybn = 1.18 \times 0.33 = 0.39$, we can see that this model is algebraically identical to the Type A model. Therefore, this shortcut to a Type B model actually simply replicates the Type A model for this one-sector case. This procedure, which is used in most operational input-output models, is identical to the Type A procedure except for the difference introduced due to the multisector feature of operational I-O models.

6-3 A TWO-INDUSTRY PROCESSING SECTOR EXAMPLE (TYPE I)

A primary reason for input-output analysis is to look at the differences from industry to industry in the effects of an exogenous change. We now consider the simplest of all input-output models, a two-sector model. In this case, we divide all industry between manufacturing and nonmanufacturing.

In table 6-3, we set out the accounts for this two-industry economy. The numbers given are for manufacturing as industry 1 and nonmanufacturing as industry 2 for 1977 in Michigan.

TABLE 6-3

Two Industry Input-Output Model Accounts

	Inputs (down)		*Final Sales*
	Manu-facturing	Nonmanu-facturing	

	Manufacturing	Nonmanufacturing	
Output *Manufacturing* *(across)*	Q(1,1) 38.7	+ Q(1,2) 25.7	+ CG(1) + IL(1) − M(l) + XFG(1)= Q(1) 19.4 + 6.0 − 56.4 + 64.0 = 97.4
Nonmanufact.	Q(2,1) 20.9	Q(2,2) 1.4	+ CG(2) + IL(2) − M(2) + XFG(2) = Q(2) 45.6 + 10.2 − 27.7 + 19.7 = 70.1
Factor Incomes	YLP(l) 23.9 H(1) 13.9 Q(1) 97.4	YLP(2) 31.1 H(2) 11.9 Q(2) 70.1	

CG(1) Total state use of manufacturing goods by consumers and state and local government.

H(1) Manufacturing profits earned in the state.

IL(1) Use of manufacturing inputs for residential and nonresidential construction, new equipment purchases, and inventory changes within the state.

M(1) Purchases within the state of manufacturing goods produced outside of the state.

Q(1) Manufacturing output in the state.

Q(2) Nonmanufacturing output in the state.

Q(1,1) Inputs from manufacturing (1) to manufacturing (1).

Q(1,2) Inputs from manufacturing (1) to nonmanufacturing (2).

Q(2,1) Inputs from nonmanufacturing (2) to manufacturing (1)

XFG(1) Sales outside of the state of manufactured goods produced within the state

YLP(1) Labor and proprietors' income earned in manufacturing in the state.

Here, $Q_{1,2}$ is the amount from industry 1 that is used in the production of industry 2, and $Q_{1,1}$ shows shipments of some industry 1 subindustries to other subindustries in industry 1. When industries are broadly defined, this sort of intraindustry shipping is to be expected (e.g., the automobile industry uses steel). Here, $Q(1)$ indicates the total sales of industry 1, whereas FS (1) = CG (1) + IL (1) − M (1) + XFG (1) is the total final sales of industry 1: i.e., $Q_1 - Q_{1,1} - Q_{1,2}$ or $CG_1 + IL_1 - M_1 + XFG_1$. Also, notice that all inputs to any industry (a column) must equal the outputs (a row).

The value added VA_1 for industry 1 is $YLP_1 + H_1$, and value added VA_2 for industry 2 is $YLP_2 + H_2$. While total value added from all industries, $VA_1 + VA_2$, equals total final sales from all industries, $FS_1 + FS_2$, this does not mean that VA_1 in industry 1 is equal to final sales FS_1 in that industry.

Before developing a full closed input-output model with endogenous consumption (usually called a Type II model),we develop a processing-sector-only model. In this model (I-O Type I), we assume that all final demand, except imports (M), is exogenous. We also assume, as we did in the one-industry case above, that we have a fixed-input production function. This means that production is like a precise recipe. If you need five cents of steel per dollar of car production, you will continue to need five cents of steel per dollar of car production. Using the numbers in table 6-3, we formulate our model.

First, we find the amount of intermediate inputs required for each dollar of output of Q_1.

$$a_{1,1} = Q_{1,1} \div Q_1 = 38.7/97.4 = 0.40 \qquad (6\text{-}40)$$

$$a_{2,1} = Q_{2,1} \div Q_1 = 20.9/97.4 = 0.21 \qquad (6\text{-}41)$$

Thus, twenty-one cents of nonmanufacturing (2) input is required for each dollar of manufacturing (1) output, and inputs from other manufacturing firms are forty cents for each dollar of manufacturing output. These are called the technological coefficients. Likewise,

$$a_{1,2} = Q_{1,2} \div Q_2 = 25.7/70.1 = 0.37 \qquad (6\text{-}42)$$

$$a_{2,2} = Q_{2,2} \div Q_2 = 1.4/70.1 = 0.02 \qquad (6\text{-}43)$$

Now we let

$$M_1 = m_1 Q_{1,1} + m_1 Q_{1,2} + m_1 CG_1 + m_1 IL_1 \qquad (6\text{-}44)$$

$$m_1 = \frac{M_1}{Q_{1,1} + Q_{1,2} + CG_1 + IL_1} = \frac{56.4}{89.8} = 0.63 \tag{6-45}$$

Therefore,

$$rpc_1 = 1 - 0.63 = 0.37, \tag{6-46}$$

and

$$m_2 = 27.7/78.1 = 0.35 \tag{6-47}$$

$$rpc_2 = 0.65 \tag{6-48}$$

The processing sector model can now be written as

$$Q_1 = rpc_1\, a_{1,1}\, Q_1 + rpc_1\, a_{1,2}\, Q_2 + QX_1 \tag{6-49}$$

$$Q_2 = rpc_2\, a_{2,1}\, Q_1 + rpc_2\, a_{2,2}\, Q_2 + QX_2 \tag{6-50}$$

$$Q_1 = 0.37 \times 0.40\, Q_1 + 0.37 \times 0.37\, Q_2 + QX_1 \tag{6-51}$$

$$Q_2 = 0.65 \times 0.21\, Q_1 + 0.65 \times 0.02\, Q_2 + QX_2 \tag{6-52}$$

$$Q_1 = 0.15\, Q_1 + 0.14\, Q_2 + QX_1 \tag{6-53}$$

$$Q_2 = 0.14\, Q_1 + 0.01\, Q_2 + QX_2, \tag{6-54}$$

where QX_1 and QX_2 represent exogenous demand for manufacturing (1) and nonmanufacturing (2), respectively. The simultaneous solution of equations 6-49 and 6-50 is necessary to find the change in total output, given a change in QX_1 and/or QX_2. However, even for this two-industry example, the algebraic manipulations become tedious. Since we showed above that we could find the equilibrium solution using round-by-round calculations,[3] we will assign subscripts and use the same approach in this instance.

$$Q_{1,t} = 0.15\, Q_{1,t-1} + 0.14\, Q_{2,t-1} + QX_{1,t} \tag{6-55}$$

$$Q_{2,t} = 0.14\, Q_{1,t-1} + 0.01\, Q_{2,t-1} + QX_{2,t} \tag{6-56}$$

In this model, output responds to new exogenous final demand immediately and to demand for intermediate inputs with a lag of one period. One can assume that users of intermediate inputs work out of inventories in the current period and then reorder at the end of the period. The response of the processing sector to a change in QX_1 is as follows:

Period	Q	Q_1	$Q_1 - QX_1$	Q_2	QX_1	QX_2
0	0	0	0	0	0	0
1	10.0	10.0	0	0	10.0	0
2	12.9	11.5	1.5	1.4	10.0	0
3	13.5	11.9	1.9	1.6	10.0	0
4	13.7	12.0	2.0	1.7	10.0	0
5	13.7	12.0	2.0	1.7	10.0	0
6	13.7	12.0	2.0	1.7	10.0	0

Since we have a processing-sector-only model, it is not surprising to find that the multiplier is small. In this case, it is 1.37. The exogenous demand for 10 additional production QX_1 requires 2.0 additional input from other manufacturing industries and 1.7 from the nonmanufacturing industries. These increases are called the *intermediate* or *indirect* effects of the exogenous increase.

A similar calculation can be made for QX_2, as follows:

Period	Q	Q_1	$Q_1 - QX_2$	Q_2	QX_1	QX_2
0	0	0	0	0	0	0
1	0	0	0	0	0	0
2	10.0	0	0	10.0	0	10.0
3	11.5	1.4	1.4	10.1	0	10.0
4	11.9	1.6	1.6	10.3	0	10.0
5	12.0	1.7	1.7	10.3	0	10.0
6	12.0	1.7	1.7	10.3	0	10.0

Note that the processing sector effect of a change in QX_2 is smaller than that of QX_1. Also note that QX_2 uses less inputs than QX_1.

6-4 A TWO-INDUSTRY CLOSED MODEL EXAMPLE (TYPE II)

We now turn to a model that makes final consumer and government spending endogenous. We use the method that makes consumption depend on labor and proprietors' income (YLP). Recall from section 6-2 that this is equivalent to making it depend on total income (YLP + H), because an offsetting change occurs in the propensity to consume, b vs. bn. The entire structural model can be written as follows:

$$Q_1 = rpc_1 \, a_{1,1} \, Q_1 + rpc_1 \, a_{1,2} \, Q_2 + rpc_1 \, CG_1 + rpc_1 \, IL_{p1} + XFG_1 \qquad (6\text{-}57)$$

$$Q_2 = rpc_2 \, a_{2,1} \, Q_1 + rpc_2 \, a_{2,2} \, Q_2 + rpc_2 \, CG_2 + rpc_2 \, IL_{p2} + XFG_2 \qquad (6\text{-}58)$$

$$YLP = a_{y,1} \, Q_1 + a_{y,2} \, Q_2 \qquad (6\text{-}59)$$

$$CG_1 = c_1 \, YLP \qquad (6\text{-}60)$$

$$CG_2 = c_2 \, YLP, \qquad (6\text{-}61)$$

where

$$a_{y,1} = YLP_1 \div Q_1 = 23.9 \div 97.4 = 0.245 \qquad (6\text{-}62)$$

$$a_{y,2} = YLP_2 \div Q_2 = 31.1 \div 70.1 = 0.444 \qquad (6\text{-}63)$$

$$c_1 = CG_1 \div YLP = 19.4 \div 55 = 0.353 \qquad (6\text{-}64)$$

$$c_2 = CG_2 \div YLP = 45.6 \div 55 = 0.829 \qquad (6\text{-}65)$$

Using the parameter values for Michigan and introducing lags we can set forth the entire model.

$$Q_{1,t} = 0.15 \ Q_{1,t-1} + 0.14 \ Q_{2,t-1} + 0.37 \ CG_{1,t-1} + 0.37 \ IL_{p1,t-1} + XFG_{1,t} \quad (6\text{-}66)$$

$$Q_{2,t} = 0.14 \ Q_{1,t-1} + 0.01 \ Q_{2,t-1} + 0.65 \ CG_{2,t-1} + 0.65 \ IL_{p2,t-1} + XFG_{2,t} \quad (6\text{-}67)$$

$$YLP_t = 0.245 \ Q_{1,t} + 0.444 \ Q_{2,t} \quad (6\text{-}68)$$

$$CG_{1,t} = 0.353 \ YLP_t \quad (6\text{-}69)$$

$$CG_{2,t} = 0.829 \ YLP_t \quad (6\text{-}70)$$

Again, the easiest way to find the effect of an exogenous change on the Michigan economy using the model is to use a period-by-period approach. (Try the first few rounds on your calculator or write a spread sheet program.) The response of a closed I-O Michigan model to a change in XFG_1 is as follows:

Period	Q	Q_1	Q_2	YLP	CG_1	CG_2	XFG_1	XFG_2
0	0	0	0	0	0	0	0	0
1	10.0	10.0	0	2.5	0.9	2.0	10.0	0
2	14.5	11.8	2.7	4.1	1.4	3.4	10.0	0
3	16.6	12.7	3.9	4.8	1.7	4.0	10.0	0
4	17.5	13.1	4.4	5.2	1.8	4.3	10.0	0
5	17.9	13.3	4.7	5.3	1.9	4.4	10.0	0
6	18.1	13.3	4.8	5.4	1.9	4.5	10.0	0
7	18.2	13.4	4.8	5.4	1.9	4.5	10.0	0
8	18.2	13.4	4.8	5.4	1.9	4.5	10.0	0

We can see that the total output multiplier for a change in XFG_1 is 1.82. If we wanted to find the value-added multiplier, we would have to multiply the value-added portion of Q_1 and Q_2 by these values.

$$VA_1 = va_1 \ Q_1 \quad (6\text{-}71)$$

$$VA_2 = va_2 \ Q_2 \quad (6\text{-}72)$$

From table 6-3,

$$va_1 = (23.9 + 13.9) \div 97.4 = 0.388 \quad (6\text{-}73)$$

$$va_2 = (31.1 + 11.9) \div 70.1 = 0.613 \quad (6\text{-}74)$$

$$VA = 0.388 \ Q_1 + 0.613 \ Q_2 \quad (6\text{-}75)$$

$$8.14 = 0.388 \times 13.4 + 0.613 \times 4.8 \quad (6\text{-}76)$$

Thus, the VA multiplier for XFG_1 is 0.814. To find the multipliers for XFG_2, we must repeat our round-by-round calculations for a change in XFG_2.

The response of a closed I-O Michigan model to a change in XFG_2 is as follows:

Period	Q	Q_1	Q_2	YLP	CG_1	CG_2	XFG_1	XFG_2
0	0	0	0	0	0	0	0	0
1	10.0	0	10.0	4.4	1.6	3.7	0	10.0
2	14.5	2.0	12.5	6.0	2.1	5.0	0	10.0
3	16.5	2.8	13.7	6.8	2.4	5.6	0	10.0
4	17.4	3.2	14.2	7.1	2.5	5.9	0	10.0
5	17.8	3.4	14.4	7.2	2.6	6.0	0	10.0
6	18.0	3.5	14.5	7.3	2.6	6.0	0	10.0
7	18.1	3.5	14.6	7.3	2.6	6.1	0	10.0
8	18.1	3.5	14.6	7.3	2.6	6.1	0	10.0

The output multiplier for XFG_2 is 1.81, which happens to be about the same as the multiplier for XFG_1. The value added for X_2 is

$$10.3 = 0.388 \times 3.5 + 0.613 \times 14.6 \qquad (6\text{-}77)$$

The multiplier of 1.03 for XFG_2 is much larger than the value-added multiplier[4] of 0.814 for XFG_1. A good deal of this difference is because the value added per dollar of output for Q_2 is much larger than it is for Q_1. This shows that a key advantage of using an input-output structure over the economic base model is that the multipliers are different for a similar exogenous change in alternative industries.

6-5 AN INPUT-OUTPUT AND NATIONAL INCOME AND PRODUCT ACCOUNTS COMPARISON

In this section, we extend the presentation above from a simplified illustration to a more inclusive overview. In diagrams 6-1 through 6-3, we use figures adapted from the *Survey of Current Business*, May 1984.

Diagram 6-1

Gross Domestic Product in the National Income and Product Accounts

Compensation of Employees	Personal Consumption Expenditures
Proprietors' Income	Gross Private Domestic Investment
Rental Income of Persons	Net Exports
Net Interest	Government Purchases
Business Transfer Payments	
Indirect Business Taxes	
Less: Subsidies Less Current	
Surplus of Government Enterprises	
Capital Consumption Allowances	
CHARGES AGAINST GDP	GDP

Diagram 6-2

Gross Domestic Product in an Input-Output Format

	Producers	Final Demand				
Producers		Pers. Cons. Exp.	Gross Privt. Domes. Invest.	Net Exports	Govnmt Purch.	GDP
Value Added	Compens. of Employees					
	Profit-Type Income, Net Int., & Capital Consump Allowance					
	Indirect Business Taxes					
	Charges Against GDP					

Diagram 6-3

Input-Output Use Table

		Industries			Final Demand (GDP)				Total Com Out.
		I_1	I_2	..	I_n	Pers. Cons. Exp.	Gross Privt. Dom. Inves.	Net Expt	Govt. Pur.	
Com- mods.	C_1									
	C_2									
	..									
	C_n									
Val. Add. (Chrg)	Comp. of Emps.									
	Profit Type Inc., Net Int., and Cap. Cons. Allow									
	Ind. Bus. Taxes									
Tot. Ind. Output										

I_i = industry i: $i = 1, 2, ..., n$
C_j = commodity j: $j = 1, 2, ..., n$

In the figure in diagram 6-1, the items in the National Income and Product Accounts are shown. This follows the form shown for state product accounts presented in table 2-16 in chapter 2. Here, GDP is divided into four components of spending, and the charges against GDP divided into nine components. In table 2-16, we aggregated some of the categories, and we also had to separate earnings into those by residents and those by nonresidents.

In diagram 6-2, we find the more disaggregate counter parts to form 2 on table 6-1. Note that the balance between the charges against GDP and GDP is preserved.

In diagram 6-3, we see the Input-Output Use table. This resembles table 6-3. The major difference is that the inputs have been characterized by commodity, while the uses have been shown by industry. The distinction between commodity and industry arises from the fact that a firm may produce more than one commodity. For example, a firm that is primarily engaged in manufacturing production may produce some business services. The firm is classified as being in the manufacturing industry because manufactured goods are their major product. In the Use table, the inputs are assembled by commodity. Therefore, in the Use table, the business service part of the inputs are grouped with services, so we can observe the amount of services used by each industry and each sector of final demand. The reclassification of inputs by commodities means that, even though the aggregate identity that total inputs equal total outputs is preserved, in this table the inputs to an industry (at the bottom of column) may not equal the output of the respective commodity (at the end of the row).

Another table, called a Make table, is also provided by the Bureau of Economic Analysis. In this table, the industrial sources of each commodity are shown. Thus, in the example cited above, we might find that ninety-five percent of services are supplied by the services industry and five percent are supplied by the manufacturing industry. Now, if we assume that commodities are supplied in fixed proportions by industry, we can use these proportions in the Make table to convert the Use table into an Industry-by-Industry table. For example, some of the commodity service inputs would be transferred to the manufacturing industry sector, because, in our example, services were a secondary product of the manufacturing industry. After this has been done, we would have an industry-by-industry table which would again fulfill the identity that the total output of each industry (at the end of a row) would equal the total inputs to that industry (at the bottom of the column). Therefore, it would again match the structure of table 6-3. We assume that we are using an industry-by-industry table in the rest of this book. This is necessary, because all of our employment and output data are industry based.

6-6 PARAMETERS FOR IMPLEMENTING A REGIONAL INPUT-OUTPUT MODEL

There is extensive literature dealing with input-output analysis in general and regional input-output analysis in particular.[5] For regional input-output, there are two basic approaches. The first is survey based tables. The second is nonsurvey based. The survey based tables are very expensive. For example, for a 50-industry model, there are 2,500 (50 × 50) interindustry coefficients to be estimated. Thus, in spite of the expense, a great deal of error may be anticipated in estimating these coefficients, based on a small sample.[6] For the nonsurvey approach, a national interindustry matrix is typically modified to represent the regional economy.

Here, we describe one of these approaches, which is called the regional purchase coefficient (*rpc*) approach. Other approaches include the location quotient and the supply-and-demand pool approaches. These approaches modify national coefficients if demand in an area is greater than the supply. Both approaches assume that there is no cross hauling. For still other approaches, see Miller and Blair, cited in note 5.

Two parameter sets are especially key in building an operational regional input-output model, using the regional purchase coefficient (*rpc*) approach. The first is the technological matrix (i.e., the $a_{i,j}$ values, see equations 6-40 through 6-43) and the other is the vector of the proportion of local use supplied locally (i.e., the regional purchase coefficients (*rpc*$_i$'s), see equation 6-46).

The Technological Matrix

A technological matrix can be obtained for the United States either from the Bureau of Economic Analysis (BEA) or the Bureau of Labor Statistics (BLS). The BLS matrix also includes a projected matrix for a year in the future. While individual areas may have different technology for various reasons, it has been shown that, if the differences are random, they tend to offset each other and may not be important in calculating a multiplier.[7] One method for accounting for differences in the composition of industries at the detailed (four digit) level is to weight each four digit industry coefficient by its relative importance in the particular region. The $a_{i,j}$'s are obtained from an industry-by-industry table. As illustrated above, they are obtained by dividing each cell in the column by the column total (equations 6-40 through 6-43).

The Regional Purchase Coefficient (RPC$_i$)

As explained previously, the regional purchase coefficient (rpc_i) for a good or service is the proportion of demand for that good or service within a region that is supplied by the region to itself. Here, we report on an rpc estimating equation for manufacturing industries based on the 1977 Census of Transportation, which is the only usable transportation census currently available, and on a subjective approach to the estimation of nonmanufacturing rpc's.[8]

The proportion (by value) of shipments made by producers in each state to destinations in the same state is estimated for as many two- and four-digit SIC manufactured commodities in as many states as possible from the 1977 Census of Transportation data. Since the 1977 Census reports all shipments for those commodity state combinations covered, including those less than twenty-five miles (which were excluded in 1972), its two million observations are a rich source of information. We are able to obtain 472 two-digit SIC estimates (out of a possible 21 industries $\times$ 48 states = 1,008) and 1,387 four-digit estimates.

We next calculate supply/demand ratios at the four-digit level. These estimates are based on 1977 County Business Patterns employment and wage data, which are used to estimate production (supply) and on demand estimates using a 466 sector 1977 input-output table. To ensure consistency, demands and supplies were summed across all states. Exports out of the United States plus inventory change are then added to demand, and imports are added to supply. The demands estimated at the state level are then adjusted to assure that total use is equal to total availability.

The definitional equation for the regional purchase coefficient is as follows:

$$\mathbf{RPC}_i = \mathbf{LS}_i/\mathbf{D}_i = (\mathbf{Q}_i \times \mathbf{PS}_i)/\mathbf{D}_i \qquad (6\text{-}78)$$

where

LS_i = local supply of the good or service i by the region to itself

Q_i = the corresponding total supply or output in the region in thousands of 1977 dollars

PS_i = The proportion of output i shipped to destinations within the region

D_i = demand in thousands of 1977 dollars for i

A desirable characteristic for the functional form for estimating RPC$_i$ is that it should, like the RPC itself, vary strictly between 0 and 1. In the present analysis, several functions that fulfilled this criterion are tried, including various forms of the logistic function.

The best results for explaining the variation in the RPC are obtained with

$$RPC_i = D^{[(e^{-1/x_i}) - 1]},$$

(6-79)

where

$$x_i = k(Z_{1i})^{a'_1} \times (Z_{2i})^{a'_2} \times (Z_{3i})^{a_3} \cdots (Z_{ni})^{a_n}$$

(6-80)

a'_1, a'_2 = key parameters on endogenous model variables

$a_3, a_4 \ldots a_n$ = parameters to be estimated for the equation as a whole for the explanatory variables

k = an intercept calibration term

$Z_{j, i}$ ($j = 1, 2$) = the explanatory variables that are endogenous to the model

$Z_{j, i}$ ($j = 3 \ldots n$) = e raised to the value of the explanatory variables that are exogenous to the model

A linear form of equation 6-79 for regression purposes is obtained by first substituting equation 6-78 into equation 6-79, giving the expression

$$LS = D^{e^{-1/x}}$$

(6-81)

In this equation for local supply, the i subscripts are left out for simplicity. It is transformed, through repeated logarithmic and algebraic operations, into

$$\ln \left[\frac{-1}{\ln (\ln (LS)/\ln (D))} \right] = \ln K + a'_1 \ln Z_1 + a'_2 \ln Z_2 + \sum_{j=3}^{n} a_j Z_j$$

(6-82)

It is the parameters for equation 6-82 that are estimated using ordinary least squares (OLS) methods. The results of this regression analysis appear in table 6-4.

TABLE 6-4

Estimated Parameters for the Four-Digit Regional Purchase Coefficient (RPC) Calibration Equation (Equation 6-82)

Variable	Coefficient	t-statistic
Constant term (k)	21.33	
Demand (a'_1)	0.18	8.73
Supply/demand (a'_2)	0.72	16.17
Weight/value (a_3)	0.29	12.64
Percentage of U.S. land area (a_4)	0.27	8.64
Establishments per employee relative to United States (a_5)	0.12	2.54
Midwest dummy (a_6)	-0.12	-1.98
Plains dummy (a_7)	-0.61	-6.64
East South Central dummy (a_8)	-0.58	-7.93
Pacific dummy (a_9)	0.43	4.48
SIC 21 (Tobacco) dummy (a_{10})	1.05	2.84
SIC 22 (Textiles) dummy (a_{11})	0.52	3.35
SIC 25 (Furniture) dummy (a_{12})	0.36	1.69
SIC 27 (Printing) dummy (a_{13})	0.81	3.89
SIC 30 (Rubber) dummy (a_{14})	-0.67	-3.38
SIC 32 (Stone, clay, etc.) dummy (a_{15})	0.24	2.56
SIC 38 (Instruments) dummy (a_{16})	0.37	1.95
SIC 2041 (Flour and Grain Mill Products) dummy (a_{17})	-0.64	-2.23
SIC 3599 (Machinery etc., electrical n.e.c.) dummy (a_{18})	1.16	4.25

R_2 = 0.4405 from the linear regression (equation 6-81)

A_2 = 0.7413 when transformed back to the R form (equation 6-79)

F = 58.687; degrees of freedom = 1.348

The first explanatory variables are supply and demand. The supply/demand ratio is the same concept that we used to approximate the location quotient in chapter 2. In some input-output regional calibration systems, it is used directly, much as the location quotient was used in chapter 2. Here, it is used as only part of the equation to predict the RPC.

The positive exponent on the weight-to-value ratio in table 6-4 indicates that products with a low value per ton are more likely to be supplied from within a region than those with a high value per ton. This is the case because the delivered prices of the former are increased proportionately more by transportation costs than the prices of the latter. The positive coefficient on the region's percentage of United States land area indicates that a larger region is more likely to contain its own suppliers.

The establishments/employee ratio acts as a proxy for the inverse of expected distance to the nearest supplier in the region. Therefore, the higher this ratio is, the greater the local availability and the higher the RPC. Furthermore, the more production is spread among different establishments, the greater the potential for product diversity (and for the availability of precisely the correct product) within the four-digit SIC category in the region.

The dummy variables in table 6-4 need no discussion here other than to note that the large positive coefficient on the Pacific region variable probably reflects the effect of high delivery costs for products from the old Industrial Belt on their ability to compete with locally produced products on the West Coast. This suggests further research on the determinates of RPC should take transportation costs more systematically into account.

Given the above results, we designed a step-by-step procedure for obtaining the RPC's for a model with fifty-three sectors (two-digit) and for a 500 sector (four-digit) Input-Output model. These steps use the equation 6-82 results, the two-digit observed data, and the detailed four-digit SIC information for each state. A description of this process and a sample set of RPC's and their associated supply and demand data are found in table 6-5.

There is no shipment data for the nonmanufacturing industries. This means that we must adopt another approach. One such approach is to assume that no cross-hauling exists. Using this approach, the percentage of output shipped to destinations within the region is assumed to be 100, if the supply/demand ratio is less than 1. If the supply/demand ratio exceeds 1, the R is set equal to 1. This is the supply/demand pool approach and is approximated by the location quotient approach covered in chapter 2.

However, we take an alternative approach. We first assign a subjective proportion of within-state shipments (PS) to each sector at the four-digit level. In many cases, this is 0.95, a value that allows for some sales to visitors, exports of business services, and the like. However, we make some significant exceptions to this value. Our subjective PS values for hotels and lodging places is 0.2, because a region's residents are, in most cases, only minor users of the region's commercial lodgings, especially in small areas. The subjective PS is given the value 0.5 for interregional transportation services on the assumption that only one of the terminals would be in the region in question. The PS values can easily be altered in instances where survey or other information provides a more concrete basis for estimation. Next, we apply these PS values to the four-digit supply/demand ratios to obtain estimated RPC values. These values are modified if they exceed a subjective adjustment value. This value is 0.95 or 0.9 in almost all cases except for eating and drinking establishments, where it is 0.8, and hotels and other lodging places, where it is 0.3. The values that exceed their assumed adjustment values are modified in such a way that they asymptotically approach the absolute maximum value of 1.00, except for hotels and other lodging places, where the absolute maximum is 0.6.

Finally, these four-digit RPC values are aggregated using four-digit demand weights to obtain two-digit RPC estimates. The aggregated estimates are used in the model, which in turn is used to generate the data employed in the next research step.

The following method is used in making maximum use of both two-digit and four-digit SIC and commodity shipment data, to estimate and reconcile two-digit and four-digit regional purchase coefficients:

1. We use the estimating equation 6-82, the four-digit County Patterns data, and a 500 sector input-output model to estimate the four-digit RPC's for each of the 451 manufacturing industries in each state. In cases where either the RPC or the proportion of output shipped (PS) within state is estimated to be greater than a present limit (0.95), a transformation is made to reduce it and put it on a curve that is asymptotic to one.

2. We aggregate these four-digit results to the twenty-one two-digit manufacturing sectors in the 53-sector model using the four-digit estimates and the four-digit supplies and demands. This gives us estimated RPC's and implicit PS's within state for each of the two-digit industries.

3. In cases where we observed shipment data from the 1977 Census of Transportation data, we use the observed two-digit data to estimate the PS within a state. We then compare the observed PS within state with the implicit PS within state from the four-digit calculation. We find a systematic tendency for the four-digit aggregation to underestimate the two-digit PS within state. This may be due

to a sampling bias toward four-digit industries that ship out of state.

4. We use the estimates of systematic bias from those states for which we have observations to adjust the aggregated four-digit results for those states for which there are no observations. These two-digit estimates, plus the observed values, then give us a full set of two-digit RPC's and PS's within state.

5. Although step four completed the requirements for the two-digit model, we took one further step to calibrate the four-digit RPCs. In this step, we adjusted the k value (see equation 6-82) in the four-digit industries that make up the two-digit industries in each state to find the k value that would yield a set of four-digit RPCs and PSs within a state consistent with the two-digit estimates that were observed or had been adjusted for bias. This adjustment routine included constraints on all RPCs and PSs when these values exceeded 0.95 (see step one). These adjustment values can be used for calibrating county models within a state. A sample of the RPC values for a particular industry and state are reported in table 6-5.

TABLE 6-5

Michigan — SIC 32: Stone, Clay, and Glass Products
(An example of RPC values calculated using the method described above.)

SIC	Industry name	100 × RPC	100 × PS	SDR	Demand
32	Stone, clay, and glass products	47	59	0.81	1,676,855
3211	Flat glass	56	41	1.38	104,472
3221	Glass containers	26	82	0.32	138,867
3229	Pressed and blown glass, n.e.c.	0	10	0.03	158,111
3231	Glass products from purchased glass	56	38	1.40	127,191
3241	Hydraulic cement	80	58	1.39	149,435
3251	Brick and structural clay tile	66	77	0.86	4,605
3253	Ceramic wall and floor tile	24	82	0.29	1,837
3255	Clay refractories	3	78	0.04	10,640
3259	Structural clay products, n.e.c.	63	70	0.90	2,077
3261	Vitreous plumbing fixtures	4	60	0.07	1,624
3262	Vitreous china food utensils	0	0	0.00	10,597
3263	Fine earthenware — table and kitchen	29	44	0.67	10,935
3264	Porcelain electrical supplies	41	29	1.42	30,100
3269	Pottery products, n.e.c.	5	31	0.16	15,662
3271	Concrete block and brick	79	76	1.04	51,662
3272	Concrete products, exc. block and B	79	79	1.00	87,431
3273	Ready-mixed concrete	86	86	1.00	206,014
3274	Lime	24	98	0.24	22,520
3275	Gypsum products	71	65	1.09	55,599
3281	Cut stone and stone products	60	96	0.63	11,186
3291	Abrasive products	45	57	0.79	136,928
3292	Asbestos products	0	0	0.00	154,489
3293	Gaskets, packing and selling device	29	30	0.95	63,445
3295	Minerals and earths	84	54	1.56	40,717
3296	Mineral wool	38	57	0.67	40,717
3297	Nonclay refractories	43	69	0.63	16,989
3299	Nonclay mining products, n.e.c.	35	95	0.37	19,785

RPC: Regional Purchase Coefficient. The proportion of Michigan demand fulfilled by Michigan output.

PS: The proportion of Michigan output shipped to destinations in Michigan.

SDR: The ratio of total supply to total demand in Michigan.

Demand: The implicit within state use in thousands of 1977 dollars as calculated by 500 Sector Model for Michigan.

6-7 TESTS OF A REGIONAL INPUT-OUTPUT MODEL

To test the validity of a 53-sector Input-Output model, we use the forecasting model in which economic base employment by industry is predicted for $t + 1$ as regional base share by industry in t multiplied by the change in the United States employment in that industry from t to $t + 1$, plus last year's regional base employment (see chapter 2, equation 2-125). We also predict exogenous income (see Economic Base Model B — chapter 2) as a share of the U.S. amount of this type of income (property income, transfers, taxes). The results are shown on table 6-6.

TABLE 6-6

53-Sector I-O Ex Post Forecast Error Using Shares of U.S. Employment by Industry and Exogenous Income (1967-1983)

	Mean % Error		Mean Absolute % Error	
	I-O Model	Naive Model	I-O Model	Naive Model
Connecticut	0.1	-1.4	0.6	2.4
Maryland	--	-1.8	0.4	2.2
New York	1.6	-1.2	1.6	1.3
Illinois	1.1	-0.4	1.1	1.9
Michigan	0.8	-0.6	0.8	3.3
Nebraska	0.0	-2.0	0.5	2.4
Florida	-1.1	-4.3	1.1	4.8
South Carolina	-0.7	-2.2	0.7	2.9
Colorado	-1.1	-4.5	1.1	4.5
Wyoming	-0.7	-4.5	1.3	4.8
U.S. AVERAGE	**-0.2**	**-2.1**	**0.8**	**2.9**

The mean average absolute percent error (MAPE) for this model is only .8 percent versus 2.9 percent for the naive, no-change model. This is a dramatic decrease from the MAPE of 2.3 for the economic base model over a sample period and number of regions that yielded a 2.8 MAPE for the naive model. This result would appear to indicate that I-O structure can make an important contribution to forecast performance and that the I-O model may be a good representation of the short-term relationships in regional economies.

We will now use the multi-industry framework, as well as the prototype model developed in chapter 3, as a starting point for a generalized regional model that can be calibrated and used for forecasting and policy analysis. This model is covered in the next chapter.

NOTES ON CHAPTER 6

1. This chapter is adapted, in part, from Treyz, G. (1987). "Fundamentals of Regional Macroeconomic Modeling: Part II," *The Survey of Regional Economic Literature,* June, 2: 1 – 28.

2. In areas where items are transshipped, the items that come in simply to be shipped out again are excluded from both M and XFG.

3. The computer algorithms for larger input-output models also usually use this approach.

4. The value-added multiplier is often used to refer to the total change in value added divided by the direct change in value added. In this case, under this definition, the value-added multiplier for nonmanufacturing (industry 2) would be $1.03 \div .613$ (from equation 6-74) $= 1.68$, and it would be $.816 \div .388$ (from equation 6-73) $= 2.10$ for manufacturing (industry 1).

5. Basic references in this field include Miller and Blair (1985) and K. R. Polenske (1980).

6. See Shelby D. Gerking (August 1976).

7. See B.H. Stevens and G. A. Trainer. (1980).

8. The following section is from Treyz and Stevens. (1985): 553 – 555.

CHAPTER 7

THE SPECIFICATION OF AN OPERATIONAL
FORECASTING AND SIMULATION MODEL[1]

In this chapter, we expand the simple prototype model developed in chapter 3 into a form that can be used as an operational model. We also draw on chapter 6, where multiple industries were introduced. Here, we generalize the chapter 3 model to a model with n-private nonfarm industries, m-areas, p-occupations, v-age/sex cohorts, x-factors of production, and z-components of demand. The chapter is organized with the same structure as chapter 3. In almost all cases, the original categories are sufficient because the simple model illustrates all of the major linkages in this expanded model.

Chapter 3 concludes with a diagram of the linkages in the prototype model (diagram 3-18). Here, we present this same diagram, with a change in the definitions of R_n and R_r, as diagram 7-1. Again, the diagram only shows the key linkages in the model. The reader should reread the summary to chapter 3 at this point.

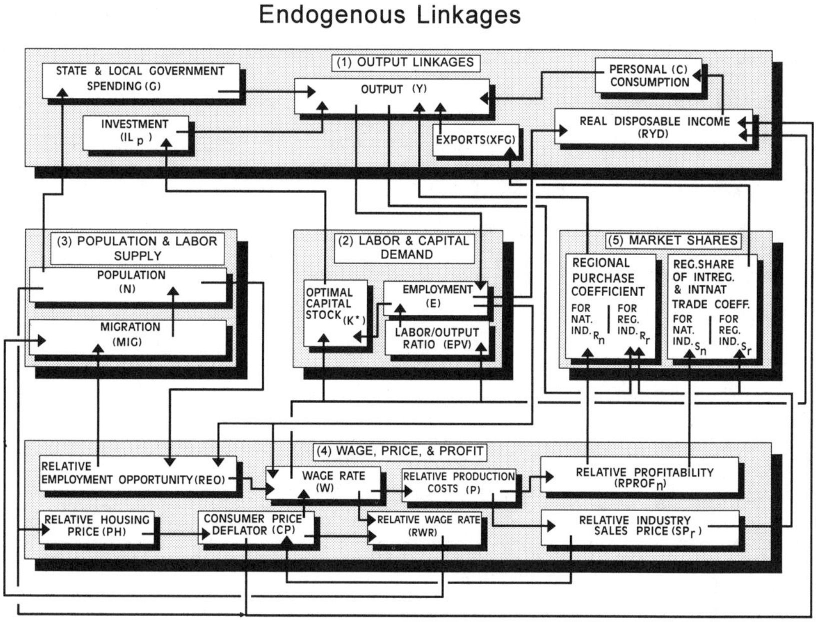

Endogenous Linkages

Diagram 7-1

We now proceed with the presentation of a generalized model in detail. The chapter 6 Input-Output (I-O) model is a special case of this model. In chapter 9, we explore the I-O and other special cases of this model. A derivation of the cost of capital is presented in the appendix for this chapter. A sample operational computerized model built using the specifications described in this chapter is available from the author and explaind in the appendix to chapter 8. It is used for the policy simulations in chapter 8.

7-1 OUTPUT LINKAGES

Output Equations

In this section, we develop a general model that uses an input-output structure with n-industries. This structure allows us to develop relationships among industries that may be key to our analysis, rather than relying on the aggregate variable relationships in the prototype model that average out industry differences.

First, we extend the Keynesian demand function,

$$Y = C + IL_p + G + XFG - M \qquad (7-1)$$

to an n-industries form. In the equation above, we only consider the final demand for consumption, investment, government spending, and net exports. In an input-output framework, as discussed in chapter 6, we consider the intermediate demand as well as final demand. *Intermediate demand* can also be thought of as the demand for an industry's output that is used as an input of production. For example, the production of steel requires coke as an input. This would be considered an intermediate demand for coke. In a multi-industry framework, output of industry i (Q_i), which is the sum of final demand and intermediate demand, can be represented as

$$Q_i = \sum_{j=1}^{n} Q_{i,j} + C_i + IL_{p,i} + G_i + XFG_i - M_i \qquad i = 1,\ldots,n \qquad (7-2)$$

where $Q_{i,j}$ is output of industry i purchased by industry j. C_i (personal consumption), $IL_{p,i}$ (planned investment spending), G_i (local and state government spending), XFG_i (exports), and M_i (imports) are the components of final demand for industry i's product.

This method of accounting can be called *accounting by destination of output or distribution*. In the prototype model, we make imports endogenous and show the locally supplied share of all final demand sectors, including exports. Here, we repeat equation 3-1.

$$Y = R (C + IL_p + G + XFG) \qquad (7\text{-}3)$$

In an n-industry model, the similar equation is

$$Q_i = \sum_{j=1}^{n} R_i \, a_{i,j} \times Q_j + R_i (C_i + IL_{p,i} + G_i) + XFG_i \qquad i = 1,\ldots,n \qquad (7\text{-}4)$$

where R_i is the regional purchase coefficient (RPC) for the output of industry i and $a_{i,j}$ is a technical coefficient. The RPC is the proportion of local use that is supplied locally. Now, all exports are supplied locally, because intermediate inputs are modeled explicitly. Therefore, XFG_i is not multiplied by the RPC (R_i) in equation 7-4. For example, in a two-sector (steel and coke) model with the inclusion of the intermediate inputs, equation 7-4 can be written out as

$$\text{steel: } Q_1 = R_1 \, a_{1,1} \, Q_1 + R_1 \, a_{1,2} \, Q_2 + R_1 (C_1 + IL_{p1} + G_1) + XFG_1 \qquad (7\text{-}5)$$

$$\text{coke: } Q_2 = R_2 \, a_{2,1} \, Q_1 + R_2 \, a_{2,2} \, Q_2 + R_2 (C_2 + IL_{p2} + G_2) + XFG_2 \qquad (7\text{-}6)$$

The regional purchase coefficient, R_i, can be calibrated using detailed four-digit SIC data (see section 6-6) and is an endogenous variable in the model (see section 7-5 for a detailed discussion). The technical coefficients can be taken from historical and projected U.S. national input-output tables provided by BLS.[2] Using these tables, the coefficients can be updated every year on the assumption that technological change occurs steadily over time.

For a *single area* n-industry model,[3] the general demand equation is equation 7-4, which shows the demand for an industry's output. We next develop the production equation. The total output of industry i (Q_i) can also be accounted for from the production side because total sales are equal to all material inputs ($Q_{j,i}$) plus value added, VA_i. Thus,

$$Q_i = \sum_{j=1}^{n} a_{j,i} Q_i + VA_i \, , \qquad (7\text{-}7)$$

or

$$VA_i = (1 - \sum_{j=1}^{n} a_{j,i}) \, Q_i \qquad (7\text{-}8)$$

The sources of the value added are the value of factor inputs used in industry i's production. The summation of the value added across all industries is total value added or gross regional product (GRP). In a two-sector model, equation 7-7 can be expressed as

$$\text{steel: } Q_1 = a_{1,1} Q_1 + a_{2,1} Q_1 + VA_1 \tag{7-9}$$

$$\text{coke: } Q_2 = a_{1,2} Q_2 + a_{2,2} Q_2 + VA_2 \tag{7-10}$$

Note that there is no need for regional purchase coefficients. The term $a_{2,1} Q_1$ is the amount of coke input used by the steel industry. It tells us the value of the intermediate input, coke, used in the production of steel. How much of that demand is filled by local output is a different question, which is answered by the output method of accounting in equation 7-4.

In general, the value added in any industry is not necessarily equal to the final demand for the product of that industry. In the aggregate, however, GRP (total value added) is equal to total final demand, and the relationship

$$\sum_{i=1}^{n} VA_i = Y = \sum_{i=1}^{n} \left(C_i + IL_{p,i} + G_i + XFG_i - M_i \right) \tag{7-11}$$

would hold in equilibrium. If $IL_{p,i}$ is replaced by IL_i, then this is an identity that is valid for any subnational area or any nation.

Next, we generalize the equations from one area to a multi-area region. This is done by dividing exports out of the area into two parts. The first part is shipments to other areas within the multi-area region, and the second is sales outside of the multi-area region. Using equation 7-4, we develop the following equation:

$$Q_i = R_i \left(\sum_{j=1}^{n} a_{i,j} Q_j + C_i + IL_{p,i} + G_i \right) + XFG_i^{k,r} + XFG_i^{k,u} \tag{7-12}$$

where $XFG_i^{k,r}$ is exports from area (k) to the rest of the multi-area (r) region and $XFG_i^{k,u}$ is exports from k to the rest of the country and to the rest of the world (u). Thus, the value XFG_i in equation 7-4 is replaced by these two variables. In chapter 3, export determination in the single sector model is $S \times XFG^u$ (equation 3-2), which is the export share (S) multiplied by external demand (XFG^u). Using a similar expression, we first show the determination of exports to the rest of the multi-area region, given by

$$XFG_i^{k,r} = S_i^{k,r} \times \left(\sum_{h=1,h \neq k}^{m} M_i^h \right), \tag{7-13}$$

where $S_i^{k,r}$ is the share of imports into other areas from area k, M_i^h is value of imports in other areas, and m is the number of areas in the multi-area region.[4]

The imports in area h are determined by

$$M_i^h = \left(1 - R_i^h\right)\left(\sum_{j=1}^{n} a_{i,j} Q_j^h + C_i^h + I_i^h + G_i^h\right)$$
$$h = 1,\ldots,m \ \ and \ h \neq k,$$

(7-14)

where R_i^h is the RPC for industry i in area h.

Exports from region k can also be to the rest of the country and the rest of the world. The equation is

$$XFG_i^{k,u} = S_i^{k,u} \times XFG_i^{u} ,$$

(7-15)

where S_i^{ku} is the regional share of interregional trade in the United States and rest of the world net of exports to the other areas in the multi-area region, and XFG_i^{u} is interregional trade in the United States and U.S. international exports.

Consumption Equations

We now introduce the determination of consumption. In the single-sector model, the consumption equation 3-3 is defined as

$$C = k_c \left(\frac{C^u}{RYD^u}\right) RYD$$

(7-16)

In a model with n-industry sectors and z-consumption components, consumption (C_i) is determined as

$$C_i = \sum_{j=1}^{z} PCE_{i,j} \ Concol_j \ C_j^u(RYD/RYD^u)$$

(7-17)

$PCE_{i,j}$ is a coefficient that denotes the proportion of consumption in the jth consumption category satisfied by industry i. $Concol_j$ is a location-specific differential consumption ratio, RYD represents real disposable income in the area. C_j^u and RYD_j^u are the consumption and real disposable income, respectively, in the United States.[5]

The value of $Concol_j$ is calculated from a survey of consumer expenditures. It indicates the amount of the jth consumption category purchased per dollar of disposable income in an area relative to that amount in the United States. In Florida, for example, it would be above 1 for health services and below 1 for snow shovel purchases.

Real Disposable Income Equations

The equations for determining personal income (YP) and real disposable income (RYD) follow the general structure of those presented for the prototype model. One difference is that W represents YLP/E in the prototype model, but it is redefined to include only wage and salary disbursements (WSD/E) in the model presented in this chapter. Here, we also need industry specific wage rates. The wage and salary disbursements for each major sector (WSD$_I$) can be calculated as

$$WSD_I = \sum_{i \in I}^{n} E_i \times W_i \, , \tag{7-18}$$

where E$_i$ is employment in industry i, W$_i$ is wage rate of industry i, and I is the major industry sector to which the relevant minor sectors (the i's) belong.

In addition to wages, employees receive other-labor income, i.e., fringe benefits. Also, proprietors' income is generated by nonwage and salaried employees. These were included in the earnings per worker in the prototype model in chapter 3 but are treated separately here. Given that these two categories (other labor income and proprietors' income) are lumped together in current BEA data for major sectors and not reported for detailed sectors, we take a ratio of these payments to employment by major industry. Thus, we develop an equation to capture regional differences in this ratio and changes in this ratio over time. The equation is

$$YOL_I = \lambda_{YOL} \times E_I \times \frac{YOL_I^u}{E_I^u} \, , \tag{7-19}$$

where YOL$_I$ is other-labor income and proprietors' income. The parameter λ_{YOL} is a region-specific coefficient and is above 1 if the region has a higher YOL$_I$ to E$_I$ ratio than the nation, and E$_I$ is employment in major industry sector I. Then, total labor and proprietors' income for major industry I in the area is

$$YLP_I = WSD_I + YOL_I, \tag{7-20}$$

and total labor and proprietors' income for all industries in the area is

$$YLP = \sum_I YLP_I \qquad (7\text{-}21)$$

Other components of personal income are personal contributions to social insurance (VSS), property income (DIR, which is dividends, interest, and rent), residential adjustment (RA), and transfer payments (VP). We introduce equations related to each component in the following paragraphs. The equations closely parallel equations 3-10 through 3-13 in the prototype model.

Personal contributions to social insurance (i.e., social security taxes) is modeled on a per employee basis as

$$VSS = \lambda_{VSS} \times WSD \times (VSS^u \div WSD^u), \qquad (7\text{-}22)$$

where λ_{VSS} is a coefficient calculated historically to adjust for regional differences in VSS per employee, and E is total employment in the area.

Property income (DIR) is modeled on a per capita rate for each of two age groups: those 65 and older (N65) and those younger than 65 (NK). First, the ratio of the per capita property income of the N65 group relative to the per capita property income of the NK group is calculated as $m65$. The following composite in property income units is found:

$$NP = NK + (m65 \times N65) \qquad (7\text{-}23)$$

Finally, property income is modeled using relative property income units as

$$DIR = \lambda_{DIR} \times NP \times (DIR^u/NP^u), \qquad (7\text{-}24)$$

where λ_{DIR} is a coefficient to adjust for regional differences in DIR per property income unit and NP is the number of property income units in the area. Thus, the model assumes that relative property income unit receipts will remain constant in the face of population changes.

The *residence adjustment* (RA) is used to convert place-of-work income (wage and salaries, other labor income, and personal contributions for social insurance reported by place of work) to a place-of-residence basis. It closely follows treatment for a single region in equation 3-10 in the prototype model. In our model, RA is formulated as a fixed share of the income on which it depends. If the residence adjustment in the last history year (RA_T) is positive, which means that some residents who live in the area work outside of the area, then it will depend on income outside of the area. For a single-area model, this is income in the rest of nation. For a multi-area model, it first draws on income arising from negative residential adjustments in other areas in the multiarea region (LOSTINC). If this is below the sum of the positive RA's, the remainder is the calibrated area proportion of applicable income in the nation. If RA_T is negative, it depends on local income (i.e., wages, proprietors' and other labor income less social security contributions) on the assumption that the same share of locally generated income will be earned by out of area workers as has been in the past. The equation for RA is

$$
RA = \begin{cases} \lambda_{RAMR} \times LOSTINC + \lambda_{RAU} \times (WDSNF^u + YOLNF^u - VSS^u), \\ \quad if RA_T \geq 0 \qquad\qquad (7\text{-}25) \\ \lambda_{RA} \times (WSDNF + YOLNF - VSS), \ if RA_T < 0 \end{cases}
$$

$$(7\text{-}26)$$

where λ_{RAMR}, λ_{RAU}, λ_{RA} are coefficients (for a single-area model, $\lambda_{RAMR} = 0$), LOSTINC is the sum of the income in the rest of the multi-area region that was generated by negative residential adjustments, and WSDNF (WSDNF^u) and YOLNF (YOLNF^u) are nonfarm wages and other labor income, respectively.

The equation for *transfer payments* (VP) is based on the assumption that transfers are directed primarily at three groups: those over 65 (N65), those under 65 who are not working (NK − E), and those not working regardless of age (N − E). Using U.S. data on transfers by type, the relative rates per group were determined so that the following equation for transfer units could be formed:

$$NV = vg \times N65 + vk \times [NK - E \times (1 + (RA/YLP))] + [N - E (1 + (RA/YLP))],$$
$$(7\text{-}27)$$

where *vg* is the transfer payment rate per capita of the over 65 group relative to the residual group, *vk* is the transfer payment rate of the under 65 not working group relative to the residual group, and $(1 + (RA/YLP))$ is an adjustment using the residential adjustment (RA) and labor and proprietors' income (YLP) to adjust employment from place-of-work to place-of-residence basis.

The equation for transfer payments is

$$VP = \lambda_{VP} \times NV \times (VP^u \div NV^u),$$
$$(7\text{-}28)$$

where λ_V is a coefficient to adjust for local differences in transfer payments per transfer unit. Finally, the equation for personal income becomes

$$YP = YLP - VSS + RA + DIR + VP$$
$$(7\text{-}29)$$

Real disposable income (RYD) for the area is

$$RYD = (YP - TAXES) \div CP \qquad (7\text{-}30)$$

where TAXES is the rest of the deductions (primarily local, state, and federal income taxes) that are taken from personal income. CP is the consumer price deflator, which is discussed in detail in section 7-4.

The TAXES equation depends on the amount of income net of transfer income. Transfer income is excluded, because most transfer payments are not taxed. It is adjusted again for regional differences (by λ_{TAXES}) and also changes as tax rates change in the United States.

$$TAXES = \lambda_{TAXES} \times (YP - VP) \times \left(\frac{TAXES^u}{YP^u - VP^u} \right) \qquad (7\text{-}31)$$

This improves on the implicit treatment of taxes in the prototype model (equation 3-7) in that it will reflect changes in U.S. tax rates by federal and state governments, on average, as they affect the local economy.

Investment Equations

In the prototype model, investment (recall equation 3-14) is determined as

$$IL_{p,t} = \alpha \left[\left(k_I K_t^* \right) - (1 - dr^u) K_{t-1} \right] \qquad (7\text{-}32)$$

In the generalized model, there are four types of investment to be considered: residential, nonresidential, equipment investment, and changes in business inventories. In a model with disaggregated industries, it is necessary to allocate demand for investment to the industries supplying the investment goods and carrying out the construction. For nonresidential and equipment investment, we can write the investment equation as

$$IL_{p,i,j} = inv_{i,j} \times IL_{p,j} , \qquad (7\text{-}33)$$

where $IL_{p,i,j}$ is type j planned investment demand ($j = 1$ for nonresidential, $j = 2$ for equipment, and $j = 3$ for residential) supplied by industry i. The parameter $inv_{i,j} = I_{i,j}^u / I_j^u$ represents the proportion of type j investment demand supplied by industry i per dollar's type j investment demand and is calculated from the appropriate column of the latest national input-output table.

The way in which the optimal capital stock (K^*) is calculated for each investment category is explained in the labor and capital demand section (section 7-2).

Introducing time explicitly into the model, we can write equations that apply for all three types of fixed capital.[6]

$$IL_{p,t} = \alpha \times \left[k_t K_t^* - \left(1 - dr_t^u \right) \times K_{t-1} \right] \tag{7-34}$$

$$K_{t-1} = \left(1 - dr_{t-1}^u \right) \times K_{t-2} + IL_{t-1} \tag{7-35}$$

Using equation 7-34, the actual capital stock in equation 7-35 can be replaced with the sum of the surviving initial capital stock (K_o) and the surviving previous investment expenditures. The investment equation is

$$IL_{p,j,t} = \alpha_j \left[k_t K_{j,t}^* - K_{j,0} \prod_{i=1}^{t} \left(1 - dr_i^u \right) - \sum_{i=1}^{t-1} IL_{j,i} \prod_{k=i+1}^{t} \left(1 - dr_k^u \right) \right], \tag{7-36}$$

where $IL_{p,j,t}$ is type j planned investment at year t, α_j is an adjustment coefficient for capital stock estimated over all states (the α_j values for residential and nonresidential investment are 0.127 and 0.061 respectively), $K_{j,0}$ is initial capital stock, and dr_i^u is depreciation rate. $K_{j,0}$ and the capital preference parameter (k_l) are region-specific estimates.

The change in business inventories equation simply shares out the national change in business inventories according to the regional share of output. It is

$$CBI_i = \left(\frac{Q_i}{Q_i^u} \right) \times CBI_i^u \tag{7-37}$$

CBI_i is change in business inventories.

Government Spending Equations

The government sector in the EDFS model has six components: federal civilian, federal military, and four state and local government components. The federal government's civilian and military spending on employment in the local area are exogenous and are maintained at a fixed share of the corresponding total U.S. values. Federal military procurement is allocated according to each local area's representation in the industries in which the federal military spending takes place.

Education, health and welfare, safety, and miscellaneous expenditures are the four state and local government components. The expenditures of state and local government are all dependent on relative population, nationally predicted state and local government expenditures, and adjustment of regional difference. The equation is

$$G_i = \lambda_G \left(N/N^u \right) \sum_{j=1}^{4} gov_{i,j} \, G_j^u \qquad (7\text{-}38)$$

In this equation, $gov_{i,j}$ is the proportion of the jth component of government demand served by industry i. One advantage of this formulation is that it has the effect of reflecting the need for state and local government to maintain per capita services in the face of changing numbers of people to serve. It can also reflect changing per capita government expenditures nationally. This equation is an extension of equation 3-16 in chapter 3.

7-2 LABOR AND CAPITAL DEMAND LINKAGES

Capital Demand Equations

In the n-industry model, two types of capital stocks have been considered: nonresidential structures and equipment. The optimal capital stock equation for these two types of capital stock is

$$K_j^* = \frac{\displaystyle\sum_{i=1}^{n} kw_i \times RLC_i}{\displaystyle\sum_{i=1}^{n} kw_i \times c_i} \times \frac{AE}{AE^u} \times K_j^{u*} \,, \qquad (7\text{-}39)$$

where K_j^* is optimal capital stock for type j capital, kw_i is industry i's share of total capital stock, RLC_i and c_i are relative labor cost and relative capital cost (see section 7-4 for details), the term of $\Sigma \, kw_i \times RLC_i$ (or $\Sigma \, kw_i \times c_i$) is the average relative wage rate (or average relative capital cost) weighted by capital in use, and AE is capital weighted employment (see equation 7-40). The reader may recall equation 3-24 for optimal capital stock for the single sector model, which does not separate capital stock into different types. Equation 7-39 directly follows equation 3-24 except for the kw_i weights and the use of AE instead of E. The equation used to determine the variable AE is

$$AE = \sum_{i=1}^{n} \frac{K_i^u / TK^u}{E_i^u / TE^u} \times E_i = \sum_{i=1}^{n} kwe_i \times E_i \qquad (7\text{-}40)$$

In equation 7-40, AE is capital using economic activity in employment terms. TK^u (= $\Sigma\ K_i^u$) and TE^u (= $\Sigma\ E_i^u$) are total capital and total employment in the nation. It is necessary to use AE instead of E in equation 7-39, because the variation in capital use per employee across industries is very large.

The optimal capital stock for residential housing is based on the following equation:

$$K_r^* = (RYD \div RYD^u)\ K_r^{*,u}\ , \tag{7-41}$$

where $RYD \div RYD^u$ simply shares out the optimal U.S. residential capital stock, based on the proportion of real disposable income in the region. The optimal capital stock of the United States for type k (k = 1, 2, 3) capital ($K_{k,t}^{*,u}$) is determined from equation 7-34 for the nation and is

$$K_{k,t}^{*,u} = IL_{p,k,t}^u \div \alpha_k + (1 - dr_{k,t}^u)\ K_{k,t-1}^u \tag{7-42}$$

Labor Demand Equations

In the general model, the Cobb-Douglas production function is extended to have x-factors of production. The equation for optimal relative labor intensity (h_i) for industry i is a generalization of the first two terms in equation 3-27 and is

$$h_i = \left[\frac{W_i}{W_i^u}\right]^{(b_u - 1)} \times \left[\prod_{j=2}^{x} \left(\frac{FC_j}{FC_j^u}\right)^{b_{j,i}}\right]\ , \tag{7-43}$$

where W_i is the wage rate for industry i, $b_{j,\,i}$ is the proportion of the jth factor's share per dollar's output in industry i (j = L for labor), and FC_j is the cost for each factor j except labor. Currently, there are three types of capital and three types of fuel in the model developed here. The factor costs will be discussed in detail in section 7-4. Relative labor intensity (L_i) comes into the model with a geometrically declining lag (see equation 3-29) to take into account that new factor shares are introduced as old capital is replaced by new capital. The equation of L_i is expressed as a moving average of the optimum as

$$L_i = L_{i,-1} + \lambda_L \times \left(h_i - L_{i,-1}\right)\ , \tag{7-44}$$

where $L_{i,\,-1}$ is the moving average of relative labor intensity from the last forecast period, and λ_L is the coefficient of a moving average that reflects the proportion of all equipment that is new equipment this year. Thus,

$$EPV_i = L_i \times \left(\frac{E_i^u}{Q_i^u}\right) \times \left(\frac{A^u}{A_i}\right),$$ (7-45)

where A and A^u are the coefficients of the Cobb-Douglas production function for the local area and the nation, respectively.[7] This corresponds with the prototype model, which is given in equation 3-30 in chapter 3. Employment is determined in the prototype model by equation 3-31,

$$E = EPV \times Y$$ (7-46)

In a multi-industry model, total employment in the area can be divided into two categories: nonfarm employment and farm employment. The nonfarm employment consists of employment of all private industries, employment of state and local government, and employment of federal civilian and military sectors. Output in private nonfarm industries is determined by demand for inputs into the production process (intermediate demand) and demand from personal consumption, government, investment, and exports (final demand) and employees per unit of output (e_i). The equation for employment in private industry i for the single area model is

$$E_i = EPV_i \times (QLI_i + QLC_i + QLG_i + QLINV_i + QXFG_i) \quad i=1,...,n$$ (7-47)

where QLI_i $(= \Sigma_j R_i \times a_{i,j} \times Q_j)$ is sales of industry i's product dependent on local intermediate demand, QLC_i $(= R_i \times C_i)$ is sales dependent on local consumer demand, QLG_i $(= R_i \times G_i)$ is sales dependent on government demand, $QLINV_i$ $(= R_i \times IL_{p,i})$ is sales dependent on local investment, and $QXFG_i$ is sales dependent on exports to outside of local area.[8]

In the multi-area regional model, exports to outside of the local area are further divided into exports to the rest of the multi-area and exports to the rest of the country. The employment dependent on exports to the rest of multi-area is determined by

$$EXRM_i = EPV_i \times QXFG_i^{kr},$$ (7-48)

where $QXFG_i^{k,r}$ is exports to the rest of multi-area region and is introduced in equation 7-12.

Federal government employment in the local area is a fixed proportion of government employment in the nation, based on the last observed proportion. The equations for federal civilian employment (EG_{FC}), and federal military employment (EG_{FM}) are

$$EG_i = \lambda_{EG_i} \times EG_i^u \qquad\qquad i = FC, FM \qquad\qquad (7\text{-}49)$$

where λ_{EGi} is a coefficient to reflect regional difference. State and local government employment (EG_{SL}) is based on maintaining per capita state and local government employment differentials from the United States and reflects changes in per capita average state and local government employment in the United States. Thus, nonfarm employment, ENF, is

$$ENF = \sum_{i=1}^{n} E_i + EG_{SL} + EG_{FC} + EG_{FM} \qquad\qquad (7\text{-}50)$$

Farm employment is estimated as a fixed share of U.S. farm employment based on the last year of history. The equation for total employment (TE) is

$$TE = ENF + EF \qquad\qquad (7\text{-}51)$$

where EF is farm employment.

Demand for Fuel

Demand for fuel is not explicit in the model. As evident in equation 7-43, the cost of fuel does enter the demands for labor and capital and plays an important role in the model. The treatment of fuel is unique in that the detailed intermediate outputs for coal mining, crude petroleum and natural gas mining, petroleum refining, and electric and natural gas utilities are excluded from the intermediate industry transactions and treated as a value added factor for purposes of calculating relative costs and labor intensity. As value added factors, fuel, capital, and labor are the Cobb-Douglas substitutes in the production function.

7-3 POPULATION AND LABOR SUPPLY LINKAGES

Population and labor supply in the region result from the interaction of the demographic section of the model with the economic section. The demographic section applies a cohort algorithm for single year-age cohorts for both males and females to the population. The *cohort algorithm* predicts the number of births and deaths that occur in the population. The excess of births over deaths gives the natural change in population. Combined with potential labor force participation rates, the labor force is built up from the cohorts. The indigenous labor force competes with potential migrants for jobs. Migrants, in turn, alter the long-run demographic structure of the population. The demographic-economic interaction becomes pronounced for rapidly growing or declining regions, and models that ignore the interaction may be misleading. Finally, the demographic section also calculates migration unrelated to economic conditions.

Migrants

The four components of net migrants are international migrants, retired migrants, former military personnel and their dependents reentering the civilian population, and economic migrants. All but economic migrants are exogenous to the economic sectors of the model.

International migration patterns by state from 1975 to 1980 as reported by the Bureau of the Census determine international migration. A fixed regional share of U.S. immigration is calculated with U.S. immigrants projected by the Bureau of the Census. The general state migrant distribution serves as the distribution of international migrants. The distributed migrants become part of the receiving region's population, to which the region's cohort algorithm applies. Survival and fertility rates apply to one-half of the migrants to reflect an average of one-half year of residency for each migrant during the year of migration.

We define retired migrants as migrants over age 65. Retired migrants respond to noneconomic factors, such as differential regional amenity levels. We calculate rates of migration for retirees by age cohorts for both males and females. The rates are defined as the sum of residually calculated migrants for the cohort for 1980 – 1990 divided by the sum of the cohort over the period in the region if total migrants are negative, or the sum of the cohort i in the United States if total migrants are positive.

$$RTMG = \sum_{k=1}^{v} rm_k \left[(1 - RTDUM_k) \times COH_k + RTDUM_k \times COH_k^u \right] \qquad (7\text{-}52)$$

RTMG denotes total retired migrants, rm_k is the rate of migration for the kth cohort as observed over the sample period. $RTDUM_k$ is one if rm_k is positive and zero if rm_k is negative. COH_k is the size of the cohort. Results of employing equation 7-52 confirm an expected pattern of migration of retirees from the snowbelt to the sunbelt with Florida and Arizona having large rates of retiree in-migration. Because military personnel and their dependents are treated as a special population, a link is required between changes in the civilian population in each region and the size of the military, including overseas personnel. The proportion of the region's population within the United States the previous year becomes the share of military personnel a region receives or loses. For personnel returning from domestic duty, we calculate associated dependents.

We define economic migrants as migrants under age 65 who were part of the civilian population in the United States the preceding year. Economic migration (ECMG) responds to both economic and amenity factors and may be expressed as

$$ECMG = f(EY/EY^u, A_c/A_c^u) \qquad (7\text{-}53)$$

where EY is expected income and A_c denotes the level of amenities. Expected income is the probability weighted sum of wages and is calculated as

$$EY = \sum_{i=1}^{n} P(E_i) \times W_i \qquad (7\text{-}54)$$

where $P(E_i)$ denotes probability of employment. Breaking the probability into two parts as

$$P(E_i) = P(E) \times P(E_i \mid E) , \qquad (7\text{-}55)$$

and specifying forecasts for the two parts as

$$P(E) = ER \div NLF \qquad (7\text{-}56)$$

$$P(E_i \mid E) = E_i \div E \qquad (7\text{-}57)$$

Equation 7-54 can be rewritten as

$$EY = (ER \div NLF) \times \left[\sum_{i=1}^{n+4} (E_i \div E) \times W_i \right] , \qquad (7\text{-}58)$$

where ER is civilian employment adjusted for place-of-residence, and E is total nonfarm private employment by place of work.

Adjusting W_i for regional cost of living and tax differentials (see equation 3-46), dividing by a similar expression for EY^u, and multiplying the numerator and denominator by $\sum_{i=1}^{n+4} (E_i \div E) \times W_i^u$, we obtain

$$EY / EY^u = \left[(ER / NLF) / (ER^u / NLF^u) \right] \times \left\{ \left[\sum_{i=1}^{n+4} (E_i / E) \times W_i \times (RYD / YP) \right] / \right.$$

$$\left[\sum_{i=1}^{n+4} (E_i / E) \times W_i^u \times (RYD^u / YP^u) \right] \right\} \times \left\{ \left[\sum_{i-1}^{n+4} (E_i / E) \times W_i^u \right] / \right.$$

$$\left[\sum_{i=1}^{n+4} \left(E_i^u / E^u \right) \times W_i^u \right] \right\} = REO \times RWR \times RWM ,$$

$$(7\text{-}59)$$

where REO, RWR, and RWM represent relative employment opportunity, relative wage rate, and relative wage rate mix, respectively. Thus, REO reflects the probability of getting a job, RWR is the real after-tax wage independent of regional industry mix differences (the same employment weights in the numerator and the denominator), and RWM is the regional mix of high-paying industries (the same wage rate in the numerator and the denominator).

Substituting equation 7-59 into equation 7-53 gives

$$ECMG = f(REO \times RWR \times RWM, A_c / A_c^u) \qquad (7\text{-}60)$$

Equation 7-60 is estimated by assuming a semi-log functional form, normalizing ECMG to the previous year's potential labor force, incorporating lagged migration responses of up to two periods, and adding a random disturbance term. The equation estimated is

$$NECM (t) = ln (\lambda_k) + \delta_1 ln (REO(t)) + \delta_2 ln (REO (t - 1))$$
$$+ \delta_3 ln (REO (t - 2)) + \delta_4 ln (RWR (t)) + \delta_5 ln (RWR (t - 1))$$
$$+ \delta_6 ln (RWR (t - 2)) + \delta_7 ln (RWM (t)) + \delta_8 ln (RWM (t - 1))$$
$$+ \delta_9 (RWM (t - 2)) + \mu (t) \qquad (7\text{-}61)$$

where λ_k denotes the region-specific relative amenity value[9] obtained by specifying a dummy variable for each region, and NECM $(t) = $ ECMG(t) / NLF $(t - 1)$. Because equation 7-61 is part of our simultaneous model, which specifies REO as an explanatory variable of the wage rate and ECMG as a component of REO, it was estimated using two-stage least squares. Also, a polynomial distributed lag of degree one was imposed on the lag weights for each variable to get the desired dynamic model properties. The results of the estimation with t-statistics presented in parentheses for 1973 to 1988 for fifty states plus Washington, D.C. are

$$\delta_1 = 0.296 \qquad \delta_2 = 0.121 \qquad \delta_3 = -0.054$$
$$(8.8) \qquad\qquad (12.0) \qquad\qquad (-2.46)$$

$$\delta_4 = 0.320 \qquad \delta_5 = 0.117 \qquad \delta_6 = -0.086$$
$$(7.1) \qquad\qquad (8.0) \qquad\qquad (-3.4)$$

$$\delta_7 = 0.196 \qquad \delta_8 = 0.117 \qquad \delta_9 = -0.206$$
$$(2.2) \qquad\qquad (-0.2) \qquad\qquad (-2.6)$$

$$R^2 = 0.63$$

The results confirm the importance of each economic factor. For substate areas, the above equation and estimates are used to calibrate a region-specific intercept using the region specific population and calculated economic migration data.

The coefficients show the effects of the variables on migration. To calculate the dynamic effects over time, it should be remembered that by the third year all of the coefficients are relevant. It is then important to consider feedbacks from the rest of the model in order to determine the pattern of migration that results for an exogenous change to the model.[10]

The equation for the natural labor force (NLF) in the area is

$$NLF = \sum_{i=1}^{v} NPR_i \times N_i , \tag{7-62}$$

where NPR_i is the natural participation rate for age/sex cohort i ($i = 1,...,v$), and N_i stands for the number of people in the ith age group. The natural participation rate for an area in a state is determined by the U.S. average unemployment rate for ith age group in 1980 and the state-specific values of the other explanatory variables, such as birth rates, racial composition, percentage of farm employment, and other social and economic variables. The value of N_i, which is the number of people in the ith age/sex cohort in the state, is available for twenty cohorts for each sex from 1971 to 1989 for all states and counties.[11] It is generated by the model for 1990 and calibrated to the United States and regional state total populations for 1990.

Population

In the simple prototype model, population in the local area is determined according to equation 3-33 in chapter 3,

$$N_t = N_{t-1} \times \frac{N_t^u}{N_{t-1}^u} + MIG$$

$$(7\text{-}63)$$

However, we will now add to the model a full-cohort survival module with several types of migrants.

For a model with a cohort-specific population module, births and deaths are included to represent the change in population due to demographic processes. Noneconomic migrants such as retired migrants, returning military and international migrants are also calculated in the model. To compute the population in such a way that it coincides with both the 1970 and 1980 censuses, it is necessary to consider the undercount in the 1970 census and its regional distribution. Between 1980 and 1990, the undercount was reasonably stable and therefore did not require adjustment. To obtain a civilian population and to estimate the civilian labor force, it is also necessary to remove military and military-dependent population.

7-4 WAGE, PRICE, AND PROFIT LINKAGES

In this section, we show how wage rates, prices for regional and national industries,[12] and profits for national industries are determined in a generalized n-industry model. We start with relative production costs, again referencing the equations in chapter 3.

Relative Production Costs

The relative production cost derived in chapter 3 (equation 3-38) is as follows:

$$P = \left(\frac{W}{W^u}\right)^a \times \left(\frac{c}{c^u}\right)^d \div \left(\frac{A}{A^u}\right)$$

$$(7\text{-}64)$$

To derive a similar relative production cost function in an n-industry and x-factor framework in which industries must purchase intermediate inputs, we first show how the function is derived in the case of n-industry and two-factors (labor and one type of capital). The total cost function for industry i (TC_i) can be expressed as

$$TC_i = W_i \times E_i + c_i \times K_i + \sum_{j=1}^{n} SP_j \times Q_{j,i}$$

$$(7\text{-}65)$$

where W_i is the wage rate of industry i, c_i is cost of capital, $Q_{j,i}$ is material inputs of

j into production of industry i, and SP$_j$ is price of material input j.

A hierarchical production function is employed where the real inputs of materials vs. value added are fixed at the top level of the hierarchy. This is called a Leontief production function. At the next level of the hierarchy, factor inputs are Cobb-Douglas and material inputs are Leontief. We can then substitute the multi-industry generalization of equation 3-22[13] into equation 7-65 and follow the derivation of equation 3-35 to obtain

$$TC_i = \frac{W_i \times E_i}{a_i} + \sum_{j=1}^{n} SP_j \times Q_{j,i} , \qquad (7\text{-}66)$$

where a_i is the share of labor in production of industry i. Also substituting the multi-industry generalization of equation 3-22 into the Cobb-Douglas production function (similar to equation 3-17) and solving for E_i, we obtain

$$E_i = VA_i \times \left(A_i^{-1}\right) \times \left(\frac{c_i}{W_i}\right)^{d_i} \left(\frac{a_i}{d_i}\right)^{d_i} , \qquad (7\text{-}67)$$

where VA$_i$ is value-added for industry i, A$_i$ is a coefficient in the Cobb-Douglas production function and represents average factor productivity, and d_i is the share of capital in production of industry i.

Substituting equation 7-67 into equation 7-66, we can write

$$TC_i = VA_i \times \left(A_i^{-1}\right) \times \left(\frac{c_i}{d_i}\right)^{d_i} \left(\frac{W_i}{a_i}\right)^{a_i} + \sum_{j=1}^{n} SP_j Q_{j,i} \qquad (7\text{-}68)$$

Dividing both sides by Q$_i$ to obtain average costs (AC$_i$), which is also equal to marginal cost in this constant returns to scale production function, we find that

$$AC_i = a_{f,i} \times A_i^{-1} \times \left(\frac{c_i}{d_i}\right)^{d_i} \times \left(\frac{W_i}{a_i}\right)^{a_i} + \sum_{j=1}^{n} a_{j,i} SP_j \qquad (7\text{-}69)$$

where $a_{f,i}$ is the factor share of production and is equal to VA$_i$/Q$_i$. A similar expression of average cost for the nation is

$$AC_i^u = a_{f,i} \times \left(A_i^u\right)^{-1} \times \left(\frac{c_i^u}{d_i}\right)^{d_i} \times \left(\frac{W_i^u}{a_i}\right)^{a_i} + \sum_{j=1}^{n} a_{j,i} SP_j^u \qquad (7\text{-}70)$$

Let $A_i^u = \left(\dfrac{c_i^u}{d_i}\right)^{d_i} \times \left(\dfrac{W_i^u}{a_i}\right)^{a_i}$ for all i, then $AC_i^u = 1$ if $SP_j^u = 1$ (for all i and

j). Also, let A_i/A_i^u be relative factor productivity (RFPROD$_i$), then relative production cost for industry i in an n-industry and two-factor framework is

$$P_i = AC_i/AC_i^u = a_{f,i} \times \frac{1}{RFPROD_i} \times \left(\frac{c_i}{c_i^u}\right)^{d_i} \times \left(\frac{W_i}{W_i^u}\right)^{a_i} + \sum_{j=1}^{n} a_{j,i} SP_j \qquad (7\text{-}71)$$

This equation can be generalized to x-factors of production and n-industries as

$$P_i = \frac{1}{RFPROD_i} \times \left(\frac{W_i}{W_i^u}\right)^{b_{L,i}} \times \left(\prod_{j=2}^{x} \frac{FC_j}{FC_j^u}\right)^{b_{j,i}} \times \left(\sum_{j=1}^{x} b_{j,i}\right) + \sum_{j=1}^{n} a_{j,i} SP_j \qquad (7\text{-}72)$$

where $b_{j,i}$ represents the proportion of a factor's share per dollar's output in industry i ($j = L$ for labor), $\displaystyle\sum_{j=1}^{x} b_{j,i} = a_{f,i}$ is the factor share of output, and FC$_j$ is factor cost for jth factor in production.

The FC$_j$ values for capital, which are discussed in the next section, are constructed using a Hall and Jorgenson[14] implicit rental cost of capital approach. They include state and federal corporate tax rates and investment credits, depreciation lifetimes, as well as property tax rates and the interest rate. The derivation of the cost of capital is lengthy. For illustrative purposes, the derivation is shown for several special cases in the appendix to this chapter. Here, we present the results from similar derivations that include all relevant features of the federal and state tax codes.

Capital Costs

The cost of capital equation calculates the implicit rental cost of capital.[15] The formulation of the equation is much like that of the factor-cost equations with the exponents representing shares that sum to one. Three types of capital are considered in our model. They are structures, equipment, and inventory. The equation for capital cost is

$$c_i = \left(CSTR_i \times PSTR\right)^{cs_i} \times \left(CEQP_i \times PEQP\right)^{ce_i} \times CINV_i^{ci_i}, \qquad (7\text{-}73)$$

where CSTR$_i$, CEQP$_i$, and CINV$_i$ are the relative rental costs of capital (net of relative differences in purchasing prices) for structures, equipment, and inventory for industry

i, respectively. PSTR and PEQP are the relative prices of structures and equipment, respectively. cs_i, ce_i, and ci_i are the proportion of capital in the ith industry accounted for by structures, equipment, and inventory, respectively. The sum of cs_i, ce_i, and ci_i should equal one.

Since equipment and structures are not explicit sectors in the model, their relative prices require separate calculation. For the relative price of equipment, the equation is

$$PEQP = \sum_{i=1}^{n} SP_i \times CWEQP_i ,$$
(7-74)

where SP_i is the price paid by a local firm for the ith input into equipment, and $CWEQP_i$ is the proportion of all inputs to equipment represented by the input from the ith industry.

The relative cost of equipment as capital for industry i is determined as

$$CEQP_i = (r + CERR)/(1 - UM_i) \times [1 - TIC^u - (1 - TCP^u) \times TIC$$
$$- DDFE - DDME_i - RDME + WM/(r + CERR)]/CEQP^u$$
(7-75)

where r is the interest rate, CERR is the rate of replacement of equipment capital, UM_i is combined national and local corporate profits tax rate for industry i, TIC (TIC^u) is local (national) investment tax credit, TCP^u is national corporate profits tax rate, DDFE is present value of federal tax savings from depreciation deductions on equipment, $DDME_i$ is present value of local tax savings from depreciation deductions on equipment, RDME is present value of local tax savings from interest deductions on equipment, and WM is equipment tax rate less the federal deduction.

The variable DDFE is determined by following equation:

$$DDFE = (1 - XSYDE) \times \frac{TCP^u}{TEL^u} \times \frac{1 - e^{TEL^u \times r}}{r}$$
$$+ XSYDE \times \frac{2 \times TCP^u}{TEL^u \times r} \times \left(1 - \frac{1 - e^{-TEL^u \times r}}{TEL^u \times r}\right)$$
(7-76)

XSYDE is the proportion of firms using sum-of-the-years digits depreciation for equipment, and TEL^u is equipment lifetime according to national laws.

The local present values of tax savings from depreciation deductions for equipment (DDME) are determined by equations that are almost exactly the same as the federal present value equations. The only exceptions are that TCP^u is replaced with VM_i, the local corporate profits tax rate and that TEL^u is replaced with TELM, the equipment lifetime according to local laws. The equations for variables $DDME_i$, UM_i, TCP_i (local corporate profit tax rate for industry i), WM, and VM_i are as follows:

$$DDME_i = (1 - XSYDE) \times \frac{VM_i}{TELM} \times \frac{1 - e^{TELM \times r}}{r}$$

$$+ XSYDE \times \frac{2 \times VM_i}{TELM \times r} \times \left(1 - \frac{1 - e^{-TELM \times r}}{TELM \times r}\right) \tag{7-77}$$

$$VM_i = TCP_i - TCP^u \times TCP_i \tag{7-78}$$

$$UM_i = TCP^u + VM_i \tag{7-79}$$

$$TCP_i = \lambda_{TCP} \times MULT_{TCP,i} \tag{7-80}$$

$$WM = TEQP (1 - TCP^u), \tag{7-81}$$

where λ_{TCP} is a coefficient that reflects the corporate profit tax rate from the last year of history, $MULT_{TCP,i}$ is the multiplicative adjustment for industries whose state corporate profit tax rate differs from the statutory rate, and TEQP is the local tax rate on equipment. The national cost of equipment capital, $CEQP^u$, is calculated in the same manner as CEQP but with local variables replaced by national average variables. For example, WM is replaced by average state equipment tax rate less the federal deduction.

The equations for structures are identical to those for equipment except that terms referring specifically to equipment replace those referring to structures. For example, local equipment lifetime (TELM) is replaced by local structure lifetime (TSLM), which is used in the local present value of tax savings from depreciation deductions for structures (DDMS). Inventory costs are calculated as

$$CINV_i = [(r / (1 - UM_i)) \times (1 - UM_i \times B)] / CINV_i^u, \tag{7-82}$$

where B is the proportion of business capital financed by bonds and loans. $CINV_i^u$ can be calculated by replacing UM_i with a national average.

Relative Fuel Costs

Relative fuel costs for industry i (RFC_i) are based on costs for commercial and industrial users as appropriate. The equation for relative fuel costs is also derived from a Cobb-Douglas function and therefore assumes possible substitution among fuels.

$$RFC_i = \prod_{j=1}^{3} \left(RFC_j\right)^{\eta_j} \qquad (7\text{-}83)$$

RFC_j is relative fuel costs for electric ($j = 1$), other fuels (mainly residual fuel oil) ($j = 2$), and natural gas ($j = 3$), and it is determined exogenously. The variable η_j is the share of jth fuel ($\Sigma_j \, \eta_j = 1$) in the total fuel value added.

Housing Prices and Relative Land Costs

Housing prices are the only prices of regional goods not built up through relative marginal costs of production. Historical housing prices are derived from the Bureau of Census Survey of Housing and Prices reported by the National Association of Realtors. Housing prices are forecast according to the same equation that is used in the prototype model (equation 3-42). It is

$$PH_t = \varepsilon \times \left[\left(N_t \div N_t^u\right) \div \left(N_{t-1} \div N_{t-1}^u\right) - 1\right] + PH_{t-1} \qquad (7\text{-}84)$$

PH denotes the relative price of housing to the United States, while t and $t - 1$ index current and last time periods respectively. Equation 7-84 simply relates the percentage change in the price of housing to a constant multiple of the percentage change in a region's share of the U.S. population. A cross-section, time-series regression of the form of equation 7-84 was run from 1970 to 1988 over all 50 states plus Washington, D.C., to obtain

$$\varepsilon = 0.445 \quad \text{T-stat} = 4.08 \quad \text{P-value} = 0.000$$

Thus, a one-percent increase in a region's share of population will cause a 0.445 percent increase in the cost of housing. Relative land cost changes are predicted using equation 7-84. Land costs affect the cost of capital through the price of structures. Our next task is to determine relative profit for national industries.

Relative Profit for National Industries

Assuming that one price prevails in all markets and that profits or losses arise when the technology in a particular area differs from the average technology in the nation, we can then show the equation for relative profitability for national industry i as

$$\pi_i = SP_i^u \times Q_i - TC_i \, , \qquad (7\text{-}85)$$

where π_i is the profit of industry i, SP_i^u is price prevailing for the product, and TC_i is total cost of production. The price prevailing in national markets assumes constant returns to scale for all inputs. We can substitute average cost (AC_i^u) for SP_i^u. Equation 7-85 can then be written as

$$\pi_i = \left(AC_i^u - AC_i\right) \times Q_i \,, \tag{7-86}$$

where AC_i is average production cost in the local area. Using equations 7-68, 7-69, 7-70 and $AC_i^u = SP_i^u = 1$, we find that profit per unit of output is

$$\pi_i = \Pi_i / Q_i = AC_i^u - AC_i$$

$$= a_{f,i}\left[1 - \frac{1}{RFPROD_i} \times \left(\frac{c_i}{c_i^u}\right)^{d_i} \times \left(\frac{W_i}{W_i^u}\right)^{a_i}\right] + \sum_{j=1}^{n} a_{j,i}(1 - SP_j) \tag{7-87}$$

Let

$$RCF_i = \left(\frac{c_i}{c_i^u}\right)^{d_i} \times \left(\frac{W_i}{W_i^u}\right)^{a_i} \tag{7-88}$$

where RCF_i is the relative cost of factor inputs for industry i. Therefore, equation 7-87 can be rewritten as

$$\pi_i = a_{f,i}\left(1 - RCF_i / RFPROD_i\right) + \sum_{j=1}^{n} a_{j,i}\left(1 - SP_j\right) \tag{7-89}$$

This equation is directly analogous to equations 3-38 and 3-39 with the addition of a term to account for intermediate inputs. RFPROD is obtained by taking the ratio of equation 7-67 to the analogous equation for employment for the United States and solving it as

$$RFPROD_i = A_i / A_i^u = \frac{VA_i / E_i}{VA_i^u / E_i^u} \times \left(\frac{c_i}{c_i^u}\right)^{d_i} \times \left(\frac{W_i}{W_i^u}\right)^{a_i - 1} \tag{7-90}$$

where VA_i is gross regional product for industry i at the state level while VA_i^u is its United States counterpart. The BEA has recently estimated these two-digit industry values by state[16] from 1969 to 1986. All of the other variables on the right-hand side of equation 7-90 can be observed or calculated as indicated previously. To reflect the time effect in the adjustment of the optimal labor intensity $(L_i$ – equation 7-44), we use the following equation to calculate RFPROD.

$$RFPROD_i = \frac{VA_i / E_i}{VA_i^u / E_i^u} \times L_i \qquad (7\text{-}91)$$

The sales price of SP_j is equal to SP_j^u for all industries in national markets, because we assume that the U.S. price will be universal. In further work, transportation costs could be introduced here, but the focus on time series analysis helps to mitigate the importance of including them because the focus is on change rather than levels.

Sales Price for Regional Industries and National Industries

For all regional industries, the SP_i value is based on the P_i value (see equation 7-71) for local markets, altered by assuming that $A_i = A_i^u$ (RFPROD = 1). The firms producing in regional markets are assumed to use a production function similar to the Cobb-Douglas function with fixed-material inputs given previously. However, in our production function, output in the area can differ from that in the United States for some share of intramarginal production. However, a production function similar to that above with $A = A^u$, is assumed to be in place for production on the margin. In regional markets, it is likely that firms will have a location advantage or disadvantage that will apply to initial sales or production. For example, a good location may mean virtually no transportation or advertising costs for the market in the neighborhood, while for sales at more distant locations, the standard marginal costs apply. Also, in a local market, some firms may have to locate at a distance and thus incur extra costs on the first items of output.

This assumption is necessary for our model to have a determinant local price for regional industries. Without a method for setting this price, we would be unable to determine whether above-average profits resulted from charging monopoly prices or from higher than average productivity. By assuming a production function with marginal productivity similar to one where $A = A^u$, we can have determinant prices reflecting the relative cost of factor inputs. For purposes of policy simulations, increases in productivity will be passed on as lower prices.

Under these assumptions, the marginal cost of production in the region relative to the United States is taken from equation 7-71 or equation 7-72 by replacing A with A^u, since firms are assumed to produce up to the point where their marginal productivity is equal to that in the United States. For national industries, we assume that the regional and national prices are identical. Thus,

$$SP_i = 1 \qquad \text{(for national industries only)} \qquad (7\text{-}92)$$

For the housing industry, SP is the observed relative price of housing in the state. In the forecast period, the last historical relative price of housing is used in conjunction with equation 7-84.

Consumer Price Deflator

In chapter 3, we introduced the equation for consumer price deflator (equation 3-43) as

$$CP = [(1 - hs^u) \times ((1 - ncs^u) \times SP_R + ncs^u) + (hs^u \times PH)] \times CP^u \qquad (7\text{-}93)$$

The multi-industry generalization of this equation is straightforward. It is

$$CP = \sum_{i=1}^{n} (SP_i \times cpweights_i) \times CP^u , \qquad (7\text{-}94)$$

where SP_i is relative sales price of i and $cpweights_i$ is the weight of the ith industry from the personal consumption column in the final demand sectors of an input-output matrix. The real estate industry weight is applied to the SP for housing in the version of CP used for calculating the relative real wage in the migration equation. However, the price of housing is replaced with the relative cost of building new housing in the CP used to deflate real disposable income. This is the case because an increase in housing prices does not reduce the real disposable income for current residents who own their own homes.

The Wage Rate Equation

The multi-industry, multi-occupation generalization of the wage equation (3-44) is

$$W_i = \left(1 + \sum_{j=1}^{p} d_{i,j} \times \Delta WD_j\right)(1 + \Delta CPR_{t-1})^\tau (1 + k^u) \times W_{i,t-1} \qquad (7\text{-}95)$$

where $d_{i,j}$ is the proportion of the jth occupation ($j = 1,...,p$) in the ith industry projected by the Bureau of Labor Statistics. ΔWD_j is the change in wage rate due to changes in demand for jth occupation and labor market conditions (see discussion in the following section). ΔCPR_{t-1} is the change in the relative consumer price deflator in the previous period,[17] and k^u is the change in U.S. wages not explained by the changes in demand.

The value of ΔCPR_{t-1} is obtained from the first difference from equation 7-94 lagged one period. The value for τ was obtained by a grid search from zero to one incrementing by one-eighth each trial. The selection criterion was the minimization of the sum of squared errors of wage multiplicative adjustments from one for all industries over all states for the historical time period. The optimal value for τ was found to be 0.25. Based on an F-test, we could reject the hypothesis that $\tau = 0$ at the 0.05 significance level. The value of k^u is calculated by extracting the change in the U.S. wage rate not explained by industry mix change and changes due to those shown in ΔWD_j in the United States. (See calculation of UW^u, equations 3-76 through 3-81).

Change in Wage Rate Due to Changes in Demand

In the simple version of the model, the change in wage rate due to demand, ΔWD (see equation 3-56), is based in part on changes in total employment (E/EA) and changes in relative employment opportunity (REO/REOA). In the generalized model, it is based on changes in occupational-specific employment demand changes and EO [EO = REO × (NLF^u/E^u) = E/NLF] for highly skilled employees and on changes in EO only for workers with shorter training periods. The equation for the change of wage rate for jth occupation is

$$\Delta WD_j = [\lambda_{WD1} \times EO/EOA2 \times (1 - DHSK)] + [(\lambda_{WD2} \times EO/EO_{-1}$$
$$\times DHSK)] + [\lambda_{WD3} \times OD_j/ODA_j \times DHSK] \qquad (7\text{-}96)$$

where λ_{WD1}, λ_{WD2}, and λ_{WD3} are coefficients, EOA2 is a moving average of EO, and DHSK is a dummy variable that is 1 for high-skilled labor and 0 for low-skilled labor. OD_j is occupation demand for jth occupation, and ODA_j is a moving average of OD_j. The variables of EOA2 and ODA_j are determined by the equations

$$EOA2 = EOA2_{-1} + 0.2 \times (EO_{-1} - EOA2_{-1}) \qquad (7\text{-}97)$$
$$ODA_j = ODA_{j,-1} + 0.2 \times (OD_{j,-1} - ODA_{j,-1}) \qquad (7\text{-}98)$$

Equations 7-97 and 7-98 are specified to capture the effects of the change in wage rates due to both shifts in occupational demand and shifts in general labor market conditions. The 0.2 values in equations 7-97 and 7-98 are determined on the basis of regression results over a range of values. The initial estimation of the equations follow the same methodology as that reported in 1985.[18] This was based on microeconomic data on a large sample of workers in the same year across states.

After an initial estimation of the λs, one final step in the determination of the λs is taken. The model is run over history with equation 7-96 and the initial λ

estimates for all fifty states plus Washington, D.C. The λs are then varied according to a grid search to minimize the sum of squared deviations of wage predictions compared to observed values for all industries across all states. Coefficients λ_{WD1} and λ_{WD2} are uniformly varied from zero to two times their initial values, while λ_{WD3} is independently varied from zero to two times its value, incrementing the coefficients during the search by one-eighth of their initial values each trial. It is found that λ_{WD3} cannot be improved upon, while optimal values for λ_{WD1} and λ_{WD2} are one-half their initial values. Thus, the final coefficients for the REMI model are

$$\lambda_{WD1} = 0.1965, \ \lambda_{WD2} = 0.7305, \ \lambda_{WD3} = 0.1335$$

In essence, the empirical estimates in equations 7-95 and 7-96 are based on time series regression over the period 1969 – 1988 for 49 industries in 50 states plus Washington, D.C.

Relative Wage Costs

There are two relative wage rates in the model. One called RWR, which we introduced in equation 7-59, is from the perspective of the potential migrant. The other one is relative labor cost (RLC_i) and is viewed from the perspective of the employer in industry i. The relative labor cost is defined as

$$RLC_i = \frac{W_i}{W_i^u \times WINDX_i} , \tag{7-99}$$

where $WINDX_i$ is an index and shows the effect of wage mix among four-digit industries within industry i (two-digit) on the wage level in i. Wage mix is included so that an area concentrated in the high-wage portion of a national industry i will not show a high relative wage cost due to the industry mix effect even if its wage cost for all parts of the regional industry are at the national average wage rate.

7-5 MARKET SHARE LINKAGES

In this section, we discuss how the regional purchase coefficient and export share are determined for national and regional industries, respectively. We start by reiterating the definition of national and regional industries. Those industries that have more than one-half of their trade in exports across all states are classified as *national*, while those that have half or more than half of their sales within the state of origin are classified as *regional*.

The two-digit national industries are the hotels and other lodging places sector and the manufacturing sectors with the exception of the stone, clay, and glass sector, the printing and publishing sector, and petroleum and coal products sector (Treyz and Rickman, 1989[19]). The regional industries consist of mining, construction, finance, wholesale and retail trade, services (except the hotels sector), and agriculture.[20] For a one-digit model, only durable and nondurable manufacturing are considered national industries.

Regional Purchase Coefficient and Export Shares for National Industries

The basic equation for determining output (recall equations from section 7-1) is

$$Q_i = R_i \times D_i + S_i^{k,u} \times XFG_i^u, \tag{7-100}$$

where R_i is the RPC and represents the proportion of local demand supplied locally by industry i. D_i is all local demand for industry i in the local area, $S_i^{k,u}$ is regional share of interregional and international trade for industry i, and XFG_i^u is interregional trade in the United States and international trade of the United States.[21]

For national industries, the equations for RPC and export shares are

$$R_{i,t} = \lambda_{R,i} \times \left(\frac{RPROF2_{i,t}}{RPROF2_{i,T}} \right)^{\vartheta_1} \times \left(\frac{R_{i,t}^u}{R_{i,T}^u} \right)^{\vartheta_2} \times \left(\frac{IMIX_{i,t}^u}{IMIX_{i,T}^u} \right)^{\vartheta_3} \tag{7-101}$$

and

$$S_{i,t}^{k,u} = \lambda_{S,i} \times \left(\frac{RPROF2_{i,t}}{RPROF2_{i,T}} \right)^{\varphi_1} \times \left(\frac{IMIX_{i,t}}{IMIX_{i,T}^u} \right)^{\varphi_2}, \tag{7-102}$$

where $\lambda_{R,i}$ and $\lambda_{S,i}$ are coefficients, $RPROF2_i$ is a moving average of $RPROF_i$ (relative profitability defined as 1 plus π_i in equation 7-89), and R_i^u is U.S. RPC for industry i. IMIX is an industrial mix that captures differential local representation in slow and fast growing three-digit industries in the local two-digit industry. The equations for RPROF2 and IMIX are

$$RPROF2_i = RPROF2_{i-1} + 0.2 \times (RPROF_i - RPROF2_{i-1}) \tag{7-103}$$

$$IMIX_{i,t} = \frac{\displaystyle\sum_{j \in i} (E_{j,b} \div E_{i,b}) \times (E_{j,t}^u \div E_{j,b}^u)}{\displaystyle\sum_{j \in i} (E_{j,b}^u \div E_{i,b}^u) \times (E_{j,t}^u \div E_{j,b}^u)}, \tag{7-104}$$

where the subscript b denotes the base year, t indicates the current time period and i indicates the two-digit industry of which the three-digit industries (j) are elements.

The first task is to estimate the values for $\lambda_{R,i}$ and $\lambda_{S,i}$ in the latest period (T) for which the required data (County Business Patterns) is available. Since all of the ratios on the right-hand side of equations 7-101 and 7-102 will be 1 in year T, this is equivalent to measuring R_i and $S_{k,u}$ in that year.

To estimate the regional purchase coefficient (R_i) for year T, we use equation 6-82 and the procedure described at length in chapter 6. Given $R_{i,T}$, exports are calculated as a residual with the base year export share ($S_{i,T}^{k,u}$) calculated by[22]

$$S_{i,T}^{k,u} = \frac{Q_{i,T} - R_{i,T} \times D_{i,T}}{X_{i,T}^{u}} = \frac{X_i^{k,u}}{X_{i,T}^{u}} \tag{7-105}$$

The value of Q_i is estimated historically by dividing the real value added (VA_i) by the share of value added in Q_i, as represented in the technological matrix $\Sigma a_{j,i}$ over the j-inputs that represent factor inputs to industry i. The values of $R_{i,T}$ and $S_{i,T}^{k,u}$ in equation 7-105 will represent $\lambda_{R,i}$ and $\lambda_{S,i}$ exactly in year T. These values will also exactly yield Q in equation 7-105 in year T.

The next task is to substitute equations 7-101 and 7-102 into equation 7-100. Then, a time series nonlinear least squares regression for 1969 – 1987 for all national industries in all states is run.[23] The elasticities for industrial mix, ϑ_3 and φ_2, and the U.S. RPC, ϑ_2, are restricted to equal one to reflect *a priori* model constructs. Moreover, ϑ_1 is restricted to equal φ_1 because changes in relative profitability are assumed to affect production for both local demand and export demand equally. The coefficients are

	Coefficient	T-Stat	P-Value
$\vartheta_1 = \varphi_1 = \psi =$	1.83	28.04	0.00
$\vartheta_2 =$	1.00	N/A	N/A
$\vartheta_3 =$	1.00	N/A	N/A
$\varphi_1 = \vartheta_1 = \psi =$	1.83	28.04	0.00
$\varphi_2 =$	1.00	N/A	N/A

where N/A denotes not applicable. The degrees of freedom were 15,243.

These results are in line with expectations from theory. If profits arising from production in one place increase relative to another, then it can be expected tha national industries will be more attracted to that area, both to serve local markets an to serve national markets. When the U.S. regional purchase coefficient drops (i.e more imports as a share of the supply to U.S. markets), firms in all areas of th United States can be expected to lose some of their local market. Likewise, in an are where the three- and four-digit industries that make up a two-digit industry are in th rapid growth part of that two-digit industry, one's share of that two-digit industry i the United States will increase, if all other things are equal.

Regional Purchase Coefficient and Export Shares in Regional Industries

For regional markets, we assert that individual firms may grow or contrac but since the market is segmented, only market expansion or contraction influence aggregate output for the industry. If high profits attract more firms to the area, sellin at marginal cost and using average technology (A^u), then these firms diminish th location rents earned by existing firms in these segmented markets by cutting the sales to intramarginal customers. The sales gained by the new firms are exactly offs by the sales loss of the existing firms. Thus, changes in the S_i^{ku} values in region markets will result from changes in production costs rather than profitability as suc Markets are also assumed to expand as a region grows. Firms in an area that grow increase their share of that market, because a larger area can support some of th more specialized sectors of a regional industry (e.g., a store selling petite shoes). other words, for specialized parts of the regional sectors, there are economies of sca that preclude local production until the market reaches a certain size.

The specification for the R_i and $S_i^{k, u}$ equations for regional industries is

$$R_{i,t} = \lambda_{R,i} \times RGRP_t^{\gamma_1} \times RGRP_{t-1}^{\gamma_2} \times \left(\frac{SPA_{i,t}}{SPA_{i,T}} \right)^{\gamma_3} \tag{7-10(}$$

$$S_{i,t}^{ku} = \lambda_{S,i} \times \left(\frac{SPA_i}{SPA_{i,T}} \right)^{\xi}, \tag{7-10}$$

and

$$SPA_t = SPA_{t-1} + 0.2(SP_t - SPA_{t-1}) \tag{7-10}$$

$$RGRP = GRPR/GRPR_T \tag{7-10}$$

GRPR is the region's share of U.S. gross domestic product. $GRPR_T$ represents the value of GRPR in the last history year (T). The $\lambda_{R,i}$ and $\lambda_{S,i}$ values are as described previously for national industries. Because cost changes are viewed as affecting market expansion for both local demand and export demand, γ_3 is restricted to equal ξ. The results based on 24,000 observations are as follows:

	Coefficient	*T-Stat*	*P-Value*
$\gamma_1 =$	0.296	115.4	0.00
$\gamma_2 =$	-0.07	-3.4	0.0007
$\gamma_3 = \xi =$	-0.563	-18.3	0.00
$\xi =$	-0.563	-18.3	0.00

This concludes our examination of the equations in the REMI model. In chapter 8, we present a forecast and simulations with a version of this model.

APPENDIX: Chapter 7

The Derivation of Cost of Capital Equations[24]

Case 1: Fixed Rate No Taxes

The first case illustrated is the derivation of the implicit rental cost of capital for a unit of capital that has a fixed lifetime in a situation where there are no taxes. It is also assumed that the rental rate for the equipment will be fixed at a

A Fixed Rental Rate of Capital (C')
Over its Lifetime (L)

C'_t

Time   L

Diagram 7-2

proportion of its purchase price, that this rental rate will be maintained for the life of the equipment, and that there is no scrap value (see diagram 7-2). The cost of capital is found by equating the present value of the future income stream with the price of capital.

$$q_o = \int_0^L C'e^{-rt}dt = \frac{C'}{-r}e^{-rt}\Big|_0^L \qquad (7\text{-}110)$$

q_o = cost of new machine or structure

L = life of capital

C' = the fixed rental rate from time = 0 until the end of its life at time L

r = the interest rate

$$q_o = \frac{C'e^{-Lr}}{-r} - \frac{C'}{-r} = \frac{C'}{r} \times \left(1 - e^{-Lr}\right) \qquad (7\text{-}111)$$

If we now solve this for $C' \div q_o$, we obtain

$$\frac{C'}{q_o} = \frac{r}{1 - e^{-Lr}} \qquad (7\text{-}112)$$

Substituting in values of $r = .1$ and $L = 12$, the implicit rental rate that we obtain is

$$\frac{C'}{q_o} = \frac{.1}{1 - e^{-1.2}} = .143 \qquad (7\text{-}113)$$

For value of $r = .1$ and $L = 10$, the implicit rental rate is

$$\frac{C'}{q_o} = \frac{.1}{1 - e^{-1}} = .158 \tag{7-114}$$

Case 2: Declining Rate No Taxes

In the second case, as in the first, there are no taxes. However, in this case, it is assumed that the rental rate declines by a certain proportion each year. This proportion will be called the replacement rate.

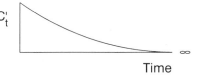

The Rental Rate of Capital (C')
Declining as the Capital Ages

Diagram 7-3

$$C'_t = C' e^{-\delta t} \tag{7-115}$$

where

C'_t = the implicit rental rate of capital at time t

C' = the fixed portion of the rental rate

δ = the replacement rate or the proportionate decline each year

$$q_o = \int_o^\infty C' e^{-\delta t} e^{-rt} dt = \int_o^\infty C' e^{-(r + \delta)t} dt \tag{7-116}$$

$$q_o = \frac{C' e^{-(r + \delta)t}}{-(r + \delta)} \Big|_o^\infty = 0 - \frac{C'}{-(r + \delta)} \tag{7-117}$$

$$q_o = \frac{C'}{(r + \delta)} \tag{7-118}$$

$$\frac{C'}{q_o} = (r + \delta) \tag{7-119}$$

Illustrating with a specific value of $\delta = .12$ and $r = .1$, the implicit rental rate using equations 7-115 and 7-119 for selected years is

$$\frac{C'_t}{q_o} = (r + \delta) e^{-\delta t} \tag{7-120}$$

$$= (.1 + .12) e^{-.12t}$$

Year	Implicit Rental Rate (C_t)
0	.22
1	.1951
2	.1731
5	.1207
:	
10	.0663
20	.0200
100	.0000014

Case 3: Case 2 Plus Federal Profits Tax

This case is similar to case 2. However, federal corporate profits taxes are now added

$$C^* = C' + T_f \tag{7-121}$$

$$C' = C^* - T_f \tag{7-122}$$

C^* = rental charge for equipment or structures including tax costs

C' = after tax return to renting firm

T_f = federal profits tax

$$T_f = \tau_f (C^* - D_t) \tag{7-123}$$

τ_f = federal profits tax rate

D_t = depreciation allowance

$$D_t = \begin{cases} \dfrac{1}{F} \times q_o & \text{if } 0 \le t \le F \\ 0 & \text{otherwise} \end{cases} \tag{7-124}$$

F = lifetime allowed for federal tax purposes

This formulation assumes straight-line depreciation.

$$C' = (1 - \tau_f) C^* + \tau_f D_t \tag{7-125}$$

$$q_o = (1 - \tau_f) C^* \int_0^\infty e^{-(r + \delta)t} \, dt + \tau_f \int_0^F D_t \, e^{-rt} \, dt \tag{7-126}$$

$$q_o = \frac{(1 - \tau_f) C^*}{(r + \delta)} + \frac{\tau_f}{F} q_o \left[\frac{1 - e^{-Fr}}{r} \right] \tag{7-127}$$

$$\left(\frac{1 - \tau_f)}{(r + \delta)}\right)\left(\frac{C^*}{q_o}\right) = \frac{q_o}{q_o} - \left(\frac{\tau_f}{F}\right)\left(\frac{q_o}{q_o}\right)\left(\frac{1 - e^{-Fr}}{r}\right) \tag{7-128}$$

$$\frac{C^*}{q^o} = \left(\frac{r + \delta}{1 - \tau_f}\right) \times \left[1 - \frac{\tau_f}{F}\left(\frac{1 - e^{-Fr}}{r}\right)\right] \tag{7-129}$$

If, in this particular instance, $r = .1$, $\delta = .12$, $\tau_f = .5$, and $F = 10$, then

$$\frac{C^*}{q^o} = \left(\frac{(.1 + .12)}{.5}\right) \times \left[1 - \frac{.5}{10}\left(\frac{1 - e^{-1}}{.1}\right)\right] \tag{7-130}$$

$$= .44\ (1 - .316) = .30$$

If $F = 1$, then

$$\frac{C^*}{q^o} = .44\ (1 - .476) = .23 \tag{7-131}$$

These values should be compared with the first-year implicit rent in equation 7-120.

It should be noted that as the term $(1 - e^{Fr}) \div (F \times r)$ approaches one (1), the implicit rental rate approaches the rate in equation 7-120. This would be the case if the government paid for τ_f percent of the machine (instant deduction of $\tau_f \times$ purchase price) but then taxed future returns at τ_f.

Case 4: Case 3 Plus State Profits Tax

This case will follow case 3, though now a state corporate profits tax will be added. In this instance, different depreciation schedules will be allowed for state and federal taxes.

$$C^* = C' + T_f + T_s \tag{7-132}$$

$$C' = C^* - T_f - T_s \tag{7-133}$$

T_s = state tax collections

$$T_f = \tau_f\ (C^* - D_t^F - T_s) \tag{7-134}$$

$$T_s = \tau_s\ (C^* - D_t^s) \tag{7-135}$$

τ_s = state profits tax rate

D_t^s = depreciation allowed for state tax purposes

$$T_f = \tau_f\, C^* - \tau_f\, D_t^F - \tau_f \left[\tau_s \left(C^* - D_t^s \right) \right] \tag{7-136}$$

$$T_f = \tau_f\, C^* - \left(\tau_f\, \tau_s\, C^* \right) - \left(\tau_f\, D_t^F \right) + \left(\tau_f\, \tau_s\, D_t^s \right) \tag{7-137}$$

$$T_s = \tau_s\, C^* - \tau_s\, D_t^s \tag{7-138}$$

$$C' = C^* - \tau_f\, C^* - \tau_s\, C^* + \tau_f\, \tau_s\, C^* + \tau_f\, D_t^F - \tau_f\, \tau_s\, D_t^s + \tau_s\, D_t^s \tag{7-139}$$

$$C' = \left(1 - \tau_f - \tau_s + \tau_f\, \tau_s \right) C^* + \tau_f\, D_t^F + \tau_s \left(1 - \tau_f \right) D_t^s \tag{7-140}$$

$$C' = \left(1 - u \right) C^* + \tau_f\, D_t^F + v\, D_t^s \tag{7-141}$$

where

$$u = \tau_f + \tau_s - \tau_f\, \tau_s \tag{7-142}$$

$$v = \tau_s \left(1 - \tau_f \right) \tag{7-143}$$

$$q_o = \left[\left(1 - u \right) C^* \int_0^\infty e^{-(r+\delta)t}\, dt \right] + \left[\tau_f \int_0^F D_t^F e^{-rt}\, dt \right] + \left[v \int_0^S D_t^s e^{-rt}\, dt \right] \tag{7-144}$$

$$\frac{C^*}{q_o} = \left(\frac{(r+\delta)}{1-u} \right) \times \left[1 - \frac{\tau_f}{F} \left(\frac{1 - e^{-Fr}}{r} \right) - \frac{v}{S} \left(\frac{1 - e^{-Sr}}{r} \right) \right] \tag{7-145}$$

For the particular case where $r = .1$, $\delta = .12$, $\tau_f = .5$, $F = 10$, $\tau_s = .1$, and $S = 10$, the result would be

$$u = .5 + .1 - .05 = .55$$
$$v = .05$$

$$\begin{aligned}
\frac{C^*}{q_o} &= \frac{.1 + .12}{.45} \left[1 - \frac{.5}{10} \left(\frac{1 - e^{-1}}{.1} \right) - \frac{.05}{10} \left(\frac{1 - e^{-1}}{.1} \right) \right] \\
&= .489\, (1 - .316 - .0316) \\
&= .489 \times .652 = .319
\end{aligned} \tag{7-146}$$

This result should be compared with the result in equation 7-130.

NOTES ON CHAPTER 7

1. This chapter is adapted in part from "The REMI Economic-Demographic Forecasting and Simulation Model" by G. I. Treyz, D. S. Rickman, and G. Shao.

2. U.S. Department of Labor, Bureau of Labor Statistics, "Outlook 2000," five articles in the *Monthly Labor Review,* Vol. 112, No. 11, November 1991, pp. 3 – 74.

3. In this model, we use an industry-industry, input-output table.

4. The superscript k, which denotes the area currently concerned, is used only when necessary.

5. The matrix $PCE = [PCE_{i,j}]$ is often called a bridge matrix.

6. This draws on a paper by D. S. Rickman, G. Shao, and G. I. Treyz (1993).

7. In an alternative version of the model, E_i^u / Q_i^u is replaced by the equation $\alpha_{0,1} \, e^{\alpha_{1,i}t} \left(Q_t / Q_{t-1} \right)^{\alpha_{2,i}}$, where $\alpha_{0,1}$ is an intercept calibrating to U.S. E_i^u / Y^u in period T, $\alpha_{1,i}$ is the inverse of the U.S. productivity growth rate for industry i, and $\alpha_{2,i}$ is an econometric estimate from a U.S. regression of the effect of cyclical output change on labor productivity in industry i. This version takes into account that labor productivity increases in response to increases in output (see Shao and Treyz, 1993).

8. Refer to equation 7-4.

9. For a comparison of calculated amenity effects from this equation with those of hedonic models, see Greenwood, et al. (1991).

10. For further discussion of this equation, see G. I. Treyz, D. S. Rickman, G. L. Hunt, and M. Greenwood, "The Dynamics of U.S. Internal Migration," *The Review of Economics and Statistics*, forthcoming.

11. "Preliminary Estimates of the Population of Counties by Age, Sex, and Race; 1980 to 1989." Available from the Statistical Information Staff, Population Division, US Bureau of the Census, Washington, D.C. 20233.

12. As discussed in chapter 3, regional industries are those industries that have more than fifty percent of their sales in intrastate trade, while national industries have fifty percent or more of their sales in interstate and international trade.

13. In an n-industry framework, a similar expression for equation 3-22 is

$$K_i^* = (W_i/c_i) \times (d_i/a_i) \times E_i$$

14. R. I. Hall and D.W. Jorgenson (1967).

15. Derivations that are more extensive than those in the appendix are available from the author.

16. BEA uses national deflators to deflate local nominal VA. We use the deflator implicit in the assumption that SP = SP^u and that intermediate input costs differ by region. Therefore, the relative value added deflator (RPVA$_i$) is RPVA$_i$ = (1 - Σ a$_{j, i}$ $\times$ SP$_j$) $\div$ a$_{f, i}$.

17. In the prototype model, the current period was used to simplify the model.

18. George I. Treyz and Benjamin H. Stevens (1985), pp. 553 – 555 and 559.

19. George I. Treyz and Dan S. Rickman (1989).

20. From the EDFS-53 sectors on table 8-1, the national industries are 1, 2, 4-16, 20-21, and 38. The regional industries are 3, 17, 19, 22-37, and 39-49.

21. Here, we only discuss the single-area model. For multi-area models, the export share to the other areas in the multi-area region responds using the same responses as those shown.

22. For multi-area models, S$_i^{kr}$ can be obtained by rearranging terms in equation 7-14:

$$S_i^{kr} = X_i^{kr} \div \left(\sum_{h=1, h \neq k}^{m} M_i^h \right)$$. Multi-area exports (X$_i^{kr}$)

are $X_{i,T}^{kr} = \left(PS_{i,T}^{mr} \times Q_{i,T}^{k} \right) - \left(R_{i,T}^{k} \times D_{i,T}^{k} \right)$, where the superscript *mr* indicates the multi-area, and k indicates the area. PS$_{i, }^{mr}$$_T$ is the estimated proportion of the total area output that stays within the major area$_{kr}$, of which area k is a subarea. The behavioral responses for S$_i^{kr}$ are based on those estimated for S$_i^{ku}$.

23. In regression analysis, the variable Q$_i^u$ was used as a proxy for XFG$_i^u$.

24. This appendix draws on work by G. I. Treyz, B. H. Stevens, R. E. Williams, C. Lawton, A. F. Friedlaender, R. M. Costrell, R. E. Hall, D. W. Jorgenson, and Gang Shao. Derivations for eight other cases are available from the author.

CHAPTER 8

REGIONAL AND MULTI-REGIONAL FORECASTS AND SIMULATIONS USING A REMI EDFS MODEL[1]

In chapter 7, the structure for an operational forecasting and simulation model was set forth. The name of the model described is the Regional Economic Models, Inc., Economic and Demographic Forecasting and Simulation (REMI-EDFS) model.

In this chapter, we use a single region, fourteen-sector version of the model. More typically, the REMI models have fifty-three sectors (see table 8-1 in the appendix) and several areas in a multi-area grouping. We chose this small, single-area model to facilitate distribution and use of the model in conjunction with this book.[2] The programs and database necessary for using this model are available on a floppy diskette for use on IBM-compatible computers.

We begin by explaining how a control forecast is made and interpreted. We then discuss policy simulations. The discussion of policy variables is presented in five major sections following the five blocks shown in diagrams 7-1 and 4-10. The structure of this chapter follows that used for the prototype model forecast and simulations in chapter 4. To do a policy study using this model, the first step is to identify the major categories of direct effects from the policy and to run the control forecast. Next, we find the particular policy variables that need to be used and establish the amount by which each policy variable is to be changed. The model is then rerun and a complete alternative forecast is created based on the policy variable changes. Finally, by analyzing the differences between the alternative and the control forecast, the effect of the policy change is seen and interpreted. This chapter is written to serve as a guide to those using the REMI demonstration model that is available from the author, as well as an overview of forecasting and policy analysis with an operational model. The key relevant tables generated by the demo model program that are discussed in the text are included at the end of this chapter.

For the REMI Demo model, we have chosen to model a county with a population of about 194 thousand and employment of about 119 thousand in 1990. This county is located on one of the Great Lakes in the Midwest. You may discover other details about this county, such as its employment for fourteen industries, production costs including labor, capital, and fuel (relative to the nation), industrial output and demand, personal income, population (by single year of age and sex), and economic migration, for each of the last twenty-one years by printing out the economic and demographic tables for the historical years 1969 – 1989. These tables, with the exception of the population by cohort tables, are included at the end of this chapter for selected years in tables 8-2 through 8-18.

You may notice that the model's last historical year is 1989. This makes 1990 the first year of forecast. Since 1990 is history from the perspective of the user, it may seem incongruous that 1990 is also a forecast year. However, due to the time lags inherent in data collection and data processing, a complete data set for any year or quarter is only available with a significant time delay. Therefore, in the typical case, the first period of forecast is a period that has already past.

Before proceeding, you need to install the model. Some basic information on installing the Demo model and using the software is in the appendix to this chapter. However, if you do not have the diskette, you may read on and refer to the results shown in the appendix to this chapter. The next section can be skipped, by those who do not have the diskette, without loss of continuity.

8-1 GENERATING RESULTS WITH THE MODEL[3]

To enter the Demo Model Menu System, move to the directory in which the model was installed and type DEMO <ENTER> (see the installation instructions in the appendix to this chapter for more information). At any menu or question box you need only press the key corresponding to your choice. At any other prompt you must type in the appropriate response followed by the <ENTER> key. Choose the **GENERATING RESULTS** option on the first menu by pressing the **2** key, and the **RUN MODEL** option on the second menu by again pressing the **2** key. Selecting this last option will start the REMI procedure, which creates a forecast. Answer "N" to the question regarding model suppressions[4] (hit the <ENTER> key after typing a response), and enter "2020" as the last forecast year. A control forecast will then be generated.

After the control forecast is created, you will be asked whether you wish to run a policy simulation. Answer "Y" to this question (in this case, only press the key corresponding to your response) and select the regular policy variable option at the succeeding **Policy Variable Changes** menu. You will then be presented with a screen of information regarding regular policy variables and asked if you wish to see a list of these variables. Enter "N" to the question, unless you want to print out the complete list. When asked which policy variable you wish to change, enter policy variable 941. This variable allows you to change industrial electric costs (rates). Enter a range of "1990,2020" at the next prompt and enter "–50.0" as the input value. This amount reflects a 50% decrease. Enter "Y" when asked if you wish to accept your changes, and enter "Y" to change another variable. Repeat the above steps for variable 942 (i.e., Electric Rates — Commercial), choosing the same years and values as was done for policy variable 941. Then, enter "N" when the program asks whether or not you want to change another policy variable. You will now be returned to the **Policy Variable Changes** menu. Press "X" at the menu to run a policy simulation that incorporates the changes you made to the policy variables. After the policy simulation is run, the **GENERATING RESULTS** menu will reappear; press the "Q" key to return to the **Demo Model Main Menu**.

At the main menu, select the **Printing Results** option and choose **Help on Printing Results** at the next menu. Read the help screen to get an idea of how to print your forecast and simulation results. Return to the **Printing Results** menu and select the **Economic** option. The REMI procedure for printing economic data will begin. Enter "1" to choose option 1 (control forecast), and select to print the primary and supplementary tables for five individual years: 1982, 1990, 1991, 2000, and 2020. When asked if you want to print more tables for the region, enter "Y." Then, select option 3 (difference) and choose the same tables for the years 1990, 1991, 1994, 2000, and 2020. Enter "N" when asked if you wish to print more tables. At the next question, press "Y" to add formfeeds. Press "N" to skip viewing the tables, and at the succeeding question, press "Y" to have your tables sent to your printer.[5] When you are returned to the **Printing Results** menu, you can then repeat the above printing steps for the population results. However, you will need to choose the **Population** results option twice: once for the control results and once for the difference results. When printing the population results, do not choose to print all the tables but only tables 1 and 2. To verify that you have printed the correct tables and for readers who do not have the demo model programs, selected economic and population tables for selected history and control forecast years are included in the appendix to this chapter as tables 8-2 through 8-18.

8-2 ANALYZING THE RESULTS

The History and Control Forecast Tables

The economic history and control forecast tables should be examined first. These tables and all of the other tables mentioned in this chapter are in the appendix. Looking at the economic results from table 8-2 (the "Super Summary Table"), we find that in 1990 this county had employment, personal income, and population as a percent of the United States of 0.086%, .073% and .078%, respectively. We find that the county's gross regional product and real disposable income in 1990 were $3.442 and $2.237 billion 1982 dollars, respectively. The index on this table identifies the subsequent tables, which provide greater detail for employment, personal income, and gross regional product data.

Table 8-3 presents the aggregation of values for the ten (10) private, nonfarm sectors for the years that were selected. The numbers in parentheses show the tables on which you will find the ten-sector disaggregate data. Looking at the top of the table, we note that total nonfarm, private employment in the county in 1990 was 104,411. Of this, 45,248 of the jobs were directly dependent on exports to the rest of the United States and the rest of the world. The remaining jobs were created by demand in the following areas: 24,034 in the purchase of inputs by local firms (called intermediate demand), 29,526 in local consumption demand, 2,275 in government purchases in the private sector, and 3,328 in local investment activity. The next section shows that relative selling price for regional industries was 94.79% of the national average. An explanation of the low price may be found in labor costs, two lines below. Here, labor costs, a component of the total costs of factor inputs, are only 90.74% of those in the nation.

Toward the middle of table 8-3, the relative factor productivity shows that total factor productivity in 1990 is slightly lower in the area than in the nation, and profitability for national industries as a percent of sales is approximately 0.2% lower on average than in the nation. Labor intensity is higher than in the nation (≈ 1.05) due to wage costs being relatively lower than other factor input costs. The multiplicative adjustments ("MULT ADJ") on tables 8-3 and 8-10 show the effect of changes not explained by the model in the past. They enter into the model as a multiplicative adjustment by industry (see item 7 in section 8-3 on policy variables 100 + N). During the history period, its value is calculated as the value that will perfectly reconcile the predictive equation with the observed values. The RPC (Regional

Purchase Coefficient) on table 8-3 indicates that 42% of local use is supplied locally. Table 8-10 (economic table 11) indicates that this proportion varies from a low of 1.5% for mining to 91.9% for retail trade. Returning to table 8-3, the industrial mix index shows that the area has a disproportionate representation in the slow growth part of the U.S. economy.[6] This will pull the local employment down. This decrease is slightly more than 2% [((1.017 ÷ 1.041) − 1) × 100] between 1990 and 2020. The next eight rows of table 8-3 present some other common economic concepts in 1982 dollars. The final row is total wage and salary disbursements in nominal dollars.

Next, we review the population tables from the control forecast. On table 8-13 (population table 1), notice that retired migrants (see **OVER 65** under the **TOTAL MIGRANTS** heading) are predicted to continue to come into the area. This Migration rate is historically based and is dependent on the size of the relevant U.S. retirement age cohorts. Table 8-14 (population table 2) shows the factors involved in estimating the number of economic migrants who enter the region annually. The number of economic migrants depends on the probability of being employed relative to that in the United States as a whole (**REO**: 1.008 in 1990), the relative, real, after-tax wage rate (**RWR**), and the relative industry mix among high- and low-paying jobs (**RWM**). Also, notice the regional constant at the bottom of the page. This constant captures the observed, relative preference shown for the area relative to other areas as estimated over the historical period. This estimate is similar to the estimate made in the prototype model, based on one year. It is -.013, meaning that $\ln \lambda_K = -.013$. Consulting equation 7-61 and summing the coefficients over all of the lags, we note that, assuming REO and RWM = 0,

$$NECM = \ln \lambda_K + .351 \; \ln RWR$$

Thus, for a net migration of zero (equilibrium),

$$0 = \ln \lambda_K + .351 \; \ln \; RWR$$
$$\ln RWR = \ln \lambda_K \div -.351 = (-.013 \div -.351) = .037$$
$$RWR = e^{.037} = 1.038,$$

indicating that this is an amenity poor area where net migration would be zero at a relative real after-tax wage that was 103.8% of that in the nation. The 103.8% is called the compensating differential, which is the wage required to offset the less than average quality of life in the area.[7]

In the appendix , we show the composition of the population by age and sex in table 8-15 (population table 4), the age composition of the migrants in table 8-16 (population table 6), the potential labor force in table 8-17 (population table 10), and the participation rates by age cohort in table 8-18 (population table 11). These participation rates are multiplied, at the single age cohort level, by the population in that cohort (see table 8-15) to obtain the potential labor force (see table 8-17).

To develop a control or baseline forecast for planning or serious use, it is necessary to look at all of the components of the forecast in light of the forecaster's knowledge of the area for which the forecast is being made. In particular, preliminary data might be available that would suggest that some additive or multiplicative policy variables should be changed to incorporate factors that were not captured in the model. Likewise, the forecaster may know about future plant closings or construction projects that would not have been forecast by the model. All of this fine tuning[8] of the forecast changes the baseline, but it only has a marginal effect on the differences between control and alternative forecasts. This is because the modifications made to the baseline are also incorporated in the alternative forecast, which includes the policy variable changes. So, when the difference is measured, the modifications are cancelled out.

The Difference Tables

Next, we turn to the tables that show the effects of reducing electrical rates by 50 percent: the second set that is created using the printing procedures. Four key tables (8-19 through 8-22) are included in the appendix to this chapter. First, make an attempt at understanding the changes you see for each of the variables, including the migration changes, as shown on table 8-22 (population table 2). Then, continue with the explanation below.

To see the most immediate effects of the electric rate reductions, turn to table 8-20, which is table 2 of the economic difference tables. There, we find that **FUEL** costs have decreased by 28.9% (-0.28943) for all years. The decrease is less than the 50 percent that was entered into the model because electricity rates represent only a portion of the fuel costs within the REMI model. The model also includes natural gas costs and residual fuel oil costs as part of total fuel costs.

The reduction in fuel costs then feeds into the total costs of factor inputs. The reduction in factor costs has an effect on each REMI industry that is dependent on whether the particular industry is national or regional. Regional industries reduce their selling prices in response to reductions in their total costs. The selling price in 1990 on table 8-20 (economic table 2) drops by approximately 1.2% (-0.01197) and remains lower than the control forecast for each year of the policy simulation.

Due to market constraints, national industries (manufacturing in the EDFS-14 model) must sell at prices determined in national markets and, therefore, cannot respond with a price change. In the case of electric rate reductions, the national industries realize increased profitability. Profits relative to the nation (table 8-20) are up by 1.5% (0.01493) in 1990.

The increased profits in manufacturing and decreased selling prices in regional industries have broad effects on the economy. Price decreases reduce the consumer price index on table 8-19 (economic table 1), which, in turn, increases the real, after-tax wage rate (RWR) shown on table 8-22 (population difference table 2). An increase in the relative real wage rate (RWR) will result in an increase in the annual number of economic migrants up through the year 2000 and a consequent increase in the potential labor force (also on table 8-22).

The increasing real disposable income and population induces higher levels of consumption and government services, thereby increasing the total level of demand in the region. This increase contributes to a total increase in demand of $87 million (0.08733) in 1990 (see table 8-20).

Effects of A Business Electric Rate Reduction of 50% In Billions of 1982 Dollars

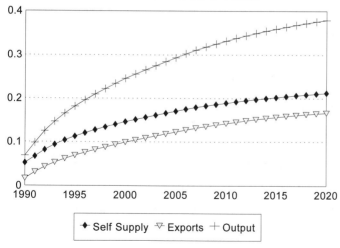

Diagram 8-1

338

The higher profitability leads to national firms locating in the region, which increases their share of local and export markets. Likewise, lower sales prices by regional firms increase market shares. All of the changes lead to greater exports and to greater self-supply. These increases and total output changes are shown in diagram 8-1.

The increases in output lead to increased demand for labor. The resulting increase in private nonfarm employment is 1,224 jobs in 1990 (see table 8-20). Diagram 8-2 shows how the increased output and reduced labor intensity due to the shift in relative factor prices interact to lead to a net increase in employment through 1996. After 1996, employment gains level off and decline slightly as the rate of reduction in labor intensity more than offsets the rate of output gain.

Effects of A Business Electric Rate Reduction of 50% As a Proportion of the Baseline Values

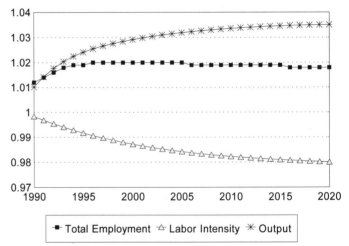

Diagram 8-2

Finally, the interaction of increased employment demand and the potential labor force (table 8-22, population table 2) and decreases in the price index (table 8-19) affects average (annual) wage rates. The annual average wage rate is obtained by dividing total wages by employment, while labor costs, reported on table 8-20, are fixed weight index. Therefore, it is possible for the average wage to drop (table 8-20, 1991), due to changes in the wage mix (table 8-22, 1991), at the same time that labor costs by industry increase (table 8-20, 1991).

Numerous other economic relationships exist within the model. Some interesting results highlight some of these relationships. For example, the average wage rate is shown to cycle over time, capital costs decrease over time, but with changing magnitude, and exports increase. We will not discuss these effects in detail at this point. However, the tables provide further detail for tracing through the effects of the electric rate changes.

8-3 CHOOSING POLICY VARIABLES

We now turn to the more difficult issue of choosing the appropriate policy variable(s) for the policy question that we wish to address. Policy variables are model variables that can be changed by the user and that provide a method of entering the direct effects of a policy into the model. When variables 941 and 942 were changed in the previous section, we were changing policy variables for electric rates. Three types of policy variables are available: regular, translator, and population. In total, there are 737 (1516) regular policy variables in use in the EDFS-14 (EDFS-53) model. To facilitate the discussion of such a large number of variables, we organize the variables into five conceptual blocks and 19 categories. These five blocks are the same as those that we have been using throughout this book (e.g., diagrams 3-1, 4-10, and 7-1, as well as table 4-1), the now familiar output linkages, factor demand, labor supply, wages, prices, and profits, and finally, market shares. An outline of the blocks and categories is presented here.

CATEGORIES OF ECONOMIC AND DEMOGRAPHIC POLICY VARIABLES

In this section, we focus primarily on describing how the different regular policy variables fit into the schematic blocks. For example, regular policy variable 1311[9] adjusts the level of dividends, interest, and rent used in the calculation of disposable income for the region. Since disposable income is a category (see previous page) within the output linkages block, variable 1311 would be found under the output linkages section below along with the other components of disposable income.

Since the translator and population variables each have distinct, unique characteristics which define them as separate groups, we discuss them separately. However, these variables have their place within the schematic blocks. Translator variables are associated with the output linkages block, because they affect groups of regular variables for industry output and demand. Population variables are associated with the labor supply block, since they directly affect characteristics of the population cohorts within the model and hence the potential labor force.

A subset of the regular variables is also discussed apart from the rest of the regular policy variables — these variables are called switches. The switch variables (see category 17 on the previous page) are important for making choices about the assumptions that you want to use in running the simulations and are usually used in conjunction with policy variables from other categories. As we discuss each category, we also discuss the associated switch variables.

Finally, we mention that this categorization is not unique. Other methods of grouping the policy variables exist. One useful method is a categorization by type of policy: forecasting and planning, economic development, transportation, energy and natural resources, taxation, budget and welfare, U.S. policies, and environmental policies. This alternative taxonomy is used in the narrative description of model applications in chapter 10.

Output

The following six categories of policy variables from the output linkages block are related through the calculation of industry output in the region. The first category, **Industry Output**, directly stimulates output, while the remaining five represent components in the calculation of output.

(1) Industry Output

Suppose that we want to show the effect in the county represented by the model of an increase in production due to additional orders from the federal government, a business in another state, or a foreign order. Suppose that this order is for one billion 1982 dollars of extra durable goods output from the area for each year into the future. We can perform this policy simulation by simply changing policy variable 601 under category 1. This is the multi-industry equivalent to increasing the PVOUTA policy variable in the prototype model. To do this, enter the menu system and run the model.

Do not suppress any of the model responses and use 2020 as your last year of forecast. Choose to run a simulation and choose to change **Regular** policy variables. Choose 601 as the variable that you wish to change and enter "1000" (you enter this amount because the variable's units are scaled to millions of dollars) as the amount of the change for each year from 1990 through 2020. Then, change variable 906 to a value of "1" for the same years. Do not change any other variables, and execute the simulation. Print out the primary and secondary tables for the difference tables. Economic tables 1 and 2 and population table 2 are in the appendix as tables 8-23 through 8-25 respectively. You may see how your output policy disturbance entered the model by examining table 13 (not shown) in the economic tables. Make an attempt at explaining the changes you see in each of the concepts, especially those on table 8-24 (table 2 of the economic tables).

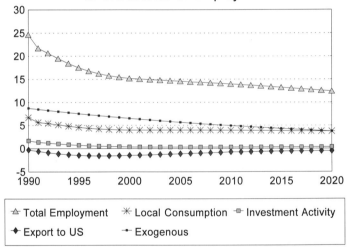

Effects of Increasing Durable Output by 1 Billion \$82s
In Thousands of Employees

Diagram 8-3

Diagram 8-3 shows the effect of the exogenous increase over a thirty year span. Here, we see that the exogenous employment increase gets smaller year by year. This is due to increasing labor productivity in the baseline forecast of this industry. The rise in productivity means that the number of employees required to produce one billion 1982 dollars of durable output decreases each year. Exports other than those included in the exogenous output decrease as competition for labor and higher wage rates drive marginal firms out. However, they recover somewhat as the labor force expands and mitigates the increase in wage costs. Investment increases in the earlier year until the capital stock is increased enough to support the expansion of economic activity.

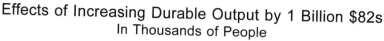

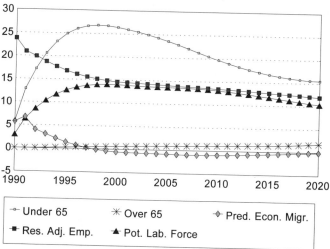

Diagram 8-4

In diagram 8-4, we note that migration is up in the first two years and remains positive through the eighth year. This increases the population under the age of 65 and the labor force. As these migrants mature and their children come into the labor force, the ratio of the increase in the under 65 population to the labor force decreases. By the tenth year the increase in the labor force almost matches the growth in employment. This means that in an open economy, the effect of the new activity on unemployment is only significant for the first ten years. By the end of the simulation, the over 65 population grows significantly as the earlier migrants who were in their thirties when they arrived begin to retire.

In addition to the regular policy variables, we also need to consider the policy switches that are found in category 17. These switching variables have an effect on the way in which other policy variables are used by the model. For example, by setting policy variable 906 equal to "1," as was done previously, the input is read as real 1982 dollars. Only when variable 906 is at its default value of "0" will the dollar input be used as nominal (current) dollars.

Industry output changes are often made to show the effect on a local economy of a policy that will lead to the opening of a new business. However, these studies are often based on the premise that all of the increased output will be exported from the area and, therefore, will not compete with existing firms. This is a valid premise only in certain cases. If, for example, a firm that was going to produce tennis balls relocated to this county, it could safely be assumed that all of the output would go to exports or import substitution, if they do not already have a tennis ball factory in the county. However, in a more general case, when a new retail store goes into business, it is not reasonable to assume that all of the retail activity of the new store would represent exports. In fact, a good deal of the retail activity in the new store might go to local markets at the expense of the preexisting stores in the area. If all of it were at the expense of existing stores, then the new store would have no net effect on local output. The easiest way to handle this problem is to divide the new output into three parts: (1) new net exports, (2) import substitution, and (3) intraindustry shifts in sales. For (1), introduce the change using the industry output policy variables below; for (2), increase the regional purchase coefficient (RPC: see the policy variables in category 16). The sales change(s) for part 3 may be ignored since the gain by the new local businesses is offset by the loss for current local businesses.

In some cases, there may be reason to think that a change in the activity (such as a strike) in an industry will *not* have an effect on the wage rate for that industry. In this case, the endogenous wage response for the industry may be shut off using variable 905 and setting it equal to 1.

---

1. Industry Output Policy Variables

Output	Policy Variable ID# In Millions of Dollars
Prototype Counterpart By Industry	PVOUTA 600 + N

where N is the number of the industrial sector as shown in table 8-1 (e.g., Nondurable Goods is industry 2, therefore, the policy variable ID is 602)

RELEVANT SWITCHES: Variables 905 and 906 (See category 17)

---

(2) Industry Demand

It is important to distinguish between demand and output (see category 1). For policy variables that affect demand, only the proportion of demand that is usually supplied locally is added to local production. You may see these proportions, by industry, on table 8-10 (economic table 11) of the economic control forecast tables. The remainder of the amount that you enter is assumed to be produced elsewhere and imported to the area. In the model, the difference between demand disturbances and output disturbances can be dramatic. Since only 4.5% of local demand for durable goods is supplied locally in the demo model county (see table 8-10, economic table 11), an exogenous increase in the demand for durable goods locally of $100 million would only result in $4.5 million of extra local output for durables, whereas such an increase in output would add the entire $100 million as local output. The only switch to be considered is variable 906. As mentioned previously, this switch determines whether your input is to be considered as real (1982) or nominal (current) dollars.

---

2. Industry Demand Policy Variables

Demand

Policy Variable ID #
In Millions of Dollars

Prototype Counterpart   PVDEMA
By Industry   650 + N

where N ranges over all private nonfarm industries – see table 8-1.

RELEVANT SWITCH: Variable 906 (See category 17)

---

(3) Disposable Income

Listed below are the policy variables that affect the different components of disposable income. Most may be changed in either dollar or percent terms. The total wage bill is also used in the calculation of disposable income, however, wage policy variables are considered under category 14.

Suppose that we wish to increase transfer payments as part of a simulation. For example, suppose that welfare payments are expanded to include a new group of people. This can be accomplished through an increase in variable 904. If we want to have this increase entered in 1982 dollars, we would also set variable 906 equal to 1. The results for these changes for an increase of 100 million 1982 dollars per year are shown on table 8-26 (table 4 of the economic tables). Note that the nominal transfers go up more than 100 million, because each 1982 dollar translates into 1.297 (see table 8-2 of the control forecast) dollars in 1990 and even more in later years. This increase is mitigated somewhat by the reduction in transfers (table 8-26) due to a reduction in people who are not employed. Also note that the total increase in personal income divided by the change in transfers is a measure of the income multiplier.

3. Disposable Income Policy Variables

Component	Policy Variable ID #	Policy Variable ID #	Prototype Counterparts
	In Millions of Dollars	As a Percent of Current Value	
Proprietors Plus Other Labor Income	1295 + N	-	
Transfer Payments	904	934	PVVPA
Contributions to Social Insurance Adj.	1310	935	PVSSA
Dividends/Interest/Rent	1311	936	PVDIRA
Residence Adjustment	1312	937	PVRAA
Personal Taxes	954	1325	PVtxA

where N ranges over all 14 major sectors.

RELEVANT SWITCH: Variable 906 (See category 17)

(4) Consumer Spending

There are thirteen components of consumer spending. Each component can be changed by an amount or a proportion, as indicated in the following table.

4. Consumer Spending Policy Variables

Component	Policy Variable ID#	Policy Variable ID#
	In Millions of Dollars	As a Percent of Current Spending
Autos and Parts	161	261
Furniture and HH Equipment	162	262
Other Durables	163	263
Food and Beverages	164	264
Clothing and Shoes	165	265
Gasoline and Oil	166	266
Fuel Oil and Coal	167	267
Other Nondurables	168	268
Housing	169	269
Household Operation	170	270
Transportation	171	271
Health Services	172	272
Other Services	173	273
Prototype Counterpart	PVCA	PVCM
TOTAL	-	1313

RELEVANT SWITCH: Variable 906 (See category 17)

Let us suppose that we consider a policy that would cause purchases of **Autos and Parts** to decrease by $30 million (1982 dollars) and **Public Transportation** expenditures to increase by the same amount. To see what would happen, we run each policy change separately and then run them together.

For the first simulation, we increase public transportation expenditures by $30 million 1982 dollars by setting policy variable 171 equal to 30 (millions of dollars) and policy variable 906 equal to 1 over the entire forecast period. We then run a simulation over the same period with variable 161 equal to -30 and variable 906 equal to 1. Finally, we run a simulation with variable 171 equal to 30, variable 161 equal to -30, and variable 906 equal to 1.

After running each individual simulation, print out the primary and secondary economic tables before running the next one; otherwise, the data tables produced in one will be overwritten by the next simulation. Since the consumption policy variables 161 – 173 work by changing the appropriate demand policy variables (see category

2), the direct effects of the simulations can be seen on economic table 13 (not shown). This table shows the exogenous output changes that were part of your simulation. For example, purchase of autos directly affects auto dealers (retail trade), as well as the auto industry. Examine and compare the simulations. You may notice a relationship between the variables in the first two simulations and those in the last. The difference tables for the last simulation (the combined changes) are shown in table 8-27 (economic table 2).

For this simulation, the model shows higher levels of exogenous employment on table 8-27. The industry specific additive effects are on economic tables 8 and 9 (not shown). If we had chosen multiplicative consumer final demand variables 261 – 273, the effects would have mainly shown up as consumption spending changes on economic table 5. For example, **Autos and Parts** would have had a large decrease since policy variable 261 directly changes the local consumption of autos and parts. This would have shown up as a change in consumption induced employment. However, policy variable 161 enters the model as an exogenous change to current levels of output and employment without directly changing consumption induced output and employment.

(5) Government Spending

Changing spending in any one of the state and local government categories is very similar to changing spending in a consumption sector. The only switch of concern is the choice between nominal and real dollars (variable 906).

Changes in federal civilian and federal military spending can not be implemented directly for a subnational region. This is true because there is no pattern of federal spending within different regions around the nation. Thus, it is difficult to model the role that federal spending plays in the average region. Such spending changes must be entered by industry (see categories 1 and 7).

5. Government Spending Policy Variables

Quantity	Policy Variable ID# In Millions of Dollars	Policy Variable ID# As a Percent of Current Spending
Federal Defense (U.S. Model Only)	-	277
Federal Civilian (U.S. Model Only)	-	278
State and Local Education	179	279
State and Local Health and Welfare	180	280
State and Local Safety	181	281
State and Local Other	182	282
Total State and Local	-	1314
Prototype Counterpart	PVGA	PVGM

RELEVANT SWITCH: Variable 906 (See category 17)

(6) Investment Spending[10]

In the consumer spending policy simulation carried out above (see category 4), the nonresidential investment required for the increase in **Transportation** (nonautomobile) demand was assumed to take place over time. That investment was made in response to the new demand for transportation services, which required capital equipment and structures, and so on. However, it is likely that construction required to provide additional public transportation services would take place prior to the increase in the use of such services. This can be simulated by using variable 175 below or using a construction translator policy variable (see category 19). In this case, we can suppress the model's endogenous investment response to the exogenous increase in output (or employment) by setting policy variable 901 equal to 1 instead of its default of 0.

350

6. Investment Spending Policy Variables

Investment	Policy Variable ID#	Policy Variable ID#
	In Millions of Dollars	Change in Percent
Residential	174	274
Nonresidential	175	275
Producers' Durable Goods and Equipment	176	276
Inventory	-	285
Total	-	1315
Prototype Investment Counterpart	PVIA	PVIM

Capital Stock

Residential Capital (only in certain cases)	1318	1316
Nonresidential Capital (only in certain cases)	1319	1317
Prototype Counterpart	PVKA	PVKM

RELEVANT SWITCHES: Variables 901, 905, and 906 (See category 17)

Effects of a One Time Reduction in the Residential and Nonresidential Structures in Billions of 1982 Dollars

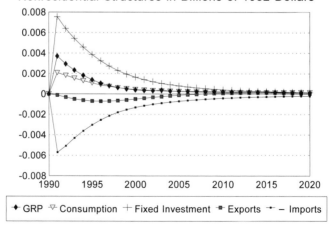

Diagram 8-5

The ability to change the actual capital stock provides some interesting alternatives. Suppose that we wanted to simulate a situation in which $40 million of the residential capital stock and $15 million of the nonresidential capital stock had been destroyed by an earthquake. We could do this by changing variables 1318 and 1319 to -40 and -15, respectively, in the first year only. You may try this simulation now. When you have printed the economic results, examine the employment affects on economic tables 2, 7, and 8 (not shown). The effects on investment and the economy are shown on table 8-28 (economic table 5) and in diagram 8-5.

This concludes the regular policy variables that relate to the output block in the model. We will return to this block when we consider translator variables and after we have looked at the regular economic and population variables for the other blocks.

Labor and Capital Demand

The variables in the following categories are related to labor and capital demand. The first category deals with demand in the labor markets, while the second considers the total factor productivity in each industry that influences the demand for all types of factor inputs.

(7) Employment

The policy variables for employment are often used as an alternative to introducing additional dollars of output (see category 1). For example, a new factory will open employing 100 people in export production in nondurables. This is simulated by entering 0.1 for variable 2. If it is expected that the real exogenous output will remain constant each year, then variable 999 is set equal to 1 and exogenous employment will drop each year as productivity increases. If exogenous output is expected to grow each year enough to absorb 100 employees even as the output per employee grows, then variable 999 remains at its default of 0. Also, switch variable 905 is used if there is a reason to believe that the usual endogenous wage response to the exogenous employment changes should be suppressed (set variable 905 equal to 1).

7. Employment Policy Variables

Employment	Policy Variable ID#	Policy Variable ID#
	In 1000s of Employees	Change in Percent
By Industry	N	100 + N
Prototype Counterpart	PVEA	

where N ranges over all Industries, Government, and Farm.

RELEVANT SWITCHES: Variables 905 & 999 (See category 17)

(8) Factor Productivity

The factor productivity concept used in the model is total factor productivity. When factor productivity is increased, the same output can be produced using less labor and capital. Thus, profits will increase for national industries and sales prices should fall for regional industries. The effects of a one-time productivity increase of 1% for durables starting in 1990 and continuing for the rest of the forecast is shown in table 8-29 (economic table 2) and diagram 8-6.

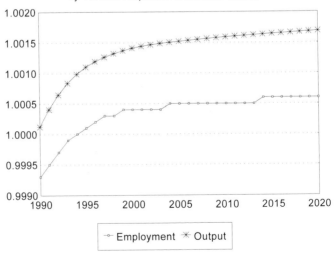

Effects of Increasing Factor Productivity for Durable Goods Production by 1% as a Proportion of Baseline Values

Diagram 8-6

We find that it takes five years before the increase in productivity increases employment. It is at this point that output has increased enough to employ the same number of workers even at the reduced number of employees needed per dollar of output. The factor productivity policy variables are shown next. We can refer to equations 4-59 and 4-63 to see how factor productivity (PVAA) enters the prototype model.

---

8. Factor Productivity Policy Variables

Productivity	Policy Variable ID#
	Change in Percent
By Industry	1000 + N
All Industries	1320
Prototype Counterpart	PVAA

where N ranges over all private, nonfarm industries — see table 8-1.

RELEVANT SWITCHES: None

Labor Supply

The occupational supply variables, along with the population variables, allow the user to change the total amount of available labor within the region. Here, we discuss the former, while population variables are considered in category 18.

(9) Occupational Supply

These variables work through occupational wage rates. An increase in supply reduces the wage. To appropriately use these variables, changes in productivity associated with occupational training must also be considered. In addition, switch variable 905 may be used when additional employees are trained who were previously not available in conjunction with an exogenous increase in employment. Low-skilled occupations are not listed because an increase in training does not directly affect the wages for low-skilled occupations in this model. If training also increases the participation rate, this can be accomplished using the participation rate policy variables described in category 18.

9. Occupational Supply Policy Variables

Occupation	Policy Variable ID#
Professional Specialty Occupations	302
Technical and Related Support	303
Construction Trades	309
Extractive and Related Workers	310
Prototype Counterpart	PVESA

RELEVANT SWITCH: Variable 905 (as an alternative way to introduce occupational training)

(Note: This table applies only to the REMI EDFS-14 model and Demo Model. The EDFS-53 model includes 20 high-skilled occupations.)

Wages, Prices, and Profits

This block includes policy variables that directly effect wage rates, costs, prices, and industry profits.

(10) Production Costs

Often a policy will increase or reduce production costs. Examples include pollution regulations (added costs) or transportation improvements (reduced costs). The policy variables in category 10 can be changed as a percentage (variable 998 default value of 0) or in millions of dollars (variable 998 set equal to 1). Again, if you choose to enter the costs in dollars, we may enter either nominal dollars (variable 906 set to its default value of 0) or real 1982 dollars (variable 906 set equal to 1). Economic table 2 is shown as table 8-30 for a simulation in which production costs are increased by 1% for durables in 1990 and the remainder of the forecast. Note that this reduces profits, but it does not increase prices because durables are a national industry.

10. Production Cost Policy Variables

Production Costs	Policy Variable ID# Cost Change in Percent
By Industry	450 + N
All Industries	1323
Prototype Counterpart	PVPA

where N ranges over all private, nonfarm industries — see Table 8-1.

RELEVANT SWITCHES: Variables 906 and 998 (See category 17)

(11) Business Taxes and Credits

Business taxes and credits are incorporated in the cost of capital equation. Changes in the variables shown on table 11 first affect capital costs, and then the effects reverberate throughout the local economy.

11. Business Taxes and Credits Policy Variables

Business Taxes	Policy Variable ID# Percentage Points
Corporate Profit — By Industry	400 + N
Corporate Profit — All Industries	951
Equipment — All Industries	952
Property — All Industries	955
Investment Credit — All Industries	953
Prototype Cost of Capital	PVccA
Depreciation — Equipment Tax Lifetime	956
Structure Tax Lifetime	957

where N ranges over all private, nonfarm industries.

RELEVANT SWITCHES: None

(12) Fuel Costs

The fuel costs variables are listed below. A sample fuel cost simulation is presented at the beginning of the chapter and in tables 8-19 through 8-22 and diagrams 8-1 and 8-2.

---

12. Fuel Cost Policy Variables

Relative Fuel Costs	Policy Variable ID# Change in Percent
Electric (Commercial)	941
Electric (Industrial)	942
Natural Gas (Commercial)	943
Natural Gas (Industrial)	944
Residual (Commercial)	945
Residual (Industrial)	946
Nearest Prototype Counterpart	PVPA

RELEVANT SWITCH: None

---

(13) Labor Costs (Other Than Wages)

If unemployment or workman's compensation tax rates are increased this increases labor costs but not wage rates. A subsidy to labor use may reduce labor cost to the employer without changing the wage rates of workers. These changes can be implemented using the policy variables shown next.

---

13. Labor Cost Policy Variables

	Policy Variable ID# Change as a % of Wage Rate
Nonwage Labor Cost	850 + N
Prototype Counterpart	PVwcA

where N ranges over all private nonfarm industries — see table 8-1.

RELEVANT SWITCH: None

---

(14) Wages

The wage rate can be changed using the policy variables under the wage rate heading. Such a change may occur due to a union settlement or a policy shift such as a change in the state minimum wage. It is also possible to change the wage bill as well as the wage rate. This may be necessary if particular employees in a policy simulation have earnings that are different than the average wage in the industry in which they are employed. For the individual private industries, this is done in employee units (see the wage bill section of the table below). Thus, if the wages for the employees to be added are 20 percent higher than they are in the industry in general, 0.2 must be added to the wage bill adjustment per employee. For the government and farm sectors, wage bill changes are made in dollar terms. In which case, we need to consider switch variable 906, which determines whether the input is entered in real or nominal units. Also, switch variable 905 can be used to suppress the wage rate effect of exogenous changes in labor demand.

---

14. Wage Policy Variables

Wage Rate

Sector	Policy Variable ID#	
	Percent Change	Percent Points
Each Private	$200+(N)$	-
State and Local	$200+(NP+1)$	-
Federal Civilian	$200+(NP+2)$	-
All of the Above	1324	-
Prototype Counterpart		PVwA

Wage Bill

Sector	Policy Variable ID#		
	Employee Equivalents	Dollars in Millions	Percent Change
Each Private	$750+(N)$	-	-
State and Local	-	924	-
Federal Civilian	-	922	-
Federal Military	-	923	-
All Nonfarm	-	921	-
Farm	-	925	-
All of the Above	-	-	931
Prototype Counterpart			-

Where NP equals the number of private, nonfarm sectors and N ranges from 1 up to NP (N: $1 \leq N \leq NP$) — see table 8-1.

RELEVANT SWITCHES: Variables 905 and 906

---

(15) Prices (Housing and Consumer)

A change in consumer prices is often an important part of a simulation. For example, prices might be raised to simulate a new sales tax or an increase in consumer electric rates. Housing price changes directly impact the real wage expected by migrants but only indirectly effect the regional economy through the effect of land prices on construction costs in the personal consumption deflator. Since most local consumers own their own home or pay rent, they don't respond immediately to changes in housing prices.

---

15. Price (Housing and Consumer) Policy Variables

Prices	Policy Variable ID# Change in Percent	Policy variable ID# Millions of Dollars of Loss in Purchasing Power
Housing and Land	971	-
Prototype Counterpart	PVPHA	
Price Index	902	960
Prototype Counterpart	PVCPA	

RELEVANT SWITCH: None (dollars are nominal dollar values)

Market Shares

This block allows the user to adjust both export and regional shares.

(16) Market Shares

The share of local markets can be increased by increasing the regional purchase coefficients, which are the proportion of local use supplied locally. The proportion of national and international markets can be changed using the export market share variable. All shares of exports may be increased by increasing variable 1322, while all local market shares can be increased by reducing imports (variable 1321).

16. Market Share Policy Variables

	Policy Variable ID#	Policy Variable ID#
	Local Market Share Change in Percent	Export Market Share Change in Percent
Market Share by Industry	1050 + N	1100 + N
All Industries	1321	1322
Prototype Counterparts	PVRA	PVSA

where N ranges over all private, nonfarm industries — see table 8-1.

RELEVANT SWITCH: None

Additional Policy Variables

As mentioned above, these variables (switches, translators, and population) have distinct characteristics that make it appropriate to consider them separately from the regular variables. The following sections provide more detail for each type.

(17) Switches (variables which are either ON or OFF)

The switches for various policy variables are shown below. All of these variables have permissible values of either 1 (ON) or 0 (OFF). They were explained previously.

17. Switch Variables

Function of Switch	Variable ID #	Default
Input in real (1982) or nominal dollars?	906	0 = Nominal
Production cost changes in percent or dollars?	998	0 = Percent
Include exogenous employment and output changes in wage rate calculations?	905	0 = YES
Activate nonresidential investment response to exogenous output or employment changes?	901	0 = YES

Function of Switch	Variable ID#	Default
Assume output demand growth will match productivity growth rate? (used when entering an output stimulus measured in employee units)	999	0 = YES

---

(18) Population Policy Variables

The next set of policy variables to be considered are the population policy variables. A full list of the population variables may be examined interactively on the computer. You will be prompted at the appropriate point; type "Y" if you want to view the list. Here, we present only a selected set.

A key policy variable used for affecting the model population is the amenity term in the migration equation. This population policy variable is variable 11; it can be used to represent a quality of life improvement (or decline). The quality improvement may come from lower morbidity or mortality, better visibility or reduced crime. For simulation purposes, however, the improvement may be quantified in terms of a real wage gain equivalent for economic migrants. This real wage gain equivalent makes the region more attractive, so a greater number of economic migrants enter the region annually. The way to do this with the model is to find the sum of the real wage coefficients, 0.351, in the migration equation ($\delta_4 + \delta_5 + \delta_6$: equation 7-61 in chapter 7) , and then, following equation 4-31 (with the sum instead of just δ_4), multiply the natural log of one plus the proportionate equivalent change by this value (.351). For example, an amenity improvement that economic migrants perceived as equivalent to a 0.4 percent increase in their wage would be entered as (ln1.004 $\times$ 0.351 $\times$ 100) = 0.1401 (approximately .4 $\times$ .351) using the amenity policy variable, which is in percent change. Economic table 2 and population table 2 for this policy variable change in 1990 are shown as table 8-31 and 8-32 in the appendix.

In diagram 8-7, the increase in migration, which is due to the increase in amenities, is immediate but decreases each year until it becomes zero in 2009. After that point, there is some loss of population as the children who came in with the original migrants become working age and join the labor force. This leads to a narrowing of the gap between the under 65 population increase and the labor force increase.

Effects of a Quality of Life Improvement Equal to .4% of Wage
In Thousands of People

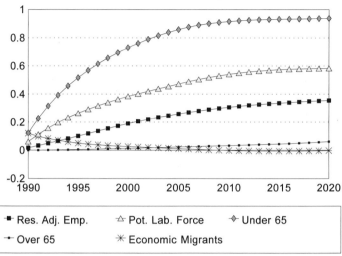

Diagram 8-7

In diagram 8-8, the effect of the increased migration is shown on the relative real after-tax rate (REO) and on the relative employment opportunity (REO). The total drop in RWR plus REO is .0041 or .41%. This almost exactly offsets the amenity gain of .4%, which resulted from the quality of life improvement.

Effects of a Quality of Life Improvement Equal to .4% of Wage
In Relative Proportions

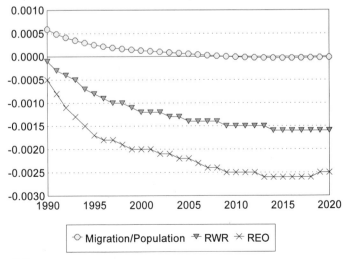

Diagram 8-8

The other population policy variables are reasonably self-explanatory. Try out several simulations using these policy variables. For example, try a simulation for a survival rate increase for males age 35 – 55 due to reduced heart attacks. Or, try a simulation in which large groups of international migrants are resettled within the county. This second simulation is interesting in that it corresponds to a situation currently occurring in some of the southern states due to emigres from Latin America.

18. Selected Population Policy Variables

	Policy Variable ID#		
	Percent Change (By Age)	Change in Percentage Points (By Age)	Percent Change (All Ages)
Birth Rate (1 – 50)	21	1	42
Survival Rate, Male (1 – 101)	22	2	43
Survival Rate, Female (66 – 101)	23	3	44
Retired Migrants, Male (66 – 101)	24	-	45
Retired Migrants, Female (66 – 101)	25	-	46
International Migrants, Male (1 – 65)	26	-	47
International Migrants, Female (1 – 65)	27	-	48
Participation Rate, Male (1 – 101)	28	8	49
Participation Rate, Female (1 – 101)	29	9	50
	Thousands of People (By Age)	Thousands of People (All Ages)	
Retired Migrants, Male (66 – 101)	4	-	
Retired Migrants, Female (66 – 101)	5	-	
International Migrants, Male (1 – 65)	6	-	
International Migrants, Female (1 – 65)	7	-	
International Migrants, (1 – 65)	-	40	
	Thousands of People	Percent Change	
Economic Migrants	10	30	
Amenity Term	-	11[*]	
Prototype Amenity		PVQOLA	
Prototype Migrants	PVMIGA		

([*]See equation 7-61; for a real wage equivalent approximation, multiply by 0.351)

(19) Translator Policy Variables

The policy variables covered previously, with the exception of the additive consumption changes, all affect just a single regular policy variable in the model. However, it is possible to ask questions that can be answered by a combination of the regular policy variables; in particular, a specific set of variables from the output block. To facilitate answering these questions, a set of 362 translator policy variables are also included with the model. These translators use a *preset* combination of regular policy variables from the output block to answer a particular question. For example, translator variable 229 (Personal Consumption Expenditures on Books and Maps) uses a combination of variables from category 2 to reflect the particular industry demands that are affected by this specific kind of purchase. There are translators for more detailed industry categories (translators 1 – 218), more detailed final demand categories (translators 220 – 357), and changes in tourism (translators 401 – 405). The detailed industry translators are aggregated from the 226 sector level and also reflect industry specific wage and value-added to output characteristics. One caution about translator variables is that by aggregating to ten private sectors, much of the detail necessary for accurate simulation may be lost. This is because the RPC for the aggregate industry (durables, for example) may be much different than the RPC for the detailed industry (such as petroleum refining) that would be applied to the translator if it were at a more disaggregate level.

A complete list of the translator variables is available by answering, "Y," to the question that asks if you want this list when you are performing a simulation. If you have < CTRL > PRNTSCRN set ON, you get a hard copy of this list.

8-4 CONCLUSION

By running a number of simulations with the Demo Model or using the tables provided and then explaining the results based on the prototype counterpart and chapter 7, we understand and appreciate the system of economic relationships built into the model. However, given the extremely different characteristics of subnational regions, we caution against generalizing the specific results for this sample Mid-Western county to predict effects in other subnational regions. Nevertheless, the basic logic of the key economic interactions found in this regional economy will be found in other areas. It is our hope that the demonstration model illustrates this economic logic and makes a link to realistic policy analysis as it is being practiced today.

APPENDIX: Chapter 8

The REMI EDFS-14 Demonstration Model
Information on Installation and Model Execution

Installation Procedures

The Demonstration (Demo) Model comes packaged on 1, 2, or 4 floppy disks, depending on the size of the diskette drive. If the drive accepts high density diskettes, either 1.2 M or 1.4 M of memory, a single floppy disk from REMI should have been received. If it is a 720 K drive or a 360 K drive, 2 or 4 disks, respectively, should have been received.

To install the Demo Model, first copy all the contents of the diskette(s) to a directory on the hard-drive. Then, move to that directory and type **INSTALL**. The program will bring up a **Yes** or **No** question. If **Yes** is selected, the model will be installed. The installation process should take between three and five minutes. Call REMI if the installation takes over fifteen minutes.

If there is a problem, please gather the following information before calling REMI:

· size of the disk drive(s)

· number of disks received

· a directory of each disk received, and

· the total number of files sent on the disk(s).

Some changes may be necessary to the **CONFIG.SYS** (the system configuration file) to properly run the model. The REMI Model runs best with **FILES = 50** and **BUFFERS = 20** or greater. If these have not been set in CONFIG.SYS, we recommend that the file be edited to include the above files and buffers statements. See the DOS manual for more information on these statements.

Using the Demo Model

The Demo Model is quite easy to use. Move to the directory where the model has been installed and type "**DEMO**." The software is mostly menu-driven. Use the arrow keys ("↑" and "↓") to move the curser to select a choice and then type <**Enter**> (the REMI Demo Model does not support a mouse). Alternatively, the number of any option's description may be entered to make the selection. There are help screens available at each menu if more information is needed while running the program.

Each option at the main menu will display another menu where selections may be further defined. Choosing the **Information** option reveals a general **Help** screen or a list of acknowledgements. The **Generating results** option runs a control forecast or a policy simulation. The **Printing results** option allows for several choices. One option is to print tables of modeling results for economic data. Another option is to print the same for population data. Lastly, time-series data of economic or population variables may be printed.

When choosing to run the model or to print modeling results, the program temporarily leaves the menu system and runs a batch procedure. In this batch procedure, the user will be prompted to answer some simple questions, and the answers will help the model prepare the simulation or to print the pertinent results. Some of the information that may be needed in response to these questions includes the following: the number of years in the forecast, the title name for the results tables, and the number(s) of the simulation policy variable(s) to be used. The information that is supplied on the choice of policy variables will probably require the most forethought. Policy variables are model variables that the *user* is able to change. They tell the model the *primary* economic effects of the policy upon the region's economy. Proper choice of policy variables is necessary to assure that the modeling results are valid. More detailed instructions on choosing policy variables is available in chapter 8.

After answering all the necessary questions and a simulation has been run or tables have been printed, the Demo Model returns to the menu system. The last menu shown before leaving the menu system will be redisplayed. At any menu the user may hit <Esc> to return to the previous menu with no effect. Hitting <Esc> at the Main Menu will exit the user from the Demo Model.

Once a control forecast or policy simulation has been run *and* the tables have been printed, the results will be stored in an ASCII file: "**TABLEXX.FS**." This file may be viewed at any time with the user's own editing software. We recommend that this file be renamed, otherwise it will be overwritten by subsequent results. You may call REMI if you have any comments or further questions.

TABLE 8-1

REMI Model Industry List

<u>INDUSTRY NAMES</u>

IND ID NUMBER	DEMO MODEL AND EDFS-14 MODEL	EDFS-53 MODEL
1	DURABLES	LUMBER
2	NONDURABLES	FURNITURE
3	MINING	STONE, CLAY, ETC.
4	CONT.CONSTRUCTN	PRIMARY METALS
5	TRANS + PUB UTIL	FABRICATED METLS
6	FIN/INS/REAL EST	NONELEC MACHIN
7	RETAIL TRADE	ELEC EQUIPMENT
8	WHOLES. TRADE	MOTOR VEHICLES
9	SERVICES	REST: TRANS EQUIP
10	AGRI/FOR/FISH	INSTRUMENTS
11	STATE & LOC GOV	MISC MANUFACT
12	FED GOV, CIVILIAN	FOOD
13	FED GOV,MILITARY	TOBACCO MANUFCT
14	FARM	TEXTILES
15		APPAREL
16		PAPER
17		PRINTING
18		CHEMICALS
19		PETRO PRODUCTS
20		RUBBER
21		LEATHER
22		MINING
23		CONSTRUCTION
24		RAILROAD
25		TRUCKING
26		LOC/INTRURB TRAN
27		AIR TRANSPORT
28		OTHER TRANSPORT
29		COMMUNICATION
30		PUBLIC UTILITIES
31		BANKING
32		INSURANCE
33		CREDIT + FINANCE
34		REAL ESTATE
35		EATING + DRINKNG
36		REST OF RETAIL
37		WHOLESALE
38		HOTELS
39		PERS + REPAIR SERV

40	PRIV HOUSEHOLDS
41	AUTO REPAIR/SERV
42	MISC BUSINES SERV
43	AMUSEMENT + REC
44	MOTION PICTURES
45	MEDICAL
46	MISC PROF SERV
47	EDUCATION
48	NONPROFIT ORG
49	AGRI/FOR/FISH SER
50	STATE + LOC GOV
51	FED GOV, CIVILIAN
52	FED GOV, MILITARY
53	FARM

NUMBER OF INDUSTRIES:

	EDFS-14	EDFS-53
PRIVATE	10	49
GOVERNMENT	3	3
NONFARM TOTAL	13	52
FARM	1	1
GRAND TOTAL	14	53

TABLE 8-2

DEMO MODEL: HISTORY (1969–1989) & CONTROL FORECAST (1990–2020)

TABLE 1: SUPER SUMMARY TABLE.
(TABLE # REFERENCES IN PARENTHESES)

	1982 HIST	1990 FCST	1991 FCST	2000 FCST	2020 FCST
TOT EMPLOY (3)	95.089	119.064	120.423	132.363	137.744
EMP % OF US	.084	.086	.086	.086	.084
TOT PRIV NF EMP (2)	81.152	104.411	105.782	117.669	123.116
PR NF EMP % OF US	.090	.092	.092	.091	.089
GRP 1982 $ (5)	2.441	3.442	3.521	4.321	5.510
PERS INCOME (4)	1.997	3.430	3.679	6.885	25.282
PERS INC % OF US	.075	.073	.073	.072	.073
DISP INCOME (4)	1.685	2.900	3.104	5.698	21.001
PCE-PRICE INDX-82 (4)	96.954	129.641	136.043	209.056	576.696
REAL DISP INCOME (4)	1.737	2.237	2.281	2.726	3.642
POPULATION (3)	180.000	194.371	195.247	200.817	219.852
POP AS % OF US	.078	.078	.077	.074	.073

(NOTE — FOR ALL TABLES: EMPLOYMENT AND POPULATION IN THOUSANDS OF PEOPLE, DOLLAR CONCEPTS IN BILLIONS OF NOMINAL DOLLARS UNLESS OTHERWISE INDICATED.)

INDEX TO AVAILABLE TABLES

TABLE 8-3

DEMO MODEL: HISTORY (1969 – 1989) & CONTROL FORECAST (1990 – 2020)
TABLE 2: SUMMARY TABLE FOR PRIVATE NONFARM SECTORS.
(DETAILED TABLE # REF IN PARENS)

		1982 HIST	1990 FCST	1991 FCST	2000 FCST	2020 FCST
PRIVATE NONFARM EMPLOYMENT (IN THOUSANDS OF PEOPLE) AND ITS DECOMPOSITION BY SOURCE OF DEMAND:						
TOTAL EMPLOY	(7)	81.152	104.411	105.782	117.669	123.116
INTERMEDIATE	(7)	17.592	24.034	24.512	28.733	31.038
LOCAL CONSUM	(7)	23.289	29.526	29.984	33.786	37.952
GOVT DEMAND	(7)	1.666	2.275	2.288	2.419	2.266
INVEST ACTIV	(8)	2.068	3.328	3.346	3.545	4.042
EXPORT TO US	(8)	36.537	45.248	45.652	49.187	47.818
EXP - MULTREG	(8)	.000	.000	.000	.000	.000
EXOGENOUS	(8)	.000	.000	.000	.000	.000
COSTS AND SELLING PRICES RELATIVE TO THE U.S.:						
SELLING PRICE	(9)	.97175	.94792	.94783	.94844	.95515
FACTOR INPUTS	(9)	.96797	.95120	.95120	.95348	.96510
LABOR	(9)	.93772	.90736	.90755	.91125	.92891
FUEL	(9)	1.02119	.98212	.98212	.98212	.98212
CAPITAL	(10)	1.01760	1.03193	1.03168	1.03170	1.03407
INTRM INPUTS	(10)	.97802	.96027	.96002	.95888	.96322
OTHER VARIABLES:						
REL FACT PROD	(10)	.99381	.99458	.99458	.99458	.99458
REL PROFIT MFG	(10)	1.02256	.99795	.99808	.99754	.99047
LABOR INTENS	(11)	1.04995	1.04714	1.04769	1.05100	1.04964
MULT ADJ	(11)	.97664	1.00001	1.00001	1.00001	1.00001
EMP % OF U.S.	(11)	.090	.092	.092	.091	.089
RPC = SS/DEM	(11)	.446	.418	.420	.428	.426
AV WAGE-THOU	(12)	13.938	18.924	20.015	32.998	111.615
INDL MIX INDX	(12)	1.07601	1.04142	1.03928	1.01981	1.01742
IN BILLIONS OF 1982 $'S						
DEMAND	(12)	4.12273	6.14915	6.26728	7.48598	9.61862
IMPORTS	(12)	2.28517	3.57696	3.63669	4.27868	5.51650
SELF SUPPLY	(13)	1.83756	2.57219	2.63060	3.20730	4.10212
EXPORTS	(13)	3.07501	4.16788	4.25849	5.19924	6.71650
INT-REG TRD	(13)	.00000	.00000	.00000	.00000	.00000
EXOG PRDN	(13)	.00000	.00000	.00000	.00000	.00000
OUTPUT	(14)	4.91257	6.74007	6.88909	8.40654	10.81862
GRP(VAL ADD)	(14)	2.19678	3.16913	3.24727	4.03211	5.21400
IN BILLIONS OF NOMINAL $'S						
WAGE&SAL DISB	(14)	1.13111	1.97584	2.11728	3.88291	13.74160

TABLE 8-4

DEMO MODEL: HISTORY (1969 – 1989) & CONTROL FORECAST (1990 – 2020)

TABLE 3: EMPLOYMENT TABLE. (IN THOUSANDS OF PEOPLE)

	1982 HIST	1990 FCST	1991 FCST	2000 FCST	2020 FCST
MANUFACTURE	21.227	24.609	24.583	24.554	20.847
AS A % OF U.S.	.110	.123	.123	.124	.126
DURABLES	5.909	7.896	7.888	7.787	5.944
NONDURABLES	15.318	16.713	16.695	16.767	14.903
NON MANUFACT	59.925	79.802	81.200	93.115	102.269
AS A % OF U.S.	.084	.085	.085	.085	.084
MINING	.060	.103	.100	.085	.071
CONT CONSTRUC.	3.674	5.224	5.286	5.914	6.512
TRANS + PUB UT	6.297	8.269	8.387	9.283	9.118
FIN, INS,+ RE	4.360	5.887	5.983	6.616	6.389
RETAIL TRADE	18.164	22.109	22.376	24.538	25.829
WHOLESALE TRD	5.809	7.462	7.562	8.305	8.017
SERVICES	20.871	29.834	30.571	37.246	45.020
AGRI/FOR/FISH	.690	.914	.934	1.129	1.314
TOTAL GOVRMENT	11.383	12.563	12.585	12.928	13.184
AS A % OF U.S.	.061	.060	.060	.059	.059
ST & LOCAL GOV	9.810	10.241	10.269	10.659	10.972
FED. GOVT. CIVI.	.722	.948	.950	.971	.872
FED. GOVT. MILI.	.851	1.373	1.365	1.298	1.340
FARM EMPLOY	2.554	2.090	2.055	1.766	1.444
AS A % OF U.S.	.071	.067	.067	.067	.067
TOTAL EMPLOY	95.089	119.064	120.423	132.363	137.744
AS A % OF U.S.	.084	.086	.086	.086	.084
POPULATION	180.000	194.371	195.247	200.817	219.852
AS A % OF U.S.	.078	.078	.077	.074	.073

TABLE 8-5

DEMO MODEL: HISTORY (1969 – 1989) & CONTROL FORECAST (1990 – 2020)
TABLE 4: PERSONAL INCOME TABLE. (IN BILLIONS OF DOLLARS)

	1982 HIST	1990 FCST	1991 FCST	2000 FCST	2020 FCST
WAGE AND SAL DISB	1.30313	2.25521	2.41495	4.40867	15.62672
PROPRI INCOME*	.00000	.00000	.00000	.00000	.00000
OTHER LABOR INC	.27579	.53043	.56607	1.00341	3.57926

DERIVATION OF PERSONAL INCOME BY PLACE OF RESIDENCE:

	1982 HIST	1990 FCST	1991 FCST	2000 FCST	2020 FCST
TOT LAB + PROP INC	1.57891	2.78564	2.98102	5.41208	19.20597
AS A % OF U.S.	.082	.081	.081	.081	,080
LESS SOC INSR CNT	.10185	.20330	.21904	.42252	1.49762
PLUS RESID ADJ	-.06115	-.10455	-.11183	-.20204	-.71681
PLUS DIV,INT,RENT	.32193	.54149	.58813	1.25088	4.79147
PLUS TRANS PAY	.25963	.41070	.44058	.84628	3.49935
PERSONAL INCOME	1.99748	3.42998	3.67887	6.88468	25.28236
AS A % OF U.S.	.075	.073	.073	.072	.073
LESS TAXES	.31293	.53043	.575061	1.18671	4.28097
DISPOSABLE PER. INC	1.68455	2.89955	3.10381	5.69796	21.00139
PCE - PRICE INDEX	96.954	129.641	136.043	209.056	576.696
REAL DIS PER INC$82	1.73748	2.23660	2.28149	2.72557	3.64167
AS A % OF U.S.	.077	.076	.076	.075	.076

BREAKDOWN OF LABOR AND PROPRIETOR'S INCOME:

	1982 HIST	1990 FCST	1991 FCST	2000 FCST	2020 FCST
MANUFACTURE	.51341	.81677	.86378	1.43003	4.20205
DURABLES	.14061	.24872	.26322	.43287	1.14807
NONDURABLES	.37280	.56805	.60056	.99717	3.05398
NON MANUFACTURE	.85978	1.62455	1.75047	3.33534	12.68902
MINING	.00183	.00927	.00957	.01318	.03778
CONT CONSTRUC	.08107	.15536	.16644	.30926	1.18548
TRANS + PUB UT	.16491	.24930	.26752	.48802	1.64960
FINANCE,INS,+ RE	.04020	.09084	.09767	.17781	.58929
RETAIL TRADE	.17002	.29142	.31172	.55879	2.00509
WHOLESALE TRADE	.12301	.21701	.23256	.41941	1.38618
SERVICES	.27182	.59881	.651460	1.34210	5.72884
AGRI/FOR/FISH	.00692	.01252	.01353	.02677	.10676
TOTAL GOVERNMENT	.18003	.29690	.31617	.55576	1.98584
ST AND LOCAL GOV	.15790	.25258	.26889	.47229	1.71120
FED GOVT CIVILIAN	.01808	.03368	.03586	.06229	.19802
FED GOV MILITARY	.00406	.01065	.01141	.02118	.07662
FARM	.02569	.04742	.05061	.09095	.32906

* IF ALL 0.0'S THEN PROP INC WAS MERGED INTO OTHER LABOR INC.

TABLE 8-6

DEMO MODEL: HISTORY (1969 – 1989) & CONTROL FORECAST (1990 – 2020)

TABLE 5: GRP BY FINAL DEMAND TABLE.
(BILLIONS OF 82 US DOLLARS-RECONCILED WITH VALUE ADDED)

	1982 HIST	1990 FCST	1991 FCST	2000 FCST	2020 FCST
TOTAL GRP	2.44121	3.44159	3.52101	4.32061	5.50956
TOTAL CONSUMPTION	1.58471	2.12736	2.16852	2.58003	3.35890
AUTOS AND PARTS	.09157	.17260	.17534	.20206	.25200
FURN & HSEHLD EQ.	.06846	.13866	.14170	.17214	.23020
OTHER DURABLES	.03164	.05234	.05359	.06628	.09059
FOOD & BEVERAGES	.29968	.35724	.36276	.41638	.51636
CLOTHING & SHOES	.09005	.12933	.13142	.15177	.18984
GASOLINE & OIL	.05460	.06195	.06229	.06541	.07031
FUEL OIL & COAL	.01444	.01784	.01802	.01980	.02299
OTHER NONDURA	.09727	.12184	.12354	.13992	.17036
HOUSING	.29916	.34080	.34753	.41427	.54081
HSEHLD OPERATION	.10056	.12605	.12731	.13925	.16050
TRANSPORTATION	.04156	.05997	.06119	.07338	.09653
HEALTH SERVICES	.12440	.16727	.17215	.22293	.32087
OTHER SERVICES	.27132	.38149	.39168	.49643	.69754
TOTAL FIXED INVEST	.21354	.40537	.41469	.51584	.73166
RESIDENTIAL	.05151	.10514	.10655	.12289	.16552
NON RESIDENTIAL	.05940	.07245	.07420	.09283	.13090
PROD. DUR. EQUIP.	.10264	.22778	.23393	.30012	.43525
CBI NET IVA + MISC	-.02152	.02595	.02498	.01643	.01596
GRPVA-GRPFD	-.33290	-.00227	-.00440	-.02264	-.07690
TOTAL GOVERNMENT	.33388	.47338	.47507	.49722	.52916
FED GOV MILITARY	.05472	.12642	.12495	.11242	.07880
FED GOV CIVILIAN	.01875	.02372	.02403	.02700	.03125
ST/LOC GOV EDUC.	.11152	.13831	.13890	.14609	.15992
ST/LOC HLTH/WLFAR	.04656	.05741	.05798	.06423	.07635
ST/LOC SAFETY	.02354	.03189	.03239	.03778	.04822
ST/LOC MISCEL	.07880	.09563	.09683	.10969	.13462
TOTAL EXPORTS	3.18904	4.27446	4.36711	5.32778	6.85521
TOTAL IMPORTS	2.52555	3.86267	3.92496	4.59405	5.90444
TOT GRP BY VAL ADD	2.44121	3.44159	3.52101	4.32061	5.50956
TOT PRI NF VAL AD	2.19678	3.16913	3.24727	4.03211	5.21400
TOT GOV COMP	.20097	.22830	.22860	.23348	.25055
TOT FARM VAL AD	.04347	.04415	.04514	.05502	.04500

TABLE 8-7

DEMO MODEL: HISTORY (1969 – 1989) & CONTROL FORECAST (1990 – 2020)
PART OF TABLE 7: TOTAL, INTERMEDIATE, & CONSUMPTION EMPLOY

	1982 HIST	1990 FCST	1991 FCST	2000 FCST	2020 FCST
PRIVATE NONFARM EMPLOYMENT (IN THOUSANDS OF PEOPLE)					
DURABLES	5.909	7.896	7.888	7.787	5.944
NONDURABLES	15.318	16.713	16.695	16.767	14.903
MINING	.060	.103	.100	.085	.071
CONT CONSTRUCTION	3.674	5.224	5.286	5.914	6.512
TRANSPORT + PUB UT	6.297	8.269	8.387	9.283	9.118
FINANCE, INS, + RE	4.360	5.887	5.983	6.616	6.389
RETAIL TRADE	18.164	22.109	22.376	24.538	25.829
WHOLESALE TRADE	5.809	7.462	7.562	8.305	8.017
SERVICES	20.871	29.834	30.571	37.246	45.020
AGRI/FOR/FISH SVCS	.690	.914	.934	1.129	1.314
EMP GENERATED BY DEMND FOR INTRMED INPUTS (1000s OF PEOPLE)					
DURABLES	.164	.202	.201	.183	.134
NONDURABLES	1.861	2.031	2.032	2.079	1.842
MINING	.056	.098	.096	.081	.068
CONT CONSTRUCTION	1.041	1.552	1.586	1.903	2.048
TRANSPORT + PUB UT	1.519	1.960	1.989	2.203	2.170
FINANCE, INS, + RE	.478	.691	.705	.796	.757
RETAIL TRADE	1.953	2.382	2.422	2.763	2.972
WHOLESALE TRADE	2.433	3.157	3.207	3.593	3.418
SERVICES	7.677	11.415	11.718	14.468	16.868
AGRI/FOR/FISH SVCS	.410	.546	.557	.664	.762
EMP INDUCED BY LOCAL CONSUMPTION DEMAND (1000s OF PEOPLE)					
DURABLES	.054	.076	.076	.070	.050
NONDURABLES	.724	.732	.727	.693	.598
MINING	.001	.001	.001	.001	.000
CONT CONSTRUCTION	.000	.000	.000	.000	.000
TRANSPORT + PUB UT	.595	.819	.832	.922	.882
FINANCE, INS, + RE	.947	1.233	1.251	1.359	1.328
RETAIL TRADE	11.884	14.341	14.506	15.804	16.574
WHOLESALE TRADE	.945	1.109	1.119	1.170	1.090
SERVICES	8.083	11.132	11.388	13.660	17.292
AGRI/FOR/FISH SVCS	.056	.082	.084	.109	.136

TABLE 8-8

DEMO MODEL: HISTORY (1969 – 1989) & CONTROL FORECAST (1990 – 2020)
PART OF TABLE 9: SELLING PRICE, FACTOR COST, AND LABOR COSTS

	1982 HIST	1990 FCST	1991 FCST	2000 FCST	2020 FCST
SELLING PRICE RELATIVE TO THE U.S.					
DURABLES	1.00000	1.00000	1.00000	1.00000	1.00000
NONDURABLES	1.00000	1.00000	1.00000	1.00000	1.00000
MINING	.955940	1.12930	1.12953	1.13104	1.13729
CONT CONSTRUCTION	.99141	1.00913	1.00896	1.00842	1.01474
TRANS + PUB UT	1.02829	.98974	.98950	.98999	.99961
FINANCE, INS, + RE	.93145	.76831	.76687	.75783	.75639
RETAIL TRADE	.95583	.94270	.94237	.94310	.95397
WHOLESALE TRADE	.96397	.92134	.92116	.92296	.93393
SERVICES	.94562	.91652	.91686	.91941	.92820
AGRI/FOR/FISH SVCS	1.01921	.97156	.97135	.97205	.98045
FACTOR COSTS RELATIVE TO THE U.S.					
DURABLES	1.05331	1.00195	1.00199	1.00517	1.01977
NONDURABLES	1.00365	.99284	.99272	.99441	1.00431
MINING	.94972	1.18234	1.18309	1.18853	1.19557
CONT CONSTRUCTION	.99973	1.05165	1.05130	1.04938	1.05852
TRANS + PUB UT	1.05554	.98651	.98647	.98948	1.00112
FINANCE, INS, + RE	.94091	.94601	.94527	.94279	.94588
RETAIL TRADE	.94755	.95444	.95411	.95625	.97057
WHOLESALE TRADE	.96119	.91845	.91822	.92041	.93375
SERVICES	.93248	.91016	.91068	.91432	.92527
AGRI/FOR/FISH SVCS	1.04815	.99024	.99006	.99199	1.00309
LABOR COSTS (WAGE RATES & OTHER LABOR COSTS) REL TO THE U.S.					
DURABLES	1.07270	.99037	.99053	.99482	1.01455
NONDURABLES	1.00351	.95749	.95740	.96114	.98110
MINING	.73251	1.90825	1.91487	1.94378	1.97074
CONT CONSTRUCTION	.97760	1.06163	1.06138	1.05897	1.07247
TRANS + PUB UT	1.07713	.92510	.92508	.92880	.94791
FINANCE, INS, + RE	.73251	.71021	.70936	.70607	.71192
RETAIL TRADE	.91569	.93358	.93322	.93640	.95681
WHOLESALE TRADE	.93005	.87417	.87392	.87709	.89591
SERVICES	.88545	.84774	.84874	.85415	.86919
AGRI/FOR/FISH SVCS	1.05811	.94890	.94880	.95254	.97233

TABLE 8-9

DEMO MODEL: HISTORY (1969 – 1989) & CONTROL FORECAST (1990 – 2020)
PART OF TABLE 10: CAP COSTS, FACT PRODUCTIVITY, & PROFITABILITY

	1982 HIST	1990 FCST	1991 FCST	2000 FCST	2020 FCST
CAPITAL COSTS RELATIVE TO THE U.S.					
DURABLES	1.01744	1.02046	1.02035	1.02070	1.02257
NONDURABLES	1.01657	1.01974	1.01961	1.01981	1.02164
MINING	1.01768	1.03945	1.03939	1.04121	1.04498
CONT CONSTRUCTION	1.01825	1.02861	1.02819	1.02677	1.02814
TRANS + PUB UT	1.01734	1.04254	1.04258	1.04526	1.04970
FINANCE, INS, + RE	1.01343	1.03215	1.03155	1.02937	1.03101
RETAIL TRADE	1.02208	1.02806	1.02786	1.02776	1.02943
WHOLESALE TRADE	1.02421	1.02575	1.02560	1.02560	1.02697
SERVICES	1.01568	1.03649	1.03619	1.03628	1.03915
AGRI/FOR/FISH SVCS	1.01568	1.03649	1.03619	1.03628	1.03915
FACTOR PRODUCTIVITY RELATIVE TO THE U.S.					
DURABLES	1.01856	.97364	.97364	.97364	.97364
NONDURABLES	1.07978	1.00585	1.00585	1.00585	1.00585
MINING	.22919	.26151	.26151	.26151	.26151
CONT CONSTRUCTION	.77950	.81015	.81015	.81015	.81015
TRANS + PUB UT	.90637	.90132	.90132	.90132	.90132
FINANCE, INS, + RE	1.43707	1.47212	1.47212	1.47212	1.47212
RETAIL TRADE	.97439	.99868	.99868	.99868	.99868
WHOLESALE TRADE	.98223	.99395	.99395	.99395	.99395
SERVICES	.94849	.97597	.97597	.97597	.97597
AGRI/FOR/FISH SVCS	1.13846	1.12375	1.12375	1.12375	1.12375
PROFIT NATIONAL INDUSTRIES RELATIVE TO THE U.S.					
DURABLES	.98955	.99826	.99820	.99586	.98710
NONDURABLES	1.03861	.99781	.99802	.99835	.99212
MINING	1.00000	1.00000	1.00000	1.00000	1.00000
CONT CONSTRUCTION	1.00000	1.00000	1.00000	1.00000	1.00000
TRANS + PUB UT	1.00000	1.00000	1.00000	1.00000	1.00000
FINANCE, INS, + RE	1.00000	1.00000	1.00000	1.00000	1.00000
RETAIL TRADE	1.00000	1.00000	1.00000	1.00000	1.00000
WHOLESALE TRADE	1.00000	1.00000	1.00000	1.00000	1.00000
SERVICES	1.00000	1.00000	1.00000	1.00000	1.00000
AGRI/FOR/FISH SVCS	1.00000	1.00000	1.00000	1.00000	1.00000

TABLE 8-10

DEMO MODEL: HISTORY (1969 – 1989) & CONTROL FORECAST (1990 – 2020)
PART OF TABLE 11: LABOR INTENSITY, MULTIPLICATIVE ADJUST, & RPC

	1982 HIST	1990 FCST	1991 FCST	2000 FCST	2020 FCST
LABOR INTENSITY RELATIVE TO THE U.S.					
DURABLES	.99837	1.00151	1.00214	1.00609	1.00653
NONDURABLES	1.06579	1.04686	1.04624	1.04173	1.03106
MINING	1.16888	1.00030	.97641	.81655	.66502
CONT CONSTRUCTION	1.00909	1.00488	1.00400	.99830	.99085
TRANS + PUB UT	.95470	.98401	.98917	1.02310	1.04907
FINANCE, INS, + RE	1.29128	1.29404	1.29647	1.31348	1.32510
RETAIL TRADE	1.04958	1.03905	1.03802	1.03097	1.02047
WHOLESALE TRADE	1.01231	1.02360	1.02530	1.03629	1.04220
SERVICES	1.06391	1.06122	1.06197	1.06619	1.06602
AGRI/FOR/FISH SVCS	.99096	1.00003	1.00275	1.02034	1.03064
MULTIPLICATIVE ADJUSTMENTS ON TOTAL OUTPUT & EMPLOYMENT					
DURABLES	.81292	1.00000	1.00000	1.00000	1.00000
NONDURABLES	.94408	1.00000	1.00000	1.00000	1.00000
MINING	.35147	.99998	.99998	.99998	.99998
CONT CONSTRUCTION	.94638	1.00000	1.00000	1.00000	1.00000
TRANS + PUB UT	.93645	1.00000	1.00000	1.00000	1.00000
FINANCE, INS, + RE	1.03513	1.00000	1.00000	1.00000	1.00000
RETAIL TRADE	1.02979	1.00003	1.00003	1.00003	1.00003
WHOLESALE TRADE	.98854	1.00001	1.00001	1.00001	1.00001
SERVICES	1.00246	1.00001	1.00001	1.00001	1.00001
AGRI/FOR/FISH SVCS	1.19136	1.00000	1.00000	1.00000	1.00000
REG PURCHASE COEFF (RPC) - PROP OF LOC USE SUPPLIED LOCALLY					
DURABLES	.049	.045	.045	.045	.044
NONDURABLES	.328	.299	.299	.297	.294
MINING	.016	.015	.015	.015	.015
CONT CONSTRUCTION	.843	.853	.852	.850	.844
TRANS + PUB UT	.456	.472	.473	.477	.474
FINANCE, INS, + RE	.245	.268	.270	.280	.283
RETAIL TRADE	.900	.919	.920	.923	.915
WHOLESALE TRADE	.815	.849	.851	.860	.854
SERVICES	.710	.727	.729	.733	.728
AGRI/FOR/FISH SVCS	.568	.588	.589	.594	.591

TABLE 8-11

DEMO MODEL: HISTORY (1969 – 1989) & CONTROL FORECAST (1990 – 2020)
PART OF TABLE 13: SELF SUPPLY, EXPORTS, & EXOGEN PRODUCTION

	1982 HIST	1990 FCST	1991 FCST	2000 FCST	2020 FCST
SELF SUPPLY (BILLIONS 82$): LOCAL PRODUCTION FOR LOCAL USE					
DURABLES	.02427	.04521	.04601	.05421	.06981
NONDURABLES	.33887	.40961	.41548	.48335	.59465
MINING	.00212	.00657	.00662	.00729	.00909
CONT CONSTRUCTION	.17968	.27708	.28251	.34024	.43584
TRANS + PUB UT	.20343	.27054	.27651	.33355	.41519
FINANCE, INS, + RE	.14456	.19733	.20341	.25639	.34082
RETAIL TRADE	.29673	.41448	.42285	.50281	.63041
WHOLESALE TRADE	.18989	.30456	.31229	.38797	.49255
SERVICES	.44333	.63203	.64976	.82274	1.09028
AGRI/FOR/FISH SVCS	.01468	.01478	.01515	.01875	.02350
EXPORTS TO THE REST OF THE U.S. AND REST OF WORLD (BILLIONS 82$)					
DURABLES	.47100	.85620	.87914	1.12642	1.52375
NONDURABLES	1.61018	1.94922	1.98109	2.32977	2.92685
MINING	.00001	.00003	.00003	.00003	.00004
CONT CONSTRUCTION	.00672	.01001	.01023	.01254	.01608
TRANS + PUB UT	.37060	.48855	.49969	.60928	.77311
FINANCE, INS, + RE	.28656	.38782	.39977	.50829	.67521
RETAIL TRADE	.09075	.12465	.12728	.15336	.19088
WHOLESALE TRADE	.10720	.16999	.17458	.21971	.29054
SERVICES	.12544	.17511	.18019	.23167	.30970
AGRI/FOR/FISH SVCS	.00656	.00632	.00648	.00818	.01035
EXOG PRODUCTION STIMULATED BY POLICY CHANGE (BILLIONS 82$)					
DURABLES	.00000	.00000	.00000	.00000	.00000
NONDURABLES	.00000	.00000	.00000	.00000	.00000
MINING	.00000	.00000	.00000	.00000	.00000
CONT CONSTRUCTION	.00000	.00000	.00000	.00000	.00000
TRANS + PUB UT	.00000	.00000	.00000	.00000	.00000
FINANCE, INS, + RE	.00000	.00000	.00000	.00000	.00000
RETAIL TRADE	.00000	.00000	.00000	.00000	.00000
WHOLESALE TRADE	.00000	.00000	.00000	.00000	.00000
SERVICES	.00000	.00000	.00000	.00000	.00000
AGRI/FOR/FISH SVCS	.00000	.00000	.00000	.00000	.00000

TABLE 8-12

DEMO MODEL: HISTORY (1969 – 1989) & CONTROL FORECAST (1990 – 2020)
TABLE 14: OUTPUT, GRP, & WAGE & SALARY DISBURSMENTS

	1982 HIST	1990 FCST	1991 FCST	2000 FCST	2020 FCST
OUTPUT OF LOCAL INDUSTRIES (IN BILLIONS OF 1982 DOLLARS)					
DURABLES	.49526	.90141	.92515	1.18063	1.59356
NONDURABLES	1.94905	2.35883	2.39657	2.81312	3.52150
MINING	.00213	.00660	.00665	.00732	.00912
CONT CONSTRUCTION	.18640	.28708	.29274	.35278	.45192
TRANS + PUB UT	.57403	.75909	.77620	.94283	1.18830
FINANCE, INS, + RE	.43112	.58514	.60318	.76468	1.01602
RETAIL TRADE	.38747	.53913	.55014	.65618	.82129
WHOLESALE TRADE	.29710	.47455	.48687	.60768	.78309
SERVICES	.56877	.80713	.82995	1.05441	1.39998
AGRI/FOR/FISH SVCS	.02123	.02110	.02164	.02693	.03385
GRP (VALUE ADD): OUTPT EXCLUD INTERMED INPUTS (BILLIONS OF 82$)					
DURABLES	.20381	.38322	.39649	.54245	.73217
NONDURABLES	.53325	.68295	.69455	.82239	1.02948
MINING	.00149	.00481	.00483	.00523	.00652
CONT CONSTRUCTION	.07512	.12466	.12733	.15574	.19951
TRANS + PUB UT	.29946	.42585	.43666	.54356	.68508
FINANCE, INS, + RE	.31413	.41400	.42606	.53218	.70711
RETAIL TRADE	.22569	.32778	.33426	.39639	.49614
WHOLESALE TRADE	.17967	.28874	.29582	.36447	.46968
SERVICES	.35481	.50787	.52176	.65763	.87317
AGRI/FOR/FISH SVCS	.00933	.00925	.00951	.01204	.01514
WAGE AND SALARY DISBURSEMENTS (BILLIONS OF NOMINAL DOLLARS)					
DURABLES	.12272	.21760	.23049	.38182	1.01771
NONDURABLES	.33346	.50412	.53332	.89047	2.73669
MINING	.00040	.00453	.00469	.00668	.01949
CONT CONSTRUCTION	.05391	.10685	.11475	.21789	.84893
TRANS + PUB UT	.13093	.19365	.20810	.38409	1.30811
FINANCE, INS, + RE	.03513	.07978	.08583	.15712	.52247
RETAIL TRADE	.13892	.24282	.25993	.46906	1.68909
WHOLESALE TRADE	.10523	.18769	.20127	.36512	1.21083
SERVICES	.20544	.43024	.46961	.99201	4.31315
AGRI/FOR/FISH SVCS	.00496	.00857	.00928	.01865	.07513

380

TABLE 8-13

DEMO MODEL: HISTORY (1970 – 1989) & CONTROL FORECAST (1990 – 2020)

TABLE 1: POPULATION MODEL SUMMARY TABLE

	1982	1990	1991	2000	2020
LAST YR CIVIL POP	176.343	190.475	191.264	197.361	215.823
TOTAL DEATHS	1.514	1.697	1.713	1.850	2.504
MALE DEATHS	.800	.880	.886	.946	1.316
FEMALE DEATHS	.714	.818	.827	.904	1.188
TOTAL BIRTHS	2.796	2.770	2.722	2.301	2.190
MALE BIRTHS	1.426	1.413	1.388	1.173	1.117
FEMALE BIRTHS	1.370	1.357	1.334	1.127	1.073
THIS YR POP B4 MIGS	177.625	191.548	192.273	197.811	215.510
MALE POPULATION	86.608	93.362	93.697	96.268	104.495
FEMALE POP	91.017	98.186	98.576	101.543	111.015
UNDER 65	160.126	171.455	171.756	175.095	177.035
OVER 65	17.499	20.094	20.517	22.716	38.475
TOTAL MIGRANTS	.218	-.267	-.101	.083	1.309
UNDER 65	-.043	-.550	-.386	-.222	.972
ECON MIGRANTS	-.061	-.791	-.627	-.452	.796
INTERNAT MG.	.187	.213	.214	.206	.184
RETURNING MIL.	-.169	.027	.027	.025	-.007
MALE	-.043	-.280	-.196	-.111	.498
FEMALE	.001	-.270	-.190	-.110	.474
OVER 65	.261	.282	.285	.305	.337
MALE	.112	.121	.122	.131	.145
FEMALE	.149	.161	.163	.174	.193
TOTAL MIGR DEATHS	.010	.010	.010	.010	.011
MALE MIGR DEATHS	.005	.005	.005	.005	.006
FEM MIGR DEATHS	.005	.005	.005	.005	.005
TOTAL MIGR BIRTHS	.000	-.007	-.005	-.003	.012
MALE MIGR BIRTHS	.000	-.003	-.002	-.001	.006
FEM MIGR BIRTHS	.000	-.003	-.002	-.001	.006
CENSUS UNDERCOUNT	.000	.000	.000	.000	.000
UNDER 65	.000	.000	.000	.000	.000
OVER 65	.000	.000	.000	.000	.000
CIVIL POP B4 MULT	177.833	191.264	192.158	197.881	216.820
MULT ADJMNT	1.001	1.000	1.000	1.000	1.000
CIVIL POP WITH MULT	178.075	191.264	192.158	197.881	216.820
TOT MILITARY & DEP	1.925	3.107	3.089	2.936	3.032
TOTAL POPULATION	180.000	194.371	195.247	200.817	219.852

TABLE 8-14

DEMO MODEL: HISTORY (1970 – 1989) & CONTROL FORECAST (1990 – 2020)

TABLE 2: MIGRATION EQUATION REGRESSION COMPONENTS

	1982	1990	1991	2000	2020
DEPENDENT VARIABLE					
RESID ECON. MIGR.	.171	.000	.000	.000	.000
RESIDUAL ADJ.	-.001	.000	.000	.000	.000
PREDIC ECON. MIGR.	-.061	-.791	-.627	-.452	.796
	1982	1990	1991	2000	2020
INDEPENDENT VARIABLES					
RWR	1.015	1.011	1.011	1.009	1.020
RWM	1.005	1.028	1.028	1.029	1.025
REO	1.022	1.008	1.010	1.016	1.038
RES ADJ. EMP.	90.588	113.264	114.570	126.151	131.328
POT LAB FORCE	86.208	99.020	100.017	108.481	111.283
EMPLOY U.S.	109917.6	135254.2	136807.5	151504.4	160445.1
POTENT.L.F. U.S.	106989.3	119128.6	120588.9	132327.0	141155.2
RWR 1 PER LAG	1.019	1.014	1.011	1.009	1.019
RWR 2 PER LAG	1.019	1.023	1.014	1.009	1.019
RWM 1 PER LAG	.998	1.028	1.028	1.029	1.025
RWM 2 PER LAG	.999	1.032	1.028	1.029	1.025
REO 1 PER LAG	1.008	1.008	1.008	1.017	1.038
REO 2 PER LAG	1.031	1.010	1.008	1.016	1.038
REG CONSTANT	-.013	-.013	-.013	-.013	-.013

TABLE 8-15

DEMO MODEL: HISTORY (1970 – 1989) & CONTROL FORECAST (1990 – 2020)

TABLE 4: CIVILIAN POPULATION BY 5-YEAR COHORTS

		1982	1990	1991	2000	2020
MALE POP	0- 4	7.049	6.999	6.903	5.879	5.853
FEM POP	0- 4	6.711	6.748	6.655	5.665	5.642
MALE POP	5- 9	6.886	7.205	7.184	6.341	6.171
FEM POP	5- 9	6.471	6.959	6.937	6.112	5.944
MALE POP	10- 14	7.664	7.132	7.147	6.806	6.200
FEM POP	10- 14	7.468	6.671	6.751	6.569	5.973
MALE POP	15- 19	8.841	6.939	6.820	7.043	6.104
FEM POP	15- 19	8.658	6.729	6.506	6.819	5.908
MALE POP	20- 24	8.774	8.039	7.841	6.916	6.271
FEM POP	20- 24	9.256	7.809	7.673	6.489	6.119
MALE POP	25- 29	8.112	9.187	8.972	6.639	6.858
FEM POP	25- 29	8.492	9.498	9.084	6.481	6.710
MALE POP	30- 34	7.708	8.607	8.717	7.686	7.355
FEM POP	30- 34	7.573	9.029	9.227	7.540	7.194
MALE POP	35- 39	5.838	8.071	8.089	8.881	7.483
FEM POP	35- 39	5.985	8.229	8.395	9.273	7.320
MALE POP	40- 44	4.639	7.008	7.527	8.355	7.165
FEM POP	40- 44	4.787	6.990	7.432	8.854	6.791
MALE POP	45- 49	3.937	5.022	5.157	7.794	6.695
FEM POP	45- 49	3.880	5.382	5.473	8.047	6.593
MALE POP	50- 54	3.702	4.200	4.298	6.649	7.480
FEM POP	50- 54	3.930	4.201	4.413	6.759	7.460
MALE POP	55- 59	3.683	3.470	3.545	4.606	8.263
FEM POP	55- 59	3.846	3.742	3.694	5.108	8.915
MALE POP	60- 64	2.961	3.373	3.273	3.669	7.311
FEM POP	60- 64	3.448	3.660	3.653	3.890	8.242
MALE POP	65- 69	2.529	2.813	2.931	2.852	6.174
FEM POP	65- 69	3.293	3.418	3.495	3.420	7.195
MALE POP	70- 74	1.941	2.082	2.112	2.502	4.548
FEM POP	70- 74	2.800	3.030	3.026	3.289	5.745
MALE POP	75- ***	2.524	3.047	3.101	3.661	5.208
FEM POP	75- ***	4.687	5.974	6.128	7.285	9.932
TOTAL POPULATION		178.075	191.264	192.158	197.881	216.820

TABLE 8-16

DEMO MODEL: HISTORY (1970 – 1989) & CONTROL FORECAST (1990 – 2020)

TABLE 6: MIGRANTS BY 5-YEAR COHORTS

		1982	1990	1991	2000	2020
MALE MIG	0- 4	.001	-.050	-.035	-.020	.087
FEM MIG	0- 4	.003	-.049	-.035	-.020	.085
MALE MIG	5- 9	-.005	-.024	-.017	-.009	.044
FEM MIG	5- 9	-.003	-.022	-.015	-.009	.040
MALE MIG	10- 14	-.002	-.019	-.013	-.007	.034
FEM MIG	10- 14	-.001	-.019	-.013	-.007	.033
MALE MIG	15- 19	-.015	-.020	-.013	-.007	.038
FEM MIG	15- 19	.001	-.023	-.016	-.009	.039
MALE MIG	20- 24	-.027	-.035	-.024	-.013	.067
FEM MIG	20- 24	.000	-.039	-.028	-.016	.069
MALE MIG	25- 29	.002	-.046	-.033	-.019	.080
FEM MIG	25- 29	.000	-.041	-.029	-.017	.073
MALE MIG	30- 34	.001	-.032	-.023	-.013	.056
FEM MIG	30- 34	.000	-.028	-.020	-.012	.050
MALE MIG	35- 39	-.002	-.018	-.013	-.007	.032
FEM MIG	35- 39	-.001	-.016	-.011	-.006	.028
MALE MIG	40- 44	.000	-.011	-.008	-.005	.020
FEM MIG	40- 44	.000	-.009	-.007	-.004	.016
MALE MIG	45- 49	.001	-.008	-.006	-.003	.014
FEM MIG	45- 49	.000	-.007	-.005	-.003	.011
MALE MIG	50- 54	.001	-.006	-.004	-.003	.011
FEM MIG	50- 54	.001	-.006	-.004	-.002	.010
MALE MIG	55- 59	.001	-.005	-.003	-.002	.008
FEM MIG	55- 59	.001	-.006	-.004	-.002	.010
MALE MIG	60- 64	.001	-.005	-.003	-.002	.008
FEM MIG	60- 64	.001	-.006	-.004	-.002	.010
MALE MIG	65- 69	.021	.023	.023	.025	.027
FEM MIG	65- 69	.027	.029	.029	.031	.035
MALE MIG	70- 74	.011	.011	.012	.012	.014
FEM MIG	70- 74	.021	.022	.023	.024	.027
MALE MIG	75- ***	.080	.086	.089	.094	.105
FEM MIG	75- ***	.101	.110	.111	.119	.131
TOTAL MIGRANTS		.218	-.267	-.101	.083	1.309

TABLE 8-17

DEMO MODEL: HISTORY (1970 – 1989) & CONTROL FORECAST (1990 – 2020)

TABLE 10: LABOR FORCE BY 5 YEAR COHORTS

		1982	1990	1991	2000	2020
MALE	0- 4	.000	.000	.000	.000	.000
FEMALE	0- 4	.000	.000	.000	.000	.000
MALE	5- 9	.000	.000	.000	.000	.000
FEMALE	5- 9	.000	.000	.000	.000	.000
MALE	10- 14	.000	.000	.000	.000	.000
FEMALE	10- 14	.000	.000	.000	.000	.000
MALE	15- 19	3.988	3.031	2.945	3.062	2.655
FEMALE	15- 19	3.532	2.743	2.640	2.850	2.471
MALE	20- 24	7.302	6.735	6.576	5.820	5.293
FEMALE	20- 24	6.390	5.624	5.555	4.910	4.637
MALE	25- 29	7.562	8.532	8.328	6.138	6.340
FEMALE	25- 29	5.735	6.940	6.700	5.184	5.367
MALE	30- 34	7.341	8.166	8.268	7.259	6.947
FEMALE	30- 34	4.843	6.248	6.445	5.712	5.449
MALE	35- 39	5.583	7.691	7.705	8.424	7.097
FEMALE	35- 39	3.975	5.948	6.130	7.383	5.828
MALE	40- 44	4.409	6.637	7.125	7.876	6.754
FEMALE	40- 44	3.255	5.173	5.556	7.217	5.536
MALE	45- 49	3.684	4.682	4.805	7.232	6.212
FEMALE	45- 49	2.527	3.752	3.847	6.071	4.974
MALE	50- 54	3.353	3 789	3.876	5.972	6.718
FEMALE	50- 54	2.350	2.689	2.848	4.682	5.168
MALE	55- 59	3.076	2.838	2.891	3.667	6.579
FEMALE	55- 59	1.983	1.980	1.961	2.790	4.869
MALE	60- 64	1.872	2.088	2.021	2.212	4.407
FEMALE	60- 64	1.241	1.352	1.354	1.484	3.144
MALE	65- 69	.756	.819	.852	.811	1.762
FEMALE	65- 69	.519	.533	.545	.531	1.123
MALE	70- 74	.358	.375	.380	.441	.802
FEMALE	70- 74	.225	.241	.241	.261	.458
MALE	75- ***	.218	.251	.255	.296	.423
FEMALE	75- ***	.130	.162	.166	.198	.272
TOTAL LABOR FORCE		86.208	99.020	100.017	108.481	111.283

TABLE 8-18

DEMO MODEL: HISTORY (1970 – 1989) & CONTROL FORECAST (1990 – 2020)

TABLE 11: POTENTIAL LABOR FORCE PARTICIPATION RATES

		1982	1990	1991	2000	2020
MALE RAT.	0- 4	.000	.000	.000	.000	.000
FEMALE RAT	0- 4	.000	.000	.000	.000	.000
MALE RAT.	5- 9	.000	.000	.000	.000	.000
FEMALE RAT	5- 9	.000	.000	.000	.000	.000
MALE RAT.	10- 14	.000	.000	.000	.000	.000
FEMALE RAT	10- 14	.000	.000	.000	.000	.000
MALE RAT.	15- 19	.451	.437	.432	.435	.435
FEMALE RAT	15- 19	.408	.408	.406	.418	.418
MALE RAT.	20- 24	.832	.838	.839	.842	.844
FEMALE RAT	20- 24	.690	.720	.724	.757	.758
MALE RAT.	25- 29	.932	.929	.928	.924	.924
FEMALE RAT	25- 29	.675	.731	.738	.800	.800
MALE RAT.	30- 34	.952	.949	.948	.944	.944
FEMALE RAT	30- 34	.640	.692	.699	.758	.758
MALE RAT.	35- 39	.956	.953	.952	.949	.949
FEMALE RAT	35- 39	.664	.723	.730	.796	.796
MALE RAT.	40- 44	.950	.947	.947	.943	.943
FEMALE RAT	40- 44	.680	.740	.748	.815	.815
MALE RAT.	45- 49	.936	.932	.932	.928	.928
FEMALE RAT	45- 49	.651	.697	.703	.754	.754
MALE RAT.	50- 54	.906	.902	.902	.898	.898
FEMALE RAT	50- 54	.598	.640	.645	.693	.693
MALE RAT.	55- 59	.835	.818	.816	.796	.796
FEMALE RAT	55- 59	.516	.529	.531	.546	.546
MALE RAT.	60- 64	.632	.619	.617	.603	.603
FEMALE RAT	60- 64	.360	.370	.371	.381	.381
MALE RAT.	65- 69	.299	.291	.291	.284	.285
FEMALE RAT	65- 69	.157	.156	.156	.155	.156
MALE RAT.	70- 74	.185	.180	.180	.176	.176
FEMALE RAT	70- 74	.080	.080	.080	.079	.080
MALE RAT.	75- ***	.258	.247	.247	.242	.244
FEMALE RAT	75- ***	.084	.081	.081	.081	.081

TABLE 8-19

DEMO MODEL: EFFECTS OF COMMERCIAL AND INDUSTRIAL ELECTRIC
  50% RATE REDUCTION

TABLE 1: SUPER SUMMARY TABLE (TABLE # REFERENCES IN PARENS)

		1990 FCST	1991 FCST	1994 FCST	2000 FCST	2020 FCST
TOTAL EMPLOY	(3)	1.256	1.569	2.220	2.605	2.454
EMP % OF US		.001	.001	.002	.002	.002
TOT PRIV NF EMP	(2)	1.224	1.497	2.055	2.331	2.222
PR NF EMP % OF US		.001	.001	.002	.002	.002
GRP 1982 $	(5)	.034	.048	.080	.118	.178
PERS INCOME	(4)	.029	.037	.071	.121	.342
PERS INC % OF US		.001	.001	.001	.001	.001
DISP INCOME	(4)	.024	.030	.059	.100	.284
PCE-PRICE INDX82	(4)	-1.487	-1.622	-1.754	-2.487	-8.036
REAL DISP INCOME(	4)	.044	.050	.065	.081	.101
POPULATION	(3)	.596	1.363	3.135	5.149	4.661
POP AS % OF US		.000	.001	.001	.002	.002

(NOTE — FOR ALL TABLES: EMPLOYMENT AND POPULATION IN
THOUSANDS OF PEOPLE, DOLLAR CONCEPTS IN BILLIONS OF NOMINAL
DOLLARS UNLESS OTHERWISE INDICATED.)

INDEX TO AVAILABLE TABLES

TABLE 8-20

DEMO MODEL: EFFECTS OF COMMERCIAL AND INDUSTRIAL ELECTRIC
    50% RATE REDUCTION
TABLE 2: SUMMARY TABLE FOR PRIVT NONFARM SECTORS (DETAILED
    TABLE # REF IN PARENS)

		1990 FCST	1991 FCST	1994 FCST	2000 FCST	2020 FCST
PRIVT NONFRM EMP (1000S OF PEO) & ITS DECOMP BY SOURCE OF DEM:						
TOTAL EMPLOYMENT	(7)	1.224	1.497	2.055	2.331	2.222
INTERMEDIATE	(7)	.328	.447	.714	.954	1.136
LOCAL CONSUM	(7)	.667	.753	.960	1.061	.949
GOVT DEMAND	(7)	.011	.018	.036	.055	.048
INVEST ACTVTY	(8)	.146	.148	.159	.127	.101
EXPORT TO US	(8)	.073	.130	.186	.134	-.012
EXP — MULTREG	(8)	.000	.000	.000	.000	.000
EXOGENOUS	(8)	.000	.000	.000	.000	.000
COSTS AND SELLING PRICES RELATIVE TO THE UNITED STATES						
SELLING PRICE	(9)	-.01197	-.01247	-.01179	-.01265	-.01484
FACTOR INPUTS	(9)	-.02252	-.02351	-.02275	-.02466	-.02823
LABOR	(9)	.00235	.00067	.00149	-.00163	-.00652
FUEL	(9)	-.28943	-.28943	-.28943	-.28943	-.28943
CAPITAL	(10)	-.00333	-.00330	-.00235	-.00221	-.00350
INTRMED INPUTS	(10)	-.00603	-.00630	-.00566	-.00609	-.00763
OTHER VARIABLES:						
REL FACT PROD	(10)	.00000	.00000	.00000	.00000	.00000
REL PROFIT MFG	(10)	.01493	.01552	.01518	.01653	.01873
LABOR INTENSTY	(11)	-.00173	-.00330	-.00749	-.01350	-.02096
MULT ADJ	(11)	.00000	.00000	.00000	.00000	.00000
EMP % OF U.S.	(11)	.001	.001	.002	.002	.002
RPC=SS/DEMAND	(11)	.002	.003	.005	.007	.009
AVG WAGE-THOUS	(12)	.019	-.013	.010	-.088	-.752
INDL MIX INDX	(12)	.00000	.00171	.00159	.00092	.00073
IN BILLIONS OF 1982 DOLLARS						
DEMAND	(12)	.08733	.10833	.16050	.21480	.29840
IMPORTS	(12)	.03528	.04154	.05659	.06846	.08584
SELF SUPPLY	(13)	.05205	.06679	.10392	.14634	.21256
EXPORTS	(13)	.01650	.03103	.06155	.09913	.16690
INTRAREG TRD	(13)	.00000	.00000	.00000	.00000	.00000
EXOGENOUS PRDN	(13)	.00000	.00000	.00000	.00000	.00000
OUTPUT	(14)	.06855	.09782	.16547	.24547	.37946
GRP(VAL ADDED)	(14)	.03389	.04652	.07674	.11307	.17382
IN BILLIONS OF NOMINAL DOLLARS						
WAGE & SAL DISB	(14)	.02516	.02857	.04969	.06633	.15365

TABLE 8-21

DEMO MODEL: EFFECTS OF COMMERCIAL AND INDUSTRIAL ELECTRIC
  50% RATE REDUCTION

TABLE 1: POPULATION MODEL SUMMARY TABLE

	1990	1991	1994	2000	2020
LAST YR CIVIL POP	.000	.596	2.585	4.953	4.690
TOTAL DEATHS	.000	.001	.005	.010	.030
MALE DEATHS	.000	.001	.003	.006	.018
FEMALE DEATHS	.000	.000	.002	.003	.012
TOTAL BIRTHS	.000	.012	.049	.080	.063
MALE BIRTHS	.000	.006	.025	.041	.032
FEMALE BIRTHS	.000	.006	.024	.039	.031
THIS YR POP B4 MIGS	.000	.606	2.629	5.023	4.724
MALE POPULATION	.000	.311	1.347	2.568	2.368
FEMALE POPULATION	.000	.295	1.282	2.456	2.357
UNDER 65	.000	.604	2.607	4.931	4.364
OVER 65	.000	.002	.022	.092	.360
TOTAL MIGRANTS	.589	.749	.501	.124	-.063
UNDER 65	.589	.749	.501	.124	-.063
ECONOMIC MIGRANTS	.589	.748	.497	.118	-.067
INTERNATIONAL MG.	.000	.001	.003	.006	.005
RETURNING MIL.	.000	.000	.000	.001	.000
MALE	.302	.384	.257	.064	-.032
FEMALE	.287	.365	.244	.060	-.030
OVER 65	.000	.000	.000	.000	.000
MALE	.000	.000	.000	.000	.000
FEMALE	.000	.000	.000	.000	.000
TOTAL MIGR DEATHS	.001	.001	.000	.000	.000
MALE MIGR DEATHS	.000	.000	.000	.000	.000
FEMALE MIGR DEATHS	.000	.000	.000	.000	.000
TOTAL MIGR BIRTHS	.007	.009	.006	.002	-.001
MALE MIGR BIRTHS	.004	.005	.003	.001	.000
FEMALE MIGR BIRTHS	.003	.004	.003	.001	.000
CENSUS UNDERCOUNT	.000	.000	.000	.000	.000
UNDER 65	.000	.000	.000	.000	.000
OVER 65	.000	.000	.000	.000	.000
CIVIL POP B4 MULT	.596	1.363	3.135	5.149	4.661
MULT ADJMNT	.000	.000	.000	.000	.000
CIVIL POP WITH MULT	.596	1.363	3.135	5.149	4.661
TOT MILITARY & DEP	.000	.000	.000	.000	.000
TOTAL POPULATION	.596	1.363	3.135	5.149	4.661

TABLE 8-22

DEMO MODEL: EFFECTS OF COMMERCIAL AND INDUSTRIAL 50%
ELECTRIC RATE REDUCTION

TABLE 2: MIGRATION EQUATION REGRESSION COMPONENTS

	1990	1991	1994	2000	2020
DEPENDENT VARIABLE					
RESIDUAL ECON. MIGR.	.000	.000	.000	.000	.000
RESIDUAL ADJ.	.000	.000	.000	.000	.000
PREDICTED ECON. MIGR.	.589	.748	.497	.118	-.067
INDEPENDENT VARIABLES					
RELATIVE WAGE RATE(RWR)	.013	.011	.011	.008	.005
RELATIVE WAGE MIX (RWM)	-.001	-.001	-.001	-.001	.000
RELATIVE EC. OP.(REO)	.008	.006	.003	-.005	-.008
RESIDENCE ADJ. EMP.	1.199	1.498	2.133	2.503	2.363
POTENTIAL LAB. FORCE	.298	.685	1.595	2.687	2.832
EMPLOYMENT U.S.	.000	.000	.000	.000	.000
POTENT.L.F. U.S.	.000	.000	.000	.000	.000
RWR 1 PERIOD LAG	.000	.013	.012	.009	.005
RWR 2 PERIOD LAG	.000	.000	.012	.009	.005
RWM 1 PERIOD LAG	.000	-.001	-.001	-.001	.000
RWM 2 PERIOD LAG	.000	.000	-.001	-.001	.000
REO 1 PERIOD LAG	.000	.008	.004	-.004	-.008
REO 2 PERIOD LAG	.000	.000	.006	-.003	-.008
REGIONAL CONSTANT	.000	.000	.000	.000	.000

TABLE 8-23

DEMO MODEL: EFFECTS OF INCREASING DURABLE OUTPUT BY 1
BILLION $82'S

TABLE 1: SUPER SUMMARY TABLE (TABLE # REFERENCES IN PARENS)

		1990 FCST	1991 FCST	1995 FCST	2000 FCST	2020 FCST
TOTAL EMPLOYMENT	(3)	24.670	21.747	17.512	15.191	12.420
EMP % OF US		.018	.016	.012	.010	.008
TOT PRIV NF EMPLYT	(2)	24.365	21.077	16.202	13.773	11.557
PR NF EMP % OF US		.021	.018	.013	.011	.008
GRP 1982 $	(5)	.797	.737	.671	.663	.709
PERSONAL INCOME	(4)	.658	.702	.806	.893	2.286
PERS INC % OF US		.014	.014	.012	.009	.007
DISPOSABLE INCOME	(4)	.537	.574	.661	.730	1.871
PCE-PRICE INDX-82	(4)	3.109	4.090	4.700	3.536	5.001
REAL DISP INCOME	(4)	.352	.343	.322	.298	.290
POPULATION	(3)	5.784	12.730	24.850	26.734	17.301
POP AS % OF US		.002	.005	.010	.010	.006

(NOTE - FOR ALL TABLES: EMPLOYMENT & POPULATION IN
THOUSANDS OF PEOPLE, DOLLAR CONCEPTS IN BILLIONS OF NOMINAL
DOLLARS UNLESS OTHERWISE INDICATED.)

INDEX TO AVAILABLE TABLES

TABLE 8-24

DEMO MODEL: EFFECTS OF INCREASING DURABLE OUTPUT BY 1
 BILLION $82'S
TABLE 2: SUMMARY TABLE FOR PRIVATE NONFARM SECTORS
 (DETAILED TABLE # REF IN PARENS)

		1990 FCST	1991 FCST	1995 FCST	2000 FCST	2020 FCST
PRIVT NONFRM EMP (1000S OF PEO) & ITS DECOMP BY SOURCE OF DEM:						
TOTAL EMPLYMNT	(7)	24.365	21.077	16.202	13.773	11.557
INTERMEDIATE	(7)	7.310	5.981	4.561	4.100	4.134
LOCAL CONSUM	(7)	6.732	5.665	4.581	3.983	3.713
GOVT DEMAND	(7)	.178	.172	.228	.243	.168
INVEST ACTVTY	(8)	1.676	1.349	.718	.371	.335
EXPORT TO US	(8)	-.282	-.601	-1.457	-1.482	-.514
EXP - MULTREG	(8)	.000	.000	.000	.000	.000
EXOGENOUS	(8)	8.752	8.510	7.572	6.556	3.720
COSTS AND SELLING PRICES RELATIVE TO THE UNITED STATES						
SELLING PRICE	(9)	.02446	.03020	.02787	.01596	.00816
FACTOR INPUTS	(9)	.03787	.04661	.04121	.02108	.00983
LABOR	(9)	.05383	.06578	.05567	.02573	.01106
FUEL	(9)	.00000	.00000	.00000	.00000	.00000
CAPITAL	(10)	.01590	.02060	.02315	.01692	.00953
INTRMED INPUTS	(10)	.01865	.02333	.02273	.01461	.00803
OTHER VARIABLES:						
REL FACT PROD	(10)	.00000	.00000	.00000	.00000	.00000
REL PROFIT MFG	(10)	-.02007	-.02595	-.02350	-.01168	-.00483
LABOR INTENSTY	(11)	-.00129	-.00277	-.00733	-.00844	-.00354
MULT ADJ	(11)	.00000	.00000	.00000	.00000	.00000
EMP % OF U.S.	(11)	.021	.018	.013	.011	.008
RPC = SS/DEMAND	(11)	.015	.005	-.001	-.001	.002
AVG WAGE-THOUS	(12)	1.326	1.729	1.852	1.303	2.198
INDL MIX INDX	(12)	.00000	.01587	-.00041	-.00615	-.00132
IN BILLIONS OF 1982 DOLLARS						
DEMAND	(12)	1.33549	1.24837	1.06702	.97152	1.01857
IMPORTS	(12)	.66654	.68459	.61844	.56548	.56429
SELF SUPPLY	(13)	.66895	.56378	.44857	.40604	.45428
EXPORTS	(13)	-.02385	-.05123	-.12705	-.12979	-.05457
INTRAREG TRD	(13)	.00000	.00000	.00000	.00000	.00000
EXOGENOUS PRDN	(13)	1.00000	1.00000	1.00000	1.00000	1.00000
OUTPUT	(14)	1.64511	1.51255	1.32153	1.27626	1.39971
GRP(VAL ADDED)	(14)	.79158	.72556	.64854	.63884	.69263
IN BILLIONS OF NOMINAL DOLLARS						
WAGE & SAL DISB	(14)	.63179	.64127	.64029	.62577	1.58594

TABLE 8-25

DEMO MODEL: EFFECTS OF INCREASING DURABLE OUTPUT BY 1
    BILLION $82'S

TABLE 2: MIGRATION EQUATION REGRESSION COMPONENTS

	1990	1991	1995	2000	2020
DEPENDENT VARIABLE					
RESIDUAL ECON. MIGR.	.000	.000	.000	.000	.000
RESIDUAL ADJ.	.000	.000	.000	.000	.000
PREDICTED ECON. MIGR.	5.721	6.759	1.369	-.597	-.086
INDEPENDENT VARIABLES					
RELAT. WAGE RATE (RWR)	.021	.029	.021	.002	-.001
RELAT. WAGE MIX (RWM)	.020	.021	.019	.017	.010
RELATIVE EC. OP. (REO)	.177	.113	.017	-.012	-.002
RESIDENCE ADJ. EMP.	23.791	20.966	16.857	14.610	11.959
POTENTIAL LAB. FORCE	2.893	6.398	12.699	14.012	10.352
EMPLOYMENT U.S.	.000	.000	.000	.000	.000
POTENT.L.F. U.S.	.000	.000	.000	.000	.000
RWR 1 PERIOD LAG	.000	.021	.026	.004	-.002
RWR 2 PERIOD LAG	.000	.000	.030	.008	-.003
RWM 1 PERIOD LAG	.000	.020	.020	.017	.010
RWM 2 PERIOD LAG	.000	.000	.020	.018	.010
REO 1 PERIOD LAG	.000	.177	.032	-.010	-.003
REO 2 PERIOD LAG	.000	.000	.053	-.007	-.004
REGIONAL CONSTANT	.000	.000	.000	.000	.000

TABLE 8-26

DEMO MODEL: EFFECTS OF INCREASING TRANSFER PAY BY 100 MIL 82'S
TABLE 4: PERSONAL INCOME TABLE (IN BILLIONS OF DOLLARS)

	1990 FCST	1991 FCST	1995 FCST	2000 FCST	2020 FCST
WAGE AND SAL DISB	.05743	.06089	.06270	.06440	.21818
PROPRIETORS INC*	.00000	.00000	.00000	.00000	.00000
OTHER LABOR INC	.01287	.01214	.01197	.01466	.05337

DERIVATION OF PERSONAL INCOME BY PLACE OF RESIDENCE:

	1990	1991	1995	2000	2020
TOT LAB + PROP INC	.07030	.07303	.07468	.07906	.27155
AS A % OF U.S.	.002	.002	.002	.001	.001
LESS SOC INSR CNT	.00518	.00552	.00583	.00617	.02091
PLUS RESID ADJ	-.00269	-.00278	-.00284	-.00301	-.01034
PLUS DIV,INT,RENT	.00151	.00366	.01104	.02017	.06412
PLUS TRANSFER PAY	.12181	.13038	.16437	.21286	.59324
PERSONAL INCOME	.18575	.19875	.24142	.30292	.89767
AS A % OF U.S.	.004	.004	.004	.003	.003
LESS TAXES	.01123	.01214	.01430	.01770	.05983
DISPOSABLE PER. INC	.17451	.18661	.22712	.28522	.83784
PCE - PRICE INDEX	.304	.446	.482	.291	.290
REAL DIS PER INC$82	.12906	.12927	.13031	.13245	.14338
AS A % OF U.S.	.004	.004	.004	.004	.003

BREAKDOWN OF LABOR AND PROPRIETOR'S INCOME:

	1990	1991	1995	2000	2020
MANUFACTURE	.00561	.00617	.00255	-.00149	.00548
DURABLES	.00137	.00148	.00027	-.00091	.00051
NONDURABLES	.00423	.00469	.00228	-.00058	.00496
NON MANUFACTURE	.06151	.06183	.06311	.06902	.23554
MINING	.00014	.00011	.00006	.00004	.00023
CONT CONSTRUC	.01172	.01105	.00909	.00804	.02267
TRANS + PUB UT	.00376	.00394	.00365	.00312	.01064
FINANCE, INS, + RE	.00195	.00211	.00214	.00185	.00516
RETAIL TRADE	.01415	.01470	.01622	.01827	.05473
WHOLESALE TRADE	.00495	.00502	.00456	.00397	.01273
SERVICES	.02495	.02465	.02715	.03350	.12832
AGRI/FOR/FISH	.00025	.00025	.00024	.00024	.00104
TOTAL GOVERNMENT	.00318	.00503	.00902	.01154	.03054
ST AND LOCAL GOVT	.00292	.00472	.00874	.01139	.03035
FED GOVT CIVILIAN	.00026	.00030	.00028	.00015	.00019
FED GOVT MILITARY	.00000	.00000	.00000	.00000	.00000
FARM	.00000	.00000	.00000	.00000	.00000

* IF ALL 0.0'S, PROP INC HAS BEEN MERGED INTO OTHER LABOR INC.

TABLE 8-27

DEMO MODEL: EFFECTS OF CUTTING AUTO EXP AND INC PUBLIC
TRANSPORT EXPEND BY 30 MILLION 1982 DOLLARS
TABLE 2: SUM TABLE FOR PRIV NONFARM SECT (DET TABLE # REF IN
PARENS)

		1990 FCST	1991 FCST	1995 FCST	2000 FCST	2020 FCST
PRI NONFRM EMP(1000S OF PEO) & ITS DECOM BY SOURCE OF DEM:						
TOTAL EMPLYMNT	(7)	.341	.305	.213	.155	.174
INTERMEDIATE	(7)	.070	.056	.026	.011	.015
LOCAL CONSUM	(7)	.092	.082	.061	.046	.049
GOVT DEMAND	(7)	.002	.002	.003	.002	.002
INVEST ACTVTY	(8)	.026	.022	.013	.007	.008
EXPORT TO US	(8)	-.004	-.010	-.030	-.034	-.023
EXP - MULTREG	(8)	.000	.000	.000	.000	.000
EXOGENOUS	(8)	.156	.153	.139	.121	.124
COSTS AND SELLING PRICES RELATIVE TO THE UNITED STATES						
SELLING PRICE	(9)	.00037	.00057	.00063	.00041	.00031
FACTOR INPUTS	(9)	.00058	.00087	.00093	.00057	.00043
LABOR	(9)	.00092	.00124	.00130	.00078	.00059
FUEL	(9)	.00000	.00000	.00000	.00000	.00000
CAPITAL	(10)	.00016	.00032	.00038	.00026	.00019
INTRMED INPUTS	(10)	.00025	.00043	.00050	.00035	.00026
OTHER VARIABLES:						
REL FACT PROD	(10)	.00000	.00000	.00000	.00000	.00000
REL PROFIT MFG	(10)	-.00028	-.00046	-.00049	-.00028	-.00020
LABOR INTENSTY	(11)	-.00002	-.00005	-.00017	-.00022	-.00022
MULT ADJ	(11)	.00000	.00000	.00000	.00000	.00000
EMP % OF U.S.	(11)	.000	.000	.000	.000	.000
RPC = SS/DEMAND	(11)	.000	.000	.000	.000	.000
AVG WAGE-THOUS	(12)	.015	.024	.035	.032	.102
INDL MIX INDX	(12)	.00000	.00093	.00073	.00067	.00054
IN BILLIONS OF 1982 DOLLARS						
DEMAND	(12)	.01372	.01299	.00988	.00791	.00996
IMPORTS	(12)	.00591	.00621	.00531	.00455	.00539
SELF SUPPLY	(13)	.00781	.00677	.00457	.00336	.00458
EXPORTS	(13)	-.00033	-.00083	-.00246	-.00274	-.00204
INTRAREG TRD	(13)	.00000	.00000	.00000	.00000	.00000
EXOGENOUS PRDN	(13)	.00734	.00729	.00705	.00669	.00667
OUTPUT	(14)	.01483	.01323	.00916	.00730	.00921
GRP(VAL ADDED)	(14)	.00901	.00821	.00624	.00518	.00609
IN BILLIONS OF NOMINAL DOLLARS						
WAGE & SAL DISB	(14)	.00800	.00868	.00922	.00893	.03200

TABLE 8-28

DEMO MODEL: EFFECTS OF REDUCING RES & NON RES STRUCT BY 40 &
15 MILLION DOLLARS IN 1990

TABLE 5: GRP BY FINAL DEMAND TABLE (BILLION OF 82 US DOLLARS
RECONCILED WITH VALUE ADDED)

	1990 FCST	1991 FCST	1995 FCST	2000 FCST	2020 FCST
TOTAL GRP	.00000	.00371	.00140	.00041	.00012
TOTAL CONSUMPTION	.00000	.00209	.00109	.00044	.00015
AUTOS AND PARTS	.00000	.00017	.00009	.00003	.00001
FURN & HSEHLD EQ.	.00000	.00014	.00007	.00003	.00001
OTHER DURABLES	.00000	.00005	.00003	.00001	.00000
FOOD & BEVERAGES	.00000	.00035	.00018	.00007	.00002
CLOTHING & SHOES	.00000	.00013	.00007	.00003	.00001
GASOLINE & OIL	.00000	.00006	.00003	.00001	.00000
FUEL OIL & COAL	.00000	.00002	.00001	.00000	.00000
OTHER NONDURABLES	.00000	.00012	.00006	.00002	.00001
HOUSING	.00000	.00033	.00018	.00007	.00002
HSEHLD OPERATION	.00000	.00012	.00006	.00002	.00001
TRANSPORTATION	.00000	.00006	.00003	.00001	.00000
HEALTH SERVICES	.00000	.00017	.00009	.00004	.00001
OTHER SERVICES	.00000	.00038	.00020	.00009	.00003
TOTAL FIXED INVEST	.00000	.00755	.00386	.00166	.00015
RESIDENTIAL	.00000	.00427	.00210	.00086	.00004
NON RESIDENTIAL	.00000	.00079	.00042	.00019	.00003
PROD. DUR. EQUIP.	.00000	.00249	.00134	.00061	.00009
CBI NET IVA + MISC	.00000	.00001	.00000	.00000	.00000
GRPVA-GRPFD	.00000	-.00019	-.00002	-.00001	.00000
TOTAL GOVERNMENT	.00000	.00006	.00020	.00014	.00000
FED GOV MILITARY	.00000	.00000	.00000	.00000	.00000
FED GOV CIVILIAN	.00000	.00000	.00000	.00000	.00000
ST/LOC GOV EDUC.	.00000	.00003	.00008	.00006	.00000
ST/LOC HLTH/WLFAR	.00000	.00001	.00004	.00003	.00000
ST/LOC SAFETY	.00000	.00001	.00002	.00002	.00000
ST/LOC MISCEL	.00000	.00002	.00006	.00004	.00000
TOTAL EXPORTS	.00000	-.00012	-.00070	-.00050	.00003
TOTAL IMPORTS	.00000	.00570	.00303	.00132	.00022
TOT GRP BY VAL ADD	.00000	.00371	.00140	.00041	.00012
TOT PRIV NF VAL AD	.00000	.00368	.00130	.00034	.00012
TOT GOV COMPENSATN	.00000	.00003	.00011	.00007	.00000
TOT FARM VAL ADDED	.00000	.00000	.00000	.00000	.00000

TABLE 8-29

DEMO MODEL: EFFECTS OF INCREASING FACTOR PROD FOR DURABLE
    GOODS PROD BY 1%
TABLE 2: SUM TABLE FOR PRI NONFARM SECT(DET TABLE # REF IN PAR)

		1990 FCST	1991 FCST	1995 FCST	2000 FCST	2020 FCST
PRI NONFRM EMP(1000S OF PEO) & ITS DECOM BY SOURCE OF DEM:						
TOTAL EMPLYMNT	(7)	-.082	-.053	.022	.054	.086
INTERMEDIATE	(7)	.002	.011	.035	.046	.059
LOCAL CONSUM	(7)	-.017	-.010	.010	.019	.030
GOVT DEMAND	(7)	.000	.000	.000	.001	.002
INVEST ACTVTY	(8)	-.006	-.003	.002	.003	.003
EXPORT TO US	(8)	-.061	-.049	-.025	-.016	-.008
EXP - MULTREG	(8)	.000	.000	.000	.000	.000
EXOGENOUS	(8)	.000	.000	.000	.000	.000
COSTS AND SELLING PRICES RELATIVE TO THE UNITED STATES						
SELLING PRICE	(9)	-.00007	-.00008	.00002	.00009	.00006
FACTOR INPUTS	(9)	-.00072	-.00074	-.00058	-.00048	-.00055
LABOR	(9)	-.00017	-.00017	.00006	.00020	.00008
FUEL	(9)	.00000	.00000	.00000	.00000	.00000
CAPITAL	(10)	-.00003	-.00006	.00000	.00007	.00008
INTRMED INPUTS	(10)	-.00004	-.00007	.00001	.00007	.00006
OTHER VARIABLES:						
REL FACT PROD	(10)	.00077	.00077	.00077	.00077	.00077
REL PROFIT MFG	(10)	.00158	.00161	.00156	.00155	.00162
LABOR INTENSTY	(11)	.00000	.00001	.00001	-.00001	-.00003
MULT ADJ	(11)	.00000	.00000	.00000	.00000	.000000
EMP % OF U.S.	(11)	.000	.000	.000	.000	.000
RPC=SS/DEMAND	(11)	.000	.000	.000	.000	.000
AVG WAGE-THOUS	(12)	-.008	-.008	-.002	.003	.000
INDL MIX INDX	(12)	.00000	.00003	.00012	.00012	.00009
IN BILLIONS OF 1982 DOLLARS						
DEMAND	(12)	-.00124	.00031	.00489	.00751	.01192
IMPORTS	(12)	-.00062	.00010	.00236	.00373	.00605
SELF SUPPLY	(13)	-.00062	.00021	.00253	.00378	.00587
EXPORTS	(13)	.00153	.00286	.00643	.00895	.01371
INTRAREG TRD	(13)	.00000	.00000	.00000	.00000	.00000
EXOGENOUS PRDN	(13)	.00000	.00000	.00000	.00000	.00000
OUTPUT	(14)	.00091	.00307	.00896	.01273	.01958
GRP(VAL ADDED)	(14)	.00030	.00132	.00422	.00622	.00957
IN BILLIONS OF NOMINAL DOLLARS						
WAGE & SAL DISB	(14)	-.00237	-.00189	.00032	.00213	.00959

TABLE 8-30

DEMO MODEL: EFFECTS OF INCREAS COSTS BY 1% IN DURABLES IN 90

TABLE 2: SUM TABLE FOR PRI NONFARM SECT(DET TABLE # REF IN PAR

		1990 FCST	1991 FCST	1995 FCST	2000 FCST	2020 FCST
PRI NONFRM EMP(1000S OF PEO)& ITS DECOM BY SOURCE OF DEM:						
TOTAL EMPLYMNT	(7)	-.077	-.133	-.248	-.293	-.329
INTERMEDIATE	(7)	-.023	-.040	-.075	-.092	-.121
LOCAL CONSUM	(7)	-.021	-.036	-.069	-.084	-.103
GOVT DEMAND	(7)	-.001	-.001	-.003	-.005	-.005
INVEST ACTVTY	(8)	-.005	-.009	-.014	-.013	-.011
EXPORT TO US	(8)	-.027	-.047	-.086	-.099	-.088
EXP - MULTREG	(8)	.000	.000	.000	.000	.000
EXOGENOUS	(8)	.000	.000	.000	.000	.000
COSTS AND SELLING PRICES RELATIVE TO THE UNITED STATES						
SELLING PRICE	(9)	-.00007	-.00015	-.00038	-.00040	-.00022
FACTOR INPUTS	(9)	-.00010	-.00024	-.00057	-.00058	-.00027
LABOR	(9)	-.00017	-.00035	-.00079	-.00076	-.00030
FUEL	(9)	.00000	.00000	.00000	.00000	.00000
CAPITAL	(10)	-.00003	-.00009	-.00029	-.00036	-.00027
INTRMED INPUTS	(10)	-.00004	-.00011	-.00030	-.00034	-.00022
OTHER VARIABLES:						
REL FACT PROD	(10)	.00000	.00000	.00000	.00000	.00000
REL PROFIT MFG	(10)	-.00322	-.00315	-.00295	-.00294	-.00313
LABOR INTENSTY	(11)	.00000	.00001	.00007	.00013	.00011
MULT ADJ	(11)	.00000	.00000	.00000	.00000	.00000
EMP % OF U.S.	(11)	.000	.000	.000	.000	.000
RPC=SS/DEMAND	(11)	.000	.000	.000	.000	.000
AVG WAGE-THOUS	(12)	-.004	-.009	-.027	-.035	-.064
INDL MIX INDX	(12)	.00000	-.00006	-.00005	.00006	.00005
IN BILLIONS OF 1982 DOLLARS						
DEMAND	(12)	-.00427	-.00767	-.01565	-.02010	-.02904
IMPORTS	(12)	-.00202	-.00378	-.00806	-.01051	-.01496
SELF SUPPLY	(13)	-.00224	-.00389	-.00758	-.00959	-.01408
EXPORTS	(13)	-.00308	-.00559	-.01197	-.01656	-.02621
INTRAREG TRD	(13)	.00000	.00000	.00000	.00000	.00000
EXOGENOUS PRDN	(13)	.00000	.00000	.00000	.00000	.00000
OUTPUT	(14)	-.00532	-.00947	-.01955	-.02615	-.04029
GRP(VAL ADDED)	(14)	-.00254	-.00454	-.00956	-.01309	-.01993
IN BILLIONS OF NOMINAL DOLLARS						
WAGE & SAL DISB	(14)	-.00191	-.00366	-.00914	-.01384	-.04451

TABLE 8-31

DEMO MODEL: EFFECTS OF A QUALITY OF LIFE IMPROVEMENT EQUAL
TO .4% OF WAGES

TABLE 2: SUM TABLE FOR PRI NONFARM SEC(DET TABLE # REF IN PAR)

		1990 FCST	1991 FCST	1995 FCST	2000 FCST	2020 FCST
PRI NONFRM EMP(1000S OF PEO) & ITS DECOM BY SOURCE OF DEM:						
TOTAL EMPLYMNT	(7)	.012	.023	.078	.159	.320
INTERMEDIATE	(7)	.003	.005	.021	.045	.093
LOCAL CONSUM	(7)	.007	.013	.037	.071	.140
GOVT DEMAND	(7)	.001	.002	.005	.008	.011
INVEST ACTVTY	(8)	.001	.002	.004	.007	.011
EXPORT TO US	(8)	.001	.002	.012	.028	.064
EXP - MULTREG	(8)	.000	.000	.000	.000	.000
EXOGENOUS	(8)	.000	.000	.000	.000	.000
COSTS AND SELLING PRICES RELATIVE TO THE UNITED STATES						
SELLING PRICE	(9)	-.00004	-.00008	-.00027	-.00039	-.00056
FACTOR INPUTS	(9)	-.00008	-.00017	-.00054	-.00079	-.00111
LABOR	(9)	-.00012	-.00027	-.00085	-.00128	-.00181
FUEL	(9)	.00000	.00000	.00000	.00000	.00000
CAPITAL	(10)	-.00003	-.00002	-.00003	-.00003	-.00004
INTRMED INPUTS	(10)	-.00002	-.00004	-.00014	-.00020	-.00028
OTHER VARIABLES:						
REL FACT PROD	(10)	.00000	.00000	.00000	.00000	.00000
REL PROFIT MFG	(10)	.00004	.00009	.00031	.00048	.00068
LABOR INTENSTY	(11)	.00000	.00001	.00008	.00021	.00064
MULT ADJ	(11)	.00000	.00000	.00000	.00000	.00000
EMP % OF U.S.	(11)	.000	.000	.000	.000	.000
RPC=SS/DEMAND	(11)	.000	.000	.000	.000	.000
AVG WAGE-THOUS	(12)	-.003	-.006	-.025	-.049	-.224
INDL MIX INDX	(12)	.00000	-.00003	-.00011	-.00011	-.00005
IN BILLIONS OF 1982 DOLLARS						
DEMAND	(12)	.00077	.00141	.00417	.00821	.01756
IMPORTS	(12)	.00030	.00055	.00150	.00291	.00629
SELF SUPPLY	(13)	.00046	.00086	.00267	.00530	.01127
EXPORTS	(13)	.00004	.00013	.00091	.00228	.00587
INTRAREG TRD	(13)	.00000	.00000	.00000	.00000	.00000
EXOGENOUS PRDN	(13)	.00000	.00000	.00000	.00000	.00000
OUTPUT	(14)	.00050	.00099	.00358	.00758	.01714
GRP(VAL ADDED)	(14)	.00027	.00051	.00177	.00371	.00830
IN BILLIONS OF NOMINAL DOLLARS						
WAGE & SAL DISB	(14)	-.00006	-.00022	-.00081	-.00052	.00802

TABLE 8-32

DEMO MODEL: EFFECTS OF A QUALITY OF LIFE IMPROVEMENT EQUAL
   TO .4% OF WAGES

TABLE 2: MIGRATION EQUATION REGRESSION COMPONENTS

	1990	1991	1995	2000	2020
DEPENDENT VARIABLE					
RESIDUAL ECON. MIGR.	.000	.000	.000	.000	.000
RESIDUAL ADJ.	.000	.000	.000	.000	.000
PREDICTED ECON. MIGR.	.120	.098	.050	.026	-.003
INDEPENDENT VARIABLES					
RELATIVE WAGE RATE(RWR)	.000	.000	-.001	-.001	-.002
RELATIVE WAGE MIX (RWM)	.000	.000	.000	.000	.000
RELATIVE EC. OP.(REO)	.000	-.001	-.002	-.002	-.003
RESIDENCE ADJ. EMP.	.017	.033	.101	.190	.355
POTENTIAL LAB. FORCE	.061	.112	.263	.384	.583
EMPLOYMENT U.S.	.000	.000	.000	.000	.000
POTENT.L.F. U.S.	.000	.000	.000	.000	.000
RWR 1 PERIOD LAG	.000	.000	-.001	-.001	-.002
RWR 2 PERIOD LAG	.000	.000	-.001	-.001	-.002
RWM 1 PERIOD LAG	.000	.000	.000	.000	.000
RWM 2 PERIOD LAG	.000	.000	.000	.000	.000
REO 1 PERIOD LAG	.000	.000	-.002	-.002	-.003
REO 2 PERIOD LAG	.000	.000	-.001	-.002	-.003
REGIONAL CONSTANT	.001	.001	.001	.001	.001

400

NOTES ON CHAPTER 8

1. This chapter was written in part by Rafael Bradley. It is enhanced by having the REMI-EDFS Demo model diskette, programmed by Rafael Bradley, available with this book or from the editor (see the appendix to this chapter). However, the tables that are provided in the appendix are sufficient for understanding the key points in the chapter.

2. REMI produces two types of EDFS (Economic and Demographic Forecasting and Simulation) models: a 14-sector model, and a 53-sector model. Economic data is commonly collected with respect to the industry, which is the source of the data. Examples would include the total dollar value of cars (the data) produced by automobile manufacturers (the industry) or the number of people (the data) working in forestry consulting (the industry). The term *sector* refers to a set of industries, or possibly just one industry, grouped by similarity in products or services. This grouping is called *aggregation*. When fewer sectors are used to represent an economy, greater aggregation is implicit in the data. A tradeoff between ease of data representation and specificity occurs when the degree of aggregation is changed. More aggregation eases examination and manipulation of the data while concurrently decreasing the degree of detail available. With respect to the REMI model, this implies that the EDFS-14 model manipulates data and produces results more readily, while the EDFS-53 model offers a detailed and accurate set of results. The Demo Model forecasts as an EDFS-14 model, but it does not include the extensive set of operation and data utilities, the U.S. model programs, or the reference documents that are included with the standard REMI EDFS-14 system.

3. As a suggestion, try reading this section of the manual – **Generating Results with the Model** — through once prior to actually trying the software. Having read the instructions in advance, you may find it easier to use the model. Alternatively, if you wish, you may skip this section without loss of continuity.

4. Model suppressions are economic characteristics of the model which may be turned ON or OFF. We will consider the use of these suppressions in chapter 9 to look at special cases of the model.

5. This will not work for users whose printer is connected to some device other than **LPT1**, or whose <**CTRL**>**PRNTSCRN** is ON! If you are such a user, press "N"

at this question and, after completing the printing of both economic and population results, exit the menu system to **DOS**. You may then use your normal method of printing text files to print the results files: **TABLEXX.FS**, **XXPOP.TAB**, and **XXPOPL.TAB**.

6. A REMI model of the U.S. economy is not included with this package, but it is included with the regular REMI model.

7. Since the constant is negative, it indicates that the county will not attract migrants unless the independent variables attain above-average values. A calculation similar to that for RWR can be made for REO following the same procedure and assuming that RWR = 0. Compensating differentials for all states are reported in Greenwood et al, 1991.

8. Fine tuning is a key part of National econometric forecasts (see Haitovsky et al, 1972).

9. Some of the variables in the EDFS-14 model have numbers over 737, since the variables are organized in *nonconsecutive* groups. These groups correspond to the those in the EDFS-53 model; however, there are only 737 EDFS-14 regular policy variables in total.

10. In this section, we are assuming that you are using the demonstration model as delivered. In this case, the operational equation for investment is the stock adjustment equation explained in note 3 (p. 42) of the Treyz, Rickman, Shao paper.

CHAPTER 9

FORECASTING AND SIMULATION SENSITIVITY
TO ALTERNATIVE MODEL SPECIFICATIONS[1]

One way to evaluate the importance of particular assumptions for different parts of the REMI model is to run the same simulation but with different suppressions in each instance. Another way is to postulate alternative pure versions or closures of the model, and then to test them with the same policy change. In addition to these two ways of seeing how sensitive the model results are to the model assumptions, we can also carry out ex post sample period forecasts to test which formulation of the model produces a model that would have best explained the 1980s. In this chapter we first consider how the predicted policy effect changes as the model suppressions are released. Next we look at the standard REMI model and four special cases of the model. Finally, we conclude with statistics comparing the five versions in post sample period forecasts.

9-1 MULTIPLIER COMPARISONS

To compare the multipliers, we carry out a number of simulations with different parts of the REMI model suppressed. In each simulation, employment in the air transportation industry in Illinois is increased by 1,000 employees for each year over the period from 1990 through 2020.

Table 9-1 lists the employment and output multipliers for the air transportation industry for the years 1990, 2000, and 2020. We will discuss the results later.

Table 9-1

Employment and Output Multipliers for Air Transport in Illinois[2]

		1990	% to REMI Type I 1990	2000	% to REMI Type I 1990	2020	% to REMI Type I 1990
Type I	Employment	1.415	1.000	1.492	1.054	1.641	1.160
(Case 1)	Output	1.282	1.000	1.284	1.002	1.283	1.001
Type II	Employment	2.170	1.534	2.272	1.606	2.504	1.770
(Case 2)	Output	1.617	1.261	1.594	1.243	1.560	1.217
Case 3	Employment	2.229	1.575	2.060	1.456	2.000	1.413
	Output	1.647	1.285	1.615	1.260	1.559	1.216
Case 4	Employment	2.244	1.586	2.444	1.727	2.737	1.934
	Output	1.650	1.287	1.663	1.297	1.634	1.275
Case 5	T Employ	2.268	1.603	2.441	1.725	2.739	1.936
	P Employ	2.230	1.576	2.215	1.565	2.518	1.780
	Output	1.648	1.285	1.612	1.257	1.586	1.237
Case 6	T Employ	2.233	1.578	2.767	1.955	3.169	2.240
	P Employ	2.196	1.552	2.518	1.780	2.910	2.057
	Output	1.632	1.273	1.736	1.354	1.712	1.335
Case 7	T Employ	2.642	1.867	3.274	2.314	3.705	2.618
	P Employ	2.598	1.836	2.972	2.100	3.402	2.404
	Output	1.871	1.459	1.974	1.540	1.914	1.493
Case 8	T Employ	2.613	1.847	2.905	2.053	3.520	2.488
	P Employ	2.571	1.817	2.633	1.861	3.230	2.283
	Output	1.850	1.443	1.748	1.363	1.817	1.417
Case 9	T Employ	2.903	2.052	3.126	2.209	3.781	2.672
	P Employ	2.856	2.018	2.831	2.001	3.469	2.452
	Output	2.022	1.577	1.855	1.447	1.923	1.500
Case 10	T Employ	4.659	3.293	3.882	2.743	5.393	3.811
	P Employ	4.590	3.244	3.505	2.477	4.943	3.493
	Output	2.862	2.232	2.166	1.690	2.388	1.863

(1)   The Type I Multipliers (Case 1)

To obtain a processing sector only multiplier, almost all of the responses in the REMI model are suppressed. The endogenous responses that are suppressed are as follows:

	Responses	Immediately affected by
(a)	wage rate	occupational and general labor demand
(b)	net migration	expected real earnings
(c)	RPC	relative profitability for national industries; relative selling prices and gross regional product (GRP) for regional industries
(d)	export share	same as RPC, except GRP will not have any impact for regional industries
(e)	house and land price	local population relative to the United States
(f)	property income	population under and over 65
(g)	transfer payment	population, especially retired population
(h)	consumption	real disposable income (RYD)
(i)	investment	RYD relative to the United States for residential investment; employment and relative factor costs for nonresidential investment
(j)	government demand	population

We relax these suppressions one by one to show the contribution of each endogenous response in the REMI model.

The Type I (case 1) multipliers are shown in table 9-1 as the first panel. In the long run simulation, the employment multipliers increase when compared with the Type I multiplier in the first period. This is due to the productivity changes in air transportation that exceed those in other industries. Thus, by the year 2020, there are 16% more indirect employees for every direct air transport employee than there are in 1990.

(2)   The Type II Multipliers (Case 2)

The Type II (case 2) multipliers can be computed once the model is closed with respect to households. To accomplish this, we release the suppression of response (*h*) (i.e., personal consumption) and keep other suppressions.

The values of the employment multiplier are 2.170, 2.272, and 2.504 for 1990, 2000, and 2020 respectively. To examine the difference in multiplier values, we calculate the ratio of the multiplier values from the REMI model with endogenous consumption to the value of the Type I first year multiplier from the REMI model and list these rates as a column next to the multiplier value for each year. These show the output multiplier declining slightly each year relative to the 1990 Type I multiplier. This is probably due to the fewer employees required because of the productivity increase in air transport mentioned previously. With fewer employees, the wages to be respent are reduced and thus, induced consumption is lower. The relative increase in the Type II employment multiplier is also due to the reduction in the number of direct employees because they are in the denominator of the employment multiplier equation.

(3)   Case 3: Case 2 Plus Wage Rate Response

In this case, which is marked as case 3 in table 9-1, we release the suppression of response (*a*) (i.e., wage rate) and keep everything else the same as case 2. This relaxation is to let the wage rate change as occupational and general labor demand changes.

Slightly larger multipliers can be observed comparing case 3 to case 2 in table 9-1 for 1990. This first year increase, when wage is endogenized, is comparable to the result that we obtained in moving from case 4 to case 5 in chapter 5 for the prototype model. This is because higher wage rates increase local demand in the short run. However, increases in wage rates push labor costs up and reduce labor intensity leading to a reduction in employment in the long run. This is why the employment multiplier decreases over the years, from 2.229 in the year 1990 to 2.060 in the year 2000 and 2.000 in the year 2020. However, the output multipliers are not changed much by making wage rates endogenous as increased wages have positive demand effects, while lower employment reduces earned income effects.

(4)   Case 4: Case 3 With Suppression of Labor Intensity

As we explained in case 3, the changes in wage rate apparently cause changes in labor intensity that reduce employment in the long run forecast, as they did when we move from case 6 to case 7 in chapter 5. Here, to test this hypothesis, we suppress the normal response of labor intensity in the REMI model and keep other responses the same as in case 3.

As we expected, the employment multipliers increase over the years from 2.224 in the year 1990 to 2.444 and 2.737 for the years 2000 and 2020, respectively. This direction of change is in the opposite direction to the change in case 3, but it is in the same direction as case 2. This confirms our hypothesis that labor intensity changes caused the drop. The suppression of the labor intensity response also stabilizes the output multiplier.

(5)   Case 5: Case 3 Plus Migration and Housing Price

In this case, we restore the normal response of labor intensity and further release the suppression of responses (*b*) and (*e*) (i.e., net migration, housing prices and land prices). When expected income in the local area increases, net economic migration increases. Of course, more inward migration makes the price of the housing and land go up.

When the population response is suppressed in the REMI model, there is no increase in state and local government spending and employment. Once we incorporate the population into the model thereby making government employment endogenous, we have to calculate an employment multiplier that includes government employees. Therefore, we list two employment multipliers for cases 5 to 10 in table 9-1. "T Employ" indicates the employment multipliers for total employment (private nonfarm industries plus state and local government employees), while "P Employ" denotes the employment multipliers for private nonfarm industries only.

The multipliers in case 5 should be compared with those in case 3 to see the marginal effect of including migration and land prices. Using the "P Employ" concept, we note that the first year multiplier is the same but that the multiplier in 2000 is 7.5% higher [({2.215 − 2.060} ÷ 2.060) × 100]. By 2020, it is 25.9% higher [({2.518 − 2.000} ÷ 2.000) × 100]. This is because increasing population raises labor supply, reducing the wage growth and its effects. It is also because more people require more government services, as can be seen by the fact that the "T Employ" multiplier is greater than the "P Employ" multiplier.

The employment multipliers from case 4 are close to the "P Employ" multipliers in case 5. The "T Employ" multiplier in case 5 is slightly larger than the other two multipliers.

(6) Cases 6 to 10: Cases With Additional Suppressions Relaxed

In each of cases 6 to 10, an *additional* suppression of normal responses is relaxed from the previous case.

For Case 6 we relax the suppression of responses (*f*) and (*g*) (i.e., transfer payment and property income). In a short run forecast, when the local economy grows in response to exogenous increases in employment, transfer payments are reduced. This reduces the amount of increase in personal income and real disposable income in the area, and thereby reduces the employment multiplier slightly. When population in the area increases, the increase is made up of younger people because they are economic migrants. However, as the people age and eventually retire, transfer payments, which are primarily social security disbursements, increase. Then, employment increases because of more personal income in the area. That is why we see smaller employment multipliers (2.233 for "T Employ" in case 6 as opposed to 2.268 in case 5) in 1990 and larger employment multipliers (3.169 for "T Employ" in case 6 as opposed to 2.739 in case 5) in 2020.

For Case 7 we relax the suppression of responses (*i*) and (*j*) (i.e., investment and government demand). In addition, we set the switch policy variable 901 equal to one, which shuts off investment generated by exogenous employment. Note that the stock adjustment process, in response to endogenous economic activity, is active in this case (and also in cases 8 – 10). More real disposable income and the growth of the local economy increases the optimal capital. To fill the gap between the optimal capital stock and actual capital stock, there is more investment in residential and nonresidential structures. Therefore, employment and output are higher in case 7 than they were in case 6.

For Case 8 we relax the suppression of response (*d*) (i.e., export share). The policy switch for exogenous investment (policy variable 901) is still equal to one, suppressing the investment response to the exogenous stimulus. The exports from the area are reduced as the selling prices and profitability in the area relative to the U.S. change. The employment multiplier is reduced by 11.3% [((2.905 − 3.274) ÷ 3.274)

× 100] in 2000 and 5.0% [((3.520 − 3.705) ÷ 3.705) × 100] in 2020, due to the export response effect. The effect is relatively lower by 2020, because, by that time, the wage increase in the early years is mitigated by the increase in population and labor supply. Of course, these mitigated wage increases have a smaller effect on exports than the effects of the initial larger wage rate increases.

For Case 9, the suppressions are the same as case 8, however the switch for exogenous investment (901) is set at its default value of zero, thus incorporating an investment response to the exogenous change. This increases the multipliers.

For Case 10 we relax the suppression of response (c) (i.e., the RPC). A dramatic increase in both employment and output multipliers can be seen from case 9 to case 10. This parallels the effect of moving from case 8 to case 9 in chapter 5. This is because the RPC scale response incorporates in the model the theory that as an economy expands, it becomes more diverse. Therefore, a higher proportion of local needs can be supplied locally. This endogenous growth in the RPC obviously has important implications for the multiplier. However, this phenomenon is not as conclusively borne out by quantitative research as some of the other relationships in the model. Thus, it is suppressed in all versions of the model in current use, except for the demonstration model in chapter 8.

9-2 ALTERNATIVE CLOSURES[3]

As we learned above, regional forecasting and simulation models either explicitly or implicitly contain assumptions about demand and supply interactions in an economy. The assumptions employed in econometric, input-output and computable general equilibrium models are very different from one type to the next. In chapters 2 and 6, we examined the forecasting ability of the economic base model and an input-output model over a post sample period ending in 1983. Here, we undertake a study of five versions of the REMI model that represent five distinct models. We then present their characteristics and their post sample period records from 1980 to 1988.

The possible assumptions that could be used in constructing regional models are many. Traditional regional models such as the economic base and input-output models imply well documented assumptions (see chapters 2 and 6; Pfester, 1976; Polzin, 1977; and Richardson, 1969). Demand is perfectly inelastic and supply is perfectly elastic; thus, the models produce constant multiplier relationships between exogenous economic activity (basic) and endogenous economic activity (nonbasic). Full employment market-clearing general equilibrium models yield horizontal supply curves if factors of production are fully mobile, vertical supply curves if factors of production are immobile, and upward sloping supply curves if factors of production are partially mobile or if one factor is immobile while the other factors are mobile.[4]

Illustrations of the divergence in policy simulation responses to exogenous stimuli from Keynesian models versus neoclassical computable general equilibrium models are in Harrigan and McGregor (1989), Rattso (1982), Rickman (1992), and Robinson and Roland-Holst (1988).[5] In a review of econometric models linked with input-output models, Beaumont (1990) characterizes them as essentially demand driven models and argues that supply should be explicitly incorporated in the models consistent with computable general equilibrium models. Econometric evidence that regional labor supply is relatively inelastic while labor demand is relatively elastic can be found in Greenwood and Hunt (1984), Muth (1971), and Plaut (1982). This suggests that demand driven models do not fit the stylized facts and supply should be made an explicit component of regional models.

Given the divergent views of regional demand and supply, we use the REMI model to explore the accuracy of regional forecasts and sensitivity of economic impact assessments to alternative labor demand and supply specifications. Five versions of the REMI model are implemented with each version corresponding to different assumptions about labor demand and supply: 1) downward-sloping demand/upward-sloping supply, 2) vertical demand/horizontal supply, 3) vertical demand/upward-sloping supply, 4) downward-sloping demand/horizontal supply, 5) downward-sloping demand/vertical supply. All five versions assume perfectly mobile capital and a supply of land that responds positively to its rate of return.

Five different labor demand and supply specifications for the REMI model are shown in this section. In the REMI model shown in diagram 9-1, the general equilibrium demand for labor (GD) slopes downward, and the general equilibrium supply of labor (GS) slopes upward. The wage responsiveness of derived labor demand and the negative relationship between wage rates and the market shares give the downward slope of the general equilibrium labor demand curve.[6] Labor supply slopes upward because migration responds positively to changes in wage rates.

The first alternative specification of the labor market suppresses the endogeneity of export and local demand to wage rate and other production cost changes and suppresses labor intensity responses to wage rate changes. This produces

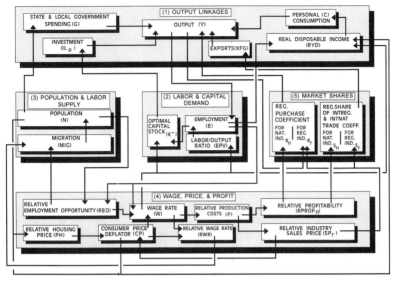

GD/GS
Downward Demand / Upward Supply (REMI)

Diagram 9-1

a vertical demand (VD) curve and is represented in diagram 9-2 as the removal of the linkages flowing from block 5 to block 1 and from block 4 to block 2. The shaded boxes, bold lines, and arrows indicate the remaining endogenous variables in the model.

VD/GS
Vertical Demand / Upward Supply (REMI Migration Only)

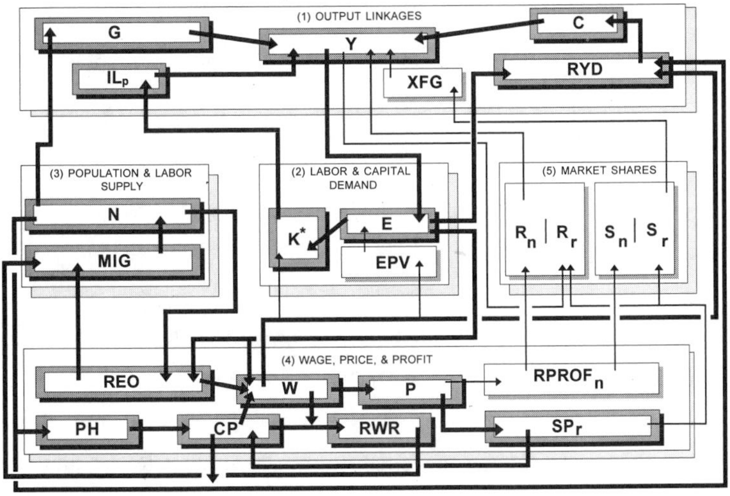

Diagram 9-2

Diagram 9-3 shows a version of the model that suppresses the labor intensity response to wage rates, market share responses to regional competitiveness, and migration responses to real after-tax wage rates and relative employment rates. Labor demand becomes completely inelastic (VD), while labor supply becomes perfectly elastic (HSI). Therefore, the model collapses to an input-output model.[7] Employment and the optimal capital stock are fixed proportions of output. Final and intermediate demands do not depend on regional competitiveness. Consumption depends on real disposable income, which is determined by employment levels and existing wage rates and price levels. The optimal capital stocks determine investment. Government spending depends solely on natural population changes.

VD/HSI
Vertical Demand / Horizontal Supply   (Input-Output)

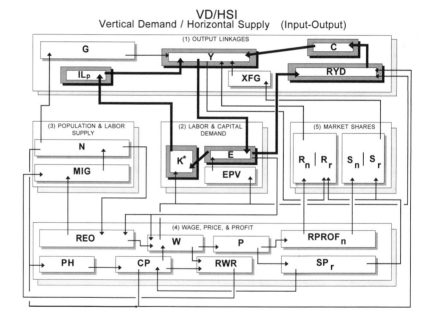

Diagram 9-3

Fixing the labor supply by suppressing the migration response and calculating the wage rate, where the number of employees demanded and supplied are equal, yields the market-clearing general equilibrium (VS) model shown in diagram 9-4. Equilibrium is defined by a "full employment" rate of employment in the region relative to the same for the United States. An exogenous positive employment shock initially pushes the employment rate above the "full employment" rate that, in turn, drives wage rates higher. This causes firms to substitute out of labor or to leave the region until labor demand again equals labor supply. The market share elasticities and a Cobb-Douglas production function determine the wage rate changes required to equilibrate labor demand and supply. Finally, since migration is suppressed this version gives identical population predictions as the VD/HSI (input-output) model.

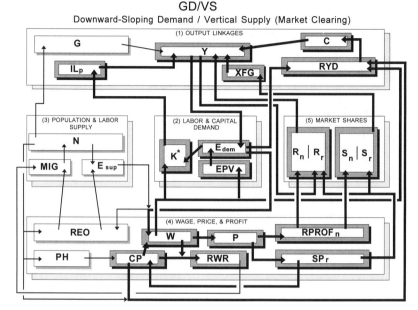

Diagram 9-4

Specifying migration as completely responsive to employment demand gives a perfectly mobile labor general equilibrium model (shown in diagram 9-5). Consistent with the immobile labor general equilibrium model, the relative regional "full employment" rate of employment defines equilibrium. Wage rates remain unchanged as migration completely responds to any change in labor demand producing a horizontal labor supply curve. The mobile labor horizontal labor supply (HSM) curve neutralizes the market share effects in block 5 and labor intensity responses in block 2. That is, a horizontal supply curve makes it irrelevant as to whether labor demand is perfectly inelastic or not. This produces a model similar to that shown in diagram 9-3. The primary difference is that migration serves to produce the horizontal supply curve in diagram 9-5, while diagram 9-3 implicitly invokes the assumption that unemployed resources exist in the region. Thus, population projections differ between the two models because of migration.[8] Employment projections differ because of population's effect on state and local government expenditures and the effect of migrant nonwage income on consumer expenditures.

414

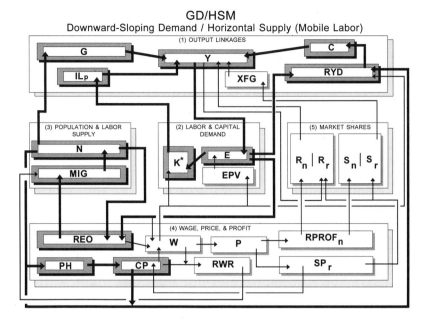

Diagram 9-5

9-3 PERFORMANCE COMPARISONS OF THE ALTERNATIVE VERSIONS
Empirical Analysis of Versions for Impact Analysis

To show the significance of the alternative specifications of labor demand and supply for impact analysis and demonstrate the channels of influence of the different closures, a sample model of Minnesota is constructed. First, a forecast is run with each version of the model for five years.[9] These are the control forecasts. Then, each version is used to generate an alternative forecast by adding ten thousand export-related jobs in miscellaneous manufacturing. These are the simulation forecasts. The differences between the control and simulation forecasts give the estimated total impacts of the increase in exports on Minnesota, as estimated by each version.[10] Multipliers each year are calculated from the direct and total impacts in the versions and averaged over the five years. Comparisons of the average multipliers for each version show the significance of the labor market closures for impact analysis.

In the standard REMI model (GD/GS), the increase in exports initially stimulates intermediate demand in the input-output component in block 1. At existing wage rates, the labor demand curve shifts outward (movement to block 2). Tightening of the labor market causes wages to increase in block 4. The migration response to the increase in wage rates and the employment rate mitigates the wage increase from what would have been expected if the supply curve had been vertical. Higher wages increase the cost of production, reducing competitiveness of local industries. This reduces exports and increases imports (movement backward along the demand curve) from what would have been expected if the supply curve had been horizontal.

The final multiplier effect includes the endogenous responses of government demand to the migration response, investment demand due to additional residential and nonresidential capital demands, and consumption demand due to increases in real income.[11] The net five-year average multiplier effects, shown in table 9-2, are 1.58 and 1.40 for employment and output, respectively.

TABLE 9-2

Average Multipliers

	Model	Employment Multiplier	Output Multiplier
1.	GD/GS (REMI)	1.58	1.40
2.	VD/GS (REMI Migration Only)	2.04	1.75
3.	VD/HSI (Input-Output)	1.82	1.61
4.	GD/VS (Market Clearing Wage)	0.00	0.12
5.	GD/HSM (Mobile Labor)	1.97	1.67

GD/GS denotes downward demand/upward supply (REMI)
VD/GS denotes vertical demand/upward supply (REMI migration only)
VD/HSI denotes vertical demand/horizontal supply (input-output)
GD/VS denotes downward demand/vertical supply (market clearing wage)
GD/HSM denotes downward demand/horizontal supply (mobile labor)

In the vertical labor demand general REMI supply (VD/GS) version, elimination of the negative effect of increased wages on other exports and on import-competing production causes the average output multiplier to increase to 1.75. The average employment multiplier increases more, proportionately, to 2.04 because of the suppression of the labor intensity response. Other induced demand produces a multiplier effect, as in the standard REMI model.

The respective output and employment multipliers for the input-output version

(VD/HSI) are 1.61 and 1.82. The suppression of migration eliminates the induced government spending and some induced consumption because of the loss of nonwage income associated with migration, causing the multipliers to be smaller than those produced by the VD/GS version. However, with the elastic supply, no loss of exports or production for import-competing demand occurs. This offsets the loss of induced demand effects to produce multipliers larger than those in the REMI version (GD/GS).

By definition, the employment multiplier for the market-clearing general equilibrium model (GD/VS) is zero. Flexible wage rates clear the labor market. In other words, after the initial outward shift in labor demand, wage rates increase, moving the economy backward along the new demand curve until the point of intersection with the vertical supply curve. Other export and import-competing employment are crowded out. Because of the substitution out of labor into other primary factors, the output multiplier equals 0.12, not zero.[12]

The respective output and employment multipliers for the perfectly mobile labor version (GD/HSM) are 1.67 and 1.97. They are larger than the multipliers produced by the input-output version (VD/HSI) with immobile labor and assumed unemployment. This occurs, because migration completely responds to the increase in employment in (GD/HSM) inducing additional government spending (because of the increased tax base) and consumption (through migrant nonwage income). However, the predicted change in population would differ dramatically from that of the input-output model (VD/HSI).[13] Though close, the multipliers are smaller than those from the VD/GS version, because wage rates are unresponsive lessening the increase in consumption.[14]

Comparison of Forecasts Across Versions

The REMI modeling system is used to run forecasts for the fifty states plus Washington, D.C., with each version of the model. The last year that historical data is available usually defines the last year of history and, subsequently, the first year of the forecast. However, to test the forecast accuracy of the model versions, 1980 is defined as the last year of history, and forecasts are run from 1981 to 1988. Known values for U.S. variables drive the state models during the forecast period. Exogenous state variables, which include state tax rates and fuel costs, equal their 1980 values throughout the forecast. Parameters of the model derived from national studies or national data are also known. Parameters calibrated to the region are based on historical data earlier than, or in, 1980. Therefore, post-sample forecasts are obtained for 1981 to 1988.

Table 9-2 presents Mean Absolute Percent Errors (MAPEs) averaged over all fifty-one regions for forecasts of total employment, population, and nominal wage rates for the first year of the forecast and the last year of the forecast.[15] The MAPE for the last year of the forecast represents the cumulative error over the entire forecast. Below each MAPE is the standard deviation of the absolute percent errors (APEs) across the states. The table also includes F-tests for the equality of the MAPE's assuming homogeneous variances, Levene's tests (Levene, 1960) for equality of variances, and Welch tests (Welch, 1947) for equality of the MAPE's allowing for heterogeneous variances if the null hypothesis of homogeneity of variances is rejected.[16]

TABLE 9-3

Post-Sample Forecast Accuracy Comparisons

	Model	Employment (MAPEs) (1981)	(1988)	Population (MAPEs) (1981)	(1988)	Wage Rates (MAPEs) (1981)	(1988)
1.	GD/GS	1.58 (.012)	4.99 (.033)	0.40 (.004)	3.65 (.030)	0.86 (.009)	6.69 (.058)
2.	VD/GS	1.40 (.011)	5.49 (.039)	0.39 (.004)	3.55 (.031)	0.82 (.009)	7.12 (.058)
3.	VD/HSI	1.44 (.012)	5.85 (.043)	0.57 (.006)	4.75 (.037)	0.82 (.009)	7.34 (.066)
4.	GD/VS	1.45 (.012)	7.63 (.065)	0.57 (.006)	4.75 (.037)	3.07 (.027)	7.33 (.060)
5.	GD/HSM	1.75 (.013)	5.55 (.041)	1.05 (.008)	6.02 (.042)	0.74 (.008)	7.81 (.072)
	Eq. of Means (F-test)	0.71	2.53[b]	11.57[a]	4.07[a]	26.09[a]	0.20
	Eq. of Var. (Lev. Test)	0.96	4.54[a]	7.27[a]	1.80[d]	23.91[a]	0.40
	Eq. of Means (Welch Test)		1.69[d]	8.07[a]	3.81[a]	9.05[a]	

[a] Indicates significance at or below .01 based on two-tailed test.
[b] Indicates significance at or below .05 based on two-tailed test.
[c] Indicates significance at or below .10 based on two-tailed test.
[d] Indicates significance at or below .20 based on two-tailed test.

GD/GS denotes downward demand/upward supply (REMI)
VD/GS denotes vertical demand/upward supply (REMI migration only)
VD/HSI denotes vertical demand/horizontal supply (input-output)
GD/VS denotes downward demand/vertical supply (market clearing wage)
GD/HSM denotes downward demand/horizontal supply (mobile labor)

No one version uniformly produces the most accurate forecasts of all variables. For employment, the VD/GS (REMI migration equation) version produces the lowest first-year MAPE, and the GD/GS (REMI) model produces the lowest MAPE in the last year of the forecast. However, for the first-year MAPE, the null hypothesis that the means are equal cannot be rejected. The F-test rejects the equality of the MAPE's for the last year of the forecast. The equality of variances is also rejected. This leads to the Welch test, which also rejects the equality of means, but at a less significant level.

For population, the VD/GS version gives the lowest first- and last-year MAPEs, with the GD/GS producing nearly identical results. Based on F-tests, the equality of the means can be rejected for both 1981 and 1988. The equality of the variances is also rejected for the 1981 and 1988 APEs. However, the equality of means is still rejected, allowing for heterogeneous variances.

For forecasts of wage rates, the GD/HSM (mobile labor) version gives the smallest MAPE for the first year, and the GD/GS version gives the smallest MAPE for the last year. The equality of the means is rejected for the first-year MAPE but not for the last-year MAPE.[17]

To discover which versions differ from the others, paired comparisons of the means are performed for first- and last-year MAPEs for employment, population, and wage rates. In other words, the F-test tells us whether significant differences exist between the versions as a group, but it does not tell us which versions are different from each other. Also, paired comparisons of the standard deviations of the percent errors are computed. The standard deviations of the percent errors, not of the MAPEs, are used, because the standard deviations of the percent errors represent the risk of forecast error. Paired comparisons for employment are shown in table 9-4. Table 9-5 contains the paired comparisons for population. Lastly, paired comparisons for wage rates are shown in table 9-6.[18]

TABLE 9-4

**Paired Accuracy Comparisons for Employment Forecasts
(Absolute Values of *t*-statistics)**

		GD/GS		VD/GS		VD/HSI		GD/VS	
		1981	1988	1981	1988	1981	1988	1981	1988
VD/GS									
	1981 (mean)	0.78							
	(var.)	0.80							
	1988 (mean)		0.70						
	(var.)		0.57						
VD/HSI									
	1981(mean)	0.57		0.20					
	(var.)	0.37		0.52					
	1988(mean)		1.14		0.45				
	(var.)		1.12		0.55				
GD/VS									
	1981(mean)	0.54		0.23		0.03			
	(var.)	0.40		0.40		0.10			
	1988(mean)		2.57[b]		2.01[b]		1.62[d]		
	(var.)		2.36[b]		1.89[c]		1.44[d]		
GD/HSM	1981(mean)	0.68		1.44[d]		1.23		1.20	
	(var.)	0.76		1.57[d]		1.08		1.16	
	1988(mean)		0.77		0.08		0.36		1.93[c]
	(var.)		0.87		0.28		0.26		1.68[c]

[a] Indicates significance at or below .01 based on two-tailed test.
[b] Indicates significance at or below .05 based on two-tailed test.
[c] Indicates significance at or below .10 based on two-tailed test.
[d] Indicates significance at or below .20 based on two-tailed test.

GD/GS denotes downward demand/upward supply (REMI)
VD/GS denotes vertical demand/upward supply (REMI migration only)
VD/HSI denotes vertical demand/horizontal supply (input-output)
GD/VS denotes downward demand/vertical supply (market clearing wage)
GD/HSM denotes downward demand/horizontal supply (mobile labor)

TABLE 9-5

**Paired Accuracy Comparisons for Population Forecasts
(Absolute Values of *t*-statistics)**

		GD/GS 1981	GD/GS 1988	VD/GS 1981	VD/GS 1988	VD/HSI 1981	VD/HSI 1988	GD/VS 1981	GD/VS 1988
VD/GS									
	1981(mean)	0.17							
	(var.)	0.20							
	1988(mean)		0.15						
	(var.)		0.26						
VD/HSI									
	1981(mean)	1.73^c		1.88^c					
	(var.)	1.91^c		2.07^b					
	1988(mean)		1.65^d		1.77^c				
	(var.)		1.38^d		1.61^d				
GD/VS									
	1981(mean)	1.73^c		1.88^c		0.00			
	(var.)	1.91^c		2.07^b		0.00			
	1988(mean)		1.65^d		1.77^c		0.00		
	(var.)		1.38^d		1.61^d		0.00		
GD/HSM									
	1981(mean)	5.18^a		5.29^a		3.54^a		3.54^a	
	(var.)	5.26^a		5.39^a		3.44^a		3.44^a	
	1988(mean)		3.29^a		3.38^a		1.63^d		1.63^d
	(var.)		3.22^a		3.44^a		1.79^c		1.79^c

[a] Indicates significance at or below .01 based on two-tailed test.
[b] Indicates significance at or below .05 based on two-tailed test.
[c] Indicates significance at or below .10 based on two-tailed test.
[d] Indicates significance at or below .20 based on two-tailed test.

GD/GS   denotes downward demand/upward supply (REMI)
VD/GS   denotes vertical demand/upward supply (REMI migration only)
VD/HSI denotes vertical demand/horizontal supply (input-output)
GD/VS   denotes downward demand/vertical supply (market clearing wage)
GD/HSM denotes downward demand/horizontal supply (mobile labor)

422

TABLE 9-6

Paired Accuracy Comparisons for Wage Rate Forecasts
(Absolute Values of *t*-statistics)

		GD/GS		VD/GS		VD/HSI		GD/VS	
		1981	1988	1981	1988	1981	1988	1981	1988
VD/GS									
	1981(mean)	0.20							
	(var.)	0.17							
	1988(mean)		0.36						
	(var.)		0.36						
VD/HSI									
	1981(mean)	0.20		0.01					
	(var.)	0.10		0.10					
	1988(mean)		0.52		0.17				
	(var.)		0.77		0.61				
GD/VS									
	1981(mean)	5.66[a]		5.74[a]		5.73[a]			
	(var.)	5.68[a]		5.74[a]		5.69[a]			
	1988(mean)		0.54		0.17		0.01		
	(var.)		0.84		0.66		0.00		
GD/HSM									
	1981(mean)	0.71		0.50		0.48		6.02[a]	
	(var.)	0.68		0.48		0.58		6.01[a]	
	1988(mean)		0.86		0.51		0.34		0.36
	(var.)		1.17		0.48		0.35		0.35

[a] Indicates significance at or below .01 based on two-tailed test.
[b] Indicates significance at or below .05 based on two-tailed test.
[c] Indicates significance at or below .10 based on two-tailed test.
[d] Indicates significance at or below .20 based on two-tailed test.

GD/GS denotes downward demand/upward supply (REMI)
VD/GS denotes vertical demand/upward supply (REMI migration only)
VD/HSI denotes vertical demand/horizontal supply (input-output)
GD/VS denotes downward demand/vertical supply (market clearing wage)
GD/HSM denotes downward demand/horizontal supply (mobile labor)

The only significant difference between any two versions in the first-year forecasts of total employment is between GD/HSM and VD/GS. As discussed next, this occurs because of the error in predicted population in GD/HSM in the first year and its effect on predicted induced expenditures. All versions have statistically smaller MAPEs of total employment for 1988 than the GD/VS version (market clearing). This suggests that in the longer run, regional economies adjust to shifts in labor demand through either changes in migration, unemployment, or participation rates.

For population, both the GD/GS (REMI) and VD/GS (REMI migration equation) versions have statistically smaller first-year and last-year MAPEs and variances than the other three versions. In addition, the versions with completely immobile labor (VD/HSI and GD/VS) are more accurate than the mobile labor version (GD/HSM). Taken together, these results suggest that migration gradually responds to employment conditions but is closer to being unresponsive than responsive, particularly in the short run.

The GD/VS version has a statistically greater MAPE and variance for the first year of forecast of wage rates than each alternative version. Thus, wage rates appear relatively constant in the short run. By 1988 though, no statistical differences in the MAPE's and variances emerge between any pair of model versions.[19] [20]

9-4 Summary and Conclusions

Regional modeling continues to evolve as existing models are modified or new models are proposed. Theoretically simple models, such as economic base and input-output models, are used extensively. Other models, such as the REMI model or computable general equilibrium models, are theoretically more complete, but are they more accurate?

Using the REMI modeling system, alternative models are formulated to examine the accuracy of competing theories of regional economies in the United States during the 1980s. The comparison aids practitioners in their choice of the appropriate model for their region. It was found that the different closures affect the values of calculated multipliers. In the simulations performed, the slopes of the labor demand and labor supply curves of the standard REMI model individually reduce predicted multipliers by twenty to thirty percent. Also, a comparison of post-sample forecasts across fifty-one regions of the United States provides insights into the relative accuracy of competing theories of regional growth.

In the short run, wage rates appear relatively constant. However, the constancy of wage rates does not appear to be caused by mobile labor. Instead, labor appears only partially mobile in the first year, and labor demand appears inelastic, though not at a statistically significant level. This suggests that in the short run, labor supply shortages or excesses are accompanied by changes in the unemployment rate or participation rates. In the long run, upward-sloped labor supply (through partially mobile labor) generally out performs the other specifications for population forecasts. Labor is mobile, but it is more immobile than mobile in the period forecasted. Labor demand may be comparatively more elastic in the long-run, but it is not at a statistically significant level.

In this chapter, we have extended the approach taken in chapter 5 to encompass the REMI model. This process of constructing alternative model versions and then testing them over a post sample period extends the forecasting results that we examined in chapters 2 and 6. The process of model validation by testing over a large number of areas in a post sample period affords an opportunity to see whether or not the theoretical and empirical basis of the model provides an explanation of reality that is superior to other competing theories and estimates. Unfortunately, the comparisons in this chapter can not be extended to those in chapters 2 and 6, since the periods over which they were tested differ.

An effort to test all competing models, over the same data set, holding the extent of exogeneity constant, would help to decide which of the models best capture the fundamental factors in the period covered. Unfortunately, since differential economic movements from one state to another may be highly correlated, even this evidence may not definitively resolve the issue of which model is better for use in the future.

NOTES ON CHAPTER 9

1. This chapter draws heavily on Dan Rickman and George Treyz, "Alternative Labor Market Closures in a Regional Forecasting and Simulation Model" in *Growth and Change*, Winter 1993, and a memo by Gang Shao and George Treyz.

2. Note that government employment is not included in the REMI multipliers.

3. This section is based on "Alternative Labor Market Closures in a Regional Forecasting and Simulation Model" by Dan S. Rickman and George I. Treyz in *Growth and Change*, Winter 1993.

4. For examples of analytical regional general equilibrium models and comparisons to the economic base model, see Merrifield (1987; 1990) and Mutti (1981).

5. Economic base and input-output models are types of regional Keynesian models because of the implied assumption of perfectly elastic supply.

6. The demand and supply curves in the model are general equilibrium, because each reflects all endogenous responses in the system of equations. Thus, an exogenous change in export demand shifts the labor demand curve by an amount that includes the indirect and induced effects. Any subsequent change in the wage rates to obtain the new intersection of demand and supply also involves endogenous induced, indirect, and competitive effects. For the remainder of the article, the general equilibrium demand curve is simply referred to as the labor demand curve.

7. Though specification of input-output models varies in practice, the common elements among the models are the vertical demand curves and horizontal supply curves. This specification implicitly assumes sufficient unemployment to meet demand rather than perfect labor mobility and is often used by practitioners.

8. The population predictions of this version equal those of an input-output model that specifies migration responses that maintain a constant relative employment rate.

9. The last year of history of the model is 1988, with forecasts that run from 1989 to 1993.

10. The choice of region and industry is not critical for the comparison of the relative responses of employment and population across the versions. The same qualitative differences have been observed in other REMI models.

11. At existing tax rates, tax collections increase as real income increases (the tax base), financing the increase in government spending. If tax rates equaled zero, the induced consumption effects would be greater and there would not be an induced government spending effect. However, because of a balanced budget multiplier effect in the model, the existence of induced taxes and government spending increases net induced expenditures. The negative effects of income taxes occur through migration if tax rates are increased because potential migrants respond to real after-tax wage rates.

12. Though a Cobb-Douglas production function gives the substitution between labor and other primary factors, the substitution occurs at .0625 per year, assuming an average thirteen-year lifetime of equipment, which yields limited substitution in the short run (Treyz, Rickman and Shao, 1992, p. 231).

13. Again, since a horizontal supply curve makes the slope of the demand curve irrelevant, the GD/HSM version produces multipliers and population projections that also would be obtained from an input-output model with perfectly mobile labor and induced state and local government expenditures.

14. The labor demand curve in VD/GS is vertical with respect to the market shares and labor intensity suppression, but it is slightly upward sloping because of the induced effect of real wages on consumption, which produces slightly larger multipliers than in GD/HSM.

15. The calculation is as follows:

$$MAPE = \sum_{i=1}^{51} |A_i - P_i|/A_i \ x \ (100/51)$$

where A_i denotes the actual value and P_i denotes the predicted value. See chapter 2 for more details.

16. Since we are testing differences of MAPEs, the variances of the APEs are used to perform the F-tests, not the variances of the percent errors. The Levene and Welch tests are calculated using the BMDP analysis of variance procedure (BMDP Statistical Software, Inc., 1990).

17. The nonparametric Kruskal-Wallis test confirms all the parametric hypothesis tests of differences in means for first- and last-year forecasts of employment, population,

17. The nonparametric Kruskal-Wallis test confirms all the parametric hypothesis tests of differences in means for first- and last-year forecasts of employment, population, and wage rates. Thus, the hypothesis tests are robust with respect to the assumption of normality and the remaining tests performed are parametric.

18. The signs of the t-statistics for the MAPEs can be inferred from the relative values of the MAPEs in table 2. Also, the signs of the t-statistics for the variances all happen to correspond to the signs of the t-statistics for the MAPEs.

19. The similarity in t-statistics of the differences in MAPEs with those of the variances suggests that the differences in MAPEs are due to differences in the variances of the percent errors, not differences in the means of the percent differences. This is confirmed by the bias proportions of Theil's U-statistics. The bias proportion is near zero in most cases and never exceeds fifteen percent. The results are available from the author upon request.

20. A two-way analysis of variance of APEs by model by major Census Bureau region is run to explore possible regional differences in relative model performance. Only two interactions of model with region have any statistical significance based on F-tests: 1988 population forecasts ($p = .053$) and 1988 wage rate forecasts ($p = .078$). The immobile labor version gives comparatively more accurate population forecasts for states in the Northeast, and the perfectly mobile labor version gives comparatively more accurate population forecasts for states in the West. During the 1980s the Northeast experienced dramatic increases in housing prices (not predicted by the REMI model) that inhibited in-migration and induced greater labor force participation rates to satisfy the employment growth. For 1988 wage rate forecasts, the market-clearing version is comparatively more accurate for the Northeast, reinforcing the argument above that wage rates rose increasing labor force participation instead of in-migration.

PART III:

APPLICATIONS AND SUMMARY

CHAPTER 10

POLICY ANALYSIS APPLICATIONS OF
FORECASTING AND SIMULATION MODELS[1]

Regional forecasting and policy analysis models are used to forecast the economic effects of a wide range of policy initiatives. The usefulness and accuracy of the predictions by these models depends as much on the inputs to the models and the interpretation of the results as it does on the models themselves. In this chapter, we present a sample of studies that have been done with models that use the structure set forth in chapter 7, as implemented by REMI.

The major uses of the regional models can be divided into the following categories:

1. forecasting and planning
2. economic development
3. transportation
4. energy and natural resources
5. taxation, budget, welfare
6. United States policies
7. environmental policies

We consider each category in turn.

10-1 FORECASTING AND PLANNING

Economic forecasting is difficult for several reasons. The exogenous variables must be forecast, the dynamic structure of the real economy must be captured in the model, and the effects of processes such as speculative episodes that are not included in the model must be foreseen. In addition to these difficulties, the forecaster must ascertain the current values of the variables in the model.

Given the difficulties of economic forecasting, it may be useful to think of a model as an instrument that can correctly capture many of the complex interactions in an economy, but may not include some of the aspects of the economy that might be foreseen by expert observers. In this instance, the model serves as an organizing instrument. It provides a structure within which various experts can bring their knowledge together to generate a coherent and consistent picture of the most likely future, as well as alternative possible futures. In this section, we discuss the various steps in making a forecast. We also cite articles that discuss forecasting and planning uses of the REMI model.

To make a forecast for a subnational area, we need forecasts for the exogenous variables. The largest category of such variables for the prototype and REMI models are the national variables. Of particular importance are forecasts of national and international demand by industry.

To provide the industry detail needed for these exogenous variables, as well as other key national variables, a U.S. model based on the REMI model structure has been developed (Shao and Treyz, 1993). The model was constructed using current and projected input-output tables for the United States from the Bureau of Labor Statistics (Monthly Labor Review, 1991). This forecast is based on a smooth trend of technological change, productivity change, and final demand change between the two input-output tables. Once this forecast is in place, a new final demand vector can be obtained from any vendor of United States forecasts and input into the model to replace the original final demand vector year by year. This generates a national forecast by industry that embodies current forecasts of cyclical behavior of the U.S. economy. The results of this forecast can then be used as the exogenous variable set for a regional model forecast.

Giarratani and Houston (forthcoming) show the effect of alternative national forecasts on the REMI forecasts for the Pittsburgh region of a particular BLS trend forecast and a particular cyclical forecast by Wharton Econometric Forecasting Associates (WEFA). In table 10-1, we present some of the results that they present in the first table in their article.

TABLE 10-1

**Comparison of BLS and WEFA United States Forecasts
and the REMI Pittsburgh Region Forecasts
for Selected Years**[2]

	(A) United States			(B) Pittsburgh Region		
	Percentage Differences between BLS & WEFA Forecast			Percentage Differences between BLS & WEFA Forecast		
	1987	1991	1995	1987	1991	1995
TOTAL EMPLOYMENT	-0.2	2.2	4.7	0.3	4.4	7.6
TOT PRIV NF EMPLOY	-0.3	2.2	5.0	0.3	4.7	8.1
GNP 1977 $	-0.1	2.9	5.0	0.0	4.3	8.3
PERSONAL INCOME	-0.7	7.6	14.8	0.0	9.3	17.6
DISPOSABLE INCOME	-0.7	5.8	12.1	0.0	8.1	15.9
PCE-PRICE INDEX-77	0.0	6.4	12.2	0.0	6.4	12.7
REAL DISP INCOME	-0.5	-0.3	0.2	0.0	5.6	5.3
POPULATION	0.1	0.2	0.7	0.2	0.7	0.8

From table 10-1, we can see that the differences between the alternatives for the Pittsburgh forecast are greater than the differences between the alternative U.S. forecasts on which the REMI Pittsburgh forecasts were based. This is apparently due to the fact that the Pittsburgh economy has a greater cyclical sensitivity than the national economy. For both forecasts, Pittsburgh showed somewhat slower growth than the nation. Giarratani and Houston also point out that, for both the national and local forecasts, individual industries have even greater disparities from one forecast to another.

Next, we consider the problem of calibrating the model to account for current preliminary data. Since final revised data may only appear with a one to three year lag, this means that adjustment to the model forecast must be accomplished with a mix of preliminary data and the model forecast. This is somewhat complicated by the large revisions that are sometimes made to preliminary data. Thus, in some instances, the possibility that the model forecast might be as good a predictor of the final revised data as the preliminary data should not be ruled out.

Nevertheless, adjusting the forecast over the period that is already history to take into account preliminary data is a necessary step toward making a forecast. This is usually accomplished through either additive or multiplicative adjustments to the model. For example, if preliminary data indicates that employment in the lumber industry has increased by 2% over the last year while the model has predicted that it would increase by 1%, then the output equation for lumber may be multiplied by 1.01 for the year in question and for subsequent years. In addition to changing the value in this transition period, a change in a multiplicative adjustment will influence the model's response to policy change. Another approach would be to use additive adjustments. Since the model is quite linear within a range, these additive adjustments will have very little influence on the policy responses of the model.

After preparing a forecast of national variables to use as exogenous inputs and calibrating the model to partial preliminary data, the next step is to incorporate outside-of-model information. An example of this type of information would be an exogenous reduction in output for a defense-related industry next year to reflect an anticipated plant closing based on the termination of a defense contract. Another example would be adjustments to projected housing construction based on high rental vacancy rates and an overhang of single family homes for sale.

Finally, a forecast is made. Even at this point, more adjustments might be made based on expert opinion regarding certain industries, labor market factors not captured in the model, or business climate changes based on political factors.

The underlying purpose for which a forecast is made may also be relevant to the construction of the forecast. This is because the purpose for which a forecast is made may be associated with a loss function. A loss function indicates what the loss is from forecast inaccuracies. For example, a forecast of the amount of fuel needed to fly a plane from Boston to the Azores that will determine how much fuel will be put in the tank of the plane will have a loss function which will show much more loss if the plane runs short of fuel then if it ends the flight with a little extra fuel. Thus, a forecast that is biased upward may be the optimal forecast in this case. Sometimes forecasts of tax revenues are biased downward, because the cost to a state government of coming up short is greater than the cost of coming out ahead. Ideally, however, instead of biasing the forecast, it is preferable to make an unbiased forecast that includes confidence intervals. One way to create these confidence intervals is to make an optimistic and a pessimistic forecast in addition to the unbiased forecast.

One way to generate these alternative forecasts is to use alternative national inputs as described above. Another way was suggested by Giarratani and Houston (forthcoming) mentioned above. In this article, they analyzed the relative cost variations and trends in key industries and identified a ninety-five percent confidence interval for a trend line cost forecast. By superseding the model's relative cost predictions through policy levers for costs, first using the upper bound and then the lower, they created a pessimistic and optimistic forecast for Pittsburgh. The spread for total employment between the optimistic and pessimistic forecast was 4.3 percent in the eight year of forecasts. The spread for individual industries ranged from a low of 1.8 percent for food processing to a high of 54.3 percent for instruments. When Giarratani and Houston used the uncertain range of export trends, the uncertain range for total employment in the eight years of forecast was 9.5 percent.

Point forecasts or range forecasts can be used for many purposes. Short-term quarterly forecasts are often used by state governments and business firms. A track record of a quarterly precursor to the REMI model for Massachusetts (Lanzillo et al, 1985) showed that any error that might have been inherent in the state model was more than offset by fine tuning of the forecast for Massachusetts in the presence of errors in the U.S. forecast. This observation was based on the fact that, for four out of six major variables, the Massachusetts forecasts were more accurate than the predictions for the same variables in the U.S. forecasts on which it was based.

Economic and demographic forecasts can also be extended by the use of satellite models. For example, a tax revenue model may be added. In this case, economic variables that are useful in predicting the tax base are extracted from the economic and demographic model and input into the satellite model. Income components can be used to predict the economic base for income taxes, consumption variables can be used for sales taxes, and industry output variables can be used for corporate taxes (see Treyz et al, 1980, and Treyz and Williams, 1982).

Another type of satellite model that can be developed is a household income distribution model (Treyz, et al, 1981). For such a model, variables that determine the parameters of an income distribution function, such as a displaced log-normal distribution, can be based on the economic and demographic forecast. When the annual distribution of income is predicted, it can be input into a model to predict tax collections. If family income is converted from annual to working period rates (Treyz et al, 1980) then a family income distribution model can be used as an input to a welfare case load model that will predict the number of households that will be eligible for welfare assistance.

As an alternative to models of categories of income, it is possible to use economic and demographic forecasts to update micro databases that contain thousands of individual family records. With such a micro database, it is possible to calculate income and sales taxes due by family and then to determine the incidence of taxes as well as total projected collections. Still another type of satellite model for forecasting is an electric load forecasting model (NEPLAN Load Forecasting Committee, 1991). Other satellite models could include models to predict air and water pollution and sales for various types of private firms.

We conclude this forecasting and planning section by citing the lessons that the Maine State Planning Office drew from their experience using a REMI model to develop a comprehensive long-range economic forecast to support policy making by the Governor and the Legislature (Irland, et al, 1984). A paraphrased list of the lessons they learned are as follows:

1. Do not contract out the entire forecasting process. Concentrate on those aspects of interest to manipulate the model in user defined ways and to focus model development to suit user needs.

2. Set priorities. Add only necessary submodels.

3. Write reports for interested nontechnical readers; illustrate them well.

4. Avoid making specific policy recommendations but clearly spell out the implications of the analysis.

5. Carefully state the bad news, but do not be afraid to state it accurately. Presented properly and constructively, the bad news may be the most important finding.

6. Involve a team of outside private sector people who can provide a different perspective and can ask tough questions.

10-2 ECONOMIC DEVELOPMENT

As indicated in the last section, a baseline forecast for a region may reveal certain problems that are likely to emerge. It is common to think of these problem areas as stemming from predictions of employment decline in some industries. While this is the typical case, it is also possible that an economy may be headed into a period of unsustainable growth, which will be a precursor of an unpleasant roller coaster ride, such as that experienced by the Northeast and California in the late 1980s and early 1990s. In this case, the appropriate policy in the mid eighties would have been one that deferred demand in the immediate future to a later date.

Many economic development studies involve the prediction of the effects of a new plant opening in the region. For a simple simulation, these questions can be answered by using industry output policy variables or special translator policy variables that represent the characteristics of narrowly defined industries. Two exemplary studies of plant location that went beyond the mechanical use of these policy variables were carried out by the University of Michigan and the Michigan Department of Commerce. One study was of the possibility of a Mazda assembly facility (Fulton et al, 1984) locating in Michigan. For this study, the authors undertook an extremely detailed analysis to answer two questions:

1. What are the state's relative locational advantages and disadvantages for the potential industry?

2. Given a decision to locate in Michigan, what is the impact on the state economy of the new activities generated?

To answer the first question, they looked at the historical series generated as a part of the REMI model construction for each state. They concentrated on constructing two measures, the local availability of inputs and relative production costs. To analyze the availability of local inputs, they looked at the column of purchases of inputs by the automobile industry in the input-output table. Next, they examined the regional purchase coefficients (RPC's) for those input industries to find a weighted average of input RPC's. Using this process, they found that the percentage of required inputs for Motor Vehicle Assembly supplied locally were 43.3 percent in Michigan, but were only 19.0, 13.8, and 23.1 percent for their three competitor states which were South Carolina, Nebraska, and Indiana respectively. They also noted that Michigan had a large underutilized labor pool of surplus labor with the requisite skills and that many of the suppliers were targeted to the automobile industry.

To examine relative production costs, they focused on the costs and the components of costs in the supplying industries. They found that Michigan was at a relative disadvantage in this area, with intermediate cost between 2 and 4 percent higher than in the rest of the country. They found that Michigan's disadvantage in wage cost in the automobile industry was even greater, showing that, based on an index of 100 for Michigan, the wage costs indexes for South Carolina, Nebraska, and Indiana were 49.7, 62.5, and 85.1 respectively. However, when the authors adjusted for relative productivity in the auto industry to develop a measure of unit labor costs, the resulting indexes were 72.4, 73.5, and 97.2, showing a reduced advantage for the competing states. In some of the supplying industries, Michigan even had a cost advantage when measured by the unit labor costs indexes.

The second major question above, asking about the effect of this plant locating in Michigan on the state's economy, was answered using a 466 sector Input-Output model conjoined with a 53 sector REMI model. This was done in such a way that the results from the processing sector of the input-output model for automobile assembly could be used as the initial disturbance in the REMI model (Stevens et al, 1981). To accomplish this, the employment and wage effects of a processing sector only (Type I multiplier) simulation were aggregated from the detailed I-O model to the 53 sectors in the Policy Analysis model. Then, calculations were made to find the set of inputs that would generate these same employment and wage effects in the REMI model with all of the appropriate suppressions made so that the REMI model would operate as a processing sector only I-O model (see chapter 9, case 1). These calculations could be made using equations 7-4 and 7-47 from chapter 7 and solving for the employment policy variables for each industry to be used as inputs to the EDFS model. Wage adjustments are also calculated to take account of differences in average wages at a more detailed industry level.

To supplement the intermediate input calculations made by the model, the Michigan Employment Security Commission conducted a survey of manufacturers to determine the percentage of their employment devoted to supplying the automobile assembly industry. Comparing the implicit survey predictions to the I-O model's predictions, the authors of the study decided to adjust the intermediate jobs created from the direct effect of 1000 jobs upward by 400 jobs distributed among the six industries that showed higher deliveries in the survey than assumed by the model.

The predicted economic effects from a Mazda automobile assembly plant started with predictions for the initial construction in 1985 of 1,250 employees and $35 million in personal income and increased to 12,201 employees and $682 million in personal income in 1990 after the construction had been completed, and the plant was in full operation directly employing 2,500 people. The employment multiplier for construction in different years ranged from 2.10 to 2.64 during the construction period, while the automobile assembly employment multiplier ranged in different years from 4.40 to 4.89. As an appendix to their study, the authors did a number of sensitivity tests. They found that if the direct and indirect wage effects had been suppressed, then the 1990 employment multiplier would have been 5.12 instead of the 4.67 in the standard model. They also found that if the 400 extra supplier jobs that had not been added for every 1,000 assembly jobs, then their employment multiplier would have dropped from their reported 4.4 to 3.6. Shortly after the study was presented, Mazda announced that it would locate in Michigan.

In another subsequent study of a Mitsubishi-Chrysler plant, the same authors presented information that indicated that the potential benefits to the Michigan economy from this facility would be less then the costs that would have been incurred by the state in providing location incentives for the plant. The state of Michigan subsequently withdrew from this competition. These two examples show that economic analysis, when carefully and accurately done, can make an important input into the decision making process.

In addition to providing useful information for potential firms that may locate in the local area and in providing an assessment of the implications of those decisions for the economy, models are often used to evaluate projects that require direct or indirect state funding. In assessing such proposals, it is essential to include all parts of the proposal. If funding from the local government is required, then either taxes must be increased or government spending must be reduced. Because a great deal of discretion is involved in deciding which tax to increase or what government program to cut, the need to balance the budget is *not* automatically programmed in the model. This has led Edwin Mills to conclude

> **By ignoring the need of state and local governments to raise money to finance proposed projects, the models make it appear that there are particular benefits to government projects that would not flow from similar private projects.**[3]

Therefore, it should be emphasized that it is incumbent on every user of a model to include the whole project in the model analysis. Since only one number (usually the number of jobs created) is typically reported to the public, it is *not* sufficient to simply include a caveat explaining that the economic effects of the financing costs have been excluded!

A study by Carlson et al (1991) shows how alternative assumptions that include all aspects of a project can turn a predicted net gain in jobs of 8,000 for an expanded convention center into a net job loss of over 300 jobs. Even studies that do not involve public financing, such as permitting horse racing, must take into account the negative effects, such as decreased consumer spending on other consumption, as well as the job creating aspects.[4]

An adjustment for reduced other spending was also made in a study of the effects of the Kansas City Chiefs and Royals on the state of Missouri.[5] In this case, accounting for alternative expenditures that consumers might have made reduced the net job effect of these franchises by 635 jobs. Tourist expenditures were also a part of this study, as they are for many economic development applications. These can be input via tourism translators that incorporate spending disturbances for a typical tourist day by different types of tourist, or they can be input by increasing consumption vectors for particular types of spending based on surveys of local tourist expenditures. Overall, the study showed a net job gain of 4,418 jobs and additional tax revenues of $9.2 million. It is important to note that when the economy is stimulated, it usually raises the probability of employment and the real wage. In both cases, this leads to migration into the area that then requires more government services. In this particular study, 118 new government employees were required. The expense of increased government employment and purchases must be deducted from any predicted revenue increases before any net gain to the state and local government budgets is inferred.

The range of economic development issues that can benefit from use of model analysis is wide. In addition to those mentioned above, some of the economic development issues for which studies have been done include: a proposed building moratorium in a county, installation of a superconducting supercollider, industrial targeting, reducing activity at a nuclear test site, the effect of a nuclear waste site, the effect of a university, spinoffs from a port project, alternative allocations of government start-up loans, off shore drilling, a shopping and entertainment complex, and casino gambling. Economic development issues are also included under other topics that we present in this chapter.

10-3 TRANSPORTATION

The direct effects of transportation infrastructure investments fall into various categories. The key categories are as follows: (1) construction and construction financing effects; (2) operating effects; (3) environmental effects; (4) tourism effects; (5) cost savings for businesses; and (6) cost savings (including safety improvements) for consumers and commuters.

The construction effects (1) are handled in a straightforward manner by using construction translator policy variables for the types of construction involved. The construction financing effects are addressed by changing appropriate tax rates or reducing alternative government expenditures by the appropriate amounts. The operating effects (2) are of significance for public transportation facilities. These are input into the model by increasing employment in the appropriate sector (e.g., interurban transport), reducing consumer expenditures on other types of transportation, and increasing taxes to pay subsidies. The environmental effects (3) apply mainly to substituting public transportation for private automobile transportation and are considered in the environmental section below. Tourism effects (4) are discussed in the proceeding section.

The use of a REMI model to evaluate economic development benefits for highway decision making are discussed in an article by Weisbrod and Beckwith (1992). They propose changes in real disposable income gains, plus auto user benefits, as the appropriate measure for the development benefits gained from a highway project. They then compare these benefits to the costs to derive a cost/benefit ratio. In their article, they describe how the cost reductions to business and auto users are calculated. They also present findings that show how reductions in the cost of doing business effect the regional economy.

In the remainder of this section, we focus on the way that costs savings to business (5) and benefits to automobile users (6) can be incorporated in the model analysis. The savings to automobile users is a reduction in cost (less commuting time) or increase in benefits (safer travel) that will not be reflected by price indexes. Therefore, it should be treated as an amenity gain, and the amenity term in the migration equation should be adjusted by an amount that reflects the dollar value of non-monetary gains. This will increase the net number of migrants into the area and have ramifications in the labor market and the rest of the model.

The effect of the improved roads is to reduce trucking costs. This reduction is accomplished by increasing the policy variable for productivity in the trucking industry. In addition, some productivity gains should also be introduced for industries that supply their own trucking.

Transportation improvements that lead to reduced costs will reduce sales prices for regional industries. These reductions will be appropriately transmitted through the model. However, transportation cost reductions that directly reduce sales prices are different than other price reductions. They apply equally to competing imports to the extent that they reduce costs for imports. Therefore, the competitive response in the model for regional industries that increases local market shares when there are reductions in sales prices must be offset by appropriate reductions in the market share when these decreases stem directly from reduced transportation costs. This reduction can be calculated by using the proportion of total cost due to trucking in the industry in question, the percentage cost change in trucking, and the market share elasticity response for local markets. If a primary goal of policy is to use transportation infrastructure improvements to foster economic development, then the increase in the variable of interest (e.g., employment, real disposable income, or real per capita income for current residents) per dollar of cost would be the appropriate measure for evaluating competing projects.

10-4 ENERGY AND NATURAL RESOURCES

Fuel costs are an important cost to the economy of any region even though they are often a small percentage of the total cost for most industries, because energy use is pervasive and regional fuel prices are volatile. In addition, fuel price changes often depend on the policy changes that are made.

The REMI model has been used to look at the effect of energy price changes that have related to electric rates and to natural gas rates. In most cases, the motivation has been to present evidence for or against the proposed policy on the basis of its implications for the regional economy. In one case, it was used to argue for a restraining order to prevent a price increase. It was argued that some of the people suffering a loss would be those who would indirectly lose their jobs. However, since it would be impossible to identify which specific job losses were due to the higher prices, it would not be possible to compensate these people.

A fuel price increase simulation is accomplished by increasing the appropriate fuel price variable for industrial and commercial users and by decreasing consumer purchasing power through the consumer expenditure price index, to reflect the extra amount that consumers will have to pay for electricity. To complete any simulation, the effects on the production side must also be considered. Since fuels are often imported, the effect of changing energy strategies may be to substitute local production for imports (e.g., a wood-gas process for electricity production to replace imported oil — see Himeljarb et al, 1977) or to replace local production (e.g., high-sulfur coal in Illinois for imported western coal) with an external energy supply. Thus, even when the regional employment effects of fuel price changes are in one direction, the choice of energy source may have direct effects that will change the sign of the predicted employment effects.

In nonenergy related natural resource uses (e.g., Taconite mining in Minnesota or the fishing industry in New Bedford, Massachusetts), the way in which this natural resource is utilized will have important regional economic effects. An example of the type of choice that sometimes confronts policy makers is the debate over whether or not the value of commercial fishing, which has reduced certain fish stocks so that sport fishing is in a steep decline in Sarasota, Florida, has a larger economic benefit than the potential loss of recreational fishing and its related tourism expenditures.

10-5 TAXATION, BUDGET, AND WELFARE

State governments face many fiscal decisions that have consequences for their states' economy. These decisions involve changes in tax rates, budgetary spending, and transfer payments. Here, we consider each category in turn.

There are three major categories of state taxes: business, sales, and income. Business taxes influence the implicit rental cost of capital as shown in the cost of capital equations in chapter 7. However, the relationship between the changes in the cost of capital and the change in the size and timing of business tax receipts may be unique to that particular tax provision. For example, a change in the corporate tax rate that increases the cost of capital by one percent next year may yield enough revenue to change the investment tax credit by enough to cut the cost of capital by two percent. Thus, a tax change that is revenue neutral might reduce the cost of capital in the short term and stimulate investment in the state. The complicated interactions of state and federal business tax provisions are incorporated in a policy analysis model by assuming rational decision making and using mathematical derivations (Hall and Jorgenson, 1967). To carry out tax simulations, the revenue consequences must also be estimated.

Sales taxes enter the model as an increase in consumer prices. If taxes are collected on all items sold in the state, then this does not effect the relative price of local and imported goods. It may, however, affect the price of one consumer good relative to another. To the extent that outside-of-model studies demonstrate elasticities of price response among consumer categories, the shifts among them must be input into the model as shifts among consumption final demand components. Of course, the decreased purchasing power caused by increased sales taxes reduces local purchases and, thus, local employment. Sales tax increases also deter inward migration by driving a bigger wedge between nominal personal and real disposable income. Changes in income taxes reduce purchasing power by directly reducing disposable income and, therefore, has many of the same impacts in an economy as a sales tax change.

A study of the effects of a revenue neutral shift in taxes, accomplished by increasing the manufacturing investment tax credit by 15 percentage points, which was financed by raising sales taxes with a refund for low income groups, was done for Massachusetts (Treyz, 1981). This study showed that in the twelfth year of the simulation there would be a 13,000 job gain in manufacturing and a 4,000 job loss in nonmanufacturing. Real per capita disposable income would be increased by one-quarter of one percent. A recent study of Michigan (Fulton and Grimes, 1991) showed that a cut in personal taxes offset by a decrease in the manufacturing investment tax credit would lead to a net loss of jobs. The proposed change was not implemented.

Ancillary income distribution and micro data-based models, as mentioned in the forecasting and planning section above, may be linked with a REMI model to provide more detailed tax analyses and more accurate feedbacks. For example, if an income tax with exemptions or progressive rates is in place, this model could take these factors into account in feeding back tax collection estimates to the model.

Local governments may change property taxes. These changes affect the cost of capital and directly reduce consumer purchasing power. Of course, these tax changes will be combined with changes in local government spending.

Shifts in the state budget spending priorities, in addition to those directly aimed at economic development, can have important economic consequences. In each case, any secondary effects not captured directly in the model should be entered as additional policy variables. For example, a shift from state and local spending on safety to education may have consequences for labor productivity as well as for the amenity attractiveness of a local area relative to other areas. While amenity changes are hard to measure, studies are available that have examined the relationship of public spending per pupil on student performances (Card and Kruger, 1992) and on the amenity attractiveness of reducing student-teacher ratios (Hoehn et al, 1987).

As an example of predicting the economic effects of changes in transfer payments, we consider a study of proposed changes in Massachusetts (Treyz, 1981) in Aid to Families with Dependant Children (AFDC). For this study, a proposed 17.5 percent increase in the welfare payment rate is eligible for a fifty percent federal reimbursement. Other funding is obtained from increases in state sales, income, and corporate taxes. By the twelfth year of the simulation, it shows a decrease of six thousand jobs. However, real per capita disposable income is increased by one-hundredth of one percent. This apparent anomaly is explained by the increase in federal funds coming into Massachusetts that more than offset the lost income from the reduction in employment.

Overall, policy analysis models have been used to analyze many taxation, budget and welfare questions. For each policy, care must be taken to consider factors not included, as well as those embodied in its equations.

10-6 NATIONAL POLICY CHANGES

Changes in economic policy at the national level can influence a subnational area through its effect on the national economy as a whole or through its relative and direct effects on the region or regions being analyzed. In the first case, it is always necessary to perform a national simulation as part of carrying out regional analyses. In the second case, it is only necessary to carry out the national simulation if the reverberation of the policy on the nation as a whole creates significant feedbacks for the subnational area in question.

Studies with regional and multi-regional models and the U.S. model analyzing changes in U.S. defense spending illustrate the issues described above. In a study of the impact of increasing the size of Fort Drum in upper New York state on the area in which it is located, it is not necessary to include changes in the United States and other regional economies in the analysis. This is done because the policy effect is strictly local and the feedbacks to the rest of the United States are small enough to be ignored (Menz, 1989). However, a study of the effect of the defense buildup from 1981 to 1985 on all of the states (Anderson et al, 1986) in the United States, as well as the U.S. economy, required a full multi-regional and national analysis.

The defense buildup in the early 1980s, compared to equivalent increased spending across all final demand sectors, had significant effects on the regional distribution and composition of economic activity, as well as on the total national economy. A study of these effects that included use of a multi-regional REMI model that included all of the states, as well as the United States (ibid), showed that thirty-five states had net employment losses due to the buildup compared to the alternative spending scenario.

In order to carry out any study of this kind, the conceptual framework for the national economy must be considered. The most straightforward assumption for short term analysis is that the economy will respond in a Keynesian way. In this framework, a U.S. model with fixed national regional purchase coefficients (RPCs) and export shares is appropriate. While this was the version of the model chosen for the defense buildup study, other model closures may be appropriate for other studies. For a long term study, it would be likely that the population of the United States and the national rate of labor force participation would be unaltered by most policies. This, in turn, would imply that the number of people employed is preset if we also note the economic long term tendency is to return to a natural unemployment rate. Thus, a model where wage rates and prices respond to restore the control forecast's employment would be appropriate. We consider such applications later in this section.

For the defense buildup study, an alternative had to be defined against which the buildup that actually occurred could be compared. For this alternative, it was assumed that in the absence of the buildup, monetary and fiscal policies that would have increased final demand by the same dollar amount as the military spending spread over all final demand components in the same proportion. To find this alternative, a model baseline that replicated the historical data set was generated. This was accomplished by using the historically observed multiplicative adjustments that were required to make each equation track the economy exactly. To the extent that the model is nonlinear, this adjusted baseline will appropriately reflect the influences of the error terms in the historical period on the difference between the baseline and the alternative (Treyz, 1972). To generate the alternative, the military procurement expenditures were removed from each state and within state final demand was increased according to the proportion determined for the United States as a whole. Two additional factors had to be considered. The first one was that the U.S. forecast was different, and the second was that effects on nearby states were more important in generating indirect demand for inputs than those in distant states. These problems were addressed by solving the U.S. model first to obtain changes in demand from the rest of the United States, then solving for major regions to obtain demands from the rest of the region, and finally solving for each state within the major region multi-regional models.

Another multi-regional simulation that requires attention to the assumptions made is in progress and concerns the effect of cutting automobile exports by twenty percent. In this case, two closures are being considered. In the first, the extra automobile sales from U.S. production would be treated as an exogenous increase in sales. In the second, nonautomobile imports would be increased enough to offset the drop in auto exports. The rationale behind the second closure would be that exchange rates would adjust to maintain imports, because, at the macroeconomic level, a negative trade balance is due to a domestic savings rate that is not adequate to support domestic investment (see chapter 2).

In looking at transportation, educational, or environmental policies at a national level, the national effects must be analyzed in addition to the regional effects. If this is done, the simple summation of the regional effects may be subject to a fallacy of composition, because some of the regional gains may be at the expense of other regions. Programs that raise overall national productivity may influence the total potential of the nation to produce. This may also be the result if production is moved from parts of the country with low productivity to those with high productivity. This result, along with the national implications of wage increases in one region as opposed to another when one region is a price leader, is set forth in a multi-regional model of France (Courbis, 1980).

An ultimate objective of regional and international modelers must be to provide better information so that national and international policies can take into account the mitigation of regional and national economic distress. As mentioned above, the United States has completed a decade when U.S. regional disparities in unemployment have shifted around the country and have been very significant. This history is likely to make the issue of regional policy at a national level an increasing priority for federal policy makers.

10-7 ENVIRONMENTAL POLICIES

A growing concern about the environment has lead to national and local legislation that is directed toward the reduction of all types of pollution. New rules,

448

regulations, and marketable permit plans designed to improve the environment have important regional socio-economic effects. The operational model presented in this book has been used extensively to predict these effects.

In a paper summarizing a socio-economic assessment of the 1991 Air Quality Management Plan (AQMP) for the Los Angeles basin, Lieu and Treyz (forthcoming) divide the types of direct effects of the plan into the following three categories of policy variables: (1) costs — changes in the cost of doing business; (2) spending — changes in the composition of spending; and (3) amenities — benefits to individuals. Each of these aspects of the implementation of the AQMP are analyzed separately using a multi-area model of the basin and then a simulation, including the net effect of all three aspects, is presented.

Cost increases by industry were applied based on engineering and equipment cost estimates, net of savings from operating more efficient equipment, and using recycled materials. These cost increases reduced profitability for industries that sell mainly in the national markets and, therefore, cannot change their prices. In this category of industries, the largest profit reductions were one-percentage point on sales in the leather and furniture industries. For the other industries that sell mainly in regional markets and can change their prices, the increase in selling prices for eating and drinking establishments was four percent. The average increase over all regional industries was six-tenths of one percent. The net effect of the cost increases was to reduce employment and real disposable income, as shown on diagrams 10-1 and 10-2.

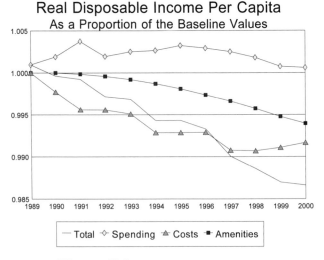

Diagram 10-1

Changes in the composition of spending affected employment both positively and negatively. Construction of new public transportation facilities, funded by borrowing, increased employment demand. The operation of the new transportation facilities also increased employment, because, even when considering the reduction in spending caused by raising the revenues for this transportation, the net effect was to substitute local employment for general consumption, such as a car purchase, which includes a high-import component. However, reducing health care expenditures (a local industry) and increasing general consumption had a negative employment effect. In the end, the positive employment effects of construction and public transportation dominated in the period considered, as shown on diagrams 10-1 and 10-2.

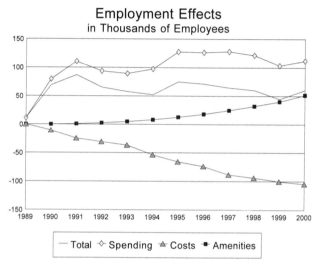

Employment Effects
in Thousands of Employees

Diagram 10-2

The employment gains in amenity attractiveness were estimated based on out-of-pocket individual savings on medical care, mortality reduction benefits based on 3.7 million dollars per life saved, and visibility benefits estimated using a hedonic approach and housing prices. The effect of the increased amenities was to increase population, which reduced wage rates and increased transfer payments. The net effect was to increase employment but to decrease real per capita income, as shown on diagrams 10-1 and 10-2. The net total effect of the policies was to increase employment but to reduce measured real disposable income. This latter measure excludes the nonmonetary amenity gains to individuals.

A current air pollution control strategy is being studied using the same model to evaluate a proposal to issue marketable permits to polluters. These permits would be traded and would be reduced each year. The lease value of the permits becomes an opportunity cost to the firms holding them as assets. The permit approach compared to command and control should reduce the net cost of pollution control as the market finds the least cost way to cut pollution. However, the regional effects on employment of this program have not yet been subject to an analysis that uses the model in an appropriate way.

Uses of the operational type models described here are planned for all areas in the United States by the Environmental Protection Agency. In these applications, the U.S. model will have to be run with average effects before each of the regional models is run. Models have been used to look at the effect of adopting the California gas standards in the Northeast on the economies of each of the Northeastern states. Other applications in the environmental area have included analysis of the economic effects of a nuclear waste dump in Nevada, the effect of industrial water rationing in Atlanta on downstream economies, and the options for solid waste disposal in Minnesota (McCarron). In general, any environmental policy that will effect the economy can be simulated. In most cases, the categories of variables used in analyzing the Los Angeles basin air quality improvement initiatives will be those used in other environmental studies.

10-8 CONCLUSION

In this chapter, we have considered various applications of a forecast and policy analysis model. The number of applications is constantly expanding. In most cases, the direct effect of any proposal can be translated into policy variables. In the case where there are direct effects for which no current policy variable exists, new policy variables can be added to the model. In some cases, this may be accomplished by adding the policy variables to an existing equation. In other cases, a preprocessing module or an extension of the model may be required to test the policy question at hand. However, the most frequent requirement will be to carry out a study or research that will enable the user to give appropriate values to the policy variables already coded in the model.

NOTES ON CHAPTER 10

1. This chapter is from G. I. Treyz, "Policy Analysis Applications of REMI Economic Forecasting and Simulation Models," *International Journal of Public Administration* (forthcoming).

2. Abstracted from Giarratani, Frank and David B. Houston. (forthcoming).

3. Mills, Edwin S. "Economics in the Service of Ideology," Northwestern University, January 1992, unpublished paper, pp. 13.

4. See Allmon, Carolyn I. (1987).

5. "The Economic Impact of the Kansas City Chiefs & Kansas City Royals on the State of Missouri," February 1989 (34 pages). Mid-American Regional Council and Mayor Hoffman McCann.

CHAPTER 11

A REGIONAL AND MULTI-REGIONAL
MODELING STRATEGY

The regional modeling strategy chosen can be critical to the rate of progress in the development and application of regional (and multi-regional) models. While specific issues that should be considered as part of a strategy, such as specification (Klein, 1969), the concept of accuracy (Jensen, 1980), various model structures (Bolton, 1985), and the role of econometrics (Leamer, 1983) have been discussed, little has been written about an overall strategy for advancing the science and application of regional modeling.

Regional model building is directed toward the practical purpose of developing an instrument to improve the quality of decision making in the public and private sectors. An explicit strategy directed toward that end that includes a commitment to the scientific method, as well as a maintained paradigm, may be more fruitful than other strategies. We present four components of a comprehensive strategy in the next section. In the following four sections, we discuss each component in turn.

11-1 THE FOUR COMPONENTS OF THE STRATEGY

The components of the suggested strategy are as follows:

1) Adopt a modeling structure at a behavioral level where universally consistent and persistent relationships can be identified and estimated

2) Establish a framework and procedure for cumulative research and model building progress

3) Define a paradigm that is general enough to allow development, but specific enough to focus research and

4) Find an institutional structure that ensures necessary interactions between model builders and users.

These four components form an integrated approach and raise institutional, as well as academic, issues.

11-2 STRUCTURAL MODELING AND ESTIMATION OF UNIVERSAL COEFFICIENTS FROM POOLED DATA SETS

In the physical sciences, the key to discovering useful relationships and laws is to find a level of explanation where causal relationships are stable and universal within a given tolerance. To use a physical example to illustrate this principle in a regional context, we might estimate a relationship between air pressure and the boiling point of water, based on cross section regional data. This relationship could then be used to predict the boiling point of water for any town in Colorado or in South Carolina. If instead we regress boiling points on miles from the coast for each city or town in Massachusetts (based on the idea that altitude is related to distance from the sea in Massachusetts, and that air pressure is related to altitude) we might obtain a workable equation for Massachusetts. This equation, however, would have to be reestimated and possibly respecified for South Carolina and would not work at all for Colorado. This example illustrates the advantage of specifying model equations at a level where the estimated causal relationships hold universally.

Models that postulate a structure at a level where coefficients change in unsystematic ways over space (and perhaps over time) may fit sample periods well, but they will not lead to the discovery of the key structural relationships necessary for scientific explanations of regional economies. This may be the case more often than we realize, because traditional tests for statistical significance are likely to produce misleading inferences when equations are estimated using short regional time series and procedures that search over a range of specifications (see Granger, 1980 for a discussion of problems with nonstationary series). However, structural estimation can offset regional data limitations in part by expanding the data set to include the universe of regions.

Reliable coefficient estimates are vital for a simultaneous model, because the entire system's performance can be altered by a single coefficient. It is important to go beyond time series data to obtain information about structural parameters from sources such as interindustry data and micro data sets. As a final model test, extensive "forecasts" over historical data for many regions, using the entire model structure, can provide a valuable validity test for the model.

11-3 A FRAMEWORK FOR CUMULATIVE PROGRESS

Any regional or multi-regional economic-demographic model has many parts, and they must all work together (see: Isard and Anselin, 1982; Bolton, 1985; and Cassing and Giarratani, 1986, for examples of other model structures). Any comprehensive regional model is complex, and building it represents a complicated data processing and programming task. This requires computational, as well as theoretical, integration. The strategy suggested here calls for starting with a core model and then developing and extending it within a basic paradigm.

11-4 A REGIONAL MODELING PARADIGM

Setting forth a paradigm in which model building will take place is at once restrictive and liberating (see Kuhn, 1962, for a discussion of the role of paradigms). It is restrictive because a basic structure is in place that defines the focus and limits of the research and development agenda until such time that a new paradigm is proposed. It is liberating because attention can be focused on one part of the agenda at a time and maintained hypotheses are in place which are continually tested.

The importance of having a defined paradigm should not be underestimated. As Leamer (1983) has pointed out, research findings are often influenced by the context in which the investigation takes place. Thus, it is unlikely that the researcher who seeks to estimate the effect of changes in relative regional profitability on industrial location will find that location is determined by the amenity preferences of company presidents.

We use the word paradigm to indicate a set of theoretical hypotheses that are internally consistent and together provide a basis for defining a structure for a model that is closed with respect to the endogenous variables in the model. An example of such a paradigm would be a regional or multiregional input-output model. Other suggested paradigms in addition to the paradigm presented in this book are numerous. For a proposed general paradigm and a review of models that have been implemented, see Bolton (1985). The most extensive framework was proposed by Isard and Anselin (1982), implemented in part for Australia (Smith, 1986) and further discussed in Isard, 1986.

We suggest that a rigorous internally consistent paradigm may best serve the development of regional and multiregional models for policy application. Such a paradigm can help to define the research agenda and provide a premise about the way that behavior will be explained. It should be sufficiently broad so that new parts of the model can be added to replace areas where simplifying assumptions have been made. The paradigm, as well as the particular equations in the model, must also be formulated with an eye to data availability. Part of the contribution of theoretical development will be to make good use of the data that exists.

11-5 BUILDER/USER INTERACTIONS

Regional models are tools to use as an aid in decision-making. They must be designed to answer relevant questions. A modeler should interact and work with users of regional models in order to focus on the reasons for building the models and the need to explain the logic behind the implications of the theory and estimations embodied in the model.

However, even though the builder/user link is important, it must be kept in its proper perspective. A modeler's first commitment must be to using the scientific method and to building accurate models. Publication and peer review of research and development work are essential for maintaining the quality of the model being built and for the scientific advancement of the field.

11-6 CONCLUSION

The field of regional economic models is in its infancy. Faster computers and new developments in economics, regional science, and econometrics will certainly open up new modeling approaches in old and new basic paradigms. The models presented in this book give an indication of how simple models have evolved into credible models that are widely used for dynamic policy analysis. Surely, these models will, in turn, be replaced by models that advance the field of regional economic model building and use even further. We hope that this book will promote the wider use and development of regional models and thereby increase the proportion of policies that are based on research findings.

GLOSSARY

Symbol	Key Occurrences	Explanation
ε	page 109	elasticity of housing price changes to changes in population density
α	page 98	adjustment speed of investment response to a gap between K^* and K in the prototype model
α_j	page 300	an adjustment coefficient for capital stock type j estimated over all states
β_1, β_2	page 105	migration response to relative employment opportunity (REO) and relative wage rate (RWR) in the migration equation for the prototype model
γ_1, γ_2	page 323	diversity of industry response of regional purchase coefficient to relative GRP for regional industries
$\gamma_3 = \xi$	page 323	own price elasticity of market share for regional industries
δ	page 325	the replacement rate (i.e., the proportionate rate of decline in rental rate of capital)
$\delta_1,\ldots,\delta_9$	page 307	coefficients on RWR, REO, and RWM in migration equation
λ_1, λ_2	page 114	employment and relative employment opportunity coefficients in the change in the wage rate due to changes in demand equation in the prototype model
λ_{DIR}	page 297	a coefficient to adjust for regional differences in DIR per property income unit
λ_{EGi}	page 304	a coefficient to reflect regional difference in the share of federal civilian ($i = 1$) and military ($i = 2$) employment
$\lambda_{R,i}$	page 320, 321	a coefficient calibrated to the regional purchase coefficient for regional industries estimated with the latest available year of CBP data

$\lambda_{S,i}$	page 320, 321	a coefficient calibrated to the local share of extraregional output for national industries for the latest available year of CBP data
λ_{TAXES}	page 299	a coefficient to adjust for regional differences in tax rates
λ_{TCP}	page 313	a coefficient that reflects the corporate profit tax rate from the last year of history
λ_V	page 298	a coefficient to adjust for local differences in transfer payments per transfer unit
λ_{VSS}	page 297	a coefficient to adjust for regional differences in VSS per employee
$\lambda_{WD1} - \lambda_{WD3}$	page 318	response parameters in the change in wage due to demand equations
μ	page 118	economic diversity response for the prototype model (set at zero in the default model)
$\xi = \xi$	page 118	own price elasticity of market share for regional industries
π_i	page 315	the profit rate per dollar of output for industry i
τ	page 112, 317	elasticity of wage response to changes in consumer prices
τ_f	page 326	federal profits tax rate
τ_s	page 327	state profits tax rate
ψ	page 117, 321	the coefficient which gives the effects of relative profitability on the regional purchase coefficient (or regional supply proportion in the prototype model) and the regional share of extraregional trade for national industries
$\vartheta_1, \vartheta_2, \vartheta_3$	page 320	coefficients in the national industry regional purchase coefficient equation
φ_1, φ_2	page 320	coefficients in the national industry extraregional market shares equation
a	page 101	labor share of output
a'_1, a'_2	page 282	parameters on endogenous model variables in the RPC equation

460

I	page 296	the major industry sector to which the relevant minor sectors (the i's) belong
IL	page 10	residential and nonresidential construction, new equipment purchases, and inventory changes within the state
IL(1)	page 271	use of manufacturing inputs for residential and nonresidential construction, new equipment purchases, and inventory changes within the state
$IL_{p, i, j}$	page 299	type j planned investment demand ($j = 1$ for nonresidential, $j = 2$ for equipment, $j = 3$ for residential) supplied by industry i
IL_p	page 16	planned local investment (new buildings, houses, and equipment)
$IL_{p, i}$	page 292	planned investment spending on the output of industry i
$IL_{p, t}$	page 161	amount of current planned investment
IL_{up}	page 16	unplanned changes in inventories, usually caused by failure to set output equal to sales
IMIX	page 320	an industrial mix index that captures the effect of differential location representation in slow and fast growing national three-digit industries on the local two-digit industry
$inv_{i, j}$	page 299	parameter that represents the proportion of type j investment demand supplied by industry i per dollar's type j investment demand
IR	page 12	investment in the rest of the country from the state (a negative value indicates a net flow of rest of country investment into the state)
k	page 282	an intercept calibration term in the regional purchase coefficient equation
K	page 31	a multiplier for predicting total output or employment changes based on changes in economic base employment or net economic base, respectively
K	page 98	capital stock

LIA	page 103	a moving average of labor intensity with geometrically declining weights over time for the prototype model
LOSTINC	page 298	income arising from negative residential adjustments in other areas in the mulitarea region
LQ(i)	page 46	the location quotient for industry i in the local region
lsc	page 243	land share of consumption
M	page 12	imports
M(1)	page 271	purchases within the state of manufacturing goods produced outside of the state
MAPE	page 58	mean absolute percent error
MIG	page 105	migration
M_i^h	page 295	the value of imports of industry i in area h
MPE	page 58	mean percent error
$MULT_{TCP, i}$	page 313	multiplicative adjustments for industries whose state corporate profit tax rate differs from the statutory rate
N	page 97	population
N65	page 297	people 65 years of age and older
ncs^u	page 109	national industry share of nonhousing construction
NECM	page 307	the ratio of this period's economic migrants to last period's natural labor force
NK	page 297	people younger than 65 years of age
NK – E	page 298	people under 65 who are not working
NLF	page 307	natural labor force
NP	page 297	number of property income units in the area
NPR_i	page 308	natural participation rate for age/sex cohort i

470

rm_k	page 305	the rate of migration for the kth cohort over 65 as observed over the sample period relative to the local population in that cohort if negative and relative to the national population in that cohort if positive
RPL	page 244	relative price of land
RPOC	page 244	relative price of the composite consumer commodity
$RPROF_i$	page 315	relative profit $[(\pi_i + 1)$ from equation 7-89] for industry i
$RPROF_N$	page 117	relative profitability
RPROFA	page 117	moving average of relative profitability with geometrically declining weights
$RPROF2_i$	page 320	moving average of $RPROF_i$ with geometrically declining weights over time for industry i
RRW	page 244	relative real earnings rate
$RTDUM_k$	page 305	is equal to one if rm_k is positive and zero if rm_k is negative
RTMG	page 305	total retired migrants
RW	page 244	relative nominal wage rate
RWM	page 307	relative wage rate mix
RWR	page 105	relative real after-tax wage rate
RYD	page 94	real disposable income
s	page 76	regional share of interregional and international trade coefficient
S	page 10	local savings by individuals and local (including state) government surplus
saea	page 114	speed of adjustment for EA
salia	page 103	speed of adjustment for labor intensity
sapr	page 117	speed of adjustment for profit response
sareo	page 116	speed of adjustment for REOA

UM$_i$	page 312	combined national and local corporate profits tax rate for industry i
UPH	page 131	unexplained changes in housing prices
UW	page 131	unexplained wage changes
UW^u	page 111	the United States wage change that is not due to demand shifts
UYLP	page 66	labor and proprietors' income earned outside of the state by residents of the state
V	page 66	net transfer payments including payments to and from the social security system
VA$_i$	page 310	value-added for industry i
VD	page 411	vertical demand
VD/GS	page 415	vertical demand/upward supply (REMI migration only)
VD/HSI	page 415	vertical demand/horizontal supply (input-output)
vg	page 298	the transfer payment rate per capita of the over 65 group relative to the residual group
vk	page 298	the transfer payment rate of the under 65 not working group relative to the residual group
VM$_i$	page 313	the local corporate profits tax rate
VP	page 96	transfer payments
VSS	page 96	social security contributions (taxes)
w	page 75	parameter for earned income per employee
W	page 96	variable for the earnings rate
WD	page 111	used as first difference (Δ) for the change in the wage rate due to demand
WD$_j$	page 317	WD for occupation j
WINDX$_i$	page 319	an index that shows the effect of wage rate mix among four-digit industries within industry i (two-digit) on the wage level in i

REFERENCES

Adams, R. M., J. D. Glyre, B. A. McCarl, and S. L. Johnson. (1989). "Reassessment of the Economic Effects of Ozone on U.S. Agriculture." *Journal of the Air Pollution Control Association* 39: 960–968.

Almon, Clopper, Margaret B. Buckler, Lawrence M. Horwitz, and Thomas C. Raimbold. (1974). *1985: Interindustry Forecasts of the American Economy.* Lexington, MA: D.C. Heath.

Allmon, Carolyn I. (Fall 1987). "Horse Racing in Minnesota: What Impact on the State's Economy?" *Minnesota Tax Journal* 2(4): 68–71.

Amos, Orley M. (1991). "Divergence of Per Capita Real Gross State Product by Sector: 1963 to 1986." *Review of Regional Studies* 21: 221–234.

Anderson, Marion, Michael Frisch, and Michael Oden. (1986). "The Empty Pork Barrel: The Employment Cost of the Military Build-up 1981–1985." *Employment Research Associates*: 19 pages.

Baird, C. (1983). "A Multiregional Econometric Model of Ohio." *Journal of Regional Science* 23: 501–516.

Barbera, A. J., and V. D. McConnell. (1990). "The Impact of Environmental Regulations on Industry Productivity: Direct and Indirect Effects." *Journal of Environmental Economics and Management* 18: 50–65.

Batey, P. W. J., and A. Z. Rose. (1990). "Extended Input-Output Models: Progress and Potential." *International Regional Science Review* 13: 27–49.

Beaumont, P. M. (1990). "Supply and Demand Interaction in Integrated Econometric and Input-Output Models." *International Regional Science Review* 13: 167–181.

Beeson, Patricia, and Randall W. Eberts. (August 1989). "Identifying Productivity and Amenity Effects in Interurban Wage Differentials." *Review of Economics and Statistics* 71: 443–452.

Blair, P. D., and A. W. Wyckoff. (1989). "The Changing Structure of the U.S. Economy: An Input-Output Analysis." In *Frontiers of Input-Output Analysis*, R. E. Miller, K. R. Polenske, and A. Z. Rose, eds. New York: Oxford University Press, 294–307.

Blomquist, Glenn C., Mark C. Berger, and John P. Hoehn. (March 1988). "New Estimates of Quality of Life in Urban Areas." *American Economic Review* 78: 89–107.

BMDP Statistical Software Inc. (1990). *BMDP Statistical Software Manual: Volume 1.* Berkeley, Los Angeles, and Oxford: University of California Press.

478

Bolton, Roger. (1985). "Regional Econometric Models." *Journal of Regional Science* 25(4): 495–520.

Burress, David, Michael Eglinski, and Pat Oslund. (1988). "A Survey of Static and Dynamic State-Level Input-Output Models." Institute for Public Policy and Business Research, University of Kansas Research Discussion Paper.

Card, David, and Allan B. Kruger. (January 1992). "Does School Quality Matter? Returns to Education and the Characteristics of Public Schools in the U.S." *Journal of Political Economy* 100: 1–40.

Carlson, Virginia L., Nickolas C. Theodore, Patricia Wright, and John D. Zukosky. (June 1991). "Alternative Employment Impacts of the Proposed McCormick Place Expansion: Final Report." Presented by the School of Urban Planning and Policy Center for Urban Economic Development at the University of Illinois at Chicago.

Carter, A. P. (1970). *Structural Changes in the American Economy*. Cambridge, MA: Harvard University Press.

Cassing, S., and F. Giarratani. (1986). "A Simulation-Oriented Regional Econometric Model." *Environment and Planning A* 12: 1611–1628.

Cassing, S., and F. Giarratani. (1992). "An Evaluation of the REMI Model for the South Coast Air Quality Management District." *Environment and Planning A* 24: 1549–1564.

Chalmers, James A., and Terrance L. Beckhelm. (1976). "Shift and Share and the Theory of Industrial Location." *Regional Studies* 10: 15–23.

Coen, Robert M. (1975). "Investment Behavior, the Measurement of Depreciation, and Tax Policy." *American Economic Review* 65: 59–74.

Connaughton, John E., and Roland A. Madsen. (1990). "The Changing Regional Structure of the U.S. Economy." *Growth and Change* 21: 48–60.

Conway, Richard S., Jr. (1980). "An Econometric Model of the Hawaii Construction Industry." Hawaii Department of Planning and Economic Development.

Conway, Richard S., Jr. (1990). "The Washington Projection and Simulation Model: A Regional Interindustry Econometric Model." *International Regional Science Review* 13: 141–165.

Conway, Richard S., Jr., and Charles T. Howard. (1980). "A Forecasting Model for Regional Housing Construction." *Journal of Regional Science* 20: 1–10.

Costa, Jose de Silva, Richard W. Ellson, and Randolph C. Martin. (1987). "Public Capital, Regional Output, and Development: Some Empirical Evidence." *Journal of Regional Science* 27: 419–437.

Courbis, Raymond. (1980). "Multiregional Modeling and the Interaction Between Regional and National Development: A General Theoretical Framework." In *Modeling and the Regional Economic System*, F. Gerald Adams and Norman J. Glickman, eds. Lexington, Massachusetts: Lexington Books, 107–130.

Dervis, K., J. DeMelo, and S. Robinson. (1982). *General Equilibrium Models for Development Policy*. Cambridge: Cambridge University Press.

Dolde, W., D. Epple, M. Harris, L. Lave, and S. Leinhardt. (1977). "Dynamic Aspects of Air Quality Control Costs." *Journal of Environmental Economics and Management* 4: 313–334.

Engle, Robert F. (1974). "A Disequilibrium Model of Regional Investment." *Journal of Regional Science* 14: 367–376.

Evans, Alan W. (November 1990). "The Assumption of Equilibrium in the Analysis of Migration and Interregional Differences: A Review of Some Recent Research." *Journal of Regional Science* 30: 515–531.

Fulton, George A., and Donald R. Grimes. (October 1991). "Example Policy Experiment for Michigan." Memorandum: 1–7.

Fulton, George A., Donald R. Grimes, and Alan L. Baum. (1984). "Industrial Location Decisions and Their Impact on the Michigan Economy: The Mazda Automobile Assembly Case." Papers presented to the Economic and Social Outlook Conference at the University of Michigan at Ann Arbor, November 15 and 16, 1984.

Gallaway, Lowell E. (1969). *Geographic Labor Mobility in the United States 1957 to 1960*. Research Report No. 28, Social Security Administration, Office of Research and Statistics.

Gerking, Shelby D. (August 1976). "Input-Output as a Simple Econometric Model." *Review of Economics and Statistics* 58(3): 274–282.

Giarratani, Frank. (1974). "Air Pollution Abatement: Output and Relative Price Effects, a Regional Input-Output Simulation." *Environment and Planning A* 6: 307–312.

Giarratani, Frank, and David B. Houston. (forthcoming). "Simulating Sources of Uncertainty in Policy Forecasting with a Large Scale Regional Econometric Model." *Geographical Analysis*.

Glickman, N. (1971). "An Economic Forecasting Model for the Philadelphia Region." *Journal of Regional Science* 11: 15–32.

Gowby, J. M., and J. L. Miller. (1987). "Harrod-Robinson-Read Measures of Primary Input Productivity: Theory and Evidence from U.S. Data." *Journal of Post Keynesian Economics*: 591–604.

480

Granger, C. W. J. (1980). *Forecasting in Business and Economics*. New York: Academic Press.

Graves, Philip E., and Thomas A. Knapp. (July 1988). "Mobility Behavior of the Elderly." *Journal of Urban Economics* 24: 1–8.

Graves, P. E., and P. D. Linneman. (1979). "Household Migration: Theoretical and Empirical Results." *Journal of Urban Economics* 6: 383–404.

Greenwood, M. J. (1975). "Research on Internal Migration in the United States: A Survey." *Journal of Economic Literature* 13(2): 397–433.

Greenwood, M. J. (1985). "Human Migration: Theory, Models, and Empirical Studies." *Journal of Regional Science* 25(4): 521–544.

Greenwood, M. J., and G. L. Hunt. (1984). "Migration and Interregional Employment Distribution in the United States." *American Economic Review* 74: 957–969.

Greenwood, M. J., G. Hunt, D. S. Rickman, and G. I. Treyz. (December 1991). "Migration, Regional Equilibrium, and the Estimation of Compensating Differentials." *American Economic Review* 81(5): 1382–1390.

Griffen, J. M., and P. R. Gregory. (1976). "An Intercountry Translog Model of Energy Substitution Responses." *American Economic Review* 66: 845–857.

Haitovsky, Yoel, G. I. Treyz, and Vincent Su. (1974) *"Forecasts With Quarterly Macro-Economic Models."* Studies in Business Cycles, No.23, National Bureau of Economic Research. New York: Columbia University Press.

Hall, J. V., A. M. Winter, M. Kleinman, F.W. Lurmann, V. Bnajer, S. D. Colome, R. D. Rowe, L. G. Chestnut, D. Foliart, L. Coyner, and A. F. Horwatt. (1989). "Economic Assessment of the Health Benefits from Improvement in Air Quality in the South Coast Air Basin." California State University Fullerton Foundation; copy available from South Coast Air Quality Management District, El Monte, CA.

Hall, Robert E. (1986). "Market Structure and Macroeconomic Fluctuations." *Brookings Papers on Economic Activity* 2: 285–338.

Hall, Robert E., and Dale W. Jorgenson. (1967). "Tax Policy and Investment Behavior." *American Economic Review* 57: 391–414.

Harrigan, F., and P. G. McGregor. (1989). "Neoclassical and Keynesian Perspectives on the Regional Macroeconomy: A Computable General Equilibrium Approach." *Journal of Regional Science* 29: 555–573.

Harris, John R., and M. F. Todaro. (1970). "Migration, Unemployment, and Development: A Two-Sector Analysis." *American Economic Review* 60: 126–142.

Hausman, J. A. (November 1978). "Specification Tests in Econometrics." *Econometrica* 46: 1251–1271.

Helms, L. Jay. (1985). "The Effects of State and Local Taxes on Economic Growth: A Time Series-Cross Section Approach." *Review of Economics and Statistics* 67: 574–582.

Himeljarb, David, and Toru Otawa. (December 1977). "Wood-Gas-Facility Electricity Generation." Science Resource Office of the Massachusetts Legislation, 1–5.

Hoehn, John P., Mark C. Berger, and Glenn C. Blomquist. (1987). "A Hedonic Model of Interregional Wages, Rents, and Amenity Values." *Journal of Regional Science* 27: 605–620.

Holz-Eakin, Douglas. (1991). "Public Sector Capital and the Productivity Puzzle." Paper presented at the 104th meeting of the American Economic Association, New Orleans, LA.

Hulten, C. R., and R. M. Schwab. (1984). "Regional Productivity Growth in U.S. Manufacturing: 1951–78." *American Economic Review* 74: 152–161.

Irland, Lloyd C., Charles S. Colgan, and Charles T. Lawton. (Fall/Winter 1984). "Forecasting a State's Economy: Maine's Experience." *The Northeast Journal of Business & Economics* II(1): 7–19.

Isard, W. (1986). "Reflections on the Relevance of Integrated Multiregion Models: Lessons from Physics." *Regional Science and Urban Economics* 16: 165–180.

Isard, W., and L. Anselin. (1982). "Integration of Multiregional Models for Policy Analysis." *Environment and Planning A* 14: 359–376.

Isard, W., D. Boyce, et al. (1984). "Integration of Multiregional Models." A research proposal submitted to the National Science Foundation.

Jansen, P. K., and T. ten Raa. (1990). "The Choice of Model in the Construction of Input-Output Coefficient Matrices." *International Economic Review* 31: 213–227.

Jensen, R. C. (1980). "The Concept of Accuracy in Regional Input-Output Models." *International Regional Science Review* 5(2): 138–154.

Jones, R., and J. Whalley. (1988). "Regional Effects of Taxes in Canada, an Applied General Equilibrium Approach." *Journal of Public Economics* 37: 1–28.

Judge, George G., W. E. Griffiths, R. Carter Hill, Helmut Lutkepohl, and Tsoung-Chao Lee. (1985). *The Theory and Practice of Econometrics*, Second Edition. New York: John Wiley and Sons.

Klein, L. (1969). "The Specification of Regional Econometric Models." *Papers of the Regional Science Association* 23: 105–115.

Kort, John R. (1983). "A Multiregional Test of the Conway-Howard Construction Model." *Journal of Regional Science* 23: 413–418.

Krupnick, A. J., and P. R. Portney. (1991). "Controlling Air Pollution: A Benefit-Cost Assessment." *Science* 252: 522–528.

Kuhn, T. S. (1962). *The Structure of Scientific Revolutions.* Chicago: University of Chicago Press.

Lanzillo, J., M. Larson, G. I. Treyz, and R. Williams. (Winter 1985). "The Massachusetts Economic Policy Analysis Model Track Record: 1977–1983." *Massachusetts Business and Economic Report* 13(1): 5–6.

Leamer, E. E. (1983). "Let's Take the Con Out of Econometrics." *American Economic Review* 73(1): 31–43.

Leontief, W. (1953). *Studies in the Structure of the American Economy.* New York: Oxford University Press.

Levene, H. (1960). "Robust Tests for Equality of Variance." In *Contributions to Probability and Statistics*, I. Olkin, ed. Palo Alto: Stanford University Press.

Lieu, Sue. (1991). "Regional Impacts of Air Quality Regulation: Applying an Economic Model." *Contemporary Policy Issues* IX: 24–34.

Lieu, Sue, and George I. Treyz. (1992). "Estimating the Economic and Demographic Effects of an Air Quality Management Plan: The Case of Southern California." *Environment and Planning A* 24: 1799–1811.

Lieu, T. S. (1986). "Impacts of Air Pollution Control Costs: An Input-Output Approach." *The Annals of Regional Science* 20: 55–65.

Maddala, G. S. (1977). *Econometrics.* New York: McGraw-Hill.

Malhotra, Devinder M., and Gasper A. Garofalo. (1988). "Analysis of Regional Productivity with Capital as a Quasi-Fixed Factor." *Regional Science and Urban Economics* 18: 533–547.

Maloney, M. T., and B. Yandle. (1984). "Estimation of the Cost of Air Pollution Control Regulation." *Journal of Environmental Economics and Management* 11: 244–263.

Marschack, J. (1953). "Economic Measurements for Policy and Prediction." In *Studies in Econometric Methods*, T. C. Koopman and W. C. Hood, eds. New York: John Wiley and Sons, 1–26.

McCarron, Robert J. "Rule Making Process Relating to Incinerator Ash and Nonpoint Ground Water Contamination." Minnesota Pollution Control Agency, Memorandum.

McCombie, J. S. L. (1986). "On Some Interpretations of the Relationship Between Productivity and Output Growth." *Applied Economics* 18: 1215–1225.

Menz, Frederick C. (1989) "Regional Economic Effects — Fort Drum." Unpublished paper, Fort Drum Steering Council Presentation on June 2, 1989, 1–17.

Merrifield, J. (1987). "A Neoclassical Anatomy of the Economic Base Multiplier." *Journal of Regional Science* 27: 283–294.

Merrifield, J. (1990). "A Practical Note on the Neoclassical Economic Base Multiplier." *Journal of Regional Science* 30: 123–127.

Mid-American Regional Council and Mayor Hoffman McCann. (February 1989). "The Economic Impact of the Kansas City Chiefs & Kansas City Royals on the State of Missouri."

Miller, R. E., and P. D. Blair. (1985). *Input-Output Analysis: Foundations and Extensions*. Englewood Cliffs, NJ: Prentice-Hall.

Mills, Edwin S. (January 1992). "Economics in the Service of Ideology." Unpublished paper, Northwestern University, 1–16.

Mofidi, Alaeddin, and Joe. A. Stone. (1990). "Do State and Local Taxes Affect Economic Growth?" *Review of Economics and Statistics* 72: 686–691.

Moomaw, Ronald L. (1981). "Productivity Efficiency and Region." *Southern Economic Journal* 48: 344–357.

Moomaw, Ronald L., and Martin S. Williams. (1991). "Total Factor Productivity Growth in Manufacturing: Further Evidence from the States." *Journal of Regional Science* 31: 17–34.

Moore, Craig L., and David J. Ehrlich. (1976). "Modeling Interstate Shifts in Employment." *Northeast Regional Science Review* 7: 143–152.

Morgan, W., J. Mutti, and M. Partridge. (1989). "A Regional General Equilibrium Model of the United States: Tax Effects on Factor Movements and Regional Production." *Review of Economics and Statistics* 71: 626–635.

Muth, R. F. (1971). "Migration: Chicken or Egg?" *Southern Economic Journal* 37: 295–306.

Mutti, J. (1981). "Regional Analysis from the Standpoint of International Trade: Is It a Useful Perspective?" *International Regional Science Review* 6: 95–120.

National Association of Realtors. (1990). *Home Sales Yearbook*. Copy available from 777 14th Street, Washington, D.C.

The NEPOOL Load Forecasting Committee, NEPLAN (New England Power and Planning) Staff. (April 1991). "NEPOOL Forecast of New England Electric Energy and Peak Load: Executive Summary, 1991–2006."

484

Newman, Robert J. (1983). "Industry Migration Growth in the South." *Review of Economics and Statistics* 65: 76–86.

Newman, Robert J., and Dennis H. Sullivan. (1988). "Econometric Analysis of Business Tax Impacts on Industrial Location: What Do We Know, and How Do We Know It?" *Journal of Urban Economics* 23: 215–234.

Ochoa, E. M. (1986). "An Input-Output Study of Labor Productivity in the U.S. Economy, 1947–72." *Journal of Post Keynesian Economics* 9(1): 111–137.

Pai, G. (1969). "Environmental Pollution Control Policy: An Assessment of Regional Economic Impacts." Unpublished Ph.D. dissertation, Department of Urban Studies and Planning, Massachusetts Institute of Technology, Cambridge, MA.

Pasurka, C. A., Jr. (1984). "The Short-Run Impact of Environmental Protection Costs to U.S. Product Prices." *Journal of Environmental Economics and Management* 1: 380–390.

Pfester, R. L. (1976). "On Improving Export Base Studies." *Regional Science Perspectives* 8: 104–116.

Plaut, T. R. (Fall 1981). "An Econometric Model for Forecasting Regional Population Growth." *International Regional Science Review* 6(1): 53–70.

Plaut, T. R. (1982). "Economic Base, Labor Force Migration and Regional Employment Growth in the United States." *Papers of the Regional Science Association* 50: 75–94.

Polenske, K. R. (1980). *The U.S. Multiregional Input-Output Accounts and Model.* Lexington, MA: Lexington Books.

Polzin, P. E. (1977). "Urban Labor Markets: A Two Sector Analysis." *Growth and Change* 8: 11–15.

Portney, P. R., D. Harrison, Jr., A. J. Krupnick, and H. Dowlatabadi. (1989). "To Live and Breathe in L.A." *Issues in Science and Technology*: 68–73.

Rattso, J. (1982). "Different Macroclosures of the Original Johansen Model and Their Impact on Policy Evaluation." *Journal of Policy Modeling* 4: 85–97.

Reaume, David M. (1983). "Migration and the Dynamic Stability of Regional Economic Models." *Economic Inquiry* 21(2): 281–293.

Regional Economic Models, Inc. (REMI). (March 1992). *Model Documentation for the REMI EDFS-53 Forecasting and Simulation Model.* REMI Reference Set, Volume 1.

Renshaw, Vernon, Edward A. Trott, Jr., and Howard L. Friedenburg. (May 1988). "Gross State Product by Industry, 1963–86." *Survey of Current Business*: 30–46.

Richardson, H. W. (1969). *Regional Economics*. New York: Praeger.

Richardson, H. W. (1985). "Input-Output and Economic Base Multipliers: Looking Backwards and Forward." *Journal of Regional Science* 25: 607–661.

Rickman, D. S. (1992). "Estimating the Impacts of Regional Business Assistance Programs: Alternative Closures in a Computable General Equilibrium Model." *Papers in Regional Science* 71: 421–435.

Rickman, D. S., G. Shao, and G. I. Treyz. (1993). "Multiregional Stock Adjustment Equations of Residential and Nonresidential Investment." *Journal of Regional Science* 33(2): 207–219.

Rickman, D. S., and G. I. Treyz. (1991). "Regional Competitiveness and Relative Industrial Growth: A Structural Approach." Unpublished paper, Amherst, MA: Regional Economic Models, Inc. (REMI).

Rickman, D. S., and G. I. Treyz. (1992). "Industry Level Estimates of Location Response to State Differentials in Profitability in the United States." Unpublished paper, Amherst, MA: Regional Economics Models, Inc. (REMI).

Rickman, D. S., and G. I. Treyz. (Winter 1993). "Alternative Market Closures in a Regional Forecasting and Simulation Model." *Growth and Change* 24: 32–49.

Roback, Jennifer. (December 1982). "Wages, Rents, and the Quality of Life." *Journal of Political Economy* 90: 1257–1278.

Roback, Jennifer. (January 1988). "Wages, Rents, and Amenities: Differences Among Workers and Regions." *Economic Inquiry* 26: 23–41.

Robinson, S., and D. Roland-Holst. (1988). "Macroeconomic Structure and Computable General Equilibrium Models." *Journal of Policy Modeling* 10: 353–375.

Rose, A., and W. Miernyk. (1989). "Input-Output Analysis: The First Fifty Years." *Economic Systems Research* 1(2): 229–271.

Rosen, Sherwin. (1979). "Wage-Based Indexes of Urban Quality of Life." In *Current Issues in Urban Economics*, Peter Mieszkowski and Malcom Straszheim, eds. Baltimore: Johns Hopkins University Press, 74–104.

Rowe, R. D., and L. G. Chestnut. (1985). "Economic Assessment of the Effects of Air Pollution on Agricultural Crops in the San Joaquin Valley." *Journal of the Air Pollution Control Association* 35: 728–734.

SCAQMD. (1991a). "Final Socio-Economic Report for 1991 Air Quality Management Plan." South Coast Air Quality Management District, El Monte, CA.

SCAQMD. (1991b). "Air Quality Trends In California's South Coast and Southeast Desert Air Basins, 1976–1990." Appendix II-B to the final 1991 Air Quality Management Plan, South Coast Air Quality Management District, El Monte, CA.

SCAQMD. (1991c). "Future Ozone Air Quality Analysis." Technical report V-C of the 1991 Air Quality Management Plan, South Coast Air Quality Management District, El Monte, CA.

SCAQMD. (1991d). "Visibility Assessment for the South Coast Air Basin." Technical report V-G of the 1991 Air Quality Management Plan, South Coast Air Quality Management District, El Monte, CA.

SCAQMD. (1991e). "Exposure Modeling for the South Coast Air Basin." Technical report V-G of the 1991 Air Quality Management Plan, South Coast Air Quality Management District, El Monte, CA.

Schultz, T. Paul. (1982). "Lifetime Migration Within Educational Strata in Venezuela: Estimates of a Logistic Model." *Economic Development and Cultural Change* 30: 559–593.

Shao, Gang, and George I. Treyz. (1993). "Building U.S. National and Regional Forecasting and Simulation Models." *Economic Systems Research* 5(1): 63–77.

Shapiro, H., and G. Fulton. (1985). *A Regional Econometric Forecasting System.* Ann Arbor, MI: University of Michigan Press.

Shoven, J. B., and J. Whalley. (1984). "Applied General Equilibrium Models of Taxation and International Trade: An Introduction and Survey." *Journal of Economic Literature* 22: 1007–1051.

Sivitanidou, Rena M., and Karen R. Polenske. (Winter 1988). "Assessing Regional Economic Impacts With Microcomputers." *American Planning Association Journal*: 101–106.

Smith, C. (1986). "An Empirically Implementable Integrated Multi-Regional Model for Australia." *Regional Science and Urban Economics* 16: 181–195.

Stevens, B. H., and James R. Bower. "Shift in Value Added Minus Payroll and the forecasting of Growth for industries in Maine." *Regional Science Research Institute Discussion Paper Series*, No. 125, Peace Dale, Rhode Island.

Stevens, B. H., and G. A. Trainer. (1976). "A New Approach to the Prediction of Regional Industrial Growth and a Preliminary Test for the Boston SMSA." *Regional Science Research Institute Discussion Paper Series*, No. 87, Amherst, MA.

Stevens, B. H., and G. A. Trainer. (1980). "The Generation of Error in Regional Input-Output Analysis and its Implication for Non-Survey Models." In *Economic Impact Analysis: Methodology and Application*, Saul Pleeter, ed. MA: Martin Nijhoff, 68–84.

Stevens, B. H., G. I. Treyz, D. J. Ehrlich, and J. R. Bower. (1983). "A New Technique for the Construction of Non-Survey Regional Input-Output Models." *International Regional Science Review* 8(3): 271–286.

Stevens, B. H., G. I. Treyz, and J. K. Kindahl. (1981). "Conjoining an Input-Output Model and a Policy Analysis Model: A Case study of the Economic Effects of Expanding a Port Facility." *Environment and Planning A* 13: 1029–1038.

Szyrmer, J. (1989). "Trade-off Between Error and Information in the RAS Procedure." In *Frontiers of Input-Output Analysis*, R. E. Miller, K. R. Polenske, and A. Z. Rose, eds. New York: Oxford University Press, 258–278.

Todaro, Michael P. (1969). "A Model of Labor Migration and Urban Unemployment in Less Developed Countries." *American Economic Review* 59: 138–148.

Todaro, Michael P. (1970). "Labor Migration and Urban Unemployment: Reply." *American Economic Review* 60: 187–188.

Todaro, Michael P. (1976). "Urban Job Expansion, Induced Migration, and Rising Unemployment." *Journal of Development Economics* 3: 211–225.

Topel, Robert H. (1986). "Local Labor Markets." *Journal of Political Economy* 94: S111–S143.

TRCEC. (1985). "Assessment of Material Damage and Soiling from Air Pollution in the South Coast Air Basin." TRC Consultants Inc.: copy available from California Air Resources Board, PO Box 2815, Sacramento, CA 95812.

Treyz, G. I. (June 1972). "An Econometric Procedure of Ex Post Policy Evaluation." *International Economic Review* 13: 212–222.

Treyz, G. I. (1980). "Design of a Multi-Regional Policy Analysis Model." *Journal of Regional Science* 20(2): 191–206.

Treyz, G. I. (1981). "Predicting the Economic Effect of State Policy Initiatives." *Growth and Change* 12(2): 2–9.

Treyz, G. I. (November 1986). "The Fundamentals of Regional Macroeconomic Modeling: Part I." *Survey of Regional Economic Literature*. Pilot Issue: 11–34.

Treyz, G. I. (June 1987). "Fundamentals of Regional Macroeconomic Modeling: Part II." *The Survey of Regional Economic Literature* 2: 1–28.

Treyz, G. I. (1991). "Causes of Changes in Wage Variation Among States." *Journal of Urban Economics* 29: 50–62.

Treyz, G. I. (forthcoming). "Policy Simulation Modeling." In *Microcomputer Based Input-Output Modeling: Applications to Economic Development*, Daniel M. Otto and Thomas G. Johnson, eds. Boulder, CO: Westview Press.

Treyz, G. I. (forthcoming). "Policy Analysis Applications of REMI Economic Forecasting and Simulation Models." *International Journal of Public Administration.*

Treyz, G. I., G. E. DuGuay, C. L. Chen, and R. E. Williams. (1981). "A Family Income Distribution Model for Regional (Massachusetts) Policy Analysis." *Journal of Policy Modeling* 3(2):   77–92.

Treyz, G. I., G. E. DuGuay, R. Williams, and C. L. Chen. (December 1980). "The Distribution of Earned Family Income at Working Period Rates as Derived from CPS Micro Data." *Review of Public Data Use* 8(4): 355–359.

Treyz, G. I., A. F. Friedlaender, E. M. McNertney, B. H. Stevens, and R. E. Williams. (1977). "The Massachusetts Economic Policy Analysis (MEPA) Model." Massachusetts Economic Policy Analysis Project, Economics Department, University of Massachusetts, Amherst, MA.

Treyz, G. I., A. F. Friedlaender, and B. H. Stevens. (February 1980). "The Employment Sector of a Regional Economic Policy Simulation Model." *Review of Economics and Statistics* 62: 63–73.

Treyz, G. I., M. J. Greenwood, G. L. Hunt, and B. H. Stevens. (1988). "A Multi-Regional Economic-Demographic Model for Regions in the United States." In *Recent Advances in Regional Economic Modelling*, F. Harrigan and P. G. McGregor, eds. London: London Papers in Regional Science #19, Pion Limited, 55–82.

Treyz, G. I., D. S. Rickman, G. L. Hunt, and M. J. Greenwood. (forthcoming). "The Dynamics of U.S. Internal Migration." *The Review of Economics and Statistics.*

Treyz, G. I., D. S. Rickman, and G. Shao. (1992). "The REMI Economic-Demographic Forecasting and Simulation Model." *International Regional Science Review* 14(3): 221–253.

Treyz, G. I., and B. H. Stevens. (1980). "Location Analysis for Multiregional Modeling." In *Modeling the Multiregional Economic System*, F. G. Adams and N.J. Glickman, eds. Lexington, Massachusetts: D.C. Heath Lexington Books, 75-87.

Treyz, G. I., and B. H. Stevens. (1983). "The Derivation of the REMI Cost of Capital Equation." Unpublished paper, Amherst, MA: Regional Economic Models, Inc.

Treyz, G. I., and B. H. Stevens. (1985). "The TFS Regional Modeling Methodology." *Regional Studies* 19(6): 547–562.

Treyz, G. I., B. H. Stevens, and D. J. Ehrlich. (1979). "An Eclectic Core Model for State Policy Analysis and Forecasting." Handbook Two of *Regional Economic Analysis for Transportation Planning.* Prepared for the National Cooperative Highway Research Program, National Academy of Science.

Treyz, G. I., B. H. Stevens, and D. J. Ehrlich. (1981). *A State Core Forecasting and Policy Simulation Model, Projects 8-15A.* National Cooperative Highway Research Program, National Academy of Science.

Treyz, G. I., and R. E. Williams. (1982). "Efficient Information Use and State-Tax Revenue Analysis and Forecasting." Revenue Estimating Procedure, NATA Conference of Revenue Estimating. Published by the Federation of Tax Administrators, Washington, D.C.

Treyz, G. I., R. E. Williams, and T. Gormley. (1980). "The Massachusetts Revenue Analysis and Forecasting (MRAF) Model." MEPA Project, Economics Department, University of Massachusetts, Amherst, MA. Mimeographed.

Trijonis, J., M. Thayer, J. Murdoch, and R. Hageman. (1985). "Air Quality Benefit Analysis for Los Angeles and San Francisco, Based on Housing Values and Visibility." Copy available from California Air Resources Board, PO Box 2815, Sacramento, CA 95812.

U.S. Bureau of the Census. *1977 County Business Patterns.* Published by the U.S. Department of Commerce. Washington, D.C.: U.S. Government Printing Office

U.S. Bureau of the Census. (1982). *Current Population Survey.* Matched file by the Bureau of Labor Statistics 1980/81, Data Users Services Division, Washington, D.C.

U.S. Bureau of the Census. (1983). *County and City Data Book, 1983.* Washington, D.C.: U.S. Government Printing Office, various issues.

U.S. Bureau of the Census. *1987 County Business Patterns.* Published by the U.S. Department of Commerce. Washington, D.C.: U.S. Government Printing Office

U.S. Bureau of the Census. (1988). *Current Population Survey* matched file by the Bureau of Labor Statistics 1986/87, Data users Services Division, Washington, D.C.

U.S. Bureau of Economic Analysis. *Local Area Personal Income.* Washington, D.C.: U.S. Government Printing Office, various issues.

U.S. Bureau of Economic Analysis (BEA). (May 1984). *Survey of Current Business* 64(5). Washington, D.C.: U.S. Government Printing Office.

U.S. Bureau of Economic Analysis (BEA). (1985). "Experimental Estimates of Gross State Product by Industry." *BEA Staff Paper 42.* Washington, D.C.: Government Printing Office.

U.S. Bureau of Economic Analysis (BEA). (1987). "Regional Information Systems (REIS)." (CD ROM)

490

U.S. Bureau of Economic Analysis (BEA). (December 1989). *Business Statistics 1961–88: A Supplement to the Survey of Current Business* 26th edition. Washington, D.C.: U.S. Government Printing Office.

U.S. Bureau of Economic Analysis (BEA). (October 1990). *Survey of Current Business* 70(10). Washington, D.C.: U.S. Government Printing Office.

U.S. Bureau of Economic Analysis (BEA). (April 1991). *Survey of Current Business* 71(4). Washington, D.C.: U.S. Government Printing Office.

U.S. Bureau of Economic Analysis (BEA). (November 1991). *Survey of Current Business* 71(11). Washington, D.C.: U.S. Government Printing Office.

U.S. Bureau of Economic Analysis (BEA). (December 1991). *Survey of Current Business* 71(12). Washington, D.C.: U.S. Government Printing Office.

U.S. Bureau of Labor Statistics, U.S. Department of Labor. (1983). *Consumer Expenditure Survey*. Washington, D.C.: U.S. Government Printing Office.

U.S. Bureau of Labor Statistics, U.S. Department of Labor. (1989). *Monthly Labor Review*. Washington, D.C.: U.S. Government Printing Office.

U.S. Bureau of Labor Statistics, U.S. Department of Labor, Office of Employment Projections. (1990). *Outlook 2000: Aggregate Economic Projection*. Washington, D.C.: U.S. Government Printing Office.

U.S. Bureau of Labor Statistics, U.S. Department of Labor. (November 1991). "Outlook 2000." *Monthly Labor Review* 112(11): 3–74. Washington, D.C.: U.S. Government Printing Office.

U.S. Clean Air Act Amendments of 1990, Public Law 101-549, 15 November. Washington, D.C.: U.S. Government Printing Office.

U.S. Department of Commerce. (1982). *1977 Census of Transportation*. Washington, D.C.: U.S. Government Printing Office.

U.S. Department of Health and Human Services, Office of the Assistant Secretary for Planning and Evaluation. (1983). *The Multiregional Input-Output Accounts, 1977*. Washington, D.C.: U.S. Government Printing Office.

U.S. Department of Labor, Bureau of Labor Statistics. (November 22, 1991). "Consumer Expenditures in 1990." *News* 91-607. Washington, D.C.: U.S. Government Printing Office.

Vaccara, B. (1970). "Changes Over Time in Input-Output Analysis." In *Applications of Input-Output Analysis*, Vol 2., A.P. Cater and A. Brody, eds. Amsterdam: North-Holland, 230–260.

Walter, W. H., W. W. Cure, J. O. Rawlings, L. J. Zaragoza, A. S. Heagle, H. E. Heggestad, R. J. Hojut, L. W. Dress, and P. J. Tample. (1984). "Assessing Impacts of Ozone on Agricultural Crops: II. Crop Yield Functions and Alternative Exposure Statistics." *Journal of the Air Pollution Control Association* 34: 810–817.

Welch, B. L. (1947). "The Generalization of Student's Problem When Several Different Population Variables are Involved." *Biometrika* 34: 28–35.

Weisbrod, Glen, and James Beckwith. (January 1992). "Measuring Economic Development Benefits for Highway Decision-Making: The Wisconsin Case." *Transportation Quarterly* 46(1): 57–79.

Wheat, Leonard F. (1986). "The Determinates of the 1963–77 Regional Manufacturing Growth: Why the South and West Grow." *Journal of Regional Science* 26: 635–659.

Whiteman, J. L. (1987). "Productivity and Growth in Australian Manufacturing Industry." *Journal of Post Keynesian Economics* 9(4): 576–593.

INDEX

494

500

502

504

506